POPE JOHN PAUL II

Other Books by The Poynter Institute

September 11, 2001: A Collection of Newspaper Front Pages

Pope John Paul II

MAY 18, 1920–APRIL 2, 2005

A Collection of Newspaper Front Pages
Selected by The Poynter Institute

Andrews McMeel
Publishing

Kansas City

$\mathcal{D}$edicated to the journalists who created the
newspaper pages published here and throughout
the world on the occasion of the death
of Pope John Paul II

05 06 07 08 09 RR3 10 9 8 7 6 5 4 3 2 1

ISBN: 0-7407-5110-7

Library of Congress Control Number: 2005925755

Attention: Schools and Businesses
Andrews McMeel books are available at quantity discounts with bulk purchase for educational,
business, or sales promotional use. For information, please write to: Special Sales Department,
Andrews McMeel Publishing, 4520 Main Street, Kansas City, Missouri 64111.

CONTENTS

NATIONAL NEWSPAPERS

INTERNATIONAL NEWSPAPERS

INTRODUCTION

THE FRONT-PAGE POPE
AND THE BELLS OF SARTEANO

The night before he died, I found myself in the sea of pilgrims, journalists and tourists streaming into St. Peter's Square beneath the private residence of Pope John Paul II.

Photographers stood, ready to shoot, their long lenses trained on the top-floor windows of the papal apartment. I eavesdropped as a reporter from New York discovered small-world connections with a seminarian from Queens. Travelers from the pope's Polish homeland shared the cobblestones with nuns reciting the rosary in Italian.

Scanning faces, catching snippets of conversation and song and prayer, I wondered at the forces filling the square. Affection? Faith? Curiosity? The approach of a historic moment felt as close as the bite in the brisk Friday evening air.

I was in Italy on a family vacation, a tourist on Roman holiday. Planning for this book had been under way for nearly a year when I left the office, so when my mobile phone chirped with updates and questions about the pope, it was a little eerie to look out my hotel room window and see the Vatican across the street.

But more than tourist or journalist, I felt like an accidental pilgrim, somehow put in the midst of a story that had touched more lives, mine included, than any before it.

It was not the first time I'd stood in a crowd awaiting news from the pope, often puzzling about dimensions of the man and his story that, for the most part, have defied the best efforts of journalists to discover and report. As a reporter covering Poland in the early 1980s, I struggled to convey what it was about John Paul that sent a tingle down my spine as his popemobile rumbled toward Victory Square in Warsaw or the Shrine of the Black Madonna in Czestochowa.

How did he influence events beyond his apparent control? How did he touch people, nonbelievers and believers alike, in ways they never thought possible? Papal biographer George Weigel portrays a man comfortable with people different both in background and belief, suggesting by way of example that childhood days with Jewish teammates on the soccer fields of Wadowice had sown lifelong fruits.

"Farewell, to you my friend, Karol," begins a letter published on the front page of the Israeli newspaper, *Yedioth Ahronoth* (p. 119). In Hebrew, a banner headline declares across the top of the page: "Israel: Pope John Paul II was a great friend of the Jewish people."

Perhaps it was a young adulthood that suffered both Nazism and Stalinism that helped make possible a papacy so devoted to young people. A poet, a playwright, an actor and a philosopher before he was elected pope in 1978, Karol Wojtyla was many things to many, many people.

A man whose impact stretched far past the walls of Vatican City, John Paul often inspired as much debate as devotion. As one Catholic among the globe's 1.1 billion, I wondered why a man who unleashed so much freedom in his homeland would choose to limit it so fervently in his church. Why would a man with such a strong devotion to Mary, the mother of Jesus, leave so many Catholic women feeling as if their aspirations were being ignored by their church? The pope cut across ideology, his deep convictions denouncing the materialism of capitalism along with the godlessness of communism. Liberals loved his opposition to the death penalty and to the U.S.-led invasion of Iraq. Conservatives applauded his views on such issues as abortion and same-sex marriage. Few of us lined up behind everything he said. But many of us had the feeling that, one way or another, he was speaking to all of us.

Perhaps more than anyone in recent memory, John Paul qualified as a citizen of the world, spending 10 percent of his papacy abroad in the course of visiting 129 countries—two-thirds of the world.

If the role of the journalist is to present the world in all its complexity, John Paul's 26-year papacy ranks as one of the great stories of our time. But how to tell it?

John L. Allen, Jr., Vatican correspondent for the *National Catholic Reporter*, says the best way to understand this pope is to examine his papacy from multiple points of view. That's what we're attempting with this collection of 144 newspaper pages from various points around the globe, from South Bend to Santiago, from Nairobi to New Delhi.

The pope's long struggle with Parkinson's disease gave journalists plenty of time to plan coverage of his passing. Many editors have known for months what would appear on their front pages when the day finally arrived. Over dinner in Warsaw last October, Mariusz Ziomecki, the editor of the Polish tabloid *Super Express*, breathed a sigh of relief when he said, "The page is set."

Other editors decided closer to deadline. One or two conceded that it was our request for advance permission to use their page, e-mailed at various points in recent months, that nudged them into figuring out how they'd tell this story.

Some papers told the story of John Paul's death as if the reader had not yet heard. "John Paul II Dies at 84," *The Washington Post* (p. 15) declared across the top of its Sunday, April 3, edition. The *Post* also found a way on its front page to reflect the complexity of the man and his papacy, reporting some of the ways he had disappointed as well as inspired.

Other papers chose a more iconic approach, selecting one or two dimensions of John Paul to highlight. *The Orange County Register* (p. 8) combined one of the pope's favorite themes—"Have no fear"—with a photograph taken of him during his more vigorous years. The *Ottawa Citizen* (p. 104) and *Tygodnik Powszechny* (p. 134), the leading Catholic paper in Poland, let powerful images tell the story on their own.

Many papers pursued local angles or their particular approach to the news. *The Wall Street Journal* (p. 96) analyzed what it characterized as John Paul's "hands-off" management style but concluded that his charisma compensated nicely.

The journalists who produced these pages realize it's impossible to tell a story of this magnitude on a single page. But we hope that assembling their collective work in the pages that follow will provide readers with a chance to consider John Paul's legacy in ways they hadn't before.

You'll find no souvenir editions of the Dewey-defeats-Truman variety here, no papers prematurely reporting the pope's death or rashly predicting his successor. But that's not to say the coverage was error-free.

By the time I returned to my hotel room from St. Peter's on April 1, for example, my in-box was topped with e-mails noting news reports that the pope had lost consciousness, that he had generated a flat EKG and, finally, that he had died. I flipped on CNN International and found veteran correspondent Jim Bitterman quoting an Italian cardinal who described the pope as headed toward death but not there yet.

The next day I boarded a train to Tuscany. I caught up with my family in Sarteano, a medieval walled hill town about 90 minutes north of Rome. Shopping at the village meat market late that afternoon, I asked the shop owner's sister-in-law, Julia Kawamura, if she'd heard any late word on the pope's condition.

"Oh, he died yesterday," said Kawamura, an American furniture designer who has lived in Italy for eight years. In Sarteano the night before, a family member had told her about Italian media reports that the pope was dead—and she had not heard the subsequent corrections. Perhaps media credibility is not an issue unique to the United States.

When the pope actually died later that day, journalists got the news via an e-mail from the Vatican. In Sarteano, we heard another way. In our rented flat up the steep stone stairs on Vicolo del Sassogrosso, we had neither television nor Internet connection. And I'd accidentally broken the antenna off my shortwave radio. Just before crawling into bed, we heard bells tolling in the distance for what seemed like a very long time. One floor above, our nine-year-old Presbyterian grandson, Mitch, announced the news to his sisters, his parents and his aunt: The pope has died.

As a journalist, I found it an interesting way to get the news. No analysis, no speculation, just a clear and urgent message from church bells in a remote Italian village.

First thing the next morning, I headed to the newsstand on Sarteano's main piazza and found people making their selections from a long shelf of Italian and other European papers.

On the front of *La Stampa* (p. 122), readers found a grid of faces in mourning. *Il Manifesto* (p. 120), the communist paper often at odds with the church, played off a popular Italian expression that roughly translates as "One pope has died, and another one is in the works." *Il Manifesto* offered an affectionate twist: *"Non se ne fa un altro."* In other words: "There won't be another like this one."

The newsstand had no Polish papers, so I set out across the village in search of Internet access. At the director's office of the village campground, and at a 16th-century convent now operated as a restaurant and inn, I found high-speed access—and generous Italian hosts willing to share it.

Once online, I found the front page of my friend Ziomecki's tabloid. Among the more irreverent publications in Poland, *Super Express* (p. 133) on this occasion turned quite somber: Translated, the headline read "Farewell, Father" above a photo of the pope and a dove.

Gazeta Krakowska (p. 131), published in the city where John Paul served as archbishop before heading to Rome, repeated the motto of his papacy: *"Totus Tuus,"* Latin for "Totally Yours," beneath a photo of a younger John Paul lighting a candle.

Gazeta Wyborcza (p. 132), the paper founded by the Solidarity trade union that the pope fueled with such confidence with his first papal visit to his homeland in 1979, presented a stark page in black and white and red. Above a smiling photo of the pope and an excerpt from his 1979 message to Poles, the headline said: "John Paul II is gone."

Seven days after hearing the bells of Sarteano, I boarded our return flight from Venice to JFK and caught sight of the flat-screen TV in the departure lounge at Marco Polo Airport. The body of the front-page pope would soon be placed in the ground beneath St. Peter's Basilica.

Bill Mitchell
Director of Publishing
The Poynter Institute
April 18, 2005

$1.50

Final Edition

Anchorage Daily News

Sunday, April 3, 2005 — ALASKA'S NEWSPAPER — www.adn.com

High-profile convention center plan goes to vote

■ **DOWNTOWN:** Aggressive campaign, vocal opposition to be weighed in April 5 election.

By RICHARD RICHTMYER
Anchorage Daily News

Voters will have the final say Tuesday on whether to transform the center of downtown Anchorage by building a new convention center.

The convention center proposal, Proposition 2, has been the highest-profile and most controversial item on the ballot, which also includes six Assembly races, two School Board races and five other bond propositions.

An advocacy group — backed largely by hotels, labor unions and tourism-related businesses — has raised at least $460,000 and mounted an aggressive multimedia campaign in favor of raising the city's bed tax to fund a new convention center. It also has targeted community and civic organizations through a grassroots effort.

Mayor Mark Begich, whose administration negotiated a development deal and crafted the convention center ballot proposition, also has been stumping for the convention center. He describes the proposed center as the starting point for a new wave of public improvements in Anchorage that will keep the city vibrant and growing, similar to Project 80s, a building boom two decades ago that was driven by the flood of new state oil money that produced the Egan Center, the Sullivan Arena, the performing arts center

See Back Page, CENTER

Q. What are we being asked to approve in Tuesday's election?

A. Voters, on a single ballot question, will be asked to do four things:
• Raise the city's hotel-room tax to 12 percent from 8 percent.
• Use the extra money to pay for a new convention center downtown on a square block fronting Seventh Avenue, between the Conoco Phillips and Atwood buildings; renovate the Egan Center and support future operating costs of both centers.
• Lower the threshold needed to pass the tax to a majority vote from the 60 percent vote required for other sales-tax hikes.
• Ban using property taxes to pay for the new center's construction or operations

Q. How big would the new convention center be?

A. 193,000 square feet, with roughly 93,000 square feet of exhibit and meeting space. The rest would be lobbies, offices, kitchens, bathrooms, storage rooms and so forth. The existing Egan Center has 45,000 square feet of meeting and exhibit space.

Q. How much would the new convention center cost?

A. The total project budget is $93 million.

See Back Page, Q&A

■ **IRAQ:** Iraqis pick a Sunni to lead the parliament; earlier, militants attacked Abu Ghraib prison, injuring 44 Americans. **Page A-10**

■ **HIGH SCHOOL HOOPS:** New state champs: West, 4A boys; Juneau, 4A girls; Heritage Christian, 3A boys; Monroe Catholic, 3A girls. **Page C-1**

■ **FINAL FOUR:** Illinois and North Carolina win berths in the final. **Page C-1**

CATHOLIC SPIRITUAL LEADER OF 27 YEARS DIES

AN ERA PASSES

John Paul II

1920

2005

Cardinals will elect successor

■ **CONCLAVE:** Search for unity will challenge evolving Catholicism.

By LAURIE GOODSTEIN
The New York Times

When the 117 Roman Catholic cardinals who are eligible to elect a successor to Pope John Paul II gather in the Sistine Chapel to cast their ballots, the worldwide suspense about the outcome will be shared even by the cardinals in the conclave.

There is no clear front-runner, unlike in some past papal elections, many church experts agree. So the cardinals will be weighing a host of factors, including the candidates' country of origin, age, experience and personality.

Among the most critical questions facing the cardinals is, should the papacy be returned to an Italian, or should the cardinals make the bold gesture of choosing a pope from the Third World, where Catholicism is both thriving and threatened by competing faiths?

"A Third World pope would clearly indicate that this is no

See Back Page, SUCCESSOR

PLINIO LEPRI / Associated Press archive 2005
Leading an epic life, Pope John Paul II rose from Nazi- and Soviet-controlled Poland to lead the Roman Catholic Church in a time of social upheaval.

As death came, pope still taught

■ **MISSION:** Pole will be remembered for travels, charisma, steadfastness.

By LARRY STAMMER
Los Angeles Times

Pope John Paul II, whose indomitable will and uncompromising belief in human dignity helped bring down communism in Eastern Europe and reshaped Christianity's relationship to Judaism, was indisputably the most influential pope of the 20th century. He died Saturday in his Vatican apartment at 84.

The first non-Italian elected pope in 455 years, John Paul energized the papacy through much of his reign, traveling as evangelist and champion of religious freedom even as he imposed a rigorous moral discipline and more centralized authority on his sometimes rebellious billion-member church.

In his final months, as his health declined markedly, he valiantly pressed ahead with his mission, choosing to project his gradual incapacitation as a final Christian message of redemp-

See Page A-12, JOHN PAUL II

In Alaska visits, pope took time with ill, disabled

■ **STOPOVERS:** John Paul celebrated Mass in Anchorage, spoke with Reagan in Fairbanks during two visits in the 1980s.

By PETER PORCO
Anchorage Daily News

Pope John Paul II, who died Saturday, made two brief but historic visits to Alaska. In February 1981, he celebrated Mass on the Delaney Park Strip in Anchorage before more than 40,000 people, and in May 1984 the pope held a short meeting with President Ronald Reagan in Fairbanks.

On neither occasion was Alaska a primary destination. Instead, John Paul made Alaska a refueling stop on his way to somewhere else — back to Rome after a 12-day Asia trip in '81 and to South Korea in '84 at the start of another journey.

Nevertheless, both Alaska visits were huge. The 1981 stopover was the first time a pope had set foot in Alaska, and it inspired what was said to be the largest gathering of Alaskans in the state to that time. The 1984 meeting with Reagan at Fairbanks International Airport represented one of the loftiest diplomatic en-

counters ever held on Alaska soil.

Each of the visits brought scores of dignitaries and hundreds of reporters. The bishops of Fairbanks, Juneau and Anchorage and many of the state's political leaders came to see John Paul, as did an array of politicians from the Lower 48.

Leader of the world's Roman Catholics, John Paul extended himself to the clergy of other faiths. He reached

See Page A-13, ALASKA

> *When the pope came through in his popemobile waving, and also when he was giving the blessing, you just had a sense that he was talking to you.*
>
> — Carl Rose, who brought his family to Anchorage from Skagway to see the pope in 1981

INSIDE

■ **TIMELINE:** Karol Jozeph Wojtyla was born in Wadowice, Poland, on May 18, 1920. He was elected pope in 1978. **Page A-12**

■ **REACTION:** Alaskans remember a principled man with a quick wit. **Page A-13**

■ **CATHOLICS:** Illustration shows breakdown of religious affiliations in Alaska, including 53,000 active Catholics. **Page A-13**

■ **ATHLETE:** John Paul was perhaps the most athletic pope in history, and skiing, hockey, soccer, hiking and swimming were among his pastimes. **Page C-5**

PONTIFF VISITED ALASKA IN 1981 AND 1984

FRAN DURNER / Daily News archive 1981
Former Gov. Wally and Erma Lee Hickel and Pope John Paul in Anchorage, 1981

GREG ANDERSON / Daily News archive 1984
President Reagan and Pope John Paul in Fairbanks, 1984

MARC OLSON / Daily News archive 1981
Archbishop Francis Hurley and Pope John Paul in Anchorage, 1981

1

THE FINAL TWO Illinois, N. Carolina to vie for NCAA title **SPORTS, C1**

2005 BASEBALL PREVIEW

D-BACKS have high hopes for season **SPECIAL SECTION**

Up to **$161** in coupons

THE ARIZONA REPUBLIC

SUNDAY, APRIL 3, 2005   azcentral.com $2.00

John Paul II dead at 84

First Polish pontiff led Catholic Church through tumultuous quarter-century

VATICAN CITY — John Paul II, the voyager pope who helped conquer communism and transformed the papacy with charisma and vigor, died Saturday night after a long battle with Parkinson's disease that became a lesson to the world in humble suffering.

"Our most beloved Holy Father has returned to the house of the Father," Archbishop Leonardo Sandri, a senior Vatican official, told pilgrims in St. Peter's Square. The throng of 70,000 momentarily stood in stunned silence, stared at the pavement and shed tears. Then, following an Italian custom that signifies hope at a time of death, at 9:37 p.m. (12:37 p.m. Arizona time) the mourners broke into sustained applause.

More from Rome and what lies ahead. A24

Gabriel Bouys/Getty Images

What's next
Pope's body expected to arrive at St. Peter's Basilica on Monday to lie in state. Also on Monday, the College of Cardinals is expected to set a funeral date, probably Wednesday, Thursday or Friday.

Arizonan's life changed
When the pope visited the Valley in 1987, a baby was passed through the crowd to him. Now 18, Naomi Miguel says, "I'd probably be living a different life if I hadn't been blessed by the pope." **A25**

Full coverage A19-A27
The next pope: How successor will be chosen. **A24**
Editorial: Remembering a 20th-century giant. **A27**
Read about and view slide shows of the pope's visits to the Valley, at pope.azcentral.com.

Coming Monday: A special section
A colorful commemorative section looks at the life of Pope John Paul II in words and pictures, including his memorable visit to the Valley.

Spring forward, but not in Arizona
Most of the nation switched to daylight-saving time this morning, but not Arizona, except on the Navajo Reservation. That means the state will be three hours behind the East Coast and on the same time as the West Coast. Hawaii, the part of Indiana in the Eastern time zone, Puerto Rico, the Virgin Islands and American Samoa also do not observe daylight-saving time.

Valley & State
Phoenix may pass own anti-meth law: City officials say if state lawmakers refuse to make it harder to buy an over-the-counter ingredient used to make methamphetamines, then the city will pass its own ordinance. **B1**

Group begins border patrols: Volunteers for the monthlong controversial Minuteman Project set up on the U.S.-Mexico border to watch for undocumented immigrants. **B7**

Viewpoints
National ID cards: Like it or not, the time may be right as a way to help curb illegal immigration. **V1**

Nation & World
Iraq prison hit: Insurgents attack Abu Ghraib, detonating two suicide car bombs and firing rocket-propelled grenades before U.S. troops repel the assault. At least 20 U.S. soldiers and 12 detainees are wounded. **A3**

Travel
Overweight baggage fees on rise: See how various airlines are charging for excess baggage. **T1**

Weather
High clouds today: Above-average temperatures, light winds. High 87. Low 61. **B10**

Classified: Looking for a great deal? Find it inside Republic Classified, **CL1**, behind the Viewpoints section.

A Gannett Newspaper:
115th year, No. 320
Copyright 2005,
The Arizona Republic

azcentral.com

On the Internet: For continuous news updates, visit azcentral.com

Domestic violence claiming more victims on periphery

By Judi Villa
The Arizona Republic

The first shotgun blast tore through Loren Kirkeide's arm.

In his garage, Kirkeide heard his girlfriend, Patty Hardman, scream. The second blast ripped into her chest, killing her as she sat in her car.

Kirkeide knew Hardman's ex-boyfriend had been harassing her for months but until then, "We didn't realize the danger we were in," he said.

Across the state every year, people like Kirkeide who are not involved in abusive rela-

Inside
ASU's broken system: It's up to Michael Crow to fix problems with athletes' conduct. **Sports. C1**

A different look: What coach Dirk Koetter should have said. **Viewpoints. V1**

tionships are falling victim to domestic violence.

Children, new boyfriends, parents, even acquaintances are being hurt or killed because they know the person

See **DOMESTIC VIOLENCE** Page A5

SUNDAY

Los Angeles Times

FINAL

On The Internet: WWW.LATIMES.COM   SUNDAY, APRIL 3, 2005   COPYRIGHT 2005/778 PAGES/†CC IE SG SD $1.50 Designated Areas Higher

Pope John Paul II Dies

Amid Mourning, Cardinals Head to Rome for Funeral and Conclave

POPE JOHN PAUL II
He was the most influential pope of the 20th century. John Paul told 12,000 cheering youths in Switzerland in June that "after almost 60 years of priesthood, it is beautiful to be able to spend yourself until the end for the cause of the reign of God."

By RICHARD BOUDREAUX
Times Staff Writer

VATICAN CITY — Pope John Paul II died Saturday, ending a long, painfully public struggle against a host of debilitating ailments and a globetrotting reign that made him one of the towering figures of his time. He was 84.

The Polish prelate who led the Roman Catholic Church for 26 years succumbed in his apartment at the Vatican's Apostolic Palace at 9:37 p.m., papal spokesman Joaquin Navarro-Valls said.

Weakened for more than a decade by Parkinson's disease, the pope was overcome by fever, infection and heart and kidney failure last week after two hospitalizations in as many months. He slipped in and out of consciousness Saturday, surrounded by the only family he had: five Polish priests and bishops and four Polish nuns who had looked after him for years.

The Vatican gave no precise cause of death.

"Our Holy Father John Paul has returned to the house of the Father," Archbishop Leonardo Sandri, the Vatican undersecretary of state, told the 60,000 people standing vigil in St. Peter's Square below the pope's still-lighted third-floor apartment windows. The crowd fell into tearful silence, then broke into applause, an Italian sign of respect.

"We all feel like orphans this evening," Sandri said.

Bells tolled in mourning across Rome and condolences poured in from around the world. President Bush said, "The Catholic Church has lost its shepherd, the world has lost a champion of human freedom, and a good and faithful servant of God has been called home."

The Vatican scheduled a memorial Mass for today outside St. Peter's Basilica and said the pope's body would be taken into the vast church no earlier than Monday. The College of Cardinals, comprising the church's red-robed "princes," is to meet Monday to set a funeral date.

Most popes in recent centuries have asked to be buried in the crypts below the basilica, but the Vatican declined to say whether the pope had left instructions. Some have suggested
[See Pope, Page A36]

A Ballot Like No Other

By RICHARD BOUDREAUX
AND TRACY WILKINSON
Times Staff Writers

VATICAN CITY — Sometime in the next 20 days, the cardinals of the Roman Catholic Church will file silently into the Sistine Chapel and lock out the world. Praying for guidance only from the Holy Spirit, they will begin the task of electing a successor to Pope John Paul II.

Never do cardinals have more power to reshape the church than they do during an interregnum. This time, the church and its 1 billion believers await their choice with pent-up anxiety, deeply divided over John Paul's 26½-year tenure.

Yet this College of Cardinals was reshaped profoundly by John Paul. All but three of the 117 electors were elevated by this pope, and the sheer weight of like-minded appointees is all but certain to result in a pontiff who also is conservative on questions of faith and morals.

It is not a college of carbon copies, however, and if history is any guide, the cardinals will elect a man who differs in other ways — perhaps unexpected ways — from his predecessor. Any number of contenders, each quite different from John Paul and from
[See Succession, Page A44]

The Unflagging Evangelist

A Tragic Youth Laid the Foundation for Karol Wojtyla's Life of Compassion

By LARRY B. STAMMER
Times Staff Writer

Pope John Paul II, whose indomitable will and defense of human dignity helped bring down communism in Eastern Europe and reshaped Christianity's relationship to Judaism, was indisputably the most influential pope of the 20th century.

The first non-Italian elected pope in 456 years, John Paul energized the papacy through much of his reign, traveling as evangelist and champion of religious freedom even as he centralized authority in his church. His efforts to impose a rigorous moral discipline on his 1-billion-member flock often chafed liberals.

In his final months, as his health declined markedly, he pressed ahead with his mission, choosing to project his gradual incapacitation as a final Christian message of redemption through suffering.

In his 26-year papacy, John Paul made 104 trips outside Italy to 129 nations, going as a pastor to countries such as Brazil, where Catholics are the majority, and Japan, where they are a minority.

He preached along the equator and inside the Arctic Circle. He preached on sere Andean mountaintops and on lush tropical islands, in famous European cathedrals and in bullet-pocked African country churches. And he preached amid the wreckage of fratricidal wars in Sarajevo and Beirut.

On his travels to Poland, it was his unflinching support for the Solidarity trade union movement that helped embolden first his homeland and then half the European continent to topple communist regimes.

A witness to the Holocaust as a young man, John Paul led the Roman Catholic Church on a pilgrimage of repentance and reconciliation with Jews, culminating in the establishment of diplomatic relations with the state of Israel.

In his final years, he made a crowning pilgrimage to the Holy Land and became the first Roman Catholic leader in nearly 1,300 years to visit Greece, trying to bridge the centuries-old theological divide with Eastern Orthodoxy.

By 2003, John Paul's journeys had been scaled back, but he continued to press on. His final trip   *[See Obituary, Page A38]*

SPECIAL SECTION

Unity: At word of the pope's death, a wave of sorrow pulls the faithful into Rome streets. **A35**

Analysis: John Paul II was a radical Christian humanist who was also strict on doctrine. **A37**

Editorial: The pope's long reign was revolutionary — and it polarized the faithful. **A43**

Succession: The who, how, where and when of deciding who will fill the papal throne. **A45**

Southland: Leaders and worshipers of many faiths have fond memories of the pope. **A46**

GERARD MOLINA *Los Angeles Times*
Claudia Valenzuela of Chile grieves in St. Peter's Square.

SECOND SEASON

How the Dodgers' Owner Got His Financial Lineup in Place

The first of two parts.

By THOMAS S. MULLIGAN
Times Staff Writer

When he sold the Dodgers to Fox Sports Enterprises in 1998, having lost $12 million the previous season, Peter O'Malley declared Major League Baseball's era of family ownership over.

Player salaries had grown too high for a baseball-only business to succeed, O'Malley said. He figured that corporate owners such as Fox Sports, a unit of media giant News Corp. with the ability to cross-promote the team through its TV properties, were the wave of the future.

This week, Frank McCourt begins his second season of trying to prove O'Malley wrong.

The question is the same today as when the Boston real estate man emerged 18 months ago as the owner-to-be: Is his wallet fat enough to keep the Dodgers competitive against teams owned by billionaires, well-heeled partnerships and Fortune 500 corporations?

Because McCourt put up little cash, his purchase has been seen as a high-wire act. But sports business experts say revenue-boosting moves in the off-season, combined with the underlying strength of the Dodgers — the team's large and loyal fan base — have convinced them that McCourt has a better-than-even chance of success.

"It's a great turnaround opportunity — a great brand, a great market with deep fan loyalty and very positive demographics," said New York investment banker Salvatore Galatioto, who for years ran the sports finance business at Lehman Bros. and recently opened
[See McCourt, Page A12]

INSIDE

STEVEN LAM *For The Times*

MAGAZINE

Ideas and Styles That Wear Well

The men's fashion issue looks at a season of high polish and glamorous returns, including vintage clothing, above.

Weather: Partly cloudy, breezy and noticeably cooler after morning low clouds and fog. L.A. Downtown: 69/52. **B18**

News Summary **A2**

Time change
Daylight saving time began at 2 a.m. today. Clocks should be moved ahead one hour.

They're In — but Not Home Free

Many Californians have 'interest-only' loans. They might be living on borrowed time.

By DAVID STREITFELD
Times Staff Writer

OAKLAND — Rachael Herron's new condo will ensure her financial salvation — unless it provokes her ruin.

Herron put no money down for her tidy one-bedroom, borrowing the entire purchase price of $211,000. To keep her monthly payments as low as possible, she got an adjustable-rate mortgage that won't require her to pay any principal for three years.

Thanks to her "interest-only" loan, the 911 police dispatcher was able to afford, barely, her first home. She now has a stake in California's sizzling real estate market. As her home increases in value, she plans to use some of that equity to pay down her credit cards.

But Herron is also setting herself up for a day of reckoning: Nov. 1, 2007.

That's when she has to start paying off her loan principal. If interest rates are higher than when she bought her home last fall — something many economists consider probable if not inevitable — her monthly payment will increase by as much as a third.

"I don't know what I'll do," said Herron, 32. "I'm already working overtime to pay my bills."

Confronted with soaring home prices, Californians are adopting a "buy now, pay later" strategy on a massive scale. The boom in interest-only loans — nearly half the state's home buy-
[See Loans, Page A28]

Rebels Wound 20 U.S. Troops in Attack on Abu Ghraib Prison

By EDMUND SANDERS
Times Staff Writer

BAGHDAD — More than three dozen insurgents launched an audacious strike Saturday evening against the notorious Abu Ghraib prison, wounding 20 U.S. troops and a dozen Iraqi detainees.

The large-scale attack represented a rare direct assault against a well-fortified U.S. position in Iraq. It was also one of the more sophisticated strikes against American troops since President Saddam Hussein was toppled from power two years ago.

Between 40 and 60 heavily armed men swarmed the prison, detonating two car bombs and peppering the facility with rocket-propelled grenades and small-arms and mortar fire.

"First they attacked at one corner to make us think that's where they were coming from, then they attacked at another corner," said Lt. Col. Guy Rudisill, military spokesman for detainee affairs. "This was a well-coordinated attack. This is something that we have not seen before."

At least one insurgent was killed, military officials said.
[See Iraq, Page A11]

7 85944 00150 3

San Francisco Chronicle

★★★★★•   SUNDAY, APRIL 3, 2005   415-777-1111 $1.50

POPE JOHN PAUL II | 1920-2005

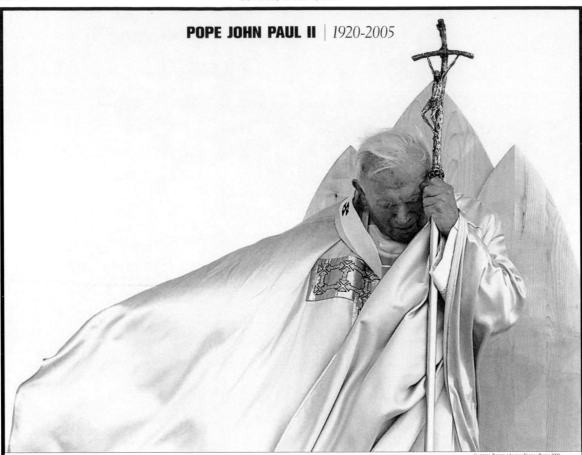

GABRIEL BOUYS / Agence France-Presse 1999

As wind billows his robe, Pope John Paul II celebrates a Mass of beatification in Maribor, located in the former Yugoslav republic of Slovenia, in 1999.

Beloved, charismatic and controversial, John Paul II transformed the papacy

By Don Lattin
CHRONICLE RELIGION WRITER

Pope John Paul II — one of the most charismatic and influential religious leaders of the 20th century — died Saturday at his apartment in Vatican City, ending a 26-year papacy in which he played a critical role in the downfall of communism and promoted traditional moral values as an alternative to the unbridled materialism of the West.

His death, announced by the Vatican at 11:37 a.m. (PST), marked the end of a reign that transformed the very idea of what it means to be the pope. In the 2,000-year history of the church, only one man has occupied the throne of Peter longer than John Paul, and none has so artfully used the media to take its message to every corner of the world.

The 84-year-old pope, suffering in recent days from breathing problems, kidney failure and high fever, died as tens of thousands of prayerful, tearful pilgrims gathered below his still-lighted third-floor window in St. Peter's Square.

"We all feel like orphans this evening," Archbishop Leonardo Sandri, a top Vatican official, told the crowd.

John Paul was born as Karol Josef Wojtyla in Wadowice, Poland, on May 18, 1920, with Eastern European roots that would define his pontificate, the second-longest after Pope Pius IX, who served from 1846 to 1878.

His life mirrored the struggles and spiritual battles of the 20th century — the rise and fall of Adolf Hitler and

▶ POPE: Page A12

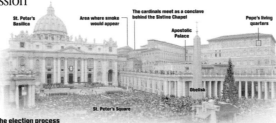

The papal succession

When a pope dies

The head of the Sacred College of Cardinals – the camerlengo – verifies the death and the pope's fisherman ring and papal seal are broken. Within 15 to 20 days, the Sacred College of Cardinals forms a conclave to choose a new pope. Currently 117 cardinals are considered eligible to vote.

After a Mass of the Holy Spirit in St. Peter's Basilica, the cardinals meet in an area behind the Sistine Chapel and are sworn to secrecy and isolated from the world. Only cardinals under the age of 80 can take part in the balloting until a majority decides who will be the new pope.

St. Peter's Basilica
Area where smoke would appear
The cardinals meet as a conclave behind the Sistine Chapel
Apostolic Palace
Pope's living quarters
Obelisk
St. Peter's Square

The election process

❶ **Traditionally, each cardinal votes four times a day, twice in the morning and twice in the afternoon, until they reach a two-thirds majority. The votes are read aloud before the assembly.**

❷ **If this majority is not reached, the ballots – which are destroyed after every vote – are burned in a way to create a black smoke.**

❸ **Crowds gathered in St. Peter's Square witness the election's progress. If voting continues to be unsuccessful for 10 days, the cardinals may agree to a simple majority vote — half plus one.**

❹ **When a majority is reached, the new pope chooses a name and the final ballots are burned in a way to make white smoke, signaling a successful election.**

❺ **The camerlengo announces on the balcony of the Vatican; "Habeum papam!" ("We have a pope!") and the new pontiff appears and gives his blessing to the waiting world.**

Sources: The Vatican; Time magazine; Associated Press

Heirarchy of the Roman Catholic Church

Supreme pontiff (pope)
Elected by
College of Cardinals

Cardinal
Chosen by pope, usually from among the bishops

Archbishop
Highest-ranking bishop, heads archdiocese or province

Bishop
Heads diocese (large number of parishes)

Monsignor
An honorary title

Deacon
Parish cleric

Pastor
Head of parish

Abbot
Superior of a monastery

Parish priest
Administers Mass

JOHN BLANCHARD / The Chronicle

INSIDE: The world mourns as church faces challenges of leadership, war, poverty and the developing world. A12 to A20

San Jose Mercury News

$1.00 | FINAL EDITION | F ....
SERVING NORTHERN CALIFORNIA SINCE 1851

MERCURYNEWS.COM

APRIL 3, 2005 | SUNDAY
THE NEWSPAPER OF SILICON VALLEY

Federal setback to BART funding

TROUBLED LINE TO S.J. WON'T BE ABLE TO MEET NEW EFFICIENCY MARK

By Barry Witt and Gary Richards
Mercury News

New federal standards make it unlikely that the proposed BART extension to San Jose will ever be part of a Bush administration budget — a critical blow to a project that was already struggling to find funding.

Federal officials have long worried that the extension will not carry enough riders to justify its $4.2 billion cost, and now they are planning to measure it against a new cost-effectiveness standard it cannot possibly meet.

The move comes just as a business group promoting the plan for a Bay Area Rapid Transit District extension released a poll showing there is still not enough voter support to approve a tax that would bolster local funding for the project. However, support is growing for a new quarter-cent sales tax, the group said, and they remain hopeful they can reach the two-thirds-majority threshold that would be needed for a ballot measure next year.

Local transportation officials, including San Jose Mayor Ron Gonzales, have always planned on a federal contribution to cover $834 million — about 20 percent — of the cost of the 16.1-mile extension from Fremont through downtown San Jose and into Santa Clara. They have rebuffed calls by the Federal Transit Administra-

See BART, Page 19A

WHY IT MATTERS

Santa Clara County voters approved a sales tax in 2000 to help pay for the $4.2 billion BART-to-South Bay extension. With the economy lagging, tax revenue is falling short and more money is needed.

Homeowners dig deep for more space underground

By Dan Stober
Mercury News

Roger McCarthy loved the house from the moment he saw it, on a stroll with his wife through downtown Palo Alto. A charming Victorian 100 years old, it lacked one feature to make it the home of his dreams: a basement, two stories deep.

So, McCarthy bought the house, then had it jacked up and placed on steel beams so workers could dig a 22-foot hole underneath.

"It's not a *statement* basement," McCarthy says. But it will be large enough to house a freight elevator, a forklift and an overhead crane — all of which McCarthy, an engineer who likes to tinker, needs to work with his collection of large antique machine tools. And that's just the bottom floor. One level up will be space for McCarthy's office, his 4,000-volume library and his collection of high-end model boats.

Silicon Valley's craze for bigger homes has quietly gone underground. Basements are in vogue — the bigger and deeper the better — making room for subterranean home

See BASEMENTS, Page 19A

Time change

Daylight-saving time began today at 2 a.m. Set clocks one hour ahead.

A LIFE OF FAITH
SPECIAL MEMORIAL SECTION INSIDE

POPE JOHN PAUL II | 1920-2005

Church's shepherd, world's statesman

Youths at congregation in San Jose get lesson from pope's suffering

By Laura Kurtzman
Mercury News

When the news came that Pope John Paul II had died at last, Monsignor Adolfo Valdivia was celebrating Mass in Spanish at St. Maria Goretti Church in San Jose.

He declared how glorious it was that they happened to be in church at just that moment and commanded the young people to kneel on the hard floor around the altar.

Valdivia later said his intention was to demonstrate the truth the pope had so powerfully lived, particularly in his last years of intense physical suffering: that neither life nor the spiritual path is always easy.

"The Holy Father had this beautiful gift to embrace the children and you, the teenagers," he told those who had

See SAN JOSE, Page 12A

INSIDE

NO CLEAR FAVORITE FOR NEW PONTIFF
PAGE 14A

GLOBAL VOICES OF PRAISE POUR IN
PAGE 15A

MERCURY NEWS.COM
Sign a guest book for the pope and get updated local and world reaction to his death.

By Ken Dilanian, Matthew Schofield and Patricia Montemurri
Knight Ridder

VATICAN CITY — After a two-day end-of-life drama that sparked an unprecedented global outpouring of attention, the first news of Pope John Paul II's death Saturday came via one of the most modern of communication forms, a papal official's e-mail to journalists.

When the news was announced to an estimated 70,000 people gathered in St. Peter's Square, some wept uncontrollably, others stared in disbelief and still others bowed their heads in prayer.

Some broke into applause — an Italian tradition in which mourners often clap for important figures.

"Our Holy Father John Paul has returned to the house of the Father," Undersecretary of State Archbishop Leonardo Sandri told the crowd.

See POPE, Page 13A

DOUG GRISWOLD — MERCURY NEWS ILLUSTRATION

5

The Fresno Bee

SOUTH VALLEY EDITION

FresnoBee.com

$1.50

SUNDAY, APRIL 3, 2005

Letter from the editor

To Our Readers:

Good morning, and welcome to the new look of your Fresno Bee.

I say "your" because this redesign is about you, our readers. For the past 18 months, a team of Bee journalists has worked under the charge to provide a design and typography that is cleaner, easier to read and better organized. What you see today are the results of that undertaking.

Among the most important changes:

■ New typefaces for both text and headlines that our tests and surveys have shown are much easier to read than our previous ones. Our new text type is rounder and less dense, and we've added a slight amount of space between lines for better readability.

■ A change in the number of columns on section fronts and other open pages — from six to five — to provide better display of photos and graphics.

■ Fewer graphic elements at the top of each section, which can distract readers' eyes from our principle objective: the very best presentation of our news content. On most days, references to stories in other sections will appear only in a strip at the bottom of the front page. Weather and air quality information (and, yes, Scoopy) will also appear daily in that bottom strip. Our index has moved from the front page to a redesigned 5-Minute Bee on Page 2 of the front section.

■ Labels at the top of all inside pages will now provide a quick idea of each page's content: Nation, World, State, Local, Television, Movies, etc.

■ A complete overhaul of our Scoreboard page in Sports features a larger and more readable typeface. Box scores for major sports, such as the NBA or Major League Baseball, will move from Scoreboard and be packaged with the game stories for each of those sports elsewhere in the section. In addition, we have created a new Page 2 for Sports that includes the day's or weekend's calendar of events — locally or on radio and television. We've also added a new feature on that page, From The Sideline, which focuses on sports personalities.

We hope you like what you see. And after you have read a few issues, we would love to hear from you. Executive News Editor Kris Eldred, a key member of our redesign team, can best answer your questions and is in charge of compiling your comments and thoughts. She can be reached at 441-6463 or keldred@fresnobee.com. Or you can, of course, contact other editors if you prefer.

Thank you for reading The Bee.

Charlie Waters
Executive Editor

Insurgents attack prison in Baghdad

By Edmund Sanders
Los Angeles Times

BAGHDAD, Iraq — More than three dozen insurgents launched an audacious strike Saturday evening against the notorious Abu Ghraib prison, wounding 20 U.S. soldiers and a dozen Iraqi detainees.

The large-scale attack represented a rare direct assault against a well-fortified U.S. position in Iraq. It also was one of the more sophisticated strikes against U.S. troops since coalition forces toppled Iraqi President Saddam Hussein two years ago.

▶ Iraqi officials see more tips on insurgents. Page 13

Between 40 and 60 heavily armed men swarmed the prison, detonating two car bombs and peppering the facility with rocket-propelled grenades and small arms and mortar fire.

"First they attacked at one corner to make us think that's where they were coming from; then they attacked at another corner," said Lt. Col. Guy Rudisill, military spokesman for detainee affairs. "This was a well-coordinated attack. This is something that we have not seen before."

See IRAQ, Page 14

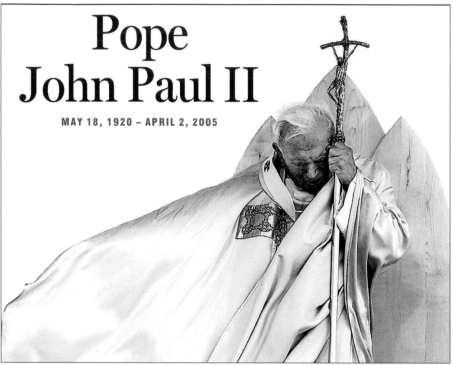

Pope John Paul II

MAY 18, 1920 – APRIL 2, 2005

GABRIEL BOUYS/AGENCE FRANCE-PRESSE FILE
Pope John Paul II celebrates a Mass of beatification of Anton Martin Slomsek in Maribor, Slovenia, on Sept. 19, 1999. The pope died Saturday night at the age of 84.

Pontiff was a teacher even in his final days

By Daniel Williams and Alan Cooperman
Washington Post

VATICAN CITY — John Paul II, the voyager pope who helped conquer communism and transformed the papacy with charisma and vigor, died Saturday night after a long battle with Parkinson's disease that became a lesson to the world in humble suffering.

"Our most beloved Holy Father has returned to the house of the Father," Archbishop Leonardo Sandri, a senior Vatican official, told pilgrims in St. Peter's Square. The throng of 50,000 momentarily stood in stunned silence, stared at the pavement and shed tears. Then, following an Italian custom that signifies hope at a time of death, the mourners broke into sustained applause.

John Paul died at 9:37 p.m. local time in the Vatican's Apostolic Palace on a clear and cool night, with a small group of Polish prelates and nuns at his bedside. The first indication of the pope's passing was the illumination of several windows in his private quarters overlooking St. Peter's Square. An e-mail announcement followed. A half-hour later, the

FRANCO ORIGLIA/GETTY IMAGES
People react after receiving word of the pope's death Saturday in St. Peter's Square at Vatican City. A crowd of 50,000 had gathered in the square.

bells of all of Rome's churches rang out in mourning.

The news evoked an outpouring of emotion for the man all over the world. In Paris, mourners packed special midnight services; church bells sounded in Cuba. President Bush called John Paul "a champion of human freedom" and "a good and faithful servant of God. ... We're grateful to God for sending such a man, a son of Poland."

The pope's body will lie in state in St. Peter's Basilica starting Monday afternoon. The date of his funeral will be set by a gathering of cardinals on Monday morning, but under guidelines he had set, it should take place within four to six days of his death. Within 15 to 20 days, the College of Cardinals will meet in the Sistine Chapel to elect a successor as

▶ Pontiff leaves lasting legacy.
▶ World reacts to the news.
Stories, Page 16

▶ Who will be his successor?
▶ El Papa reached Hispanics.
▶ Fresno Bee editorial.
Stories, Page 17

↗ Check out fresnobee.com for:
▶ Interactive: His life and legacy.
▶ Photography: A special slideshow.
▶ Audio: Homilies and prayers.

bishop of Rome and supreme pontiff of the Roman Catholic Church.

The pope, 84, had slipped in and out of consciousness throughout Saturday. The last medical bulletin from the Vatican, issued in the early evening, said he had developed a sudden fever in late morning. The pope had suffered from Parkinson's disease for years; his death was the culmination of a chain of medical setbacks that began in early February with influenza that forced him into a Rome hospital.

Spokesman Joaquin Navarro-Valls said the pontiff received the Viaticum, a rite for the approach of death, during an 8 p.m. bedside Mass and died surrounded by his closest

See POPE, Back Page

Valley recalls pope in prayer, services

John Paul II's legacy reaches across all faiths.

By Ron Orozco
The Fresno Bee

Bill Harvey sat in Our Lady of the Sierra Catholic Church in Oakhurst shortly after noon Saturday when he learned that Pope John Paul II had died.

Harvey, 76, prayed for the pope and wiped away tears.

"He'll be missed," Harvey said. "He really fulfilled his title throughout the world. He was a loved pope — by children, by adults, by everyone."

In the central San Joaquin Valley, Catholics such as Harvey wept over the pope's death, applauded his life and expressed relief that he no longer suffered.

A papal spokesman announced the pope's death in Vatican City at 11:37 a.m. PST. John Paul's death at age 84 ended a long struggle with debilitating illness.

Harvey had come to Our Lady of the Sierra, built in 1999 and one of the Valley's newest Catholic church-

es, specifically to pray for the pope. He was in the last pew at 12:10 p.m. Saturday when he learned about the death.

Harvey gasped, gathered his thoughts, and returned to prayer. After he finished, he said, "I can't recall another pope that passed away that all denominations had prayed for."

News of the pope's death, in fact, resonated through many faith communities.

St. Frances Cabrini Catholic Church in Woodlake began receiving calls within minutes of the pope's death, said Father Jesse Venzor.

"We've had many people call asking about services. We've even had calls from Christians who aren't Catholic who want to come and show their respect for the Holy Father," Venzor said. "The Holy Father was truly a man for all religions. He transcended the Catholic faith."

TOMAS OVALLE/THE FRESNO BEE
Monsignor Anthony Janelli prays for Pope John Paul II during a special Mass on Saturday night at St. John's Cathedral in downtown Fresno.

Non-Catholics said they appreciated what John Paul did for world peace, and they plan to closely watch the direction of the Catholic Church after cardinals elect a new pope.

Norma Madruga, who attends a Seventh-Day Adventist church in

Fresno, said, "My concerns are politically — how it affects our world. A lot of people depend on what the pope and Catholic Church have to say."

Bishop John Steinbock, leader of

See VALLEY, Back Page

SUNDAY   SERVING THE MONTEREY PENINSULA AND SALINAS VALLEY $1.50

Monterey County The Herald

Sunday, April 3, 2005

www.montereyherald.com

Spring forward
Daylight-saving time began at 2 a.m. Sunday.
Set clocks forward one hour

1920 - 2005

DEATH OF POPE TOUCHES WORLD

MILLIONS MOURN WHILE THEY HONOR PONTIFF'S LEGACY

By KEN DILANIAN,
MATTHEW SCHOFIELD
and PATRICIA MONTEMURRI
Knight Ridder Newspapers

VATICAN CITY — Pope John Paul II died Saturday after a two-day end-of-life drama that sparked an unprecedented global outpouring of attention to his life, his legacy and what lies ahead for the Roman Catholic Church.

The first news of his death came via an e-mail to journalists by the papal spokesman, and then it was announced to an estimated 70,000 people gathered in St. Peter's Square. Some wept uncontrollably, others stared in disbelief, and still others bowed their heads in prayer.

"We all feel like orphans this evening," Undersecretary of State Archbishop Leonardo Sandri told the crowd.

The bells of St. Peter's Basilica tolled in a solemn signal of mourning. People streamed into the square and the crowd overflowed into nearby streets.

Many said they knew what happened when they saw the light flick on in the window of John Paul's apartment, three stories above Bernini's colonnade.

"He was so strong, and he always spoke about our problems," said Cotbrina Tosti, 26, who was born the year he ascended to the papacy, and who stood, in tears, in the packed, hushed crowd. "He had his opinions and sometimes they were not ours, but he spoke without judgment and he always spoke with love."

In Washington, President Bush said that "the Catholic Church has lost its shepherd, the world has lost a champion of human freedom, and a good and faithful servant of God has been called home." He said the pontiff "launched a democratic revolution that swept Eastern Europe and changed the course of history. . . . We will always remember the humble, wise and fearless priest who became one of history's great moral leaders."

From the moment that senior church officials told the world on Friday that the pope was dying, the international news media focused on the Vatican with rare intensity, engaging Catholics and non-Catholics alike in the pope's fate. Perhaps not since the Sept. 11 attacks in New York has any single event so dominated the world's attention, a reflection of John Paul II's charisma, humanity and spirituality, which transcended religious doctrine.

In the United States and Britain, 24-hour news channels covered almost nothing else, beaming a

> "We will always remember the humble, wise and fearless priest who became one of history's great moral leaders."
> — President Bush

Please see **Pope page A9**

Go to:
montereyherald.com
for a photo slide show of the pope's life and to post your condolences in our online guest book.

inside
Cardinals head toward Vatican. **A7**
County dignitaries look back on pope's life. **A7**
Pope brought Catholicism to masses. **A8**
Visit to county in 1987 was blissful. **A10**

Pope John Paul II greets the crowd at Laguna Seca in Monterey on Sept. 17, 1987.

VERN FISHER/Herald File

Thousands descended on Peninsula 18 years ago to see the pontiff

Pope's 1987 visit to county sparks fond memories

By JOE LIVERNOIS
Herald Staff Writer

He walked among us here in Monterey County in 1987, the most celebrated Christian to grace the area since Father Junipero Serra built his church in Carmel more than 200 years ago.

In fact, Pope John Paul II's visit to the area was meant to honor the memory of Serra, who is buried in Carmel Mission Basilica. It was a day still vivid in the minds of the thousands who had the chance to meet or at least see the pontiff.

"It's one of my earliest memories from childhood," said Paul Del Piero, who was a mere 3 years old when the pope stepped off the plane at the Monterey Peninsula Airport, shook hands with local dignitaries and wandered over to where Paul Del Piero was standing with his mother, Tina.

The pope bent down and kissed Paul on the cheek. He then blessed Tina Del Piero's pregnant

Please see **Visit page A9**

Carmelite Monastery nuns greeted Pope John Paul II when he stopped by Carmel Mission Basilica on a Sept. 17, 1987, visit to Monterey County.

HERALD FILE

7

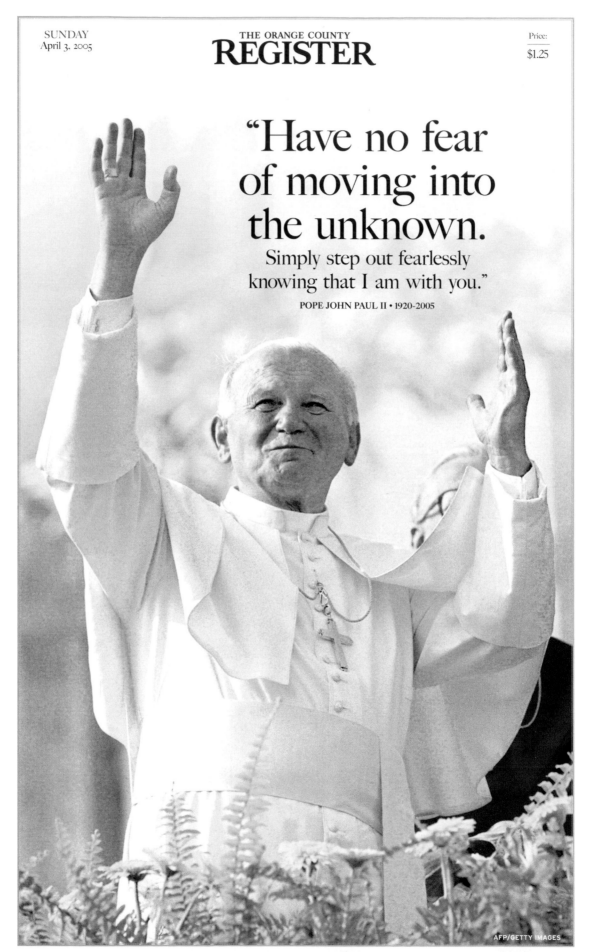

SUNDAY
April 3, 2005

THE ORANGE COUNTY
REGISTER

Price:
$1.25

"Have no fear
of moving into
the unknown.
Simply step out fearlessly
knowing that I am with you."

POPE JOHN PAUL II • 1920-2005

AFP/GETTY IMAGES

POPE MEMORIAL COVERAGE IN THIS SECTION

● **The passing**
As a priest addressed 70,000 people keeping vigil in St. Peter's Square, bells tolled, confirming the death of Pope John Paul II.
News 3

● **The world responds**
Leaders, the faithful and thousands more poured onto streets, and poured out their emotions, at the death of a man who took his faith to the world.
News 4

● **The county reacts**
Mission San Juan Capistrano's basilica bell pealed a somber message for 30 minutes. And a Polish emigre to Orange County reflects on the pope's legacy in his homeland.
News 10, 12

SPECIAL
COMMEMORATIVE
SECTION INSIDE

● **The legacy**
A man who faced down Nazis and communism, and brought a strong, abiding traditional vision to Catholicism.
8-page section behind News

**DAILY NEWS
COVERAGE BEGINS
ON NEWS 13**

The Orange County Register is a Freedom Communications newspaper. Copyright 2005
Customer service toll-free 1 (877) OCR-7009 (627-7009)
Read us online www.ocregister.com

How athletes cope when the cheering stops / SPORTS • C1

Cloudy,
late rain
62|47
Weather • B8

FOUNDED 1857 VOLUME 293, NO. 93

The Sacramento Bee

SUNDAY April 3, 2005 ★★   www.sacbee.com   • • • •   Final edition   **$1.50**

POPE JOHN PAUL II: 1920 – 2005

A world weeps

HEROIC BATTLE WITH ILLNESS ENDS HISTORIC PAPACY

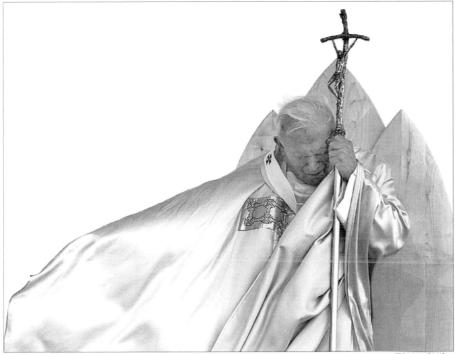

Pope John Paul II celebrates a Mass of beatification in Maribor, Slovenia, in September 1999. The pope, who died Saturday night, journeyed to about 130 countries during his quarter-century pontificate. And despite failing health, he continued traveling almost to the end of his life.

AFP/Getty Images/Gabriel Bouys

'We all feel like orphans'

BEE NEWS SERVICES

VATICAN CITY – John Paul II, the voyager pope who helped conquer communism and transformed the papacy with charisma and vigor, died Saturday night in his Vatican apartment, ending a long public struggle against debilitating illness. He was 84.

"We all feel like orphans this evening," Undersecretary of State Archbishop Leonardo Sandri told the crowd of approximately 70,000 that gathered in St. Peter's Square below the pope's still-lighted apartment windows.

A Mass was scheduled for St. Peter's Square for 10:30 a.m. (1:30 a.m. PDT) today. The pope's body was expected to be taken to St. Peter's Basilica no earlier than Monday afternoon, the Vatican said.

Bells pealed in mourning after the Vatican announced that the pope had died at 9:37 p.m. The assembled flock fell into a stunned silence before many in the crowd broke out in applause, an Italian tradition in which mourners clap for important figures. Others simply wept at the news of the passing of the leader of the world's 1.2 billion Roman Catholics.

He was surrounded at his death by a
▶ POPE, page A19

INSIDE
Photographs capture how the pope touched lives.
▶ Page A15

The pope left a political legacy as a Cold War fighter.
▶ Page A17

sacbee

To read more coverage of the pope's death online, please go to:
www.sacbee.com

Many laud pontiff's quest to heal, unite

SPECIAL MASSES
In addition to regularly scheduled Masses at all parishes today, the Sacramento Diocese is offering the following Masses in honor of Pope John Paul II. Auxiliary Bishop Richard Garcia will preside at each service.

Today
9:30 a.m.: Westminster Presbyterian Church, 1300 N St., Sacramento

7:30 p.m.: Spanish-language Mass at Our Lady of Guadalupe Church, 711 T St., Sacramento

Wednesday
6 p.m.: St. Ignatius Loyola Parish, 3235 Arden Way, Sacramento

By Sam Stanton
BEE STAFF WRITER

Brad Bloom was just a year out of college in 1978, the year John Paul II was elected pope at the youthful age of 58, and he still remembers his first impression of the new pontiff.

"I just remember looking at a Newsweek or something, and there's a picture of him skiing," said Bloom, now 48 and the rabbi at Congregation B'nai Israel in Sacramento. "It wasn't the image you'd expect of a pope, the usual one of someone dressed in clerical gown and robes and cloistered at the Vatican."

That exuberance for life came to embody the 26 years of John Paul's papacy. On Saturday, as word spread that his fight against illness had finally ended, his unique nature and warm embrace of others were recalled again and again throughout the Sacramento region.

"He's the only pope I've ever known," said Gina Crosthwaite, a 31-year-old youth minis-

ter from Oroville who had brought 13 children to the 53rd annual youth conference Saturday at Christian Brothers High School, a Catholic institution in Oak Park.

Crosthwaite, who came to the conference with her husband, Ray, said the pope's death left her wanting to return home.

Others among the 400 teens at the confer-
▶ REACTION, page A14

The Rev. Philip Massetti, head of the Marello Youth Retreat Center in Loomis, prays with teens Saturday in memory of the pontiff at Christian Brothers High.

Sacramento Bee/Lezlie Sterling

He cast aside ancient ways

By Jennifer Garza
BEE STAFF WRITER

Pope John Paul II reached beyond the walls of the Vatican, radically changing the papacy and how it shapes the world.

He will be remembered for his meetings with world leaders, his contributions to the end of the Cold War, his struggle to recover from a would-be assassin's bullet.

But perhaps more than anything, the pontiff will be remembered for his ability to connect with the faithful.

For centuries, leaders of the Roman Catholic Church were carried on ornate chairs and rarely left the comforts of the Vatican. Over the 26 years of his pontificate, Pope John Paul II visited 130 countries. He made seven trips to the United States.

When asked why he traveled so much, even to countries with small Catholic populations, he'd smile and say, "I must visit my people."
▶ IMPACT, page A17

'Minutemen' spur immigration debate

By Margaret Talev
BEE WASHINGTON BUREAU

TOMBSTONE, Ariz. – In terms of drawing attention to the complexities and divisiveness of illegal immigration across the U.S.-Mexico border, the Minuteman Project already has exceeded organizers' expectations.

The self-styled brigade of more than 1,000 Americans who've signed up to patrol a stretch of the border continuously over the next month, beginning Monday,

and turn in illegal immigrants to authorities convened only two days ago.

Yet, already, President Bush has called them vigilantes. The Mexican government has formally objected to their presence. Officials say Mara Salvatrucha, a violent Salvadoran gang that controls much of the border smuggling, has threatened to retaliate against so-called Minutemen who get in the way. Immigrant
▶ BORDER, back page, A20

INSIDE THE BEE

SPORTS • C1
Down to two
Illinois will take on North Carolina on Monday night for the NCAA title after the Illini whipped Louisville 72-57 and the Tar Heels ran past Michigan State 87-71.

TRAVEL • M1
Nonstop hops
From Atlanta to Washington, D.C., Sacramento International Airport now offers nonstop flights to 28 destinations.

Complete index on page A2
©2005, The Sacramento Bee

Outdated technology slows state to a crawl

Information systems stumble along as work begins on fixes.

By Clea Benson
BEE CAPITOL BUREAU

When it comes time for the state to send monthly paychecks to more than 200,000 employees, someone in the controller's office in downtown Sacramento downloads the data from a mainframe computer onto a tape the size of

an eight-track and walks it over to the room that houses the printers.

The information-transfer process takes so long that the controller's staff has to start it before the end of the pay period to get the checks mailed out on time.

And if anything goes wrong, only the old-timers on the controller's staff know how to fix it. The payroll program was written about 30 years ago in a computer language so ancient that to recent computer-science graduates, it
▶ STATE, back page, A20

9

The San Diego Union-Tribune.

SUNDAY
APRIL 3, 2005

REGIONAL
$1.75
PLUS TAX
. . . .

◄ SPECIAL SECTION INSIDE. MORE COVERAGE: A8-A10; INSIGHT, G1.

MAY 18, 1920 – APRIL 2, 2005

JOHN PAUL II

John Paul II led Roman Catholics for 26 years, making his the third-longest papacy in church history. *1999 Associated Press photo*

Death of pontiff evokes worldwide outpouring of grief

**By Daniel Williams
and Alan Cooperman**
THE WASHINGTON POST

VATICAN CITY — John Paul II, the voyager pope who helped conquer communism and transformed the papacy with charisma and vigor, died last night after a long battle with Parkinson's disease that became a lesson to the world in humble suffering.

"Our most beloved Holy Father has returned to the house of the Father," Archbishop Leonardo Sandri, a senior Vatican official, told pilgrims in St. Peter's Square.

The throng of 50,000 momentarily stood in stunned silence, stared at the pavement and shed tears. Then, following an Italian custom that signifies hope at a time of death, the mourners broke into sustained applause.

John Paul died at 9:37 p.m. local time in the Vatican's Apostolic Palace on a clear and cool night, with a small group of Polish prelates and nuns at his bedside. The first indication of the pope's passing was the illumination of several windows in his private quarters overlooking the piazza. An e-mail announcement followed. A half-hour later, the bells of all of Rome's

SEE **Pope, A9**

San Diegans pack churches to share prayers, memories

By Mark Sauer
STAFF WRITER

Church bells are tolling the sad news across San Diego this morning as Catholics here join their brethren around the world to mourn the passing of Pope John Paul II.

Some wept as they prayed or lighted votive candles; others busied themselves preparing for evening Mass or draping photos of the late pontiff in black cloth yesterday. They reflected on the legacy of John Paul, who for more than a quarter century led the world's 1 billion Catholics, including more than a million locally.

The Rev. Edward Traczyk, pastor of St. Maximillian Kolbe Polish Mission in Pacific Beach, told callers in Polish and English of plans to honor the pontiff with prayer services all this week.

"What we have on top of being Catholic is also that we are Poles. There's some closeness to him because he was one of us," said Traczyk, who is from a city 50 miles south of Krakow, Poland, where

SEE **San Diego, A8**

Baseball starting off 2005 in foul territory

Fallout from steroid scandal lingers as new season arrives

By Chris Jenkins, STAFF WRITER

For the record, it's still there: Second level, Section 4, Row 5, Seat 12.

Major league baseball isn't played at Qualcomm Stadium anymore. Virtually the entire playing surface is covered with grass, with no base paths or mound or home plate cutouts. A

single white seat amid some 65,000 dark blue ones is the lone physical reminder of the 36 years and thousands of big league games played there.

The fold-down chair was painted white with a red "M" to commemorate a 458-foot home run struck by St. Louis Cardinals slugger Mark McGwire in 1998, the year he broke Roger Maris' long-standing record of 61 homers in a single season. "Big Mac," with a body so pumped-up as to be cartoonish, went on to finish with 70. The seat's red M, like

McGwire's image, is fading.

Completely gone is any reminder of the most ferocious and maybe longest ball ever hit in Mission Valley, a grand slam that Barry Bonds of the San Francisco Giants hit with such power on June 5, 2002, that it actually dented the JumboTron scoreboard. Some new sheet metal and paint took care of that memory.

Downtown's Petco Park now houses the

SEE **Baseball, A11**

◄ SPECIAL SECTION: Baseball 2005, your Padres season preview.

IN SPORTS: Padres make their final cuts before the season begins.

IN BOOKS: Wild pitches and wild men, our scorecard of this year's baseball books.

Right to know
Opening the calendars of your county supervisors. **Local, B1**
A guide to how you can access government records. **Local, B7**

Two left standing
Illinois knocks out Louisville 72-57. North Carolina eliminates Michigan State 87-71 in the men's NCAA tournament. **Sports, C1**

Later than you think?
Be sure you set your clocks ahead; daylight-saving time began at 2 a.m.

Inside

Airfares	D2	Crossword E4	Movies F6
Bridge	E4	Dear Abby E7	Obituaries J5
Nick Canepa	C1	Editorials G2	Burl Stiff E7
Classifieds	K1	Horoscope E7	TV Week Inside
Comics	Inside	Lottery B2	Weather B8

Online at www.uniontrib.com

A COPLEY NEWSPAPER
29 sections   382 pages

APRIL 3, 2005

THE SUNDAY DENVER POST

DENVERPOST.COM | © THE DENVER POST | *Voice of the Rocky Mountain Empire* | $1 MAY VARY | *&* Rocky Mountain News | ★★

POPE JOHN PAUL II | 1920-2005

Exalted in memory

Peter Turnley | The Denver Post

Silent prayers and flowing tears fill St. Peter's Square on Saturday after the news of Pope John Paul II's death. An estimated 70,000 people crowded the square, spilling into nearby streets.

Colorado's faithful gather amid tears, prayers, praise

By Chuck Plunkett
Denver Post Staff Writer

Shortly after the Vatican confirmed the passing of Pope John Paul II, Gloria Stano climbed the extension ladder another time. She wanted to make sure the black bunting she had hung over the entrance to Notre Dame Roman Catholic Parish church in southwest Denver was just right.

Her husband, Joe, helped steady her.

In the bright sun, the black crepe formed a peak over the big wooden doors. Behind Gloria Stano, the peak of Mount Evans gleamed white in a blue sky.

Across Colorado, Catholics found ways to mark the passing of a global spiritual leader who reigned for nearly a generation.

While Gloria Stano worked, the faithful passed underneath to go inside and pray.

"I think he was awesome," Stano said. "He was on our level. He reached down to all of us."

At Our Lady of Mount Carmel in north Denver, the Rev. Tim Kremen reflected on the time he shook the pope's hand during a program in Rome.

And another, less formal time, when he saw the pontiff in St. Louis. There, a child handed the pope a hockey stick.

"He was so proud (of the gift)," Kremen said. "He perked up when children were around."

The pope's concern for youth was displayed on a grand scale in Denver in 1993, when he attended the World Youth Day festival during a summer marred by gang violence.

During the festival, John Paul visit-

> See **REACTION** on 14A

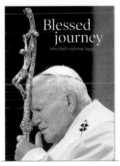

Blessed journey
John Paul's enduring legacy

Retrospective: John Paul II was an electrifying personality and a resilient and influential leader. > Special Section

Succession: The process of choosing a pope, and what traits the new pope is likely to possess. > 33A

Denver's archbishop: Charles Chaput grieves for a fatherly spirit. > 11A

Pontiff's death stirs a world of emotions

His final hours draw reflection and praise. Then mourning begins for "one of history's great moral leaders."

By Knight Ridder Newspapers

Vatican City — Pope John Paul II died Saturday after a two-day end-of-life drama that sparked an unprecedented global outpouring of attention to his life, his legacy and what lies ahead for the Roman Catholic Church.

The first news of his death came via an e-mail to journalists by the papal spokesman, and then it was announced to an estimated 70,000 people gathered in St. Peter's Square.

Some wept uncontrollably, others stared in disbelief, and still others bowed their heads in prayer.

"We all feel like orphans this evening," Undersecretary of State Archbishop Leonardo Sandri told the crowd.

The bells of St. Peter's Basilica tolled in a solemn signal of mourning.

People streamed into the square, and the crowd overflowed into nearby streets.

Many said they knew what happened when they saw the light flick on in the window of John Paul's apartment, three stories above Bernini's colonnade.

"He was so strong, and he always spoke about our problems," said Cotbrina Tosti, 26, who was born the year John Paul ascended to the papacy and who stood, in tears, in the packed, hushed crowd.

> See **DEATH** on 8A

Aging warheads set for overhaul, but many want them scrapped

By William J. Broad
The New York Times

For more than two decades, a compact, powerful warhead called the W-76 has been the centerpiece of the nation's nuclear arsenal, carried aboard the fleet of nuclear submarines that prowl the Atlantic and Pacific oceans.

But in recent months, the warhead has become the subject of a fierce debate among experts inside and outside the government over its reliability and its place in the nuclear arsenal.

The government is readying a plan to spend more than $2 billion on a routine 10-year overhaul to extend the life of the aging warheads. At the same time, some weapons scientists say the warheads have a fundamental design flaw that could cause them to explode with far less force than intended.

Although the government has denied that assertion, officials have disclosed that Washington is nevertheless considering replacing the W-76

> See **ARSENAL** on 24A

Citizen border patrol: patriots or vigilantes?

About 400 people — many of them armed — will watch for illegal migrants crossing into the U.S. through the desert.

By Michael Riley
Denver Post Staff Writer

Tombstone, Ariz. — Closely watched by nervous governments on both sides of the border, hundreds of anti-immigrant activists fanned out into the desert of southern Arizona on Saturday, launching a self-styled citizen patrol to spot illegal immigrants sneaking into the United States.

The 400 or so volunteers of what's known as the Minuteman Project got an enthusiastic send-off from Colorado U.S. Rep. Tom Tancredo, one of the nation's harshest critics of immigration policy.

Tancredo dismissed critics who say the activists are taking the law into their own hands.

"We are saying to our government, 'Please enforce the law.' That's not a radical idea; that's not a vigilante idea," said Tancredo, who received a standing ovation Friday at a packed orientation meeting before the patrols began.

"It's an American concept," he said.

On the Mexican side of the border,

patrols of soldiers were trying to dissuade groups of immigrants Saturday from crossing in areas east of Tucson that the activists plan to patrol.

On the U.S. side, the Border Patrol said it didn't want the activists' help.

"We don't support this; we don't condone it," said Andrea Zortman, a Border Patrol spokeswoman. "We feel they are going to be more of a hindrance to our job than a help."

None of that dampened the enthusiasm of the participants, some from as far away as Florida and New York, who descended on the border town of

> See **BORDER** on 23A

Rocky Mountain News

MONDAY, APRIL 4, 2005   ROCKYMOUNTAINNEWS.COM   ★ 50 cents in Denver

'Man of peace' at peace

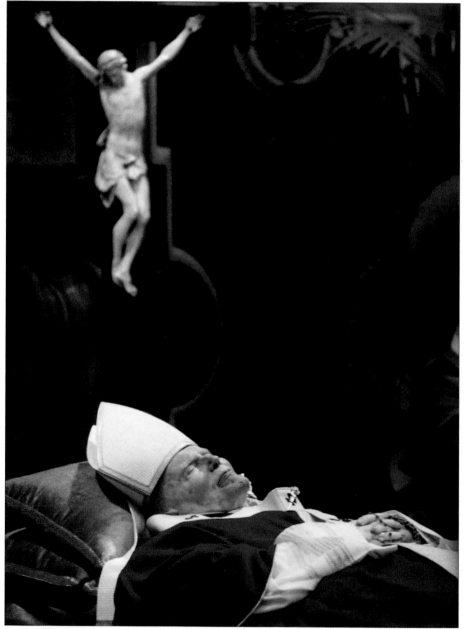

MASSIMO SAMBUCETTI/ASSOCIATED PRESS

Pope lies in state at the Vatican

The body of Pope John Paul II, dressed in a white bishop's miter and crimson vestments, lies in state in Clementine Hall at the Vatican on Sunday. An estimated 100,000 people attended a Mass at St. Peter's Square to mourn the pope. His body will be moved to St. Peter's Basilica today for public viewing. President Bush is expected to join other world leaders and attend the pontiff's funeral. **21A**

■ **Local Catholics** honor Holy Father with prayers, memories. **5A**

Battle over justice center

■ **Mayor backs** $378 million plan on May 3 ballot; foes call it too costly, urge alternatives. **6A**

COLORADO

AIDS cases up in ski resort towns

W. Slope playgrounds see highest rates of disease in rural Colorado. **4A**

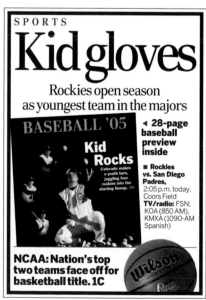

SPORTS

Kid gloves

Rockies open season as youngest team in the majors

BASEBALL '05

Kid Rocks
Colorado makes a youth turn, juggling four rookies into the starting lineup. 2H

◄ **28-page baseball preview inside**

■ **Rockies vs. San Diego Padres,** 2:05 p.m. today, Coors Field
TV/radio: FSN; KOA (850 AM), KMXA (1090-AM Spanish)

NCAA: Nation's top two teams face off for basketball title. 1C

MILE HIGH TECH

Local tech firms booming years after dot-com bust

Software makers IQNavigator, Vericept thrive. **1B**

Hartford ❦ Courant.

America's Oldest
Continuously
Published Newspaper

WEATHER
Scattered Showers.
High Of 53. B8

VOLUME CLXIX, NUMBER 93   COPYRIGHT 2005, THE HARTFORD COURANT CO.   SUNDAY, APRIL 3, 2005   ★★★ $2.00 in Fairfield County and outside Connecticut   **$1.50**

POPE JOHN PAUL II · KAROL WOJTYLA: 1920-2005

IN PEACE

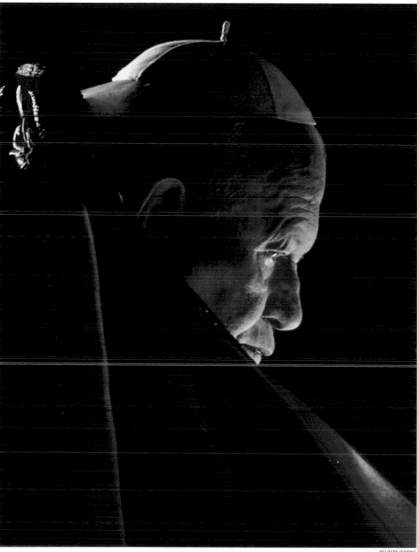

REUTERS/CORBIS

POPE JOHN PAUL II, who died Saturday at 84, was a pontiff who traveled the world and was known for his close personal connection with the Catholic faithful. He was the first non-Italian pope since the 16th century and his papacy encompassed 26 years of change. He is shown during a service in Rome in 2003.

John Paul Gave Papacy A Voice In World Change

By **DANIEL WILLIAMS** And **ALAN COOPERMAN**
WASHINGTON POST

John Paul II, the voyager pope who helped conquer communism and transformed the papacy with charisma and vigor, died Saturday night in Vatican City after a long battle with Parkinson's disease that became a lesson to the world in humble suffering.

"Our most beloved Holy Father has returned to the house of the Father," Archbishop Leonardo Sandri, a senior Vatican official, told pilgrims in St. Peter's Square. The throng of 50,000 momentarily stood in stunned silence, stared at the pavement and shed tears. Then, following an Italian custom that signifies hope at a time of death, the mourners broke into sustained applause.

John Paul died at 9:37 local time in the Vatican's Apostolic Palace on a clear and cool night, with a small group of Polish prelates and nuns at his bedside. The first indication of the pope's passing was the illumination of several windows in his private quarters overlooking St. Peter's Square. An e-mail announcement followed. A half-hour later, the bells of all of Rome's churches rang out in mourning.

The news evoked an outpouring of emotion for the man around the world. In Paris, mourners packed special midnight services, church bells sounded in Cuba. President Bush called John Paul "a champion of human freedom" and "a good and faithful servant of God."

"We're grateful to God for sending such a man, a son of Poland," he said.

The pope's body will lie in state in St. Peter's Basilica starting Monday afternoon. The date of his funeral will be set by a gathering of cardinals Monday morning, but under guidelines he had set it should take place within four to six days of his death. Within 15 to 20 days, the College of Cardinals will meet in the Sistine Chapel to elect a successor as bishop of Rome and supreme pontiff of the 1 billion-plus-member Roman Catholic Church.

The pope, who was 84, had slipped in and out of consciousness throughout Saturday. The last medical bulletin from the Vatican, issued in the early evening, said he had developed a sudden fever in late morning. The pope had suffered from Parkinson's disease for years; his death was the culmination of a chain of medical setbacks that began in early February with influenza that forced him into a Rome hospital.

His death ended the Roman Catholic Church's third-longest papacy, a reign that was at once energetic, charismatic and polarizing.

John Paul successfully encouraged the largely peaceful revolts against Soviet rule in his native Poland and across Eastern Europe. He was the most traveled pontiff in the 2,000-

PLEASE SEE **VOICE,** PAGE A12

In A City That A Young Cardinal Once Visited, Many Hoped For A Miracle

By **VALERIE FINHOLM, KATHLEEN MEGAN** And **FRANCES GRANDY TAYLOR** · COURANT STAFF WRITERS

The pews at Sacred Heart Church in New Britain started filling up Saturday shortly after the news that Pope John Paul II had died.

The Mass had been scheduled for 4 p.m., but by 3:30 most of the candles of remembrance had been lit and the pews were filled by a wide range of people, including white-haired couples neatly dressed in suits, teenagers in sweatshirts with their hair pulled back, mothers holding toddlers and single people in their 20s or 30s. Many people kneeled in silent prayer. Some were red-eyed from weeping.

New Britain, the state's most Polish town, had a special bond with the Polish pope because he had visited there when he was a cardinal.

"I'm not sure all of you here heard the news: At 2:37 this afternoon, Pope John Paul II died," said Msgr. Daniel J. Plocharczyk.

During the sermon, he spoke about having been besieged by the media since Thursday when it be-

PLEASE SEE **TEARS, PRAYERS,** PAGE A14

SPECIAL SECTION

Requiem: Karol Wojtyla made history many times during his 26-year reign. This sections looks at the pope's legacy around the world. **Section S, behind Section A**

The College of Cardinals was reshaped profoundly by John Paul himself. **Page A13.**

IN NORTHEAST MAGAZINE: BEYOND COMPLICITY

CONNECTICUT'S VOYAGE INTO SLAVERY

For centuries, Connecticut's involvement in the transatlantic slave trade has been almost entirely hidden. But a ship's log uncovered in the Connecticut State Library reveals that 250 years ago, Connecticut men in Connecticut ships were on the front lines of the slave trade. They worked the coast of Africa trading New England products for men, women and children to sell in the West Indies, the American South and the cities of our state. The log led staff writer Anne Farrow, photographer Tom Brown and videographer Alan Chaniewski to the ruins of a slave castle on the coast of Sierra Leone in West Africa. Over more than a century, 50,000 Africans were funneled through the slave-trading operation on Bunce Island before being forced to make the often deadly passage across the Atlantic. Today's Northeast is a revelatory chapter in Connecticut's buried history.

13

50403
6 04209 00150 1

REGION: Amtrak Outlines $50 Million Repair Plan For State's Bridges   **SPORTS:** N. Carolina, Illinois Advance To NCAA Men's Basketball Title Game

The Day

MARE LIBERUM · VOX LIBERA

Spring forward

Daylight-saving time began at 2 a.m., so remember to set clocks ahead one hour.

SUNDAY, APRIL 3, 2005, NEW LONDON   SERVING EASTERN CONNECTICUT SINCE 1881   VOL. 124, No. 276   132 PAGES $1.50

News · Section A   **Sports** · Section B   **Perspective** · Section C   **Region** · Section D   **Classified** · Section E   **Business** · Section F   **Daybreak** · Section G

POPE JOHN PAUL II ✦ 1920-2005

WORLD MOURNS POPE

Across 26 Years, Pope's Impact Was Extraordinary

By **ROBERT D. McFADDEN**
New York Times News Service

WHEN CARDINAL KAROL WOJTYLA of Poland was elected pope in 1978, it was quickly evident that this was to be an extraordinary pontificate, one that would captivate much of humanity by sheer force of personality and reshape the church with a heroic vision of a combative, disciplined Catholicism.

It was to be the longest and most luminous pontificate of the 20th century, and (depending on how St. Peter is counted) the second- or third-longest history — a 26-year era that would witness sweeping political changes around the world, the growth of the Roman church to nearly 1 billion baptized members from 750 million, and the beginning of Christianity's Third Millennium.

The man who would call himself John Paul II was not the traditional papal figure, compassionate and loving but ascetic and remote behind the high walls and elaborate ceremony of the Vatican. Here was a different kind of pope: complex, schooled in confrontation, theologically intransigent but deftly politic, full of wit and daring, energy and physically expressive love. He was also the

See **JOHN PAUL II** *page* **A8**

Region's clergy praise pope as force for peace

By **IZASKUN E. LARRAÑETA**
Day Staff Writer

As Pope John Paul II lay dying, leaders of local religious communities expressed sorrow, calling the pope a leader who made great strides in bringing unity among faiths.

Protestant, Jewish and Muslim leaders spoke admiringly of the Roman Catholic leader who opened up relations with believers in the world's other great religions, and hoped the next pope would do the same.

On Saturday, after the Vatican announced the pope had died at 9:37 p.m. Rome time, Bishop Michael Cote of the Catholic Diocese of Norwich said he would celebrate a Memorial Mass for the pope this afternoon at the Cathedral of St. Patrick.

"It is with great sadness that we have learned of the death of our Holy Father, Pope John Paul II," Cote said in a statement. "Today, I wish to add my

See **RELIGIOUS** *page* **A7**

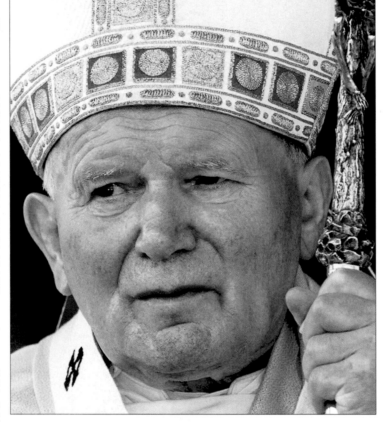

◼ *Above, the most-traveled of all pontiffs, Pope John Paul II, is shown during his first Mass in Cuba in this 1998 photo.*

DOMENICO STINELLIS
Associated Press

INSIDE

◼ The region's Roman Catholic parishioners mourn the loss Saturday of Pope John Paul II with prayer and reflection while remembering the impact he made on worshippers of all denominations. / **D1**

◼ The process used by the College of Cardinals to pick a successor to John Paul II has ancient roots. / **A6**

◼ Catholics throughout Connecticut remember the pope as one who spoke out for peace. / **D9**

College of Cardinals sets in motion process for pontiff's funeral

By **VICTOR L. SIMPSON**
Associated Press Writer

Vatican City — Pope John Paul II, who helped topple communism in Europe and left a deeply conservative stamp on the church that he led for 26 years, died Saturday night in his Vatican apartment, ending a long public struggle against debilitating illness. He was 84.

"We all feel like orphans this evening," Undersecretary of State Archbishop Leonardo Sandri told the crowd of 70,000 that gathered in St. Peter's Square below the pope's still-lighted apartment windows.

In the massive piazza that stretches from St. Peter's Basilica, the assembled flock fell into a stunned silence before some people broke into applause — an Italian tradition in which mourners often clap for important figures. Others wept. Still others recited the rosary. A seminarian slowly waved a large red and white Polish flag draped with black bunting for the Polish-born pontiff, the most-traveled pope in history.

At one point, prelates asked those in the square to stay silent so they might "accompany the pope in his first steps into heaven."

But as the Vatican bells tolled in mourning, a group of young people sang, "Alleluia, he will rise again." One strummed a guitar, and other pilgrims joined in singing the "Ave Maria."

"The angels welcome you," Vatican TV said after papal spokesman Joaquin Navarro-Valls announced the death of the pope, who had for years suffered from Parkinson's disease and came down with fever and infections in recent weeks.

In contrast to the church's ancient traditions, Navarro-Valls announced the death to journalists in the most modern of communication forms, an e-mail that said: "The Holy Father died this evening at 9:37 p.m. in his private apartment." The spokesman said church officials now would be following instructions that John Paul had written for them on Feb. 22, 1996. A precise cause of death was not given.

In the last two days of the pope's life, after it had become clear he would not recover, the tide of humanity near the Vatican had ebbed and flowed, swelling again Saturday night.

"He was a marvelous man. Now he's no longer suffering," Concetta Sposato, a pilgrim who heard the pope had died as she was on her way to St. Peter's to pray, said tearfully.

"My father died last year. For me, it feels the same," said Elisabetta Pomacalca, a 25-year-old Peruvian who lives in Rome.

"I'm Polish. For us, he was a father," said pilgrim Beata Sowa.

See **PONTIFF** *page* **A7**

Mock Terror Attacks Reveal Flaws In Response Systems

Huge New London drill this week designed to find public safety shortfalls

Insurgents Mount Attack On Abu Ghraib

At least 40 militants used rocket-propelled grenades, small-arms fire and two car bombs to attack the Abu Ghraib prison west of Baghdad Saturday, injuring 20 U.S. troops and 12 prisoners and heightening fears that militants are gearing up for more attacks.

See story **A2**

◼ *Seattle police scramble over rubble as first-responders during the 2003 terrorism-response exercise in that city.*

ELAINE THOMSON / Associated Press

By **ETHAN ROUEN**
Day Staff Writer

MUSTARD GAS HAD BEEN RELEASED at the Port Authority.

City Hall in Portsmouth, N.H., and local first responders were being stretched thin.

Federal agencies moved in to assist with the cleanup and to hunt for the terrorists who released the gas, but things seemed to get worse.

On that April day in 2000, the command center was chaotic, packed with people shouting orders. Even though it was only a drill, the first of an ongoing series of mock terror attacks mandated by Congress, the stress was beginning to wear on the taxed responders.

"As the incident commander, I had to kick everyone out," said Ricky Plummer, then the fire chief in Portsmouth. "It just got out of control."

Communication between local, state and federal agencies has been one of the biggest failings in the two TOPOFF exercises held so far. The Department of Homeland Security hopes that won't be the case this week when it tests a new National Response Plan during

How this week's drill will affect New London / A5

TOPOFF3 in New London and New Jersey.

New London City Manager Richard Brown said the drill will be less of a test of first responders — he's confident they'll perform well — and more of a test of whether agencies can work together.

The drills strive for accuracy, using actual explosions and volunteer victims with fake wounds and looking like they are impaled with shrapnel. The drills are designed to overwhelm the agencies responding to the attacks to find faults that can be corrected, officials said.

See **DRILL** *page* **A5**

Weather
Today: *Cloudy, rain.*
High 53, Low 38.
Monday: *Mostly sunny.*
High 66, Low 44.
Details, C14

The Washington Post

MARYLAND
EDITION

$1.50

128TH YEAR NO. 119   M2   MO   SUNDAY, APRIL 3, 2005   M₁ M₂ M₃ M₄ V₁ V₂ V₃ V₄

Prices may vary in areas outside metropolitan Washington. (See box on A4)

John Paul II Dies at 84

Long-Serving and Well-Traveled Pope Persevered Despite Illness

Pope John Paul II was the most traveled pontiff in the history of the church, visiting 129 countries outside Italy.

2001 PHOTO BY CLAUDIO PAPI — REUTERS

By Daniel Williams *and* Alan Cooperman
Washington Post Foreign Service

VATICAN CITY, April 2 — John Paul II, the voyager pope who helped conquer communism and transformed the papacy with charisma and vigor, died Saturday night after a long battle with Parkinson's disease that became a lesson to the world in humble suffering.

"Our most beloved Holy Father has returned to the house of the Father," Archbishop Leonardo Sandri, a senior Vatican official, told pilgrims in St. Peter's Square. The throng of about 60,000 momentarily stood in stunned silence, stared at the pavement and wept. Then, following an Italian custom that signifies hope at a time of death, the mourners broke into sustained applause.

John Paul died at 9:37 local time in the Vatican's Apostolic Palace on a clear and cool night, with a small group of Polish prelates and nuns at his bedside. The first indication of the pope's passing was the illumination of several windows in his private quarters overlooking St. Peter's Square. An e-mail announcement followed. A half-hour later, the bells of all of Rome's

churches rang out in mourning.

The news evoked an outpouring of emotion throughout the world. In Paris, mourners packed special midnight services; church bells sounded in Cuba. President Bush called John Paul "a champion of human freedom" and "a good and faithful servant of God. . . . We're grateful to God for sending such a man, a son of Poland."

The pope's body will lie in state in St. Peter's Basilica beginning Monday afternoon. The date of his funeral will be set by a gathering of cardinals on Monday morning, but under guidelines set by him, it should take place within four to six days of his death. Within 15 to 20 days, the College of Cardinals will meet in the Sistine Chapel to elect a successor as bishop of Rome and supreme pontiff of the 1 billion-plus-member Roman Catholic Church.

The pope, who was 84, had slipped in and out of consciousness Saturday. The last medical bulletin from the Vatican, issued in the early evening, said he had developed a sudden fever in late morning. The pope had

See POPE, *A33, Col. 1*

His Successor

Pontiff's Road Map Will Guide Selection

By Daniel Williams
Washington Post Foreign Service

VATICAN CITY, April 2 — Shrouded in deep secrecy and rooted in medieval tradition, the choice of the next pope will bear the legacy of John Paul II, who appointed all but three of the 117 voting cardinals who will gather beneath the frescoed ceiling of the Sistine Chapel to choose his successor. When they write the names of candidates by hand on rectangular cards for the balloting, it will be under rules that John Paul set nearly a decade ago.

John Paul's influence was so strong in every corner of the church that almost everyone in the emerging set of *papabili* — men who could be pope — shares his basic views. Joseph Ratzinger, John Paul's chief guardian of doctrine, was in full accord with the last pope's stances on sex and church discipline. Claudio Hummes of Brazil, for instance, became known for speaking out against the social harm of unrestrained capitalism, a favorite issue for John Paul.

So as Roman Catholics approach the defining moment of a papal election, all signs are that the church will stick broadly to its current course. The new pope is likely to stress a need for firm moral direction against the temptations of materialism in contemporary life. He will favor centralized Vatican authority. He is likely to firmly oppose abortion, euthanasia, contraception and the ordination of women, all issues of interest to

See SUCCESSION, *A41, Col. 1*

POPE JOHN PAUL II
1920-2005

The Church Loses Its Light
In John Paul II, World Record at Direct, Dynamic Leader

Special Section

A 12-page report looks back at the life of John Paul II, his role as a theologian, his handling of the sex abuse scandal and his embrace of the Third World. Plus, reaction to his death from across the region and around the world, a look at possible successors and a guide to the selection process. *A31-A42*

In Style: An appreciation of John Paul II, a look back at his trip to Washington in 1979 and a special KidsPost tribute.

His Legacy

A Papacy and Church Transformed

By Hanna Rosin
Washington Post Staff Writer

So much was expected of Karol Wojtyla when he became pope in 1978. Here, for the first time, was a pontiff plucked not from the Vatican's perfumed inner chambers, but a man of the world. He was not Italian; he skied, he kayaked, he acted in dramas. His fellow clerics compared him to John Wayne.

His faith, too, seemed tested. He had lost his mother early, lived in the shadow of Auschwitz, performed forced labor in a limestone quarry. "Do Not Be Afraid" was his motto at his inauguration, and one sensed that after living through Poland's brutal mid-century, he no longer was.

So even before his first papal pronouncement, he was granted a place in history as the Roman Catholic Church's first modern pope, charged with leading the centuries-old institution into the next millennium —

the "new springtime of Christianity," as he called it.

And 26 years later, it's by that yardstick that Pope John Paul II's legacy will be judged, both in the church he transformed and in the world he tried so hard to influence.

For those who expected more from the modernization — American priests ordained in the 1960s, say, Catholic women who wanted to be priests or Latin American leaders who wanted a partner in revolution — the pope not only betrayed his promise but locked the church in place for years to come.

"I'm of the generation of priests who were euphoric about the idea that the church could change," said the Rev. Andrew Greeley, an author and columnist. "And while I recognize all his great talents, I think he pulled the plug on it, and that greatly dismays me."

But to his many admirers, John Paul succeeded brilliantly

See ANALYSIS, *A32, Col. 1*

At St. Peter's Square, Raffaella Sabatini is among the thousands praying for the pope after his death was announced.

BY LUCIAN PERKINS — THE WASHINGTON POST

Spring Forward

Clocks should have been set forward one hour at 2 a.m. today.

The Post on the Internet:
washingtonpost.com

Contents © 2005
The
Washington
Post
Company

0 70628 27100 7

For the Nationals, a Chaotic Journey Home

Labyrinth of Political Challenges Preceded Today's Debut at RFK

By Lori Montgomery, Barry Svrluga *and* Thomas Heath
Washington Post Staff Writers

On a steamy morning in August, key figures in the campaign to bring baseball to Northern Virginia gathered in a Georgetown law office for a meeting with Major League Baseball. They had some shocking news.

The Virginia baseball bid, years in the making, had been gaining momentum because of the league's long reluctance to put a team in the District. But now the group had to report that Gov. Mark R. Warner (D) had joined legislative leaders in rejecting a plan to use state-supported bonds to build a stadium near Dulles International Airport.

For a long, painful moment, baseball's chief negotiator, Chicago White Sox owner Jerry Reinsdorf, said nothing. Then his team ordered the Virginians out of the room.

"We didn't know what was going to happen to us," recalled Keith Frederick, chairman of the Virginia Baseball Stadium Authority. Executive Director Gabe Paul Jr. said he remembers thinking they had just slit their own throats.

Reinsdorf was weighing two bids for the ailing Montreal Expos. Virginia's bid was falling apart. The other, from the District, had solid public financing and unwavering political support. But baseball officials weren't ready to give in to the District yet. When the meeting resumed, Reinsdorf gave Virginia two weeks to come up with a

new financing plan.

In the final weeks of the process, the Washington region was competing against itself — city vs. suburb — each side scrambling to throw more cash and sweet enticements on the baseball bargaining table. In late September, the District won its tortuous, 33-year quest for a new ballclub by agreeing to a financing plan for the stadium, the costs of which have soared to $581 million.

Today, the former Expos will play here for the first time as the Washington Nationals. But even as they take the field for an exhibition game against the New York Mets, the franchise is handicapped by the strange, chaotic circumstances of its birth

See NATIONALS, *A12, Col. 1*

INSIDE

Illinois, N. Carolina In Final
The Illini and Tar Heels will play for NCAA basketball title after topping Louisville and Michigan State. SPORTS, *E1*

Iraq Convulsions
An insurgent assault at Abu Ghraib prison wounds 18 American GIs. Meanwhile, Shiite clergy threaten protest over political impasse. WORLD, *A16*

Another Soggy Day
Almost two inches of rain fall on the area. METRO, *C1*

Education Issue
30 great local high schools; how to find good classes online. THE MAGAZINE

Today's contents are on A2

15

DOMINGO 3 DE ABRIL DEL 2005

MARIEL
25 Años Después • La Travesía, Los Testimonios

XXV aniversario del Mariel

Una revista coleccionable en esta edición

FLORIDA
elnuevoherald.com

el NuevoHerald

PREMIO ORTEGA Y GASSET

BY ORG

50¢ SUR DE LA FLORIDA

75¢ RESTO DEL ESTADO

1.25¢ FUERA DEL ESTADO

Precios varían según el área

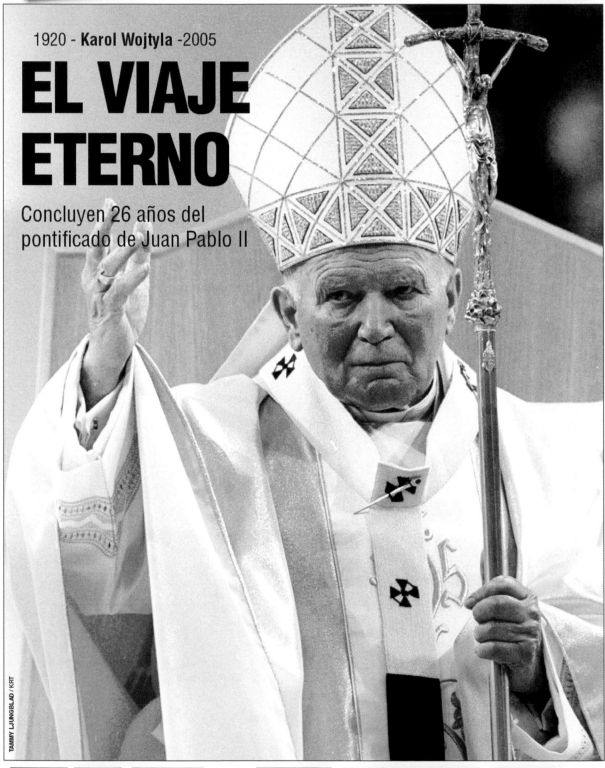

1920 - **Karol Wojtyla** -2005

EL VIAJE ETERNO

Concluyen 26 años del pontificado de Juan Pablo II

TAMMY LJUNGBLAD / KRT

EN SU NIÑEZ

▶ Karol se destacó por su inclinación a la lectura y por ser cortés y piadoso

EN SU JUVENTUD

▶ Le apasionaba la literatura, fue un destacado dramaturgo y poeta. También disfrutó viajar y relacionarse con la gente común, sobre todo en el tiempo en que fue minero.

EN SU MADUREZ ▶ Se entregó a Cristo como sacerdote, luego fue nombrado obispo y, posteriormente, cardenal.

EN ROMA

▶ En 1978 el aún joven cardenal polaco, se convirtió en el primer Papa no italiano en 456 años.

Naples Daily News

SCRIPPS
www.naplesnews.com
Sunday, April 3, 2005
$1.50

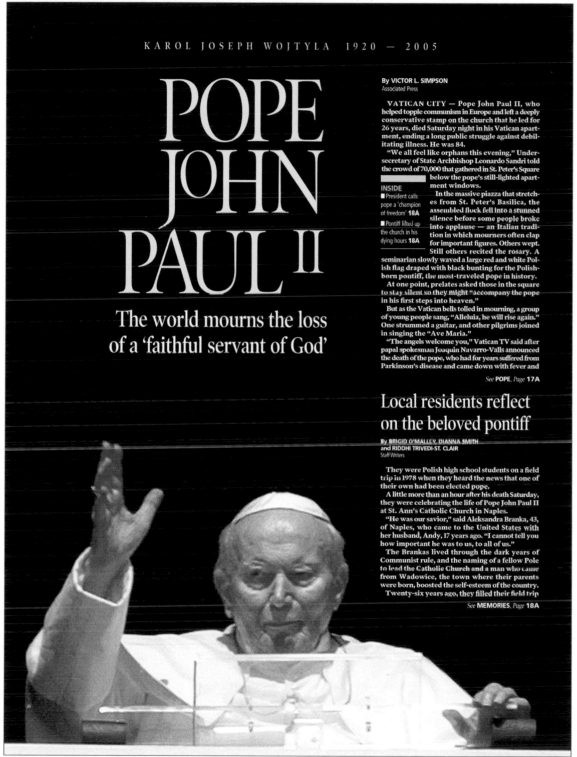

KAROL JOSEPH WOJTYLA 1920 — 2005

POPE JOHN PAUL II

The world mourns the loss of a 'faithful servant of God'

By VICTOR L. SIMPSON
Associated Press

VATICAN CITY — Pope John Paul II, who helped topple communism in Europe and left a deeply conservative stamp on the church that he led for 26 years, died Saturday night in his Vatican apartment, ending a long public struggle against debilitating illness. He was 84.

"We all feel like orphans this evening," Undersecretary of State Archbishop Leonardo Sandri told the crowd of 70,000 that gathered in St. Peter's Square below the pope's still-lighted apartment windows.

INSIDE
■ President calls pope a 'champion of freedom' **18A**

■ Pontiff lifted up the church in his dying hours **18A**

In the massive piazza that stretches from St. Peter's Basilica, the assembled flock fell into a stunned silence before some people broke into applause — an Italian tradition in which mourners often clap for important figures. Others wept. Still others recited the rosary. A seminarian slowly waved a large red and white Polish flag draped with black bunting for the Polish-born pontiff, the most-traveled pope in history.

At one point, prelates asked those in the square to stay silent so they might "accompany the pope in his first steps into heaven."

But as the Vatican bells tolled in mourning, a group of young people sang, "Alleluia, he will rise again." One strummed a guitar, and other pilgrims joined in singing the "Ave Maria."

"The angels welcome you," Vatican TV said after papal spokesman Joaquin Navarro-Valls announced the death of the pope, who had for years suffered from Parkinson's disease and came down with fever and

See **POPE**, *Page* **17A**

Local residents reflect on the beloved pontiff

By BRIGID O'MALLEY, DIANNA SMITH and RIDDHI TRIVEDI-ST. CLAIR
Staff Writers

They were Polish high school students on a field trip in 1978 when they heard the news that one of their own had been elected pope.

A little more than an hour after his death Saturday, they were celebrating the life of Pope John Paul II at St. Ann's Catholic Church in Naples.

"He was our savior," said Aleksandra Branka, 43, of Naples, who came to the United States with her husband, Andy, 17 years ago. "I cannot tell you how important he was to us, to all of us."

The Brankas lived through the dark years of Communist rule, and the naming of a fellow Pole to lead the Catholic Church and a man who came from Wadowice, the town where their parents were born, boosted the self-esteem of the country.

Twenty-six years ago, they filled their field trip

See **MEMORIES**, *Page* **18A**

Associated Press

COLLIER COUNTY SCHOOLS

Educator bonuses difficult to implement

By RAY PARKER
brparker@naplesnews.com

Elementary schoolteacher Karen Pelletier may spend extra hours helping students and even come up with more exciting lessons.

But her paycheck remains the same.

By her estimates, teachers spend about 1,400 hours off the clock throughout the year.

"If you're a go-getter in sales, you get rewarded by all the extra work," she said. "New teachers aren't so willing to do it (the extra work) for free anymore."

The past few years, Florida and other state lawmakers have been questioning the traditional teacher-pay system, wondering if it fits the rising demands of today's schools.

Many teachers and union leaders, however, contend business world incentives don't transfer to the schoolhouse, so the solution is simply to pay teachers more across the board.

Meanwhile, Gov. Jeb Bush and others want to change education's traditional pay system, which for generations has compensated all teachers the same, based on their education and experience.

Some business leaders think the single-salary schedule should be replaced to "align pay with the realities of the teacher labor market," according to a 2004 report by the Washington-based Committee for Economic Development.

Florida remains at the forefront of this effort,

See **BONUSES**, *Page* **21A**

Teachers struggle to keep up in salaries

By RAY PARKER
brparker@naplesnews.com

Almost 30 years ago, neither thought much about money or mortgages when they started out in Collier County classrooms.

But that changed as life brought new challenges.

Collier schools Superintendent Ray Baker has climbed from teacher to district chief, now making $160,000 a year, while English teacher Rebecca Rife has topped her teaching salary scale at $55,146 a year.

Along the way, the gap has widened between them, not just in dollars, but in each position's buying power.

In fact, superintendents' average salaries rose

Baker

by more than 12 percent over a 10-year period when adjusted for inflation, while the average teacher salary declined by nearly 2 percent, according to a 2004 survey of more than 500 school districts nationwide.

In other words, teachers actually lost money from 1993 to 2003.

"When I first started out I was married and it was going to be a second income," Rife, 53, said. "Not expecting to be on my own. But then circumstances changed.

"I discovered my income wasn't exactly covering all the bases, especially in Naples."

See **SALARIES**, *Page* **21A**

Orlando Sentinel

OrlandoSentinel.com   FINAL EDITION **SUNDAY** APRIL 3, 2005 $1.50

— FOUNDED 1876 —

POPE JOHN PAUL II | 1920-2005

'The angels welcome you'

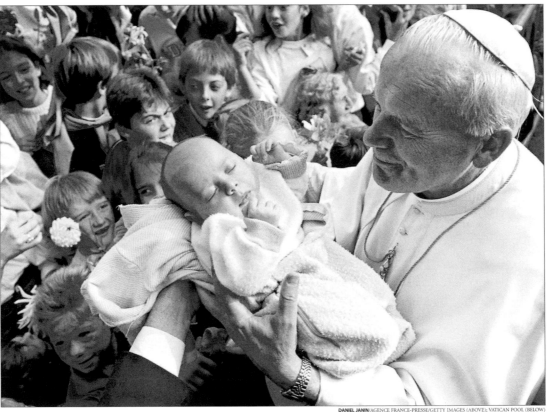

DANIEL JANIN/AGENCE FRANCE-PRESSE/GETTY IMAGES (ABOVE); VATICAN POOL (BELOW)

Pope John Paul II blesses a baby in Ars, France, in October 1986 during a visit to the Lyon area. The pontiff was visiting east and central regions of France during his 31st international pastoral visit.

World remembers Holy Father

In July 1989, Pope John Paul II hikes in the Arrier Valley near Aosta in the Italian Alps, where he was on a summer vacation.

He lived by the words "be not afraid," and he died by them as well.

Pope John Paul II, who changed the world and inspired millions with his indomitable spirit, died Saturday at 9:37 p.m. (2:37 p.m. EST) in his private apartment at the Vatican after a long, debilitating illness.

Even in death, the 84-year-old Polish pope taught by example — embracing the end of his life with prayer and love.

"I have looked for you, and you have come to me, and for this I thank you," aides quoted the dying pope as saying when told thousands of young people were among the crowd gathered in St. Peter's Square.

During the 26 years John Paul led the Roman Catholic Church, he helped tear down the Iron Curtain and traveled the globe, delivering a message of hope and faith to millions — many of whom he addressed in their native tongue.

"The angels welcome you," Vatican TV said, announcing the death of one of the 20th century's great leaders.

PONTIFF'S 26-YEAR REIGN

EXPANDED COVERAGE BEGINS ON PAGE A3

SARASOTA
Herald-Tribune

A MULTIMEDIA COMMUNICATIONS COMPANY

SUNDAY, APRIL 3, 2005 $1.25

No. 1 Illinois to meet
No. 2 North Carolina
in NCAA final
Sports

INSIDE TODAY: 2005
Baseball Preview

POPE JOHN PAUL II 1920-2005

A mourner reacts after the announcement of the death of Pope John Paul II, Saturday in St. Peter's Square at Vatican City. The Polish pontiff, who led the Roman Catholic Church for 26 years, died Saturday in his Vatican apartment. He was 84.

DALLAS MORNING NEWS

MOURNING AND PRAYER

John Paul II changed the papacy, the Catholic Church and the world

In St. Peter's Square in April 2003, Pope John Paul II watches a white dove released in honor of his repeated calls for peace.

ASSOCIATED PRESS ARCHIVE / 2003

By ROBERT D. McFADDEN
THE NEW YORK TIMES

On the night of Oct. 16, 1978, a vast, impatient throng in floodlit St. Peter's Square cheered wildly as white smoke curled from a chimney atop the Sistine Chapel, signaling the election of a new pope.

Cardinal Pericle Felici emerged minutes later to introduce Cardinal Karol Wojtyla of Poland, the first non-Italian pope since 1523. But even he had trouble pronouncing the name — voy-TEE-wah. Hardly anyone, it seemed, knew who he was. Murmurs and questions rippled through the predominantly Roman crowd.

Then a powerfully built man with slightly stooped shoulders and a small smile on his angular face stepped onto the central balcony of St. Peter's Basilica. Cheers faded into silence. The crowd waited.

He stood at the balcony rail, looking out, a Polish stranger in the fresh white robes of the pope. And there were tears in his eyes as he began to speak.

"I have come," he said in lightly accented Italian, "from a faraway country — far away, but always so close in the communion of faith."

"I do not know whether I can express myself in your — in our — Italian language," he said, pausing.

The crowd roared appreciatively, and the laughter swelled into resounding cheers.

"If I make mistakes," he added, beaming suddenly, "you will correct me."

Tumult erupted.

The cheers went on and on, and then grew into rhythmic waves that broke on the basilica facade and echoed across the square in a thundering crescendo: "Viva il Papa! Viva il Papa! Viva il Papa!"

A pope of a different sort

It was an extraordinary beginning. But almost from the start, it was evident to many of the world's Roman Catholics, and to multitudes of non-Catholics as

PLEASE SEE **POPE** ON 12A

Long public health struggle is over

Pope John Paul II, 84, died at 9:37 p.m. Saturday (2:37 p.m. EST). His death was announced to the news media by e-mail.

Sacrament administered

The Vatican celebrated a Mass for John Paul and he received the sacrament for the sick and dying in the 97 minutes before he died.

Final hours spent in prayer

The Vatican noted that the pope's final hours were marked by the "uninterrupted prayer of all those who were assisting him in his pious death...."

Memorial Mass set for this morning

A Mass is scheduled in St. Peter's Square for 10:30 a.m. (4:30 a.m. EDT) today.

INSIDE

Did you set your clocks ahead?

Clocks should have been set ahead one hour at 2 a.m. for daylight-saving time.

OUR 80th YEAR, NUMBER 182

Business Weekly revamped

Business Weekly, the Herald-Tribune's Monday business section, debuts new and expanded business coverage starting tomorrow.

An expanded business reporting staff will capture the trends, challenges and changes in the red-hot local economy.

You also will notice some changes today in the Business & Money section.

Some features that have been in the Monday newspaper — local interest rates, money market rates, national interest rates, local stock highlights and stock guru Lauren Rudd's column — move to Sunday to jump-start your investing for the week.

For more on the Business Weekly changes, see Executive Editor Mike Connelly's column on **Page 3B.**

Is sunshine going to Florida's head?

Changing demographics, politics and population intensify whatever happens in the Sunshine State.

By ABBY GOODNOUGH
THE NEW YORK TIMES

PINELLAS PARK — The packs of picketers and journalists left abruptly after Terri Schiavo died in her hospice here Thursday, and within 24 hours, the nation's attention had turned away from Schiavo, the brain-damaged woman, and her wrenching family battle.

But a familiar sense of surrealism lingered in Pinellas Park and across Florida, the state that seems to surpass any other in terms of strange but important, lurid but poignant events that say as much about America as they do about whatever sun-soaked Florida town where they unfold.

After the tug of war over Elian Gonzalez and the presidential recount of 2000, the anthrax scare after the 2001 terrorist attacks, four consecutive hurricanes in 2004 and now the

strife over Schiavo, the rest of the world moves on. But for Florida there is a curious psychic toll, a sense of emerging from an alternate universe where gripping sagas blot out the sun.

"It's kind of exciting, but it drives you crazy, too," said William McKeen, chairman of the journalism department at the University of Florida. "It's time for Wyoming to have its chance."

It was not always this way.

PLEASE SEE **FLORIDA** ON 18A

South Florida Sun-Sentinel

SUNDAY | APRIL 3, 2005   **BROWARD METRO EDITION**   c •   WWW.SUN-SENTINEL.COM | $1

POPE JOHN PAUL II
1920-2005

AP photo

REQUIEM

He was the most-traveled pope, the most ecumenical pope, and the first non-Italian pope in 455 years.

He stood up against communist giants, materialistic culture and dissidents in the Roman Catholic Church — which he ruled with a firm hand.

At 84, after battling several illnesses, Pope John Paul II died Saturday, leaving the faithful around the world in mourning.

As the Vatican begins the process of choosing a new leader for more than a billion Catholics, plans were being made to honor the life of Pope John Paul II, one who touched so many.

OBITUARY AND SPECIAL COVERAGE BEGIN ON PAGE 21A

20

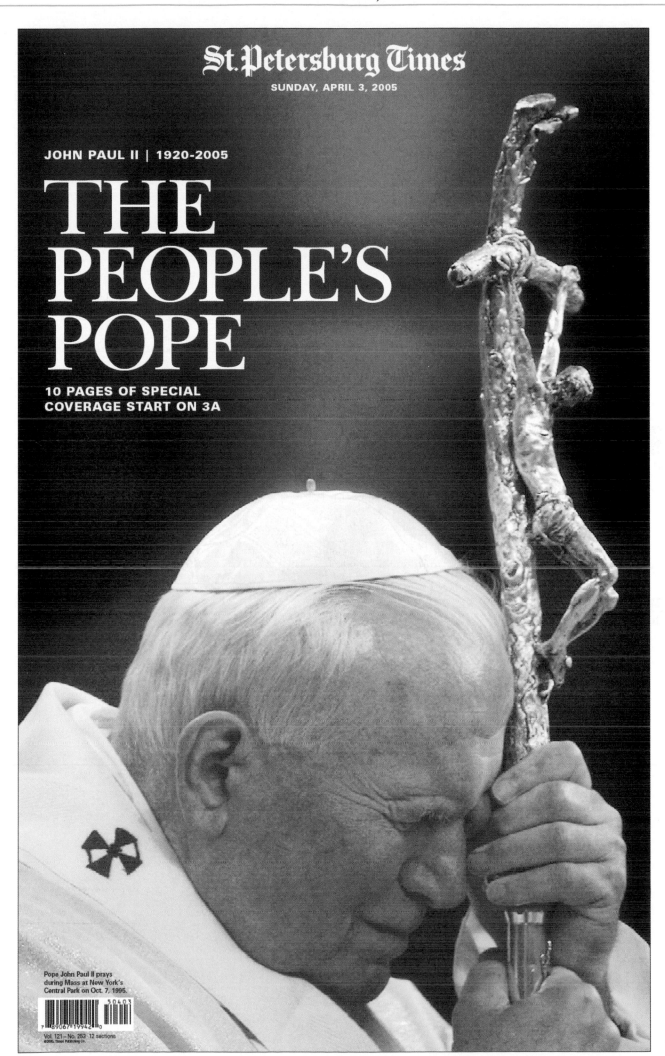

St. Petersburg Times

SUNDAY, APRIL 3, 2005

JOHN PAUL II | 1920-2005

THE PEOPLE'S POPE

10 PAGES OF SPECIAL COVERAGE START ON 3A

Pope John Paul II prays during Mass at New York's Central Park on Oct. 7, 1995.

Vol. 121 – No. 253   12 sections
©2005, Times Publishing Co.

MARIEL 25 YEARS AFTER THE RIDE TO FREEDOM
THE HERALD MARKS THE ANNIVERSARY WITH A 32-PAGE MAGAZINE INSIDE TODAY'S NEWSPAPER

The Miami Herald

SUNDAY, APRIL 3, 2005 | 102ND YEAR, NO. 201 | ©2005 THE MIAMI HERALD | FINAL | ONE DOLLAR

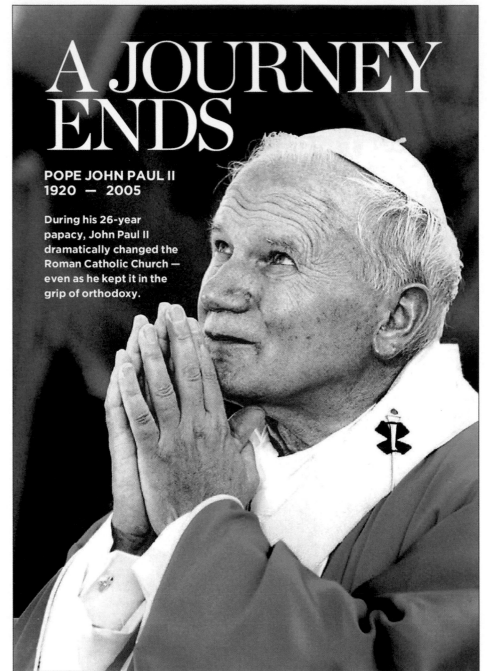

A JOURNEY ENDS

POPE JOHN PAUL II
1920 — 2005

During his 26-year papacy, John Paul II dramatically changed the Roman Catholic Church — even as he kept it in the grip of orthodoxy.

BRIAN SMITH/HERALD FILE

John Paul II helped transform the world with tireless travel and boundless spirit

BY JUAN O. TAMAYO
jtamayo@herald.com

Pope John Paul II lit the flame that exorcised 72 years of communism from Europe and electrified the world's 1.2 billion Catholics, becoming the religious superstar of the 20th century.

But when he died Saturday night in his Vatican apartment at age 84, it was his very public pain and suffering that marked the last decade of his papacy — his way of reminding his flock that redemption comes through suffering.

A memorial Mass was scheduled to be held today in St. Peter's Square at 10:30 a.m. local time (4:30 a.m. EST).

It was a 26-year papacy that both admirers and critics acknowledged kept the Roman Catholic Church in the grip of orthodoxy, while at the same time profoundly changing it.

He gave women a larger role in the lay affairs of the church and wrote almost romantically about sex. But he blocked women's way to abortion, birth control pills and the priesthood, and kept male priests celibate.

He complained that communism treats man as purely a worker, capitalism treats him purely as a consumer, and neither treats him as a dignified human being. In America, he once said, abortions and death sentences amounted to "a culture of death."

*TURN TO POPE, 28A

POPE SPECIAL EDITION

SEVEN PAGES OF COVERAGE, 27-33A

● **THE REACTION:** In South Florida, at the Vatican and around the world, mourners pay tribute, 27A

● **THE LEGACY:** John Paul II will be remembered for steering the church back toward rigid orthodoxy, 31A

● **THE SUCCESSOR:** There's a list of leading candidates to replace John Paul II, but the conventional wisdom says Vatican policy won't change significantly, 30A

● **EDITORIAL:** He opened the Catholic Church to the world, 32A

WHAT'S PLANNED

● **FUNERAL:** No date has been set. The pope is to be buried four to six days after his death.

● **MASSES:** St. Mary's Cathedral, 7525 NW Second Ave., Miami, will hold two today, one at 10 a.m. and the other, to be celebrated by Archbishop John C. Favalora, at 7:30 p.m.

● **BOOK SIGNING:** The Archdiocese of Miami has designated five churches where, through April 10, visitors can sign condolence books that will be sent to the Vatican. They are: St Mary's; Gesu Catholic Church, 118 NE Second St., Miami; La Ermita de la Caridad, 3609 S. Miami Ave., Coconut Grove; San Pablo Catholic Church, 550 122nd St. Ocean, Marathon; St. Anthony Catholic Church, 901 NE Second St., Fort Lauderdale. St. Anthony will hold special services at 6 p.m. Thursday and 8:15 a.m. Friday.

MORE ONLINE

● **HERALD.COM:** Click on Today's Extras to post condolences, view a slide show, read up-to-date coverage and see an extensive gallery of photos.

COMING UP

● A keepsake section commemorates John Paul II.

POPE JOHN PAUL II

KNIGHT RIDDER

TAMPA, FLORIDA • ONLINE AT TBO.COM   **SUNDAY**   APRIL 3, 2005 • LIFE. PRINTED DAILY.

THE TAMPA TRIBUNE
and The Tampa Times

John Paul II
1920-2005

Tribune illustration by ANDY DORSETT

Epic Life, Struggle Come To End

His papacy was marked by his campaign against poverty and injustice around the world.

By LARRY STAMMER
Los Angeles Times

Pope John Paul II, whose indomitable will and uncompromising belief in human dignity helped bring down communism in Eastern Europe and reshaped Christianity's relationship to Judaism, was indisputably the most influential pope of the 20th century.

He died Saturday in his Vatican apartment at 84.

The first non-Italian elected pope in 456 years, John Paul energized the papacy through much of his reign, traveling as evangelist and champion of religious freedom even as he imposed a rigorous moral discipline and more centralized authority on his sometimes rebellious 1 billion-member church.

In his final months, as his health declined markedly, he pressed ahead with his mission, choosing to project his gradual incapacitation as a final Christian message of redemption through suffering.

"We all feel like orphans this evening," Undersecretary of State Archbishop Leonardo Sandri told the crowd of 70,000 that gathered in St. Peter's Square below the pope's still-lighted apartment windows.

"The angels welcome you," Vatican TV said after papal spokesman Joaquin Navarro-Valls announced the death.

In contrast to the church's ancient traditions, Navarro-Valls announced the death in an e-mail that said: "The Holy Father died this evening at 9:37 p.m. in his private apartment."

The pope's body will lie in state in St. Peter's Basilica starting Monday afternoon. The date of his funeral will be set by a gathering of cardinals on Monday morning, but under guidelines he had set it should take place within four to six days of his death.

In his 26-year papacy, John Paul made 104 trips outside Italy to 129 nations, going as a pastor to countries including Brazil, where Catholics are the majority, and Japan, where they are a minority.

He preached along the equator and inside the Arctic Circle. He preached on severe Andean mountaintops and on lush tropical islands, in famous European cathedrals and in bullet-pocked African country churches.

See JOURNEY ENDS, Page 14 ▶
He had lost his whole family at age 21.

9 PAGES OF COVERAGE INSIDE

Tribune photo by FRED BELLET

Bay Area Pews Fill

Less than an hour after his death, local Catholics headed to their parishes to reflect and grieve together.

DETAILS, Page 6

Tribune file photo by BRUCE HOSKING

Schoolboy Pranks

As college classmates, Thomas Larkin taught the future pontiff how to swear. Now, the bishop remembers a friend.

DETAILS, Page 7

The Associated Press

A Nation Mourns

Many Americans had a chance to meet the pope during his seven U.S. visits, and people from many faiths respected him.

DETAILS, Page 9

Associated Press file photo (1986)

Plenty Of Memories

From his birth in a small city in Poland to his death in a Vatican apartment, Karol Josef Wojtyla lived a fascinating life.

DETAILS, Page 12

23

ATLANTA, GEORGIA

SUNDAY

The Atlanta Journal-Constitution

APRIL 3, 2005

ajc.com

★★★★★ METRO   Copyright © 2005, The Atlanta Journal-Constitution

A POPE FOR THE PEOPLE
JOHN PAUL II: 1920-2005

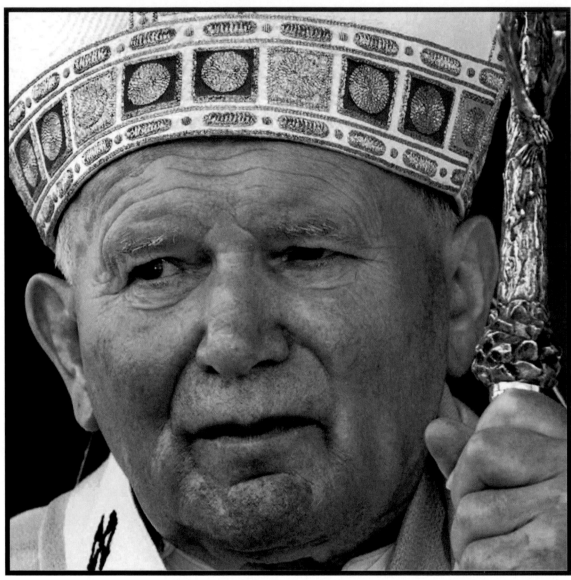

DOMENICO STINELLIS / Associated Press,1998

'We all feel like orphans'

By SHELLEY EMLING and GAYLE WHITE

The death of Pope John Paul II, whose sparkling eyes and gentle smile were known around the world, leaves 1.1 billion Roman Catholics of all races and nationalities waiting for a new spiritual shepherd.

The popular pontiff died Saturday night at his Vatican apartment.

"We all feel like orphans this evening," Vatican Undersecretary of State Archbishop Leonardo Sandri told a crowd of 70,000 that gathered in St. Peter's Square.

A one-time actor, athlete and laborer, the pope left an indelible mark on the 20th century. He symbolized a Catholic leadership that was shifting away from its Italian roots, but was rock solid in his adherence to the church's traditional teachings. His unwavering stance against artificial birth control and for an all-male, celibate priesthood frustrated some American moderates.

His tenure spanned more than a quarter-century, encompassing the downfall of communism, the church's coming of age in the Third World

Please see POPE, A14

Inside: A 4-page special report. On ajc.com: Photo galleries, a guest book and news updates.

24

SUNDAY EDITION

Star ★ Bulletin

starbulletin.com

APRIL 3, 2005 ★

75 cents

POPE JOHN PAUL II
1920–2005

Into God's embrace

One of the longest, most influential papal terms in history ends after years of deteriorating health

Star-Bulletin news services

VATICAN CITY >> The Vatican secretary of state, Cardinal Angelo Sodano, celebrated a Mass for the repose of Pope John Paul II's soul this morning on the steps of St. Peter's Basilica, calling on the tens of thousands of people gathered there to pray for "our beloved John Paul."

Applause rang out when Sodano, dressed in golden vestments, prayed for the pope at the start of the Mass.

"We entrust with confidence to the risen Christ, Lord of life and history, our beloved John Paul II who for 27 years guided the universal church as the successor of Peter," he said.

Thousands of people streamed toward St. Peter's Square for the midmorning Mass, joining the faithful who had held an overnight vigil in the plaza after learning of the pope's death. The traditional Sunday noontime prayer, which John

Please see Pope, A11

Worshippers reacted after hearing about the death of Pope John Paul II in St. Peter's Square at the Vatican yesterday.

ASSOCIATED PRESS

Kalaupapa patients have special sadness

Settlement residents reflect on a pope whom many had met and admired

By Mary Vorsino
mvorsino@starbulletin.com

Word of Pope John Paul II's death spread quickly through the small Molokai settlement of Kalaupapa, where nearly half of the 40 residents have met the man who led the Catholic Church over the last quarter-century.

"Everybody was saddened," said Kuulei Bell, a Mormon who, along with most, if not all of the residents, will attend this morning's Catholic services at St. Francis Church. She said the mood in Kalaupapa dampened almost immediately after the pope's death was confirmed yesterday morning.

"Because I saw him (in Brussels), I had some kind of personal feeling," she said. "For me, it was a special sadness."

That very personal grief of the pope's death has hit many in Kalaupapa, whose residents have had several

Please see Kalaupapa, A11

A statue of Pope John Paul II greets the morning sunrise at the Shrine of Our Lady of Czestochowa in Doylestown, Pa., in this file photo.

ASSOCIATED PRESS / FEBRUARY 2002

INSIDE : Church's image elevated by pope's final days. A8 • Isle residents react to his death. A11 • A look at his life and legacy. A12

Cazimero halau sweeps Merrie Monarch honors

By Gary C.W. Chun
gchun@starbulletin.com

HILO >> After a decade absent from the Merrie Monarch Festival, Robert Cazimero and the men of Halau Na Kamalei made up for lost time, winning the overall trophy in this year's 42nd annual hula competition.

Halau Na Kamalei swept all kane hula categories winning the kahiko or ancient dance, 'auana or modern dance and overall titles.

Cazimero's halau put together sterling performances over the two nights of competition — Friday, with "Kahikilani," and last night with the proud anthem "Kona Kai 'Opua."

In the wahine division, Na Lei

Online: Results will be posted at starbulletin.com
Tomorrow: A wrap-up of the competition in our Today section.

O Kaholoku from Kohala on the Big Island, and kumu hula Nani Lim Yap and Leialoha Amina won for the second year in a row. They also repeated in winning the kahiko competition for

Please see Hula, A6

Manu Boyd, left, and Robert Cazimero celebrated last night as the winners were announced at the 42nd Annual Merrie Monarch Festival. Cazimero's Halau Na Kamalei won the overall title and both kane halau awards.

DENNIS ODA / DODA
@STARBULLETIN.COM

62 >> 72

Partly cloudy. A5

Classifieds >> 524 STAR

Volume 124 / Number 62 / 16 sections
Copyright © 2005 / All rights reserved

8 03781 00002 9

25

With St. Peter's Basilica in the background, Pope John Paul II waves to the faithful during his weekly general audience at the Vatican on Sept. 25, 1996. –AP

SUNDAY SUN-TIMES

YOUR COMPLETE SUN-TIMES IS INSIDE • SUNDAY, APRIL 3, 2005
• LATE SPORTS FINAL • $1.50 CHICAGO, $1.75 ELSEWHERE

POPE JOHN PAUL II
1920-2005

CHICAGO, ILLINOIS

Sunday ILLINI ROLL TO NCAA CHAMPIONSHIP GAME

Chicago Tribune
FINAL

$1.79 City & Suburbs; $2 Elsewhere   SUNDAY, APRIL 3, 2005   ✪   CHICAGOLAND

158TH YEAR — NO. 93 © CHICAGO TRIBUNE

John Paul II dies

Catholics and world mourn end of an epic life

Pope John Paul II died at 9:37 p.m. Rome time Saturday. "Our Holy Father John Paul has returned home," Archbishop Leonardo Sandri announced to the crowd keeping vigil in St. Peter's Square.

AP file photo

Pope John Paul II
1920 ~ 2005

Man of indomitable faith

By Steve Kloehn | Tribune staff reporter

Pope John Paul II, who changed the course of the world through faith and sheer dint of will, will be remembered as a bold pontiff who towered over his century, then led his church into a new millennium.

Shaped by his childhood in rural Poland and fired in the kiln of World War II, the young priest Karol Wojtyla rose to lead the world's largest church, striding the globe with an authority that transcended Catholicism.

Some in his own church complained that he was a throwback to an earlier kind of pope, imperial and autocratic, bent on quashing dissent. Others said he was ahead of his time, traversing the world many times over to spread his message, the first jet-set pope.

But few in any realm have ever wrestled with the leaders and movements of their eras the way Pope John Paul II did.

From Nazi Germany to Soviet communism, from consumer culture to the slide into moral relativism, Wojtyla pitted himself against each of the great forces that swept over the world during his 84 years.

Occasionally prevailing, never surrendering, he proved that the pope needs no military divisions, that spiritual power is a force to be reckoned with even in the midst of secular

modernism.

"Be not afraid!" he called out in his first mass at St. Peter's Basilica on Oct. 22, 1978. Those were among the first words he spoke to the world as pontiff, and they became a refrain in each of his 104 trips abroad, in each of his 14 encyclicals and more than 60 other major papal documents.

"Be not afraid!"—part command, part prayer—became the driving force of his 26-year papacy, an epic reign that energized and polarized the Roman Catholic Church.

He stared down dictators and clamped down on critics. He was credited with toppling the totalitarian government of his native Poland in 1989, which led to the fall of communist Eastern Europe and the Soviet Union.

He was blamed for alienating women and liberal Catholics in the West with rigid stances against women in the priesthood, abortion, birth control and homosexuality. Church insiders chafed at the growing power of the Vat-

PLEASE SEE **FAITH**, PAGE 14

Pope raised his hand in final blessing

**By Liz Sly
and Tom Hundley**
Tribune foreign correspondents

VATICAN CITY—Pope John Paul II, the man who led the Catholic church for a generation with vision, drive and charisma, died Saturday, bringing an end to his prolonged personal suffering and to a historic era for the world.

In a brief statement issued 15 minutes after the pope's death, the Vatican announced that the 84-year-old pontiff had passed away at 9:37 p.m. local time, in the apartment that became his home in 1978 when the Polish archbishop named Karol Wojtyla was elected the 265th pope.

Moments before his death, he lifted his right hand in a weak gesture of benediction, an apparent acknowledgment of a chorus of "amens" rising from the thousands of people gathered below his window, Vatican Television reported.

Then he died, far from his homeland but surrounded by the Polish aides and confidants who had remained his closest friends throughout his 26-year papacy, including his personal secretary, Archbishop Stanislaw Dziwisz.

When it finally came, the news was no

PLEASE SEE **POPE**, PAGE 9

South Bend Tribune
SUNDAY

© 2005 South Bend Tribune Corp., 133rd year, No. 26

www.southbendtribune.com

APRIL 3, 2005

Michigan Edition $1.50

Pope John Paul II
1920-2005

By VICTOR L. SIMPSON
Associated Press Writer

VATICAN CITY — Pope John Paul II, who helped topple communism in Europe and left a deeply conservative stamp on the church that he led for 26 years, died Saturday night in his Vatican apartment, ending a long public struggle against debilitating illness. He was 84.

"We all feel like orphans this evening," Undersecretary of State Archbishop Leonardo Sandri told the crowd of 70,000 that gathered in St. Peter's Square below the pope's still-lighted apartment windows.

In the massive piazza that stretches from St. Peter's Basilica, the assembled flock fell into a stunned silence before some people broke into applause — an Italian tradition in which mourners often clap for important figures. Others wept. Still others recited the rosary. A seminarian slowly waved a large red and white Polish flag draped with black bunting for the Polish-born pontiff, the most-traveled pope in history.

See POPE/A11

A pope who touched the world

■ Rev. Theodore Hesburgh, area clergy describe the man behind an extraordinary papacy.

Tribune Staff Report

Pope John Paul II brought strength and vitality as he assumed the papacy in 1978. And he made the papacy visible as he traveled the world touching the lives of pilgrims, diplomats and politicians alike. Before his death, area clergy talked about his legacy.

Rev. Theodore M. Hesburgh, president emeritus, University of Notre Dame

The first time the Rev.

Theodore M. Hesburgh met with John Paul II shortly after the pope's election at the Vatican, the meeting began as a linguistic battle.

"I started to talk to him in Italian, figuring, what the heck, he went to school in Italy the way I did, and he's been living here," Hesburgh said.

"He answered me in English."

Hesburgh switched to French.

"I knew he knew French very well," he said. "Again he comes back in broken English. I figured there was only one thing: He was using me to learn some English."

See WORLD/A11

Tribune Photo/GENE KAISER

University of Notre Dame graduate student Heidi Kellner from Green Bay, Wis., prays the rosary at the University of Notre Dame's Grotto with some 300 other students and others devoted to the memory of Pope John Paul II.

THE INDIANAPOLIS STAR

"Where the Spirit of the Lord is, there is Liberty" II COR. 3:17

| SUNDAY, APRIL 3, 2005 |

A GANNETT NEWSPAPER ■ INDYSTAR.COM

CITY FINAL ■ $1.75

POPE JOHN PAUL II: 1920-2005

A MORAL VOICE, A HUMAN TOUCH

Hoosiers hail leader who reached across faiths

Outreach: Archbishop Daniel Buechlein called the pope a global pastor.
Steve Healey / The Star

By Robert King, Matthew Tully and Tim Evans
robert.king@indystar.com

For Indiana's Catholics, it came as a personal loss — not only of a religious leader but also of a man some saw as a father figure.

For people from other religious traditions, it was a farewell to a leader many credited with narrowing the gaps between the Roman Catholic Church and the rest of God's children.

The death Saturday of Pope John Paul II brought out strong feelings from across the spectrum of faith in Indiana. And it served as clear evidence that his legacy won't soon be forgotten.

See Hoosiers, Page A14

MASS ON MONDAY

A special memorial Mass for the pope will be at noon Monday at SS. Peter and Paul Cathedral, 1347 N. Meridian.

Long-serving, long-suffering: Pope John Paul II, who presided over the Roman Catholic Church for 26 years, died Saturday after a long battle with Parkinson's disease, which he used as a lesson to the world about suffering.
Vincenzo Pinto / AFP/Getty Images 2002 photo

John Paul's funeral to be within 4 to 6 days

Change agent: The 264th pope brought new style to an old institution.
Massimo Sambucetti / Associated Press 2004 photo

By Victor L. Simpson
Associated Press

VATICAN CITY — Pope John Paul II, who helped topple communism in Europe and left a deeply conservative stamp on the church that he led for 26 years, died Saturday in his Vatican apartment, ending a long public struggle against debilitating illness. He was 84.

"We all feel like orphans this evening," Undersecretary of State Archbishop Leonardo Sandri told the crowd of 70,000 that gathered in St. Peter's Square below the pope's still-lighted apartment windows.

In the massive piazza that stretches from St. Peter's Basilica, the assembled flock fell into a stunned silence before some people broke into applause — an Italian tradition in which mourners often clap for important figures.

See Pope, Page A15 COVERAGE CONTINUES ON A10

HIS LIFE AND TIMES

From grim childhood to papal destiny

Key moments of his life, from his study for the priesthood during the Nazi occupation to his surprise election as pope in 1978 (right). **A11**

IN INDIANA

Touching lives of Hoosiers

Louis Luke (right), of Martinsville, received a papal kiss in 2000. Read about his and other Hoosiers' encounters with the pope. **A14**

CHURCH'S FUTURE

What to expect in the days ahead

The Roman Catholic Church has elaborate procedures for picking a successor. Also, how John Paul II's legacy could influence the church. **A13**

6-PAGE SPECIAL SECTION INSIDE TODAY

MEMORIES OF THE POPE

Des Moines Sunday Register

A
DM

DesMoinesRegister.com ■ The Newspaper Iowa Depends Upon ■ Price $1.50 — April 3, 2005

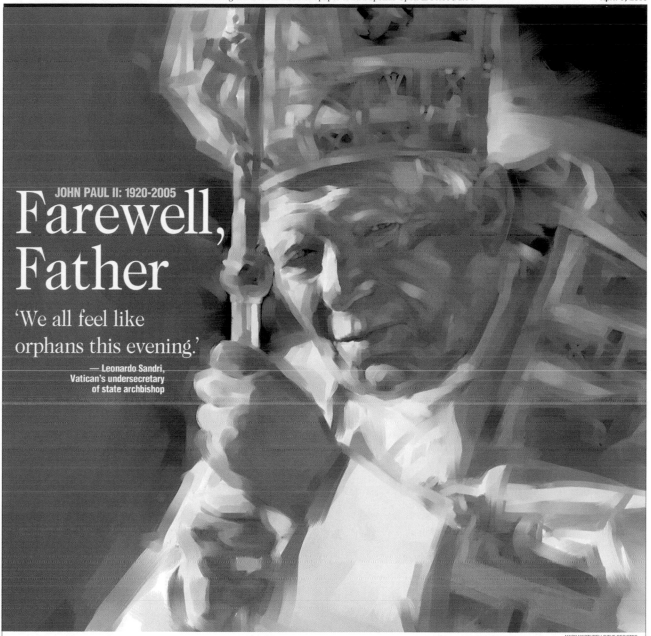

JOHN PAUL II: 1920-2005

Farewell, Father

'We all feel like orphans this evening.'

— Leonardo Sandri,
Vatican's undersecretary
of state archbishop

MARK MARTURELLO/THE REGISTER

John Paul leaves world of mourners with one last lesson

By DANIEL WILLIAMS and ALAN COOPERMAN
WASHINGTON POST

Vatican City — John Paul II, the voyager pope who helped conquer communism and transformed the papacy with charisma and vigor, died Saturday at age 84 after a long battle with illness that became a lesson to the world in humble suffering.

"Our most beloved Holy Father has returned to the house of the Father," Archbishop Leonardo Sandri, a senior Vatican official, told pilgrims in St. Peter's Square.

The throng of 50,000 momentarily stood in stunned silence, stared at the pavement and wept. Then, following an Italian custom that signifies hope at a time of death, the mourners broke into applause.

John Paul died at 9:37 p.m. local time (1:37 CST) in the Vatican's Apostolic Palace, with a small group of Polish prelates and nuns at his bedside. The first indication of the pope's passing was the illumination of several windows in his private quarters overlooking St. Peter's Square. An e-mail announcement to journalists followed. A half-hour later, the bells of all of Rome's churches rang out in mourning.

The news evoked a global

See **POPE**, Page 9A

AROUND THE WORLD
Words of praise

Leaders and people from every continent and many faiths found something in the life of Pope John Paul II to praise. **Page 6A**

IN IOWA
Special tie to Iowans

Pope John Paul II was history's most televised and most traveled pope, but Iowa's Catholics have always felt a special connection. **Page 7A**

LOOKING AHEAD
Secrecy shrouds vote

The world's Catholic cardinals now head for Rome to attend Pope John Paul II's funeral. But they will stay much longer to elect the 265th pope. **Page 8A**

PAY TRIBUTE TO JOHN PAUL II
Pope's legacy

Go to DesMoinesRegister.com to contribute your thoughts about the legacy of John Paul II. Also check the site for news updates in the wake of his death.

Pontiff's worldliness, popularity helped define his reign

The "Hands of Peace" exhibit in the Pope John Paul II Cultural Center in Washington, D.C., has been worn to a shiny patina by the countless visitors who have placed their palms inside the casting of the pope's hands.

It's a visible symbol of the defining element of Pope John Paul II's papacy — his connection to the people of the world.

In his first 25 years as pope, John Paul traveled more than 700,000 miles and visited about 130 countries. So it might be hard for some to remember that before Karol Josef Wojtyla became pope and turned the custom

SHIRLEY RAGSDALE

on its head, pilgrims and visiting dignitaries traveled to Rome to visit the Holy Father.

And in doing so, the pontiff exposed the Catholic Church to the world as no

See **RAGSDALE**, Page 9A

31

PARTLY CLOUDY
HIGH 76, LOW 53
WEATHER, 8B

Sunday Eagle
◉ *Now you know.*

APRIL 3, 2005
FINAL EDITION
$1.50

POPE JOHN PAUL II 1920-2005

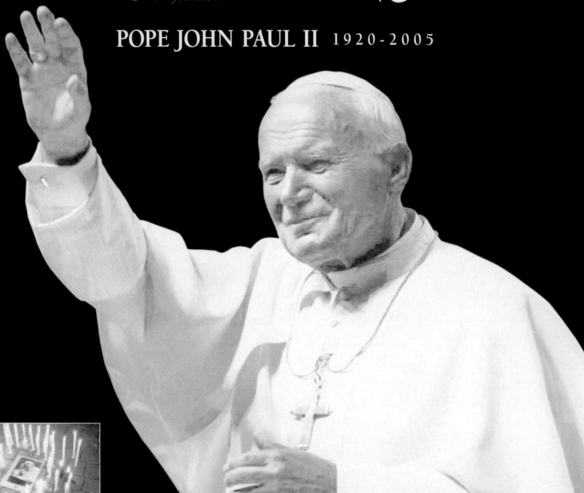

LOOKING BACK

■ **PRAISING A LEGACY:** Catholics around the world mourn, 10A

■ **IN WICHITA:** John Paul II provided moments of unforgettable grace for many who live here, 11A

■ **IMAGES AND WORDS:** Remembering the pope, 9A

■ **FOR THE YOUNG PEOPLE:** This pope gave unprecedented hope and attention to the young, 13A

LOOKING AHEAD

■ **WHO WILL LEAD?** Chances are better than ever that the next pope could be a non-European. Here's a look at possible successors, 10A

ONLINE EXTRAS

For a photo slide show of the pope's life or to post your condolences in our online guest book, go to Kansas.com.

HE SHONE

JOHN PAUL II HELPED SHAPE THE 20TH CENTURY

BY DAVID O'REILLY
Philadelphia Inquirer

Pope John Paul II, spiritual leader of the world's 1 billion Roman Catholics for a quarter of a century, died Saturday at 84.

Firmly conservative in matters of morality and theology, yet passionately progressive on behalf of the poor, immigrants and world peace, John Paul was an uncompromising moral voice and a giant on the world stage.

Even as ill health visibly overtook him, he carried his message around the world – slowed, but never stopped, by bullets, a tumor, a broken hip, arthritis, Parkinson's disease and advancing age.

As he took on such controversial topics as abortion, euthanasia, capital punishment, communist oppression and capitalist greed, John Paul found himself allied with differing factions of the secular world. But it was the issues that varied, not his stance; all his positions were grounded in his

unwavering belief in the worth and dignity of every human life.

The pontiff's failing health had become an acute public concern in recent years as he grew visibly weaker and struggled at times to walk and speak.

Yet images of John Paul in his prime – stepping off airplanes, kissing the ground of each new nation he visited, or stretching his arms out to cheering crowds in Manila, Dublin,

Please see POPE, Page 8A

Wichitans pray for soul's repose

BY ANNIE CALOVICH
The Wichita Eagle

During every Mass comes a point at which the presiding priest prays for the pope.

For 26 years, the prayer has been:

"Strengthen in faith and love your pilgrim church on earth, your servant, Pope John Paul."

The Rev. John Jirak reached that point Saturday afternoon during a wedding at the Cathedral of the Immaculate Conception in downtown Wichita.

"And I realized we can't say that anymore. It hit me like a ton of bricks," Jirak told the congregation at his next Mass, the regular 5 p.m. vigil Saturday.

With Pope John Paul II's death, the Mass drew people who normally wait until Sunday to go to Mass.

Please see LOCAL, Page 11A

Ashley Bryant prays during a Mass at St. Mary's Cathedral in Wichita on Saturday.

Jeff Tuttle/
The Wichita Eagle

$1.75 | SUNDAY, APRIL 3, 2005

The Courier-Journal

SPECIAL REPORT | A GANNETT NEWSPAPER

May 18, 1920 | April 2, 2005

John Paul II

Man who reshaped papacy dies at 84

Pope John Paul II was still a hearty individual when he celebrated Mass at Giants Stadium in 1995. The themes of his papacy were peace, justice and the sanctity of life.

Kathy Willens/Associated Press

33

From Los Angeles Times, AP and Washington Post dispatches

VATICAN CITY — Pope John Paul II, whose indomitable will and uncompromising belief in human dignity helped bring down communism in Eastern Europe and reshaped Christianity's relationship to other religions, died yesterday. He was 84.

"We all feel like orphans this evening," Undersecretary of State Archbishop Leonardo Sandri told the crowd of 70,000 that gathered in St. Peter's Square below the pope's still-lighted apartment windows.

The Vatican said the pope, whose health had declined markedly in recent months, died at 9:37 p.m. (2:37 p.m. EST).

The assembled flock fell into a stunned silence before some people broke out in applause — an Italian tradition in which mourners often clap for important figures. Others wept.

"It is the emotion of losing a grandfather, like losing a living stone to which we have clung for so long," said Monsignor Patrick Jacquin, the rector of Notre Dame.

A Mass was scheduled for St. Peter's Square for 10:30 a.m. (4:30 a.m. EDT) today.

The pope's body was expected to be taken to St. Peter's Basilica no earlier than tomorrow afternoon, the Vatican said.

It said the College of Cardinals would meet tomorrow morning. They were expected to set a funeral date.

When John Paul II was elected on Oct. 16, 1978, at age 58, he was the youngest pope in 132 years, the first Polish pope, and the first non-Italian pope in four and a half centuries.

The former Cardinal Karol Wojtyla, archbishop of Krakow, the ancient capital of his native Poland, rapidly declared a "new evangelization" and began an extraordinary series of journeys that made him one of the most familiar figures on the face of the Earth.

His message was that faith must be grounded in truth and that the key to freedom is love and service to God. His themes were peace, justice and the sanctity of life.

He warned that a spreading "cult of death," in forms ranging

See **PONTIFF**, Back page, col. 1

SPECIAL COMMEMORATIVE SECTION INSIDE

The Times-Picayune

$1.50 169th year No. 72 — **SUNDAY, APRIL 3, 2005** — METRO EDITION

Joannes Paulus PP II

1920 • POPE JOHN PAUL II • 2005

'A PASTOR TO THE WORLD'

MILLIONS MOURN THE PASSING OF POPE JOHN PAUL II

Pope John Paul II, seen here celebrating Mass in Cuba in 1998, died Saturday night in Vatican City. By church dictate, his funeral must fall on the fourth to sixth day after death.

AP FILE PHOTO

By Bruce Nolan
Staff writer

Pope John Paul II, the Polish intellectual whose strong-willed, activist papacy helped undermine the Soviet Union, redefined the office's relationship to the world and dominated the billion-member Roman Catholic Church for more than a quarter century, died Saturday after a long and conspicuously public struggle with Parkinson's disease. He was 84.

John Paul died at 9:37 p.m. in Vatican City, or 1:37 p.m. New Orleans time. Frail and immobile, he died after a urinary tract infection spread and he suffered heart and kidney failure, the Vatican said.

But the final infection was merely the latest complication in a series of disabilities that beset the pope as the neurological disease progressively tightened its grip after becoming noticeable in 1993.

John Paul lost his ability to walk more than a year ago, then more recently, his ability to speak.

Twice in February he was hospitalized, the last time to perform an urgent tracheotomy to help him breathe.

Yet until nearly the very end he maintained some semblance of a public schedule. He was wheeled from event to event; aides read his speeches as he sat, silent and nearly immobile, nearby.

Rabbi Ed Cohn of Temple Sinai may

have been the last New Orleanian to visit with John Paul in a small group. Cohn and a group of rabbis met the pope to thank him for his outreach to Judaism on Jan. 18, about two weeks before his first hospitalization and final decline. John Paul managed a muffled thank you to Cohn's greeting, Cohn said.

John Paul's final goal was to provide a silent, tortured witness to the redemptive value of suffering and the sanctity of human life, his aides said.

But in recent days he was unable to do even that. He missed all of the Vatican's Holy Week and Easter services. In his last public appearance, he was

*See **POPE**, A-10*

INSIDE • Successor likely to be picked from among a handful of cardinals, A-16 • Tradition dictates church's next steps, A-16 • Crowd at Vatican weeps upon news of his death, A-19

Illinois, North Carolina to play for NCAA title | HIGH SCHOOLERS TACKLE COLLEGE-APTITUDE ESSAYS
SPORTS, D1 · MAINE/NEW ENGLAND, B1

Maine Sunday Telegram

Final Edition
Sunday, April 3, 2005

Copyright 2005 Blethen Maine Newspapers Inc.

EST. 1862

www.pressherald.com
$1.75
$2.00 outside Cumberland, Sagadahoc, York, Knox and Lincoln counties

Volume 117 Number 38

138 pages

Pope John Paul II 1920-2005

'A good and faithful servant'

Across state, world figure is mourned, remembered

John Paul II transcended his role as Catholic leader to become a pope for every person, Mainers say.

By ANN S. KIM
Staff Writer

Peter Biel had closely followed the news of Pope John Paul II's failing health, but word of his death Saturday afternoon still came as a shock.

"I just started to cry. I just couldn't do anything. I'm a man, I don't cry ever," said Biel, 32, a South Portland resident and a parishioner at the Cathedral of the Immaculate Conception in Portland. "I cried for about two hours. I just went to my room and cried. The world lost someone really, really important."

Across Maine, people mourned the death of the 84-year-old pontiff. He was remembered not just as the leader of Roman Catholics but as a figure whose compassion and legacy extended to those outside his faith.

The Diocese of Portland asked pastors to toll their church bells upon news of the pope's death. On Monday, Bishop Richard J. Malone will celebrate Mass at the Cathedral of the Immaculate Conception for the repose of John Paul's soul.

"We are deeply saddened at the loss of this courageous prophet of truth and hope. At the same time, because we believe that at death, life is not ended but merely changed, we rejoice in the hope of eternal life that inspired his life and ministry as the Church's universal shepherd," Malone said in a statement. "His legacy will be remembered until the end of time."

Gov. John Baldacci, a Catholic, praised the pope as one of the most important world leaders of modern times.

"His grace touched millions as he traveled the globe to reach out to people," Baldacci said in a statement. "John Paul II transcended his role as leader of Catholics and became a leader for all peoples."

U.S. Sen. Olympia Snowe said in a statement: " As we mourn

*Please see **MAINE**, Page A6*

The Associated Press
Pope John Paul II, shown celebrating his first Mass in Cuba in 1998, visited 129 countries in his 26 years as leader of the Catholic Church. He made seven trips to the United States.

After 26 years as leader of the Catholic Church, Pope John Paul II dies at age 84

By DANIEL WILLIAMS and ALAN COOPERMAN
The Washington Post

VATICAN CITY — John Paul II, the voyager pope who helped conquer communism and transformed the papacy with charisma and vigor, died Saturday after a long battle with Parkinson's disease.

"Our most beloved Holy Father has returned to the house of the Father," Archbishop Leonardo Sandri, a senior Vatican official, told pilgrims in St. Peter's Square. The throng of 50,000 momentarily stood in stunned silence, stared at the pavement and shed tears. Then, following an Italian custom that signifies hope at a time of death, the mourners broke into sustained applause.

John Paul died at 9:37 local time in the Vatican's Apostolic Palace on a clear and cool night, with a small group of Polish prelates and nuns at his bedside. The first indication of the pope's passing was the illumination of several windows in his private quarters overlooking St. Peter's Square. An e-mail announcement followed. A half-hour later, the bells of all of Rome's churches rang out in mourning.

The news evoked an outpouring of emotion for the man all over the world. In Paris, mourners packed special midnight services; church bells sounded in Cuba. President Bush called John Paul "a champion of human freedom" and "a good and faithful servant of God. ... We're grateful to God for sending such a man, a son of Poland."

The pope's body will lie in state in St. Peter's Basilica starting Monday afternoon. The date of his funeral will be set by a gathering of cardinals on Monday morning, but under guidelines he had set it should take place within four to six days of his death. Within 15 to 20 days, the College of Cardinals will meet in the Sistine Chapel to elect a successor as bishop of Rome and supreme pontiff of the 1 billion-plus-member Roman Catholic Church.

The pope, who was 84, had slipped in and out of consciousness throughout Saturday. The last medical bulletin from the Vatican, issued in the early evening, said he had developed a sudden fever in late morning. The pope had suffered from Parkinson's disease for years; his death was the culmination of a chain of medical setbacks that began in early February with influenza that forced him into a Rome hospital.

Spokesman Joaquin Navarro-Valls said that the pontiff received the Viaticum, a rite for the approach of death, during an 8 p.m. bedside Mass and died surrounded by his closest Polish aides and household staff. The only Italians present were three physicians and two nurses.

His death brought an end to the Roman Catholic Church's third-longest papacy, a reign that

*Please see **POPE**, Back Page*

Staff photo by Herb Swanson
A photo of Pope John Paul II sits on the altar while two people pray at Portland's Cathedral of the Immaculate Conception Saturday afternoon.

WORLD REACTS TO POPE'S DEATH

A MADAWASKA NATIVE was inspired to join the priesthood after attending a pilgrimage to see Pope John Paul II speak 12 years ago. **A6**

NO POPE ever traveled as much or as far, delivered so many speeches, wrote so much – or so popularly – or celebrated as many Masses as John Paul. **A14**

WHAT IS THE LEGACY of John Paul? Some call him a 'clear voice for social justice,' while critics found him inflexible and having little real impact on Catholics. **A6**

THE MAN CHOSEN to replace John Paul likely will carry on his legacy without radically altering it. **A6**

THE POPE'S BATTLE with Parkinson's may help bring a new focus on the debilitating condition. **A7**

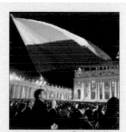

The Associated Press
A man waves the Polish flag after the death of Pope John Paul II was announced in St. Peter's Square at the Vatican.

Red Sox facing Yankees in season opener tonight

By KEVIN THOMAS
Staff Writer

NEW YORK — There will be a chill in the Yankee Stadium air tonight, a sign of early spring in the Bronx.

The last time this stadium was packed, the chill came from an autumn breeze. Then, the Boston Red Sox defeated the New York Yankees, marking one of the greatest comebacks in sports history, and causing a long-awaited celebration back in New England.

And now, just over five months later, these two teams are back,

facing each other yet again, to start the 2005 baseball season.

"It feels like that (the season never ended)," Red Sox manager Terry Francona said.

Maybe it seems that way because the buzz has not stopped. It took Boston 86 years to win a World Series, and no one seems in a hurry to stop the euphoria.

The page turns toward the

A LOOK AT THE 2005 BOSTON TEAM
D1

*Please see **SOX**, Page A9*

Police: Father killed daughter, himself

Lavinia Gelineau told co-workers she was afraid of her father, who had a history of abuse.

By TESS NACELEWICZ
Staff Writer

The father of 25-year-old Lavinia Gelineau – the widow of a Maine National Guardsman killed in Iraq – brutally beat her, then strangled her with a clothesline in the basement of her Westbrook home, authorities said Saturday.

The father, Nicolae Onitiu, 51, who was visiting from Romania, then smoked a cigarette and

hanged himself from a floor joist in the basement, said Stephen McCausland, spokesman for the Maine Department of Public Safety.

"This is a horrific case of domestic violence," McCausland said.

The bodies were discovered Friday morning at Gelineau's new green colonial home on Central Street. She lived there with her mother, Iuliana Onitiu, who had left the home last week to avoid contact with her estranged husband, McCausland said. He said there was a history of violence by Nicolae Onitiu against his wife, and the couple

Lavinia Gelineau

had separated.

Lavinia Gelineau had bought the house and moved in just weeks ago, hoping to begin a new life there after the tragic death of her husband almost one year ago. Spec. Christopher Gelineau, 23, a member of the 133rd Engineer Battalion, was killed April 20 by a roadside bomb in Mosul.

Police discovered the bodies of Lavinia Gelineau and her father after she failed to show up

for work Friday morning and her co-workers contacted police. McCausland said the two died either early Friday or Thursday night.

Autopsies were performed Saturday and it was determined that Gelineau died of strangulation, McCausland said. However, he said, she had other injuries "indicating that there was a horrific beating" that likely began in her kitchen.

"There was evidence of a fight in the home that started in the kitchen and ended in the basement," McCausland said. After smoking a cigarette, Onitiu

*Please see **GELINEAU,** Page A13*

35

THE LIFE OF **POPE JOHN PAUL II**   **SPECIAL SECTION INSIDE**   FINAL ★★★★

THE SUN

SUNDAY

April 3, 2005   F   Baltimore, Maryland : $1.66

Pope John Paul II dies

26 years as leader of Catholic Church transformed papacy

Some of the faithful hold a candlelight vigil in St. Peter's Square at the Vatican after the announcement of the pope's death at age 84. Thousands gathered to pray and sing hymns outside his apartment.

PIER PAOLO CITO : ASSOCIATED PRESS

HIS YOUNG FLOCK

Voices raised in prayer and song mark final hours

By JANICE D'ARCY
SUN STAFF

VATICAN CITY — Before news of the end came, St. Peter's Square was not somber. Cheers sporadically broke out among the young in one corner of the vast plaza. High-pitched melodies rose up nearby. Across the cobblestones, just beneath the apartment where the 84-year-old Pope John Paul II labored to breathe, there were near-constant chants, almost

joyous.
"Giovanni Paulo," the voices called.
These were the children who grew up with Pope John Paul, the only pope many of them have known.
Their presence spoke to a central contradiction in the pope's long tenure: He drew the young to him with warmth and charisma and humanity — even as he urged them to hold to the strict, traditional teachings of the church.   [*See* Youth, 15A]

LOOKING AHEAD

Tradition and politics blend in selection of the next pope

By JOHN RIVERA
AND MIKE LEARY
SUN STAFF

Sealed inside the Sistine Chapel, restored to its original splendor during the pontificate of Pope John Paul II, 117 cardinals in their blood-red robes will soon gather to select his successor in the papal conclave — one of the world's most ancient and arcane electoral processes. It famously concludes with a puff of

white smoke and the joyful Latin proclamation, *Habemus papem:* We have a pope.
Even as word of Pope John Paul's death was announced yesterday, the cardinals were preparing to journey to Rome from around the world for his funeral and pre-conclave meetings — the first will be tomorrow.
Then, no sooner than 15 days nor later than 20 days after the pope's death, the conclave will begin, fol-   [*See* Conclave, 13A]

INSIDE

CHRISTOPHER T. ASSAF : SUN STAFF
Mary McDonald of Elkton and Paul Staehle of Baltimore pray at the Cathedral of Mary Our Queen in Baltimore. (Page 11A)

16 pages of coverage

POPE JOHN PAUL II: Born as Karol Josef Wojtyla, the proud son of Poland helped break communism's hold on Eastern Europe even as he kept a strict doctrinal grip on worldwide Roman Catholicism. **Special section, 1S**

BALTIMORE VISIT: During his 10-hour stay a decade ago, Pope John Paul was ushered around by dignitaries but made a point of seeking out the common man. **Special section, 4S**

POLES MOURN: Members of the city's Polish community recall a popular soul representing more than part of the church hierarchy. **Page 11A**

FILLING CHURCHES: On a bleak rainy afternoon as their vigil comes to an end, Catholics across Maryland seek comfort and shared remembrances. **Page 11A**

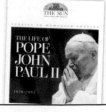

Political influence felt around world

By TODD RICHISSIN
SUN FOREIGN STAFF

VATICAN CITY — Pope John Paul II died yesterday, more than a quarter-century after beginning a reign that transformed the papacy. He succumbed to years of health problems that ravaged his body but did little to diminish his control of the Roman Catholic Church or his political influence across the globe.
The pope, 84, died during the third day of a worldwide vigil marked most poignantly by huge crowds that gathered outside his apartment above St. Peter's Square, from where he had led them in prayer for so many years.
Tens of thousands of pilgrims had journeyed to be near him at the end, offering silent prayers, gentle hymns and — from the young people he made a special effort to reach — rhythmic clapping keeping beat to energetic songs dedicated to "Papa."
"The Holy Father died this evening at 9:37 p.m. [2:37 p.m. Eastern time] in his private apartment. All the procedures outlined in the apostolic Constitution "Universi Dominici Gregis" that was written by John Paul II on Feb. 22, 1996, have been put in motion," the Vatican said in a statement sent

Pope John Paul II is shown at a Mass in Cuba in 1998. He was the most-traveled pope, visiting more than 130 countries.

to journalists by e-mail.
The pope's body was expected to be taken to St. Peter's Basilica no earlier than tomorrow afternoon, the Vatican said, and the College of Cardinals would meet tomorrow at 10 a.m. local time to set a funeral date.
News of the pontiff's death quickly reached around the globe, to churches where prayer services were being held at the moment of his death, to the more than 130 countries this most-traveled of all popes had visited and well beyond.
At St. Peter's Square, Vatican officials broke the news to the estimated   [*See* Pope, 14A]

Lottery, Page B2
VOLUME 267
NUMBER 93
$2.50
***

Boston Sunday Globe

APRIL 3, 2005

THE WEATHER
TODAY: Windy, with periods of rain. High 46-51. Low 36-41.
TOMORROW: Possible showers, then sun. High 50-55. Low 38-43.
HIGH TIDE: 5:41 a.m. 6:32 p.m.
FULL REPORT: Page B8

'A hero for the ages'

AP FILE PHOTO

Despite illness, Pope John Paul II, seen in 1996 at the Vatican, continued a busy schedule of audiences and travel in his later years.

For next pontiff, daunting challenges await

By Charles M. Sennott and Michael Paulson
GLOBE STAFF

VATICAN CITY — Nearly 27 years ago, John Paul II assumed the papacy in an era when the church confronted the real prospect of nuclear war in a world divided between East and West.

Now, the man who succeeds John Paul will face the task of overseeing a church and speaking to a world increasingly divided between North and South, between rich and poor, between secular and devout.

When the 117 voting-age cardinals gather to elect the next pope two weeks from John Paul II's death yesterday, they will invoke centuries-old rituals of transition to choose the head of the billion-member church. But that new pope will face a dizzying array of modern-day challenges, internal as well as exter-

nal, and with little consensus from church leaders about their top priorities.

In Europe, the Catholic hierarchy is threatened by an advancing secular culture and a dramatic surge of Muslim immigrants who are building mosques across the continent.

In Africa, the church faces the twin scourges of AIDS and poverty; in Latin America, it copes with the

steady migration of parts of a traditionally Catholic population toward evangelical Protestantism.

And in the United States, the church is still reeling from the clergy sexual abuse crisis and grappling with a fast-changing set of moral questions provoked by scientific advances in medicine and genetics.

"There are different issues in different parts of the world," said Har-

FUTURE, Page A22

Pope John Paul II, Catholics' dynamic leader, is dead at 84

By Michael Paulson and Charles M. Sennott
GLOBE STAFF

VATICAN CITY — Pope John Paul II died last night at age 84 as millions of Catholics prayed beneath his window and around the world, ending one of the most extraordinary and influential papacies in the 2,000-year history of Christianity.

As the bells of St. Peter's Basilica tolled, and a crowd of thousands stood in grief-stricken silence in St. Peter's Square, a grim-faced Vatican official, Archbishop Leonardo Sandri, broke the news, saying: "Our Holy Father, John Paul, has returned to the house of the Father." He died at 9:37 p.m. local time (2:37 p.m. EST), the Vatican said.

Around the world, Catholics and non-Catholics flocked to churches and public squares, called in to talk radio, and posted messages on websites in the start of a global mourning for the only pope much of the world's population has ever known. Many acknowledged the dramatic impact of John Paul's remarkable 26-year papacy — the third-longest in the history of the church — during which the pontiff helped bring an end to the communist hold on his Eastern Europe, improved relations between Catholicism and other faiths, and reshaped the leadership of the 1-billion-member Roman Catholic Church in his conservative image.

A somber President Bush — a Methodist who had clashed with the pope over the Iraq war — ordered the nation's flags flown at half-staff. Speaking from the

POPE, Page A20

Special section

Pope John Paul II

1920 – 2005

In his 26 years as pontiff, John Paul II became one of the most visible and influential religious leaders of all time. He is remembered by millions — from Rome to Boston, Jerusalem to Warsaw — as the personification of his church. In today's Globe, this section commemorates the pope's life and legacy.
Section E

A life for history
Polish native reshaped the church. | **E2**

Bridging religious divides
Reaching out to other faiths | **E4**

An empire crumbles
Call to faith was key to Soviet collapse | **E5**

Letter and spirit
Excerpts of the pope's writings | **E9**

Doctrine and dissent
Strong opinions, strong dissents | **E10**

A visit to Boston
Meeting America in 1979 | **E11**

N.E. mourns a man of charisma, courage

By Thomas Farragher
GLOBE STAFF

New Englanders bid a solemn, poignant farewell yesterday to Pope John Paul II, the vibrant young pontiff who smiled at them through raindrops at the dawn of his papacy and moved them to tears at its twilight after his long, dignified fight against infirmity.

Within an hour of his death, Catholics streamed up the steps of rain-splashed churches to salute his historic, 26-year reign and to wonder how his successor might affect their faith and its teachings.

"He was truly a blessing to the world," Gerardo Espinoza, 49, of Brighton said after praying for the pope at St. Anthony Shrine in downtown Boston. "It's amazing to see what happens when someone

becomes an instrument of God."

As mournful Masses began, the faithful — many choked with emotion — carried umbrellas and solemn remembrances of a genial Polish pope whose transformative legacy, they said, would be his charisma, courage, and conservatism.

"This pope brought everyone back to realize just what their faith was all about," said Leo Barry, 58, of Braintree. "He's going to be very hard to follow."

Bells tolled and forsythia wreaths were draped in black at St. Stanislaus in Chelsea, as parishioners at the Polish-American church dabbed their eyes and prayed for John Paul, a man who shared their rich ethnic heritage.

"Growing up in the communist

NEW ENGLAND, Page A21

REUTERS PHOTO

Worshipers were gathered in St. Peter's Square at the Vatican yesterday. For many New Englanders, the vivid image of the pope celebrating Mass in Boston 26 years ago has never faded.

Today in Real Estate
A guide to buying or selling a home this spring. **H1**

THE BIG MOVE

Turn clocks ahead
Daylight saving time began at 2 a.m. today. Set your clocks ahead one hour.

For breaking news, updated Globe stories, and more, visit:

Boston.com

14718
0 947726 1

Fishing's revival stirs waterfront debate

New Bedford prospers, at a price

By Robert Gavin
GLOBE STAFF

NEW BEDFORD — Long lamented as a declining industry, fishing is making a surprising comeback in this old whaling town, creating jobs and sparking new investment, but also reviving tensions along the waterfront.

With the size of the catch nearly doubling since 1999, and its value growing 35 percent to $176 million, New Bedford is the nation's top seafood port in terms of the dollar value of its catch. Fishing industry employment in the New Bedford area has nearly doubled to more than

1,300 since then, while more than 60 new fishing businesses, a 40 percent increase, have sprung up, according to the Center for Policy Analysis at the University of Massachusetts at Dartmouth.

As a result, New Bedford's harbor is bursting at the seams, with dock space at such a premium that boats, lashed side by side, sometimes extend four and five deep from the piers. Warren Alexander, who in the last year added five vessels to his fleet of scallopers, said the scarce dock space has become so costly and inconvenient that he may relo-

NEW BEDFORD, Page B6

PLAY BALL, CHAMPS

GLOBE STAFF PHOTO/JIM DAVIS

Red Sox pitcher David Wells worked out yesterday at Yankee Stadium in preparation for tonight's opener against the Bombers. **C1.**

Hard-liner faces test in Senate for UN post

By Peter Canellos
GLOBE STAFF

WASHINGTON — Negotiations were underway, and John R. Bolton was incensed: "Peace hopes . . . are spurious in rationale and unworkable in reality," he wrote in the blunt style that has turned heads around the world. "This cannot be allowed."

The year was 1966, and Bolton, a 17-year-old student at Maryland's McDonogh School, was laying down his anticommunist creed in a school-newspaper editorial headlined "No Peace in Vietnam."

On Thursday, almost 40 years after he put pen to paper against President Lyndon B. Johnson's failed overtures to North Vietnam, Bolton's hardline views will face their stiffest test, as the Senate Foreign Relations

BOLTON, Page A14

The Detroit News AND Free Press

Metro edition ·   7 8 9 10 11 12 13 14 15   A B C D E F

Sunday, April 3, 2005

Dale G. Young / The Detroit News
Alan Anderson tries to make a move on UNC's Jawad Williams. Anderson, named team MVP, was held scoreless in the loss Saturday.

Cinderella season ends for scrappy Spartans

■ Underdog MSU goes home defeated but not beaten, a great rebound story regardless of ending.

ST. LOUIS

You run as far as you can go, as fast as you can go, and see where it takes you. Michigan State ran as long it could, before it hit something that wouldn't move.

We knew North Carolina had the dominant stars. We wondered if they'd show up, and how MSU would respond if they did. The answer arrived with sudden clarity Saturday night, as the Tar Heels ended the Spartans' improbable Final Four run with an 87-71 victory, coolly fighting off MSU's early charge.

BOB WOJNOWSKI

Carolina simply had too much, too much talent, too much size, too much speed. The Tar Heels now advance to the championship matchup the rest of the nation craved, facing Illinois Monday night.

At least MSU (26-7) finished its season without major regret.

Carolina was better, and it would have taken an amazing effort for the Spartans to win. The unfortunate thing is, we had started to grow accustomed to their amazing efforts.

From a 38-33 halftime lead, MSU fell quickly, buried by Carolina stars Jawad Williams and Raymond Felton. It was almost as if the Spartans expended all they had in the first half, and finally ran out.

From the start, the differences were stark, but not unexpected. North Carolina glided, content to heave three-point shots. And MSU ran straight at 'em, shot, missed, rebounded, shot, missed, rebounded, scored.

Please see WOJO, Page 9A

MSU women are ready
Liz Shimek brings her work ethic to the game tonight vs. Tennessee. **Page 1C**

North Carolina too much
The Tar Heels overwhelm Michigan State with its talent. **Page 1C**

The Detroit News

Business	1B	Money&Life	4B
Class Index	1P	N.Y. Times	
County	4D	Crossword	13A
Deaths	2D	Obituary	2D
Editorials	12A	Opinions	13A
Horoscope	6P	Sports	1C
Lottery	2A	Stocks	6B
Metro	1D	Weather	2A

131st year, No. 224
© The Detroit News
Printed in the USA

 GANNETT

38

Detroit Free Press

Susan Ager	1K	Jumble	2Q
Mitch Albom	1L	The List!	2E
Books	4L	Movie Guide	7E
Crossword	7P	Real Estate	1G, 1J
Ron Dzwonkowski	2L	Sound Judgment	4E
Editorials	2L	Sunday	1L
Entertainment	1E	Travel	1M
Game On!	8E	The Way We Live	1K
Horoscope	TV Book		

Volume 174, Number 331
© 2005 Detroit Free Press Inc.
Printed in the United States

$1.50
$2 home

detnews.com

The Detroit News available online Updated all day, every day.

Recycled newsprint is used to print The Detroit News and

A TRIBUTE
POPE JOHN PAUL II
1920-2005

SPECIAL SECTION CELEBRATES HIS PAPACY
SECOND SECTION

FAREWELL

Plinio Lepri / Associated Press
Pope John Paul II brought his papacy to people around the globe, becoming well-known for his common touch and doctrinal conservatism.

INSIDE

Faithful mourn
Bells ring, black bunting goes up at Metro churches.
Page 6A

Turmoil seen
Pope's death to shake up established order.
Page 7A

Great leader
Editorial: John Paul II was a champion of social justice.
Page 12A

World mourns passing of the people's pope

By Daniel Williams
And Alan Cooperman
Washington Post

VATICAN CITY — John Paul II, the voyager pope who helped conquer communism and transformed the papacy with charisma and vigor, died Saturday night after a long battle with Parkinson's disease that became a lesson to the world in humble suffering. He was 84.

"Our most beloved Holy Father has returned to the house of the Father," Archbishop Leonardo Sandri, a senior Vatican official, told pilgrims in St. Peter's Square. The throng of 50,000 momentarily stood in stunned silence, stared at the pavement and shed tears. Then, following an Italian custom that signifies hope at a time of death, the mourners broke into applause.

John Paul died at 9:37 p.m. (2:37 p.m. Detroit time) in the Vatican's Apostolic Palace, with a small group of Polish prelates and nuns at his bedside. The Vatican chamberlain formally verified the death, which in the past was done by tapping a pope's forehead three times with a silver hammer. The chamberlain then destroyed the symbols of the pope's authority: his fisherman's ring and dies used to make lead seals for apostolic letters.

The first indication of the pope's passing was the illumination of several windows in his private quarters overlooking St. Peter's Square. An e-mail announcement followed: "The Holy Father died this evening ... in his private apartment." A half-hour later, the bells of all of Rome's churches rang out in mourning.

The news evoked an outpouring of emotion all over the world. In Paris, mourners packed midnight services; church bells sounded in Cuba. President Bush called John Paul "a champion of human freedom."

Please see POPE, Page 6A

Vatican begins plans for funeral, successor

Associated Press

Papal tradition dictates the rituals that will follow a pope's death. What to expect:

■ **Mourning period:** A nine-day mourning period, known as the "novemdiales," follows the death of a pope. The pope's body will lie in state in St. Peter's Basilica in the Clementine Chapel no earlier than Monday afternoon, the Vatican said. After the death of John Paul I in 1978, an estimated 750,000 mourners filed past the body over three days. Many more could pay homage to John Paul II.

■ **Funeral:** The funeral and burial must be held between the fourth and sixth day after death. For John Paul II, it likely will be between Wednesday and Friday in St. Peter's Square. Many of the world's leaders and other dignitaries are expected to attend.

■ **Burial:** Most popes in recent centuries have chosen to be buried beneath St. Peter's Basilica. The Vatican has not clarified whether John Paul sought such a burial. There is speculation that the Polish-born pontiff could have chosen to be interned in Krakow's Wavel Cathedral alongside Polish royalty.

■ **Conclave:** The Cardinals will gather for the first time Monday to set a funeral date, after which they'll focus on electing a new pope. Among those who will participate will be Cardinal Edmund Szoka, former leader of the Detroit Archdiocese, and Cardinal Adam Maida, current leader. The election of John Paul took two days and eight ballots.

Ankur Dholakia / The Detroit News
Beverly Lemle of Detroit prays Saturday for the pope at the Cathedral of the Blessed Sacrament in Detroit.

Unknown cardinal changed the world

Among the many firsts linked to Pope John Paul II, one goes barely noticed:

He was the first pope with a Web site. Small point, sure. But it befits a record-shattering papacy that was different from Day One, when Karol Wojtyla became the first non-Italian pope in 455 years, taking over for John Paul I, the Italian whose papacy lasted a scant 34 days.

GEORGE BULLARD

St. Peter's Square that day in 1978 had no clue what was coming. The obscure cardinal from Krakow was on nobody's short list of possible winners — or on anyone's long list, either.

Even alleged "Vatican insiders" were surprised. They chalked up the Pole as a compromise selected after a deadlock between liberals and conservatives. Bureaucrats took a wait-and-see attitude.

Nobody knew it at the time, but the modern mega-papacy was about to be born.

This new guy was different. Actor. Playwright. Poet. Traveler. He backpacked. He spoke eight languages fluently.

Those of us awaiting word in *Please see LEADER, Page 6A*

SPRING AHEAD! IT'S DAYLIGHT-SAVING TIME

ON GUARD FOR 173 YEARS

METRO FINAL
50 cents

Detroit Free Press

MONDAY
April 4,
2005

www.freep.com

Tigers preview!

The pieces are in place.
This year, the Tigers are
AL Central contenders.

**KANSAS CITY ROYALS
AT DETROIT TIGERS**
1:05 p.m. today at Comerica Park
TV/RADIO: Fox Sports Net, WXYT-AM
(1270), WTKA-AM (1050)
TICKETS: Sold out

JOHN PAUL II | SPECIAL SECTION INSIDE

Ancient papal rites draw awe, wonder

GIANNI GIANSANTI/Pool via Getty Images-Agence France-Presse
Cardinal Martinez Somalo blesses the body of Pope John Paul II as he lies in state Sunday in the Clementine Hall at the Vatican's Apostolic Palace. Said Detroit's Cardinal Adam Maida, "I've never known a pope to command such a position on the world stage."

MICHIGAN STATE 68, TENNESSEE 64

MSU WINS THRILLER; FINAL NEXT

RASHAUN RUCKER/Detroit Free Press
MSU's Kelli Roehrig, back, and Liz Shimek celebrate a berth in Tuesday night's title game.

MICHAEL ROSENBERG

INDIANAPOLIS — Frame it, seal it, get a videotape of it, enjoy it. Hold onto it forever. Michigan State beat Tennessee, 68-64, but this was so much more than a simple score, so much bigger than a single victory.

It's not just that Tennessee was the favorite in every way — to the experts, and in the hearts of most fans at the RCA Dome. It's not just that Tennessee is the biggest, boldest name in women's college basketball (the Lady Vols are booked at every Final Four through 2012).

No, it's *how* this happened. Hope and Chance had both checked out of the MSU hotel. With less than 15 minutes left, Tennessee led by 16, 49-33.

Then the Spartans came back and stunned the whole dome. In the final minute Sunday night, Kelli Roehrig scored to give Michigan State a 66-64 lead, and then the Lady Vols had one last desperate chance. And they missed.

And they got the rebound.

And the Vols shot, again and again, but then Roehrig grabbed a rebound and passed to Lindsay Bowen, who found a streaking Victoria Lucas-Perry, who sank a lay-up and the Lady Vols, all in one flash.

On to the championship game Tuesday night. Michigan State will play Baylor.

Please see MSU, Page 8A

TOM IZZO: UNLEASHED

He was blunt about the defeat. And he was blunt about his critics. He said this past season was "the hardest of my career," despite going 20-7. He likened it to a "root canal." He spilled his thoughts, then wondered if he should.

Izzo's assistants tried to stop his postgame musings.

Mitch Albom's column, Page 1C
Your Sparty shots, Page 8A

It's war of the nice girls on daytime TV in Detroit

MIKE DUFFY

Whether she's dancing across the stage, flashing her upbeat humor or breezily chatting with guests on her hang-loose syndicated daytime talk show, Ellen DeGeneres always has her sunny side up.

So don't expect her to start trash talking about the great and powerful Oprah Winfrey.

Not even as their Motor City showdown begins at 4 this afternoon, with "The Ellen DeGeneres Show" departing the friendly confines of 10 a.m. weekday mornings on WDIV-TV (Channel 4) to square off against "The Oprah Winfrey Show." The latter has long been a powerful afternoon viewer magnet for WXYZ-TV (Channel 7).

Ellen DeGeneres, left, and Oprah Winfrey will compete for metro-area viewers in the 4 p.m. time slot starting today.

"We have some of the same audience. But our shows are also very different," says DeGeneres. "Oprah's been on a long time, and she's the queen. I'd like to be the queen someday."

For now, though, Ellen DeGeneres remains the plucky new princess of daytime.

Over the course of the past 20

Please see DUFFY, Page 5A

WHAT'S NEXT FOR CHURCH

Here's a look at the coming events surrounding the death of Pope John Paul II:

TODAY: College of Cardinals meets and may set the funeral date. Funeral and burial must be held between the fourth and sixth day after death, except for "special reasons."

■ The pope's body goes on public view at St. Peter's Basilica at 5 p.m. Rome time (11 a.m. in Detroit).

TUESDAY: Hundreds of thousands of mourners are expected to file past his body. Heads of state and dignitaries gather for the funeral.

WEDNESDAY: The earliest day the funeral may be held. It will be at St. Peter's Square and could last more than two hours. The lead celebrant will be the dean of the College of Cardinals, Joseph Ratzinger.

■ At the funeral of John Paul I in 1978, the coffin was placed atop a rug in front of the altar. Cardinals, wearing red vestments and white miters, entered in order of seniority.

BURIAL: Most popes in recent centuries have been buried beneath St. Peter's Basilica. Their lead-lined coffins were carried through the "door of death," left of the main altar. The coffin was lowered into a marble sarcophagus and covered by a stone slab.

■ The Vatican has not said where Pope John Paul II will be buried. There is speculation that he could choose to be interred in Krakow's Wawel Cathedral alongside Polish royalty.

APRIL 12: The earliest day for conclave to convene to elect a new pope. The conclave is to be held 15 to 20 days after the pope's death.

■ Once the conclave starts, ballots will be held each morning and each afternoon. If no one gets the required two-thirds majority after about 12 days, cardinals may change the protocol and pick a pope by simple majority.

Public viewing gets under way today; Maida stunned by his task

PETER MacDIARMID/Getty Images-Agence France-Presse
Crowds attend a mass Sunday for Pope John Paul II in St. Peter's Square in Vatican City. He led the Catholic Church for 26 years.

DAVID CRUMM

As he struggled to describe the monumental events unfolding this week in his 1-billion-member church, Detroit Cardinal Adam Maida reached for a word usually reserved for kids: "awesome."

The cardinal meant it. At age 75, this veteran communicator found that words were failing him to describe this historic moment when faith, mystery and ritual have transfixed the world at the passing of Pope John Paul II, the world's spiritual superpower.

Awe.

It's the ancient core of religion itself, but it's rarely seen in our overstressed, entertainment-saturated world today. In 20 years of writing about religion, I've rarely seen true awe. Certainly, I sensed it around 1990 in the vast, peaceful crowds that toppled communism in eastern Europe and in the miraculous emergence of Nelson Mandela in South Africa.

But what the cardinal was doing Sunday was eloquently reminding his 1.5 million followers in southeast Michigan that the next few weeks are shaping up as one of those incredibly rare experiences of awe.

Something powerful is drawing Catholics and many non-Catholics to closely follow the upcoming funeral rituals for John Paul, followed by the ancient gathering

Please see CRUMM, Page 3A

MOURNING THE POPE, CHOOSING HIS SUCCESSOR

Readers' eulogies
"'Be not afraid' was this man's constant refrain. It is an eloquent and simple affirmation of human dignity." — Robert del Valle, Royal Oak
More letters on 7A

The world mourns
In Catholic and Protestant churches, synagogues and mosques around the world, mourners pray for the pope who touched millions of lives. **Pages 10A-11A**

Who will lead now?
As cardinals prepare for the conclave, they must choose a pope who can help heal church divisions over gender issues, poverty and secularism. **Page 13A**

Commemorative page
"Do not abandon yourselves to despair. ... We are the Easter people, and hallelujah is our song. The profound lessons the pope taught us. **Page 14A**

SUNDAY, APRIL 3, 2005   ST. PAUL   WWW.TWINCITIES.COM

PIONEER ✦ PRESS

MINNESOTA'S FIRST NEWSPAPER $1

1920 ✦ 2005

POPE JOHN PAUL II

MASSIMO SAMBUCETTI, ASSOCIATED PRESS PHOTO FROM APRIL 10, 2003

He was a modern pope who helped transform the Catholic Church and the world. Yet for all his accomplishments, John Paul II also will be remembered for his disappointments.

BY HANNA ROSIN *Washington Post*

So much was expected of Karol Wojtyla when he became pope in 1978. Here, for the first time, was a pontiff plucked not from the Vatican's inner chambers, but a man of the world. He was not Italian; he skied, he kayaked, he acted in dramas.

His faith, too, seemed tested. He had lost his mother early, lived in the shadow of Auschwitz, performed forced labor in a limestone quarry. "Do Not Be Afraid" was his motto at his inauguration, and one sensed that after living through Poland's brutal mid-century, he no longer was.

So even before his first papal pronouncement, he was granted a place in history as the Roman Catholic Church's first modern pope, charged with leading the centuries-old institution into the next millennium — the "new springtime of Christianity," as he called it.

And 26 years later, it's by that yardstick that Pope John Paul II's legacy will be judged, both in the church he transformed and in the world he tried so hard to influence. On Saturday, after years of declining health, he died at age 84.

For those who expected more from the modernization of John Paul — U.S. priests ordained in the 1960s, say, or Catholic women who wanted to be priests — the pope not only betrayed his promise but locked the church in place for years to come.

REMEMBERING THE POPE, 6A

FINAL MESSAGE 4A ▪ **A REMARKABLE LIFE ENDS** 5A ▪ **WHAT'S AHEAD** 6A ▪ **LOCAL REACTION** 8-9A ▪ **MORE** 10-11A

COMING MONDAY: FOUR-PAGE COMMEMORATIVE SECTION ON THE LIFE AND LEGACY OF POPE JOHN PAUL II

40

NEWSPAPER OF THE TWIN CITIES

Star Tribune

www.startribune.com   METRO EDITION · SUNDAY · APRIL 3, 2005 $1.75

POPE JOHN PAUL II | 1920-2005

A FINAL ACT OF FAITH

"Sliding into death I unveil the awaiting, my eyes fixed on one place, on resurrection."

From a poem by Pope John Paul II

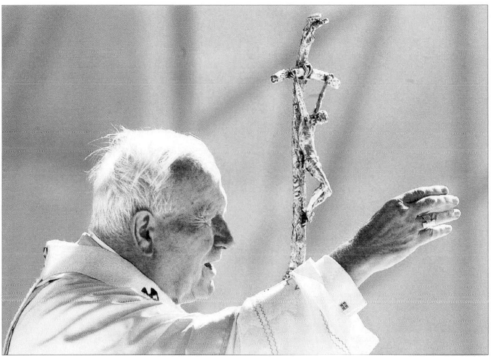

Gary Hershorn/Reuters file photo

John Paul II at a mass in New York in 1995. "All popes belong to the world, but Americans had special reasons to love the man from Krakow," President Bush said Saturday.

A pope of the people, he led with charisma and a missionary spirit

By J.Y. Smith
Washington Post

Pope John Paul II, an obscure Polish prelate who became the supreme pontiff of the Roman Catholic Church, a statesman who helped bring down communism, and a defender of the faith who insisted that the church confront the sins of its past to prepare it for the third millennium, died Saturday in the Vatican. He was 84.

Death came after his health took a sudden turn for the worse in recent days after weeks of treatment for various ailments that were compounded by Parkinson's disease.

"We all feel like orphans this evening," Undersecretary of State Archbishop Leonardo Sandri told the crowd of 70,000 that had gathered Saturday in St. Peter's Square.

At the news of John Paul's death, the assembled flock fell into a stunned silence before some people broke out in applause — an Italian tradition in which mourners often clap for important figures. Others wept.

A seminarian slowly waved a large red and white Polish flag festooned with a black ribbon.

The crowd outside the Vatican quickly swelled, with many people clutching their rosaries. As bells tolled in mourning, a group of young people sang, "Alleluia, he will rise again." Later, pilgrims joined in singing the "Ave Maria."

POPE continues on A18
— Not a traditional papal figure.

EXPANDED COVERAGE, A15-A24

Richard Tsong-Taatarii/Star Tribune

At the Basilica of St. Mary in Minneapolis, Allison Jones and her boyfriend, David Cowell, paused to pray.

NATIVE SON MOURNED: "The pope contributed to the fact that we live in a free country," said one Pole. **A16**

A SUCCESSOR CONSIDERED: Candidates hail from Africa, South and Central America, and Europe. **A20**

ACROSS MINNESOTA: Bells signaled the pope's passing and elicited prayers of sadness and gratitude. **A22**

ON STARTRIBUNE.COM: Updates on the story, photo galleries and audio on the life and passing of Pope John Paul II.

A loss felt throughout his flock

By Warren Wolfe and Nolan Zavoral
Star Tribune Staff Writers

It was a Palm Sunday, and a frail Pope John Paul II appeared at his apartment window overlooking St. Peter's Square to greet tens of thousands of cheering pilgrims.

"It was painful to see how tortured he was as he tried to speak," said Don Briel, a frequent Vatican visitor and Catholic educator at the University of St. Thomas. "And yet here he was ... again demonstrating his valiant sense that one doesn't abandon one's tasks, even embracing suffering to complete what one is called to do."

The pope was remembered by Twin Cities clergy and other religious leaders as a man of intellect, as well as spirituality.

LEGACY continues on A21

SHOOTING AT RED LAKE

Tears for a loving partner

By Jill Burcum
Star Tribune Staff Writer

RED LAKE, MINN. — It is in the depths of the night, when their baby sleeps beside her, that 14-year-old Alex Roy senses her boyfriend, Chase Lussier, is with her again.

"I always have dreams about Chase. He talks to me and says, 'I love you,'" said Roy, an eighth grader at Red Lake Middle School. "I ask him, 'Why did you leave me? Why did you leave our son?'"

Fresh tears flow down Roy's already tear-stained cheeks.

"When I start to wake up, he says, 'No, babe. Don't go. Please. Don't go.'"

Steve Rice/Star Tribune
Alex Roy, 14, held Ayden, the son she had with shooting victim Chase Lussier.

LUSSIER continues on A27

NEWS INSIDE

Abu Ghraib firefight: Iraqi insurgents attack the infamous prison near Baghdad, injuring 44 U.S. troops and 12 prisoners. **A6**

Daylight saving time began at 2 a.m. today, so we lost an hour until fall. Be sure you've set your clocks ahead one hour.

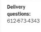

Delivery questions:
612-673-4343

Sunday, April 3, 2005
Copyright 2005
Star Tribune
Vol. XXIII/No. 364
13 sections

Power pair savor late, great romance

By Rochelle Olson
Star Tribune Staff Writer

At 50 and 78, they will soon become one of Minnesota's glamorous power couples.

Minnesota Supreme Court Chief Justice Kathleen Blatz and Republican businessman Wheelock Whitney will marry this month in a small church ceremony.

"I wouldn't have expected it. ... I wouldn't have believed it," said Blatz of her two-year romance with the man she calls her "beau." She added, "It's a great lesson. Life is more complicated than we wish and more simple than we realize."

COUPLE continues on A26

RWBGY X1234567

It's Illinois vs. UNC

Play ball!

■ 26-PAGE BASEBALL PREVIEW SECTION INSIDE

■ Illinois 72, Louisville 57 ■ UNC 87, Michigan State 71 ■ Final game Monday, 8:20 p.m ■ Complete coverage, Sports

SUNDAY POST-DISPATCH

www.STLtoday.com   APRIL 3, 2005 $1.25

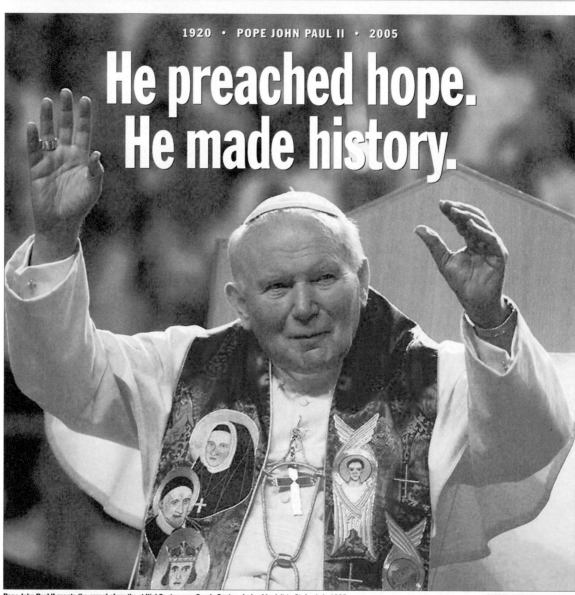

1920 · POPE JOHN PAUL II · 2005

He preached hope.
He made history.

Pope John Paul II greets the crowd of youths at Kiel Center, now Savvis Center, during his visit to St. Louis in 1999.

ANDREW CUTRARO / POST-DISPATCH

In last weeks, he seemed to be "a soul pulling a body"

BY IAN FISHER AND ELAINE SCIOLINO
New York Times

VATICAN CITY — Pope John Paul II's death ended an extraordinary, if sometimes polarizing, 26-year reign that remade the papacy.

He died in his apartment three stories above St. Peter's Square, as tens of thousands of the faithful gathered within sight of his lighted window for a second night of vigils, amid millions of prayers for his rapidly declining health from Roman Catholics around the world.

People wept and knelt on cobblestones as the news of his death spread across the square, bowing their heads to a man whose long and down-to-

earth papacy was the only one that many young Catholics around the world remembered. For more than 10 minutes, not long after his death was announced, the largely Roman crowd applauded him.

"I have looked up to this man as a guide, and now it is like a star that has suddenly disappeared," said Caeser Aturi, 38, a priest from Ghana, which the widely traveled pope visited in 1980, on a continent where the Roman Catholic church grew sizably under his reign.

Born Karol Wojtyla on May 18, 1920, in Wadowice, Poland, he was 84 years old.

The pope had been hospitalized twice since Feb. 1 and suffered for a
See Death, A5

WHAT'S NEXT

The pope's body is expected to be taken to St. Peter's Basilica no earlier than Monday.

The College of Cardinals will have a preliminary meeting at 3 a.m. Monday (St. Louis time).

A funeral date has not been set. The Vatican said it probably would be between Wednesday and Friday.

IN THIS SECTION

■ St. Louis, national and world reaction **A7-10**

IN NEWSWATCH

■ Pope's visit in 1999 energized Catholics here. **B1**

■ Secrecy will frame the next papal election. **B7**

Most-traveled pope touched lives and championed peace

BY PATRICIA RICE
Of the Post-Dispatch

The first pope to carry the message of Christianity to every corner of the Earth has died.

Pope John Paul II, 84, died at 9:37 p.m. (1:37 p.m. St. Louis time) on Saturday (April 2, 2005) in his Vatican apartment. The spiritual leader of the world's 1 billion Catholics had become increasingly frail since 2000 but had kept his schedule until last month.

"We all feel like orphans this evening," Undersecretary of State Archbishop Leonardo Sandri told the crowd of 70,000 that had gathered in St. Peter's Square below the pope's still-lighted apartment windows, The Associated Press reported.

St. Louis Archbishop Raymond Burke said the pope was "a man of such greatness that the legacy cannot be described."

"A great teacher of the faith, a great apostle who traveled the whole world to teach the message of Christ, but also a great lover of mankind, who brought nations, leaders of nations, to a greater respect for the principles of justice which are the foundations of peace," he said.

Today, as Cardinal Justin F. Rigali — former archbishop of St. Louis, now Philadelphia's archbishop — joins other cardinals from around the world hurrying to Rome for the pope's funeral and the election of his successor, tens of thousands of St. Louisans may hold dear the image of the aging pope on the metal stairs to a jet at Lambert Field.
See Pope, A4

42

The Kansas City Star.

Sunday, April 3, 2005

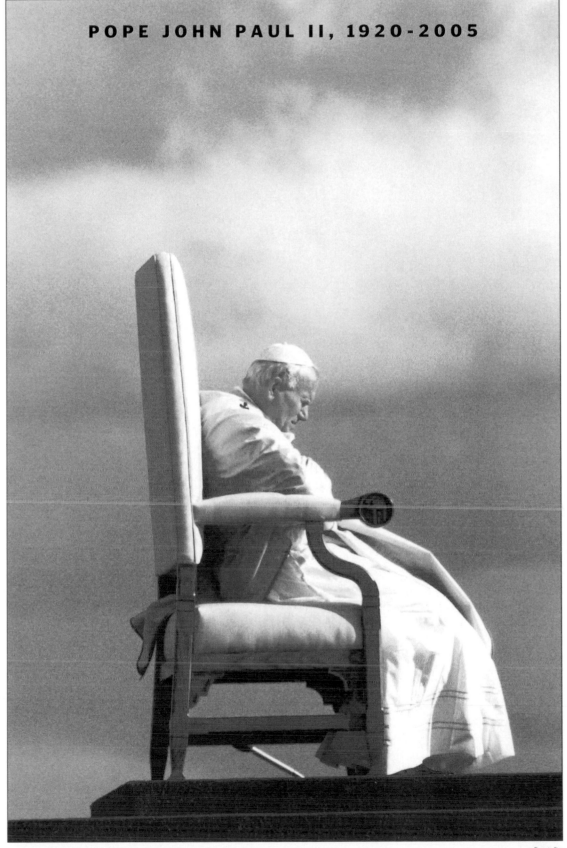

POPE JOHN PAUL II, 1920-2005

Toronto Star

Pope John Paul II celebrates Mass at the Downsview Park in Toronto on July 18, 2002.

43

PILGRIM OF PEACE

Billings Gazette

Final Four muscle

Illinois Luther Head helped the Illini dump Louisville to make the NCAA championship game. North Carolina will be the opponent.

Sports 1B

SUNDAY, APRIL 3, 2005 · *The Source* · LOCAL EDITION

POPE JOHN PAUL II 1920-2005

'The angels welcome you'

Pope John Paul II dies at age 84; world mourns

VATICAN CITY (AP) — Pope John Paul II, who helped topple communism in Europe and left a deeply conservative stamp on the church that he led for 26 years, died Saturday night in his Vatican apartment, ending a long public struggle against debilitating illness. He was 84.

"We all feel like orphans this evening," Undersecretary of State Archbishop Leonardo Sandri told the crowd of 70,000 that gathered in St. Peter's Square below the pope's still-lighted apartment windows.

In the massive piazza that stretches from St. Peter's Basilica, the assembled flock fell into a stunned silence before some people broke into applause — an Italian tradition in which mourners often clap for

important figures. Others wept. Still others recited the rosary. A seminarian slowly waved a large red and white Polish flag draped with black bunting for the Polish-born pontiff, the most-traveled pope in history.

At one point, prelates asked those in the square to stay silent so they might "accompany the pope in his first steps into heaven."

But as the Vatican bells tolled in mourning, a group of young people sang, "Alleluia, he will rise again." One strummed a guitar, and other pilgrims joined in singing the "Ave Maria."

"The angels welcome you," Vatican TV said after papal

Please see Pope, 8A

Pope John Paul II prays during three minutes of silence to commemorate the victims of the tsunami that hit Southeast Asia at the Vatican on Jan. 5.

Associated Press

Faithful praise ministry of pope

300 attend Saturday Mass at St. Patrick's Co-Cathedral

By SUSAN OLP and BECKY SHAY
Of The Gazette Staff

A few more parishioners than normal attended 5 p.m. Mass at St. Patrick's Co-Cathedral Saturday, several hours after the world learned of Pope John Paul II's death.

About 300 people filled the pews of the downtown church. Late afternoon sunshine illuminated the tall stained-glass windows.

Just inside the church hung an oil portrait of John Paul, painted by Elizabeth McNamer, a member of St. Patrick's and an adjunct professor of religion at Rocky Mountain College. The painting, she said, was made from a photograph taken of the pope during his visit to Chicago in 1980.

Please see Faithful, 10A

- ■ Procedure put in motion for secret election of pope, **9A**
- ■ Gazette reporter recalls John Paul II's installation, **10A**

The Rev. John Houlihan enters St. Patrick's Co-Cathedral for Mass, walking past a painting of Pope John Paul II by Elizabeth McNamer.

BOB ZELLAR/Gazette Staff

Crittenton Home a refuge for pregnant girls

Helena institution shelters needy pregnant teens who have nowhere else to go

By LORNA THACKERAY
Of The Gazette Staff

Everywhere Pat Seiler, executive director at the Florence Crittenton Home in Helena, went on a statewide awareness tour last fall, someone lingered behind after her slide show presentation.

"I've had them say, 'Pat, your lecture was so healing for me, because I was there,'" she said. "They always say to us, 'Thank you for a good start.'"

Elderly Montanans who lived in the home as children and middle-aged women who sought help there come to tell her their stories. In Big Timber, 25 percent of her audience had been

How to help

The Florence Crittenton Home's annual budget is about $900,000. A third of that comes from fund-raising.

Donations are tax deductible. The address is Florence Crittenton Home and Services; 901 N. Harris; Helena MT 59601.

- ■ Florence Crittenton Home has provided haven for girls for decades **MAGAZINE, 1E**

adopted from the home.

No one could listen more appreciatively or more attentively than Seiler, a slim, dark-haired woman, who exudes devotion and enthusiasm

Please see Crittenton, 7A

Pat Seiler, executive director of Florence Crittenton Home in Helena, talks with a resident. "We want to remind people that this home belongs to everyone," she said recently.

ELIZA WILEY/Independent-Record

Commemorative edition: Four special pages

Sunday World-Herald

AN INDEPENDENT NEWSPAPER OWNED BY EMPLOYEES

SUNRISE EDITION
SUNDAY, APRIL 3, 2005

POPE JOHN PAUL II: 1920-2005

He so loved the world

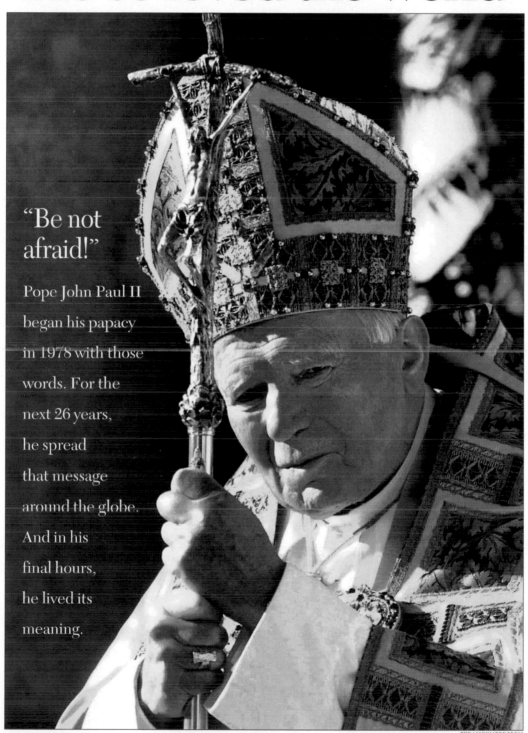

"Be not afraid!"

Pope John Paul II began his papacy in 1978 with those words. For the next 26 years, he spread that message around the globe. And in his final hours, he lived its meaning.

Pope John Paul II at the Holy Door at St. Paul's Outside the Walls Basilica, Jan. 18, 2000

THE ASSOCIATED PRESS

The former actor — and youngest pope in 132 years — proves to be a natural on the world's stage.
Page 2K

The pontiff leaves a lasting impression on Omahans who see him on visits to three central U.S. cities.
Page 3K

The Cardinals' process for electing a pope has a modern twist: sweeping for electronic listening devices.
Page 4K

SUNDAY

$2.50

LAS VEGAS
REVIEW-JOURNAL
LAS VEGAS SUN

Sunday

COMBINED EDITION • APRIL 3, 2005

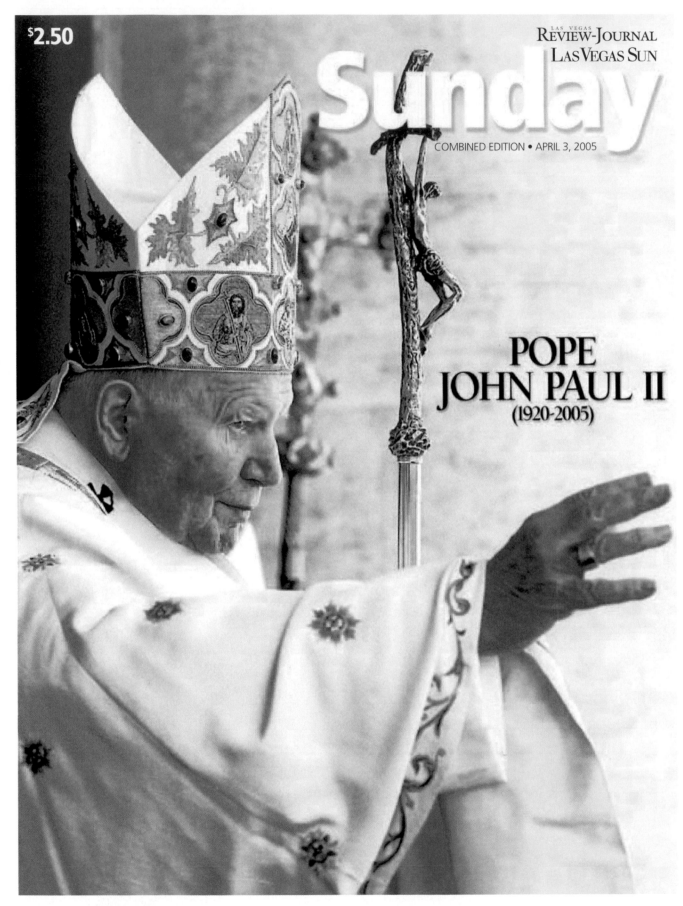

POPE JOHN PAUL II
(1920-2005)

VATICAN CITY

John Paul II, the Polish pontiff who led the Roman Catholic Church for more than a quarter-century and became history's most traveled pope, died Saturday in his Vatican apartment. He was 84. **PAGE 3A**

THE WORLD

Pope John Paul II traveled to 130 countries to bring the Gospel to everyone, leaving his message and visage firmly stamped upon the world's consciousness. Always spiritual, the journeys often were political. **PAGE 8A**

LAS VEGAS

Contrasting emotions were woven tightly around afternoon services Saturday just off the Strip at the Guardian Angel Cathedral, which serves both local Catholics and visitors from around the world. **PAGE 3A**

COMPLETE COVERAGE INSIDE / PAGES 2A-3A, 5A-14A

Heath & Fitness
How much exercise is right for you? ▶ **Special Section**

Old and New
New faces mark renewal of Sox-Yanks rivalry ▶ **C1**
◀ Matt Clement and Randy Johnson

New face
Former Miss NH Trish Regan on CBS News ▶ Clayton, **A11**

· · · · ·

STATE EDITION

"Live Free or Die"
Gen. JOHN STARK

NEW HAMPSHIRE
Sunday News

© 2005 Union Leader Corp., Manchester, NH

New Hampshire's Newspaper
theunionleader.com

☆ ☆ ☆ ☆ (X)

59th Year ● April 3, 2005
202 Pages, 15 Sections ● $1.75

JOHN PAUL II, 1920-2005

'Pilgrim Pope' goes home

Prayers rise from NH for the Pope

By SHAWNE K. WICKHAM
Sunday News Staff

MANCHESTER — As Pope John Paul II was nearing death at his Vatican apartment, the New Hampshire faithful yesterday prayed for "the grace and peace of a happy death" for the Roman Catholic Church leader.

From around the state, Catholics of all ages, from white-haired seniors to infants carried by their mothers, gathered at St. Joseph Cathedral, where Bishop John McCormack offered a 9 a.m. Mass for the dying pontiff.

Six hours later came word from the Vatican that the Pope had died.

▶ **Personal Pope:** Manchester bishop recounts private meetings with John Paul II. **A7**

At St. Marie Church on Manchester's West Side yesterday afternoon, parishioners heard their pastor, the Rev. Marc Montminy, praise the Pope as "truly a man for all seasons."

"He was a manager, a missionary, a statesman and a prophet," Montminy said, "But most of all a pastor of souls."

He called the world traveling Pope "a tramp for the Lord," and said he taught us how to live and, lately, how to die with dignity. He said it was fitting that the Pope should depart as the Roman Catholic church celebrates Divine Mercy Sunday, which John Paul II had introduced into the liturgical calendar.

Morning prayer

Earlier in the day, Jeanine Chatel of Manchester brought her mother, Germaine Chatel,

▶ See **Prayers**, Page A5

ASSOCIATED PRESS FILE

Pope John Paul II waves as a white dove is released by Roman young people in honor of his repeated calls for peace in St. Peter's Square in April 2003. The Pope died yesterday at 2:37 p.m. Eastern time.

Around the world, Catholics prayed for their leader, some lighting candles in makeshift shrines like this one, located in front of the Vatican Embassy in Berlin, Germany, last night.

ASSOCIATED PRESS

His papacy, his legacy, his example

▶ **Funeral plans:** College of Cardinals to meet by tomorrow; funeral could be as soon as Wednesday.

By VICTOR L. SIMPSON
The Associated Press

VATICAN CITY — Pope John Paul II set an example of how to live life, a dynamic preacher who traveled the world, battled Communism and proclaimed his moral code opposing abortion, casual sex and consumerism. In his final days, crushed by sickness that slowed his vigorous gait and silenced his powerful voice, he tried to set an example of how to suffer and how to die.

As he hovered near death, his system failing, the pontiff who once skied and hiked mountains refused to go to the hospital, preferring to remain in his Vatican apartment with his closest aides at his beside.

Cardinal Joseph Ratzinger, the German prelate who is the chief guardian of church doctrine, said John Paul had been aware that he was "passing to the Lord."

John Paul had often warned against a modern world that preferred to ignore its elderly, seeing them as useless appendages of society. Many said his persistence to stay on his job — even travel — set a wonderful example for the sick and the ailing.

The Polish pontiff who led the Roman Catholic Church for 26 years, known as the "pilgrim Pope" for his world travels, died yesterday in his Vatican apartment. He was 84.

Crowd of 70,000

"We all feel like orphans this evening." Undersecretary of

▶ See **Pope**, Page A18

Americans join world in mourning Pope

By ROBERT TANNER
The Associated Press

More inside

▶ **Full coverage** of the death of Pope John Paul II can be found on pages A5-A10, A16 and A18.

Quietly at home, or with heads bowed in church, Americans marked the death of Pope John Paul II, recalling him as a great leader who combined warmth with moral power, a call to care for the poor with an emphasis on liberty.

Bells tolled at Roman Catholic churches across the nation, as they did at the Vatican and around the world. Religious leaders of all faiths spoke out to honor him, as did political leaders. Flags were lowered to half-staff.

"We will always remember the humble, wise and fearless priest who became one of history's great moral leaders," said President Bush, who singled out John Paul's praise for America's Constitution. "All Popes belong to the world, but Americans had special reasons to love the man from Krakow."

Many mourners reflected on John Paul's long suffering and graceful acceptance of death. Others looked to the Polish-born Pope's clear-voiced denunciation of communism. And others re-

▶ See **Nation**, Page A6

Defining a life worth living

"Even if you see someone who's way, way disabled and you think, 'Why are they here?' They're here so you can see how lucky you are."
KATHY BATES
advocate for the disabled

◆ **After Terri Schiavo:** N.H. advocates urge protection for the disabled, but caution that the wrong steps could infringe on their civil rights.

By SHAWNE K. WICKHAM
Sunday News Staff

KATHY BATES was enjoying the pretty spring day, window-shopping on the mall in Lebanon, when a stranger's words cut into her happy daydreaming.

"I feel so sorry for you," the woman told Bates. "I wouldn't want to live the way you live."

Bates, 43, a special education teacher and a long-time advocate for the rights of disabled individuals in New Hampshire, has cerebral palsy and uses a wheelchair for mobility. Her life at the time of that encounter was especially joy-filled, she recalled.

"I had just gotten married, I just got a new job. I had a new condo. It was a sunny day . . . I was really, truly happy."

And that's how she answered the stranger who approached her: "Oh, please don't feel sorry for me," she told her. "I have a great life."

The Terri Schiavo case over the last several weeks has sparked a national discussion about end-of-life care. And part of that conversation has focused on how to define "quality of life."

Some say the decision to withhold food and water from the 41-year-old Florida woman, leading to her death Thursday, raises disquieting questions about how our society values — or de-values — the lives of severely disabled individuals.

▶ See **Disabled**, Page A14

BOB LaPREE/UNION LEADER

Watercolor painting is a bit of a struggle but a favorite pastime for Kathy Bates, who has cerebral palsy.

47

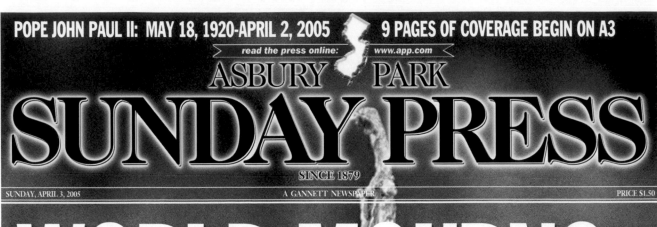

POPE JOHN PAUL II: MAY 18, 1920-APRIL 2, 2005 — 9 PAGES OF COVERAGE BEGIN ON A3

read the press online: www.app.com

ASBURY PARK
SUNDAY PRESS

SINCE 1879

SUNDAY, APRIL 3, 2005 — A GANNETT NEWSPAPER — PRICE $1.50

WORLD MOURNS POPE'S DEATH

Pontiff left his mark on Catholic Church, world for 26 years

SHORE FAITHFUL SHARE SORROW, SEEK SOLACE

By KATHY MATHESON
STAFF WRITER

They knew his death was inevitable and would likely come soon.

But when the news actually broke Saturday afternoon — Pope John Paul II, dead at age 84 — the sadness was not any easier to bear.

"We're devastated," said Jami Conilio, a 27-year-old youth minister for St. Ann's Roman Catholic Church in Keansburg.

The Vatican's announcement that the pontiff died at 2:37 p.m. EST ended what had essentially been a worldwide vigil for Pope John Paul II, who had suffered a number of debilitating illnesses and hospitalizations over the past couple of weeks.

In Monmouth and Ocean counties, the news sent thousands of Catholics to area churches in search of solace. There, they not only shared their sorrow but also their admiration for an extraordinary man who served as a

See **Sorrow,** Page **A3**

THE ASSOCIATED PRESS

VATICAN CITY — Pope John Paul II, who helped topple communism in Europe and left a deeply conservative stamp on the church that he led for 26 years, died Saturday night in his Vatican apartment, ending a long public struggle against debilitating illness. He was 84.

"We all feel like orphans this evening," Undersecretary of State Archbishop Leonardo Sandri told the crowd of 70,000 that gathered in St. Peter's Square below the pope's still-lighted apartment windows.

In the massive piazza that stretches from St. Peter's Basilica, the assembled flock fell into a stunned silence before some people broke into applause — an Italian tradition in which mourners often clap for important figures. Others wept. Still others recited the rosary.

A seminarian waved a large red and white Polish flag draped with black bunting for the Polish-born pontiff, the most-traveled pope in history.

At one point, prelates asked those in the square to stay silent so they might "accompany the pope in his first steps into heaven."

See **Pontiff,** Page **A3**

Pope John Paul II presides at a Mass at Giants Stadium in East Rutherford in 1995. (FILE PHOTO)

48

Sunday Star-Ledger

OW

FINAL EDITION

THE NEWSPAPER FOR NEW JERSEY

APRIL 3, 2005 $1.25

JOHN PAUL II

INSIDE: SPECIAL 12-PAGE SECTION CELEBRATING HIS LIFE

A BELOVED POPE IS GONE

HE CHANGED THE WORLD AND LEAVES A POWERFUL LEGACY

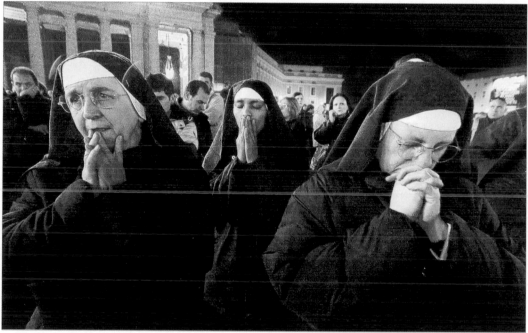

Nuns standing among the tens of thousands at St. Peter's Square pray moments after hearing the announcement of the pope's death.

MARIO LAPORTA/AFP/GETTY IMAGES

No easy choices in replacement

Understanding the selection process and how it all works.
Pages 3 & 4

A day of prayer to say goodbye

Faithful remember a "regular guy" who knew how to inspire people. Page 5

Why women won't forget John Paul

He "could make you forget you were standing in the rain."
Braun column, Page 9

BY STEVE CHAMBERS AND JEFF DIAMANT   STAR-LEDGER STAFF

VATICAN CITY — Pope John Paul II, the beloved but weary traveler who contributed to the fall of communism and later turned his sights on the materialism of the West, died yesterday in his Vatican apartment. He was 84.

His 26-year papacy was the third-longest in the history of the Roman Catholic Church.

The Vatican said John Paul died of heart and kidney failure at 9:37 p.m. (2:37 p.m. EST). The pope, dependent on a breathing tube and weakened by a bacterial infection, had received last rites Thursday, leaving his worldwide flock of 1 billion to pray for a gentle death for a man whose strength was never more evident than in his final weeks of suffering.

Archbishop Leonardo Sandri, a member of the papal household, announced the death to tens of thousands of people gathered in St. Peter's Square.

[See Pope, Page 6]

IN OTHER NEWS

Flood warnings issued as rivers on the rise

The National Weather Service issued flood warnings for all of New Jersey's northern counties and advisories for motorists to respect roadway barriers as rain poured on the state with no plans to let up until tonight.

Parts of several rivers have reached or will rise above flood level, and many residents who live in drenched areas of Lincoln Park and Wayne found drier quarters for weekend. See story, page 23

Daylight-saving time
Did you remember to set your clocks ahead one hour?

IN SPORTS

Illinois and N.C. head to final

No. 1-ranked Illinois pulls away from Louisville in the second half, and North Carolina rides hot shooting to set up NCAA showdown tomorrow.

Baseball bonus section

Put Pedro Martinez in a Mets uniform and the team suddenly has a chance to win back some fans' hearts from the Yankees. A closer look at the crosstown rivals.

A dangerous steroid subplot

A shadowy world of pills and misinformation that often preys on the young exists online, far from the big league stadiums where a steroid scandal has erupted.

INSIDE

Abu Ghraib jail attacked
Insurgents fire grenades and detonate car bombs at notorious Baghdad jail, injuring U.S. personnel.
Page 16

Housing shifts now under fire
Group targets system that allows rich towns to transfer their affordable housing requirements.
Page 23

Active Adult Communities
Special advertising section looks at condos, townhouses and rentals.
Section 11

Special Section

ABBY	S2/P2	HOROSCOPE	S2/P4
BOOKS	S10/P6-7	MOVIES	S4/P12
CLASSIFIED DIRECTORY	S1/P2	OBITUARIES	S1/P40
CONSUMER	S2/P3	OUTDOORS	S5/P22
CROSSWORD	S2/P4	SIGNAL2NOISE	S4/P10
EDITORIALS	S10/P2	WEDDINGS	S2/P6
GAMES	S2/P4	WEATHER	S1/P43

8 14186 00125 2

For The Star-Ledger's top stories starting at 3 a.m. every day check out http://www.nj.com or access E-Delivery at www.nj.com/starledger/ed.

49

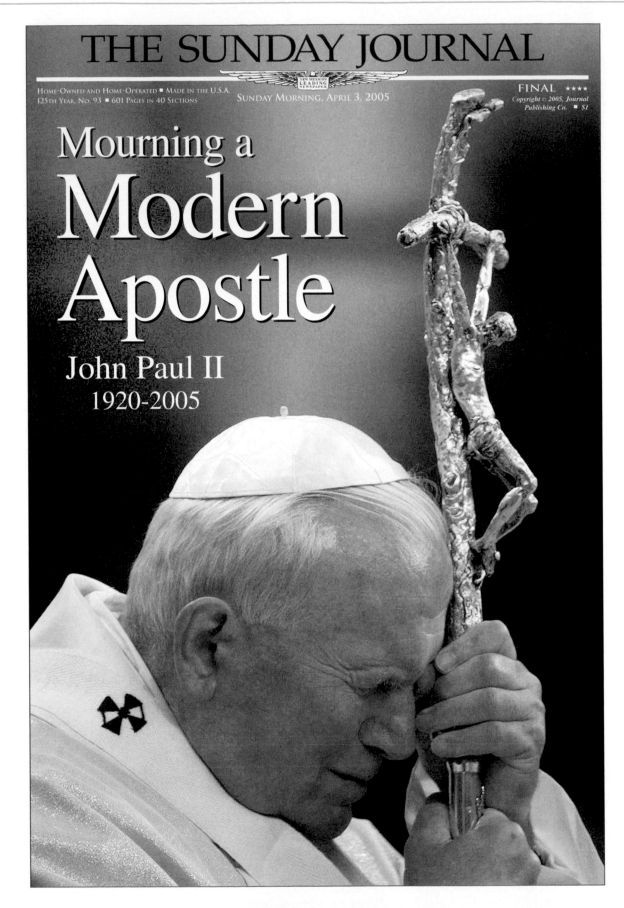

THE SUNDAY JOURNAL

HOME-OWNED AND HOME-OPERATED ■ MADE IN THE U.S.A.
125TH YEAR, NO. 93 ■ 601 PAGES IN 40 SECTIONS

SUNDAY MORNING, APRIL 3, 2005

FINAL ★★★★
Copyright © 2005, Journal
Publishing Co. ■ $1

Mourning a
Modern
Apostle

John Paul II
1920-2005

**PONTIFF WAS AN
ICON OF PEACE**

Page A3

**NEW MEXICANS
REMEMBER**

Page A6

**ACTOR TO POPE:
AN EPIC LIFE**

DIMENSION Page B8

THE SANTA FE
NEW✷MEXICAN

Locally owned
and independent
*Serving New Mexico
for 156 years*

SUNDAY
APRIL 3, 2005
ONE DOLLAR

www.santafenewmexican.com

POPE JOHN PAUL II — 1920-2005

*"Have no fear of moving into the unknown. Simply step out fearlessly
knowing that I am with you; therefore no harm can befall you."*

Graceful passage

Pope John Paul II gives his Easter Sunday blessing from the window of his Vatican apartment on March 27. The pope had tried to speak but ultimately failed and was not heard in public again.

The Associated Press

The Washington Post

So much was expected of Karol Wojtyla when he became pope in 1978. Here, for the first time, was a pontiff plucked not from the Vatican's inner chambers, but a man of the world. He was not Italian. He skied, kayaked and acted in dramas. Fel-low clerics compared him to John Wayne.

Even before his first papal pronounce-ment, he was granted a place in history as the Roman Catholic Church's first modern pope, charged with leading the institu-tion into the next millennium — the "new springtime of Christianity," as he called it.

And 26 years later, it's by that yard-stick that Pope John Paul II's legacy will be judged, both in the church he trans-formed and in the world he tried so hard to influence.

This man who changed the papacy died Saturday night in his Vatican apartment, ending a long public struggle against debilitating illness. He was 84.

The Associated Press

Father of faith: After Pope John Paul II was pro-nounced dead Saturday, Catholics from around the world began to mourn an epic figure. **Page A-8**

Wes Pope/The New Mexican

Santa Fe mourns: Archbishop Sheehan presides over a Mass at St. Francis Cathedral, where Santa Feans gathered to remember the pope. **Page A-5**

KRT

Inside the Vatican: A four-page special section chronicles the papacy, explains events at the Vati-can and captures the pope's lasting images. **Inside**

51

Weather: Cloudy, showers, 51/40   NITE ★ OWL   Sunday, April 03, 2005

DAILY ◉ NEWS

NEW YORK'S HOMETOWN NEWSPAPER

$1.00

POPE JOHN PAUL II
1920-2005

REUTERS

COMPLETE COVERAGE STARTS ON PAGE 2

SPECIAL 48-PAGE COMMEMORATIVE EDITION

Newsday

LONG ISLAND

WWW.NEWSDAY.COM   SUNDAY, APRIL 3, 2005 | NASSAU EDITION $1.50

Pope
John
Paul II

1920-2005

Staten Island Sunday Advance

SINCE 1886

APRIL 3, 2005

$1.50

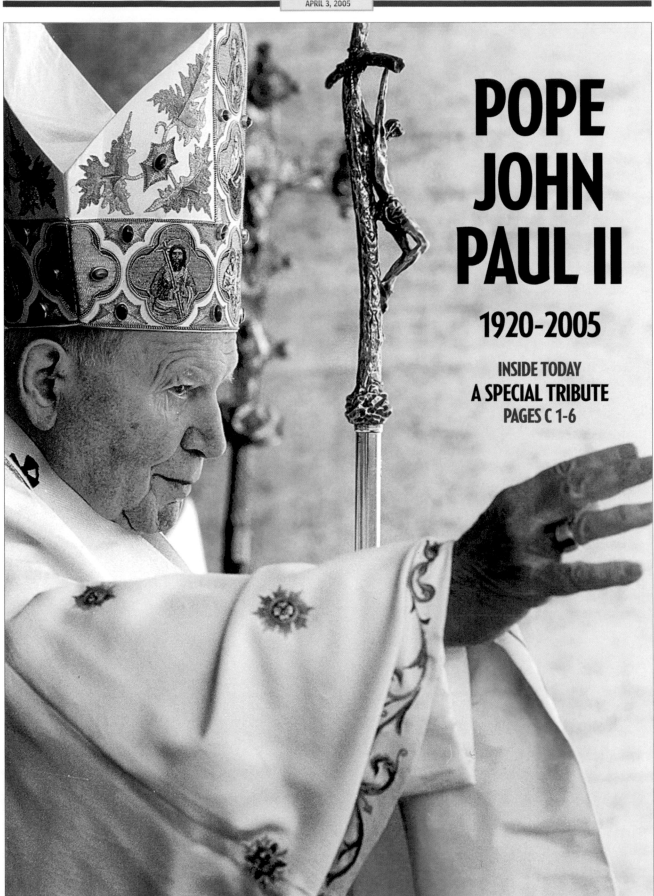

POPE JOHN PAUL II

1920-2005

**INSIDE TODAY
A SPECIAL TRIBUTE
PAGES C 1-6**

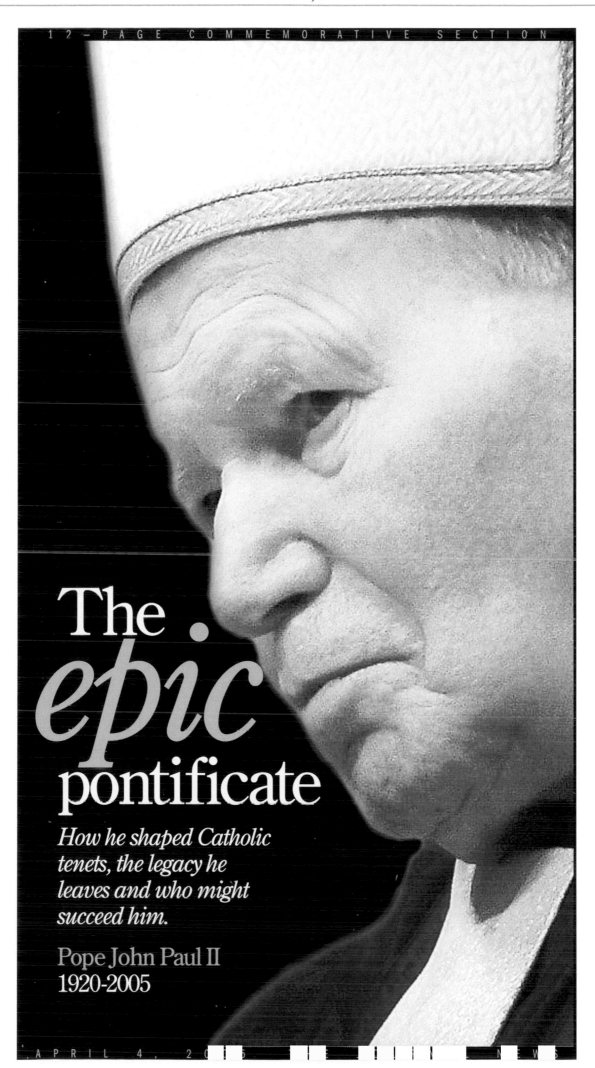

12-PAGE COMMEMORATIVE SECTION

The
epic
pontificate

How he shaped Catholic tenets, the legacy he leaves and who might succeed him.

Pope John Paul II
1920-2005

APRIL 4, 2005

"All the News That's Fit to Print"

The New York Times

Late Edition
New York: **Today,** scattered showers, cool and breezy, high 46. **Tonight,** rain ending, chilly, low 39. **Tomorrow,** breezy, milder, high 57. **Yesterday,** high 57, low 40. Weather map, Page 37.

VOL. CLIV . . . No. 53,173 | NEW YORK, SUNDAY, APRIL 3, 2005 | $4.50 beyond the greater New York metropolitan area. | $3.50

POPE JOHN PAUL II DIES AT 84

In 26-Year Reign, Reshaped Church and Papacy

Challenge Posed in Selecting a Successor

By LAURIE GOODSTEIN

When the 117 Roman Catholic cardinals who are eligible to elect a successor to Pope John Paul II gather in the Sistine Chapel to cast their ballots, the worldwide suspense about the outcome will be shared even by the cardinals in the conclave.

There is no clear front-runner, unlike in some past papal elections, many church experts agree. So the cardinals will be weighing a host of factors, including the candidates' country of origin, age, experience and personality.

Among the most critical questions facing the cardinals is, should the papacy be returned to an Italian, or should the cardinals make the bold gesture of choosing a pope from the third world, where Catholicism is both thriving and threatened by competing faiths?

"A third-world pope would clearly indicate that this is no longer a European church, that we are truly catholic in the sense that the word catholic means universal," said the Rev. Thomas Reese, editor of America, a Jesuit weekly.

To qualify as electors, cardinals must be less than 80 years old. In this election, the cardinals come from more than 60 countries, and more than 60 of them were appointed in the past four years. For many of them, the funeral proceedings and the conclave itself, 15 to 20 days after the pope's death, will offer the first opportunity to take the measure of all the potential candidates firsthand.

"Each one of those cardinals is going to walk into that conclave thinking, 'Which of these candidates is going to go over best back in my diocese, in my country,' " Father Reese said.

With all but three of the cardinal electors having been appointed by John Paul, nearly all his potential successors fit his mold of doctrinal conservatism on issues like abortion and euthanasia, birth control, homosexuality and the ordination of women. So the more pivotal factors are likely to be the candidates' nationality and professional experience.

Vatican observers have spent years now honing their ever-changing lists of cardinals who are "papabile," or potential popes. Although the chosen successor may not have made any of these lists, there are certain names that keep cropping up

Continued on Page 44

Derrick Ceyrac/Agence France-Presse

Pope John Paul II listening during a Mass at the Strasbourg cathedral in 1988 on his fourth trip to France.

Succumbs to Illness Suffered at Length and in Public

By IAN FISHER

VATICAN CITY, Sunday, April 3 — Pope John Paul II died Saturday night, succumbing finally to years of illness endured painfully and publicly, ending an extraordinary, if sometimes polarizing, 26-year reign that remade the papacy.

He died at 9:37 p.m. in his apartment three stories above St. Peter's Square, as tens of thousands of the faithful gathered within sight of his lighted window for a second night of vigils, amid millions of prayers for him from Roman Catholics around the world as his health declined rapidly.

People wept and knelt on cobblestones as the news of his death spread across the square, bowing their heads to a man whose long and down-to-earth papacy was the only one that many young and middle-aged Catholics around the world remembered. For more than 10 minutes, not long after his death was announced, the largely Roman crowd simply applauded him.

"I have looked up to this man as a guide, and now it is like a star that has suddenly disappeared," said Caeser Aturi, 38, a priest from Ghana, which the widely traveled pope visited in 1980, on a continent where the Roman Catholic church grew sizably under his reign.

He was born Karol Wojtyla on May 18, 1920 in Wadowice, Poland. He was 84 years old.

Hospitalized twice since Feb. 1 and suffering for a decade from Parkinson's disease, John Paul's health hit its last crisis on Thursday, when the Vatican announced that a urinary tract infection had caused a high fever and unstable blood pressure.

In the next day, his kidneys and cardio-respiratory system began to fail. On Saturday morning, his chief spokesman, Dr. Joaquín Navarro-Valls, announced grimly that the Pope had begun to fade from consciousness.

His last hours were spent, Dr. Navarro-Valls said in a statement early on Sunday, by "the uninterrupted prayer of all those who surrounded him." At 8 p.m. Mass was celebrated in his room, the statement said, and he was administered the final Catholic rite for the sick and dying for the second time, having already received it on Thursday.

He was surrounded at his death by a close circle of aides from Poland: his two personal secretaries, Archbishop Stanislaw Dziwisz and Monsignor Mieczyslaw Mokrzycki; Cardinal Marian Jaworski, Archbishop Stanislaw Rylko; the Rev. Tadeusz Styczen, as well as three Polish nuns who have long worked in his residence. His personal doctor, Renato Buzzonetti, two other doctors and two nurses were also there.

After a doctor certifies his death, tradition calls for the Vatican camerlengo, Cardinal Eduardo Martinez Somalo, who will run the Vatican until a new pope is chosen, to call out his baptismal name three times. He then strikes the pope's forehead with a silver hammer to ensure he is dead. The hammer is then used to destroy the papal ring, the symbol of his authority.

The Vatican said the body of John Paul II would lie in state at St. Peter's Basilica no sooner than Monday. The Italian news agency ANSA reported that his funeral — to be at-

Continued on Page 44

Giuseppe Cacace/Getty Images

The Vatican's doors will not reopen until a new pope is elected.

Krakow and Beyond: Prayers, Tributes and Awe

By RICHARD BERNSTEIN

KRAKOW, Poland, April 2 — They were already there when the end came, perhaps 10,000 or 20,000 people, all gathered under bare trees in the large square under the window of the archbishop's residence where Pope John Paul II used to stand and talk to people on pastoral visits in this city.

There were not very many tears, though some people did weep. It was more a kind of awed and pensive stillness under the dark sky. Candles lined the windows of the residence; in the distance was the sound of a siren. And then, around 10 p.m. on Saturday, the people who had been standing through a chilly evening for hours praying for the pope learned he was dead. They sank collectively to their knees.

The Roman Catholic Church lost one of its most charismatic and influential leaders, but Poland lost one of the great men of this country's turbulent and tragic history. So Krakow was out, lighting candles, saying prayers, pressing knees onto cold pavement or trampled grass, and remembering the man who represented to them nothing less than the savior of the national Polish soul.

"He was like Moses," said Przemyslaw Kalicki, who was standing in the square with his wife, Paulina, and their 13 year-old son Maciej, just minutes after the pope's death became known. "He led us through the Red Sea of Communism."

As Mr. Kalicki spoke, the 16th-century bell of the Wawel Cathedral across town, the biggest bell in Poland, began to ring, and the members of the Kalicki family stopped to listen. The bell, which has a deep and mystical timber, has been rung only on historic occasions.

The sense of history was indeed present. An era began here in 1978, when the city's son, Karol Wojtyla, was elected pope and Poland was a Communist dictatorship. And it ended with Poland democratic and secure, at least in part because of his moral authority.

Continued on Page 46

Janek Skarzynski/Agence France-Presse — Getty Images

In Wadowice, Poland, the hometown of Pope John Paul II, women wept yesterday after hearing of his death.

Drug Makers Race to Cash In on Fight Against Fat

By STEPHANIE SAUL

OBESITY INC.
Wanted: A Magic Pill

LOUISVILLE, Ky. — The L-Marc Research clinic stands at the geographic center of an American epidemic, where the meat-and-potatoes Midwest meets the chicken-fried South, and just across the street from a McDonald's.

The clinic is a leading recruitment post in the drug industry's multi-billion-dollar war on fat. Desperate to be thin, overweight people eagerly respond to L-Marc's local newspaper ads for volunteers to test experimental weight-loss drugs. For each trial, the clinic is forced to turn away dozens of volunteers.

"I've had people crying on the phone," said Heather Hausberger, the dietitian who screens applicants. "They've tried everything. Nothing seems to work. A lot of people are looking for the quick fix, the magic pill."

Many drug makers, too, are seeking that magic pill. From pharmaceutical giants to tiny start-ups, the industry is spending billions of dollars developing obesity drugs. An estimated 200 possibilities are now in the research pipeline or under test among patients at dozens of clinics like L-Marc, according to MedMarket Diligence, a health care research firm.

Some drug makers say they are tackling fat in response to public health warnings of a national obesity epidemic — one that has been linked to diabetes, heart disease and other conditions and now accounts for more than $100 billion of the United States' $1.8 trillion annual medical bill. The obese are defined as those with a so-called body mass index of 30 or more. By that measure, obese people now make up one-third of the adult population.

But many drug industry analysts

Continued on Page 22

Aging Warheads Ignite a Debate Among Scientists

By WILLIAM J. BROAD

For over two decades, a compact, powerful warhead called the W-76 has been the centerpiece of the nation's nuclear arsenal, carried aboard the fleet of nuclear submarines that prowl the Atlantic and Pacific Oceans.

But in recent months it has become the subject of a fierce debate among experts inside and outside the government over its reliability and its place in the nuclear arsenal.

The government is readying a plan to spend more than $2 billion on a routine 10-year overhaul to extend the life of the aging warheads. At the same time, some weapons scientists say the warheads have a fundamental design flaw that could cause them to explode with far less force than intended.

Although the government has denied that assertion, officials have disclosed that Washington is nevertheless considering replacing the W-76 altogether.

"This is the one we worry about the most," said Everet H. Beckner, who oversees the arsenal as director of defense programs at the National Nuclear Security Administration.

Some arms-control advocates oppose the 10-year overhaul program, saying it could produce not only refurbishments but also deadly new in-

Continued on Page 27

JOHN PAUL II

A SPECIAL SECTION John Paul II was a politically deft figure who transcended geographical and ideological boundaries. **PAGE 39**

UNEASY FLOCK Under John Paul II, a drifting Catholic Church gained new rigor and a clear direction. But that direction has dismayed many American Catholics. **WEEK IN REVIEW**

AN EDITORIAL Keeper of the flock for a quarter of a century. **PAGE 46**

INSIDE

Help Wanted in China: Cheap Labor Falls Short

There is a growing shortage of factory workers in two of China's southern provinces at the heart of its export-driven economy, and analysts caution that it could be the start of a long-term trend that could eventually erode China's leadership position for cheap labor. **PAGE 4**

The Filibuster's Defender

With his encyclopedic knowledge of Senate rules and procedure, Senator Robert C. Byrd of West Virginia has emerged as the Democratic leader in fighting to preserve filibusters of judicial nominees. **PAGE 26**

Reaction Shifts on Shootings

The Columbine High School rampage in 1999 inspired gun-control proposals in Congress and the states but recent highly publicized shootings in Chicago, Atlanta, Wisconsin and Minnesota have led to calls to ease gun laws. **PAGE 25**

Apathy Worries AIDS Experts

Despite warnings from New York City health officials about a rare, possibly more virulent strain of H.I.V., many AIDS activists hold out little hope that the news will prompt substantial or lasting changes in the behavior of gay men. **PAGE 29**

Top Teams Advance

Top-ranked Illinois and top-seeded North Carolina advanced to the N.C.A.A. men's basketball title game tomorrow. Illinois defeated Louisville, 72-57, for its first berth in the title game. North Carolina defeated Michigan State, 87-71. **SPORTSSUNDAY**

New Season, Old Faces

Randy Johnson and Roger Clemens are at the head of a class of pitchers who are thriving well into their 40's. Stephen King ponders the state of Red Sox fans. **BASEBALL PREVIEW, SECTION 8A**

A Reminder

Daylight saving time resumed at 2 a.m. today. Clocks were set ahead one hour.

Job Market/Section 10
In New York City and the metropolitan region.

Updated news: nytimes.com

BUSINESS
Chained to your desk?
Take a vacation already. **F1**

ARTS | LIFE
New Age stuff is
coming of age. **B1**

LOCAL
A mystery woman saved
three people from a fire. **C1**

SUNDAY
April 3, 2005

101st Year, No. 131
Newsstand price $1.75

THE SUNDAY
POST ★ STAR
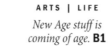

Your life. *Est. 1904* Your newspaper.

THE WEATHER

Today:
Windy.
Periods
of rain.
High 49.
Tomorrow: Mostly cloudy.
High 48. **Details, Page A8**

POPE JOHN PAUL II: 1920-2005
HE'S GONE TO GOD

Sadness, memories fill hearts

By BRENDAN McGARRY
bmcgarry@poststar.com
and STEPHEN DRAVIS
Special to The Post-Star

Within two hours after the death of Pope John Paul II on Saturday, hundreds of parishioners filled the pews at St. Mary's Church in the heart of downtown Glens Falls.

They grieved for the loss of a man whom they looked upon as a great spiritual leader. He was warm, brilliant and deeply devout, and he spread good will to the faithful and non-believer alike, they said.

The pope, Joseph Tocci said, opened his arms to all of mankind and touched millions of people's lives.

"He was concerned about the poor and needy," he said. "All in all, he was a great man and made a great mark on the world."

Pausing to place a cane on the steps of the cathedral, Louise Fortini said she was sad to hear news of his death, despite the much-publicized anticipation.

"We're losing a great man," she said. "He was a very fine example for all of us."

During the homily, the Rev. Thomas Babiuch, a native of Warsaw, Poland, shared his first encounter with the Polish pope.

Babiuch was 10 or 11 when the pope visited Poland. Rains that summer soaked the fields with mud.

The pope stopped his motorcade to screams and shouts of followers. He got out of the car and walked in the rain and mud, dirtying his shoes and cassock, to greet the crowds.

He lifted one baby into the air, saying, "This is the future of the church," Babiuch said.

"This is the pope that I'm going to remember, a pope who was very human, with compassion for the people," he said.

The pope, Babiuch said, experienced and condemned the atrocity of war, helped peacefully defeat totalitarian systems and traveled extensively to fight poverty.

"He may not be present with

KNIGHT RIDDER ILLUSTRATION

He was a pope for the people

By PHIL McCOMBS
The Washington Post

No pope ever took the show on the road like John Paul II.

Within hours of his election, this cheerful, energetic yet deeply mystical and pious man was holding an international news conference in several languages, sending Vatican bureaucrats scurrying in a panic to find out what he was saying.

In short order, he began fulfilling Christ's "great commission" to spread the Gospel worldwide by launching an unprecedented series of evangelical pilgrimages that by the quarter-century mark of his pontificate had taken him to 102 countries.

Almost single-handedly, it seemed, John Paul II, who died Saturday at

More Inside

A look back
at the pope's life
Page A4
A look ahead
at the selection
of a new pope.
Page A5
Death could
shine a light
on Parkinson's
disease. **Page A5**

the age of 84, wrenched the papacy from near-medieval somnolence into the modern world of jet planes, Jumbotrons and electronic mass media.

The crowds he drew were enormous — a gathering of more than 5 million in Manila may have been the largest in human history — and people embraced him in a very intense, immediate, intimate way.

"To see a million people rise up and roar like you'd see at a collegiate football game when he was coming down in the 'Pope Copter' was very moving," recalled college student Dustin Katona of World Youth Day in Toronto in 2002. "My heart was racing. I was literally on my buddy's shoulders taking pictures."

"It was wild," Ysella Fulton-Slavin, a college English instructor, recalled of the pope's 1987 visit to Detroit. "We were in this football stadium, they were selling Pope-Corn and Pope-on-a-Rope and I'm thinking, 'This is crazy.' But all of a sudden he

Please see **REGION**, *Page A6*

Please see **POPE**, *Page A7*

Rainy day

NATHAN PALLACE–THE POST-STAR
The waters of Lake Lonely in Saratoga Springs creep up over the shoreline Saturday morning in the parking lot of the Lake Lonely Boat Livery. For a rainy weather update, see PAGE C3.

Area is enemy territory for Red Sox fans

By SCOTT DONNELLY
sdonnelly@poststar.com

More Inside

Complete Major League Baseball
2005 preview, including tonight's
Red Sox-Yankees game. **Page D1**

Since their team's Oct. 27 World Series win, Boston Red Sox fans have found renewed confidence to wear the team's colors with pride.

Just one problem.

Sox memorabilia isn't so easy to find here in Yankees land.

"You cater to the customer, and if the customer is a Yankees fan, which a majority of the people here are, then that's what you order," said Hank Pelton of Big Uglies in Glens Falls. "With Red Sox fans, everybody's been kind of hidden in a cave, but now

they're out."

As a result, Pelton is working now to get some Red Sox T-shirts and hats in stock, including the Yankees hater's hat that looks like a Yankees hat but features an "H" where the "N" would normally be, Pelton said.

Still, since some of the licensing firms that own the rights to market team merchandise

Please see **FANS**, *Back Page*

Steroid users? Cheaters.

By WARREN ALBER
alber@poststar.com

More Inside

Adults feel the same. **Page D1**

When on the playground or during free time in class, Max Comer does not like playing with cheaters.

But like each of his classmates in Cara Cogan and Amy Jordan's second-grade class at Schuylerville Elementary School, Comer is

willing to give second chances.

Don't come around asking for third or fourth chances, though, because in Room 19 on "Apple Drive" in Schuylerville Elementary, it's

Please see **KIDS**, *Back Page*

The Charlotte Observer

SUNDAY, APRIL 3, 2005   +   ====== www.charlotte.com ======   C D E F   • Price varies by county | **$1.50**

JOHN PAUL II | 1920-2005

AT PEACE

WORLD MOURNS DEATH OF BELOVED PONTIFF

ERICH SCHLEGEL – ASSOCIATED PRESS PHOTO

Evangelina Sosa cries Saturday as she sings praises for the pope at the Basilica of Our Lady of Guadalupe in Mexico City.

By David Crumm
and Patricia Montemurri
Knight Ridder

Pope John Paul II died Saturday after a two-day end-of-life drama that sparked an unprecedented global outpouring of attention to his life, his legacy and what lies ahead for the Roman Catholic Church.

The first news of his death came via an e-mail to journalists by the papal spokesman, and it was then announced to about 70,000 people gathered in St. Peter's Square. Some wept uncontrollably; others stared in disbelief.

The pope's death at age 84 came after his long, slow decline from Parkinson's disease and old age accelerated in recent weeks into a series of health emergencies that required three hospitalizations and the inser-

SEE **JOHN PAUL II** | 12A

PLINIO LEPRI – ASSOCIATED PRESS PHOTO

Pope John Paul II – shown at the Vatican in January – rose from a humble boyhood in Poland to become one of the longest-ruling popes in history. A global ambassador and conservative theologian, he was known for his strong leadership and folksy charisma.

Tar Heel players get ready to take on Michigan State on Saturday evening in the NCAA tournament semifinals in St. Louis. The Tar Heels won 87-71 Saturday night to force a finals matchup with top-ranked Illinois.

DAVID T. FOSTER III – STAFF PHOTO

FINAL FOUR 2005 | COMPLETE GAME COVERAGE IN SPORTS

UNC awakens, gets dream finals matchup

By Michael Gordon
Staff Writer

ST. LOUIS — The great majority of those who came to St. Louis chasing a dream were, according to one 19th century account, "profoundly ignorant of what was before them."

Let the history books show that the North Carolina Tar Heels seemed fully aware of what stood between them and the chance at their fourth national cham-

pionship, surging in the second half to overwhelm Michigan State, 87-71, in the semifinals of the NCAA tournament Saturday night.

Before a crowd of more than 45,000 at the Edward Jones Dome and a worldwide audience of millions on the sport's biggest stage, the tournament's top seed and biggest enigma answered its doubters in the Show-Me State showdown. The Tar Heels hammered the Spartans with a dis-

play of speed, power and athleticism that turned a 5-point halftime deficit into a lead that grew and grew some more until the final whistle stopped the beating.

North Carolina (31-4) meets Illinois, the country's top-ranked team, in a dream matchup to decide college basket-

SEE **TAR HEELS** | 7A

ON WWW.CHARLOTTE.COM/SPORTS
View a slideshow of game photos

NEWS UPDATES AT WWW.NEWSOBSERVER.COM • FINAL EDITION, $1.50   SUNDAY, APRIL 3, 2005   ©2005 THE NEWS AND OBSERVER PUBLISHING COMPANY • RALEIGH, N.C. +

SPRING FORWARD

Due to the change in time — clocks ahead one hour — and the late UNC basketball game, some papers might be delivered late this morning.

SCHOOLS RECLAIM DROPOUTS

As high school dropout rates rise, school systems devise strategies to better engage students and prepare them for the future. Q – PAGE 25A

THE SUNDAY NEWS & OBSERVER

WAR IS FOCUS AT FULL FRAME

This year the annual Durham film festival has created a special program — eight of the event's 78 films — that looks at wars in different ways and from many angles. Among other highlights at the festival is a documentary about artist Geoffrey Holder. ARTS & ENTERTAINMENT – PAGE 1G

TAR HEELS CRUISE INTO TITLE GAME

UNC's Jawad Williams, who had struggled in the NCAA Tournament, reacts after dunking for two of his 20 points Saturday.
STAFF PHOTO BY SCOTT LEWIS

Go ahead and celebrate, Carolina fans. You had to wait awhile. Only three years removed from its worst season ever, a North Carolina men's basketball team that still includes some of the players from that 8-20 finish has returned to the national championship game for the first time since 1993, when the Tar Heels last won the title.

UNC defeated Michigan State, 87-71, Saturday night, and the Tar Heels (32-4) will face No. 1-ranked Illinois (37-1) at 9:21 p.m. Monday in what promises to be an entertaining matchup of fast paced basketball.

EXPANDED COVERAGE IN SPORTS

Pirate ship ID is premature, scholars say

State too eager to claim wreck as Blackbeard's, article argues

BY JERRY ALLEGOOD
STAFF WRITER

GREENVILLE — Three archaeologists are mounting the first major challenge to the state's claim that an undersea wreck near Beaufort Inlet is probably the flagship of the famous pirate Blackbeard.

The critics — two East Carolina University professors and the state of Michigan's underwater archaeologist — say there is no conclusive evidence to justify identifying the wreck as the Queen Anne's Revenge. They contend that pressure to capitalize on the Blackbeard connection has caused alternative theories for the wreck's identity to be overlooked.

"It's an exciting shipwreck and an important shipwreck," said Wayne R. Lusardi, the Michigan researcher who previously worked on the Blackbeard project. "It just may not be the one everyone hopes it is."

Lusardi and ECU faculty members Bradley Rodgers and Nathan Richards attacked state claims in an article in the April edition of The International Journal of Nautical Archaeology. Both sides said the article in the British publication, which has about 2,000 subscribers worldwide and is the preeminent journal in its field, was the first to dispute the identity of the wreck.

The article is likely to be a lively topic at a conference at ECU on Thursday and Friday called "Examining the Shipwreck Believed to be Queen Anne's Revenge: Science, Mystery, and the Pirate Era in North Carolina." Lusardi, Rodgers and Richards

SEE **SHIPWRECK**, PAGE 20A

Pope John Paul II
1920-2005

The mourning begins

Pope who shaped both Catholicism and the 20th century dies

On April 10, 2003, as U.S. forces invaded Iraq, the pope supported calls for peace in St. Peter's Square.
AP FILE PHOTO

BY DANIEL WILLIAMS
AND ALAN COOPERMAN
THE WASHINGTON POST

VATICAN CITY — John Paul II, the voyager pope who helped conquer communism and transformed the papacy with charisma and vigor, died Saturday night after a long battle with Parkinson's disease that became a lesson to the world in humble suffering.

"Our most beloved Holy Father has returned to the house of the Father," Archbishop Leonardo Sandri, a senior Vatican official, told pilgrims in St. Peter's Square. The throng momentarily stood in stunned silence, stared at the pavement and shed tears.

Then, following an Italian custom that signifies hope at a time of death, the mourners broke into sustained applause.

John Paul died at 9:37 local time in the Vatican's Apostolic Palace on a clear and cool night, with a small group of Polish prelates and nuns at his bedside. The first indication of the pope's passing was the illumination of several windows in his private quarters overlooking St. Peter's Square. An e-mail announcement followed.

A half-hour later, the bells of all of Rome's churches rang out in mourning.

The news evoked an outpouring of emotion all over the world. In Paris, mourners packed special midnight services; church bells sounded in Cuba. President Bush called John Paul "a champion of human freedom" and "a good and faithful servant of God. ... We're grateful to God for sending such a man, a son of Poland."

The pope's body will lie in state in St. Peter's Basilica starting Monday afternoon. The date of his funeral will be set by a gathering of cardinals Monday morning — but under guidelines he had set, it should take place within

SEE **POPE**, PAGE 14A

An endearing, enduring legacy as a lover of life

BY YONAT SHIMRON
STAFF WRITER

Pope John Paul II was too weak to attend a symposium in November celebrating the 40th anniversary of the Vatican's efforts at Christian unity. But during an evening service, his aides wheeled him in.

Despite the pope's failing body, his spirit filled the room.

"He was just radiant," said Geoffrey Wainwright, a professor of Christian theology at Duke Divinity School who attended the symposium at the Vatican. "He's a humanly attractive person and a genuinely charismatic figure."

Whatever may be the legacy of the 265th pope, who died Saturday, his warmth and spiritual humility endeared him to millions, including thousands in North Carolina who never met him but were touched by him through television, books or events in other cities.

Except in his final days, he was never one to retire to the grandeur of the Vatican palace, preferring to kiss the ground of the many countries he visited and to meet with political leaders as well as ordinary lay people.

John Paul II, who advocated a "culture of life" against abortion, the death penalty and euthanasia, was himself a lover of life, unwilling to concede anything to old age, even when his body was plagued with the tremors of Parkinson's disease and his voice failed.

A moral theologian and philosopher, John Paul II

Those waiting in St. Peter's Square at the Vatican hear that the pope has died.
AP PHOTO BY GREGORIO BORGIA

SEE **LEGACY**, PAGE 16A

Lynette Miracle has Stage IV breast cancer and says her doctors missed the diagnosis. She asks why her doctors could practice despite histories of addiction.
STAFF PHOTO BY JULI LEONARD

Patient blames medical board

2 doctors with drug problems missed her cancer for months

BY KRISTIN COLLINS
STAFF WRITER

CLINTON — The first doctor who looked at the lump in Frances Lynette Miracle's breast was a painkiller addict with a record of 25 drug convictions. The second had a history of cocaine addiction.

By the time Miracle traveled from her home in rural Eastern North Carolina to Duke University Medical Center in 2002, she had incurable breast cancer.

Miracle does know that she would never have trusted them with her health if she had known their histories.

"It's not like these doctors are

her for six months in 2001 and 2002 — were abusing drugs at the time. Both later surrendered their licenses to practice, however, and one was suspected of being intoxicated at work.

She also doesn't know whether the cancer might have been cured had they treated the lump in her breast more aggressively.

changing oil in a car," says Miracle, 46, her face swollen and her head bald from chemotherapy. "When you have got someone with a drug problem over and over and over, there has to come a point where someone says you can't be a doctor anymore."

Miracle, of Sampson County, has hired a lawyer and is following federal procedures to file a lawsuit against the clinic where the two doctors worked. But more than

SEE **CANCER**, PAGE 6A

AKRON, OHIO

Sunday
AKRON BEACON JOURNAL

SUNDAY, April 3, 2005 A B C   News Online www.ohio.com

$1.50
In some areas $1.00
MO   Home Delivery 800-777-2442

© Copyright 2005 Beacon Journal Publishing Co.

NCAA
MEN'S FINAL FOUR
Saturday

Illinois	72
Louisville	57
North Carolina	87
Michigan State	71

CHAMPIONSHIP GAME
Monday on WOIO (Ch. 19)
Illinois vs. North Carolina, 9:18 p.m.

WOMEN'S FINAL FOUR
Today on ESPN
LSU vs. Baylor, 7 p.m.
Tennessee vs. Michigan State, 9:30 p.m.

Business section
The Sunday Business section is on Pages B4-B7 today because of the death of Pope John Paul II.

■ Taking Action columnist Betty Lin-Fisher shows how to compare deals on free checking accounts in area.
PAGE B4

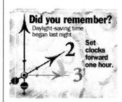

Did you remember?
Daylight-saving time began last night
Set clocks forward one hour.

Extra copies of today's Beacon
Commemorative copies of today's Beacon Journal, including the front news sections and the special section on Pope John Paul II, are available, starting today, at the front desk of the Beacon Journal, 44 E. Exchange St., downtown Akron. Price is $1.

Today's weather
Some a.m. snow; clouds breaking and windy
47° High
33° Low

NewsChannel 5 forecast, Page B12

POPE JOHN PAUL II 1920 – 2005

Pope's legacy alive in works

Candles encircle an image of Pope John Paul II in St. Peter's Square, where thousands gathered to pray for the ailing pontiff, who died Saturday at age 84.

26-year papacy catalyst for change worldwide

By David Crumm and Patricia Montemurri
Detroit Free Press

For a quarter century, Karol Wojtyla was the world's spiritual superpower.

As Pope John Paul II, his decisions shaped the lives of more than 1 billion Catholics around the world – by far the largest organized religious group on Earth.

He used his personal charisma in a tireless campaign for a Catholic vision of human rights that helped to topple Communism, defend the poor and build bridges to other faiths, especially Judaism.

John Paul died at 9:37 p.m. (2:37 p.m. EST) Saturday in his Vatican apartment after a long public struggle against debilitating illness.

His followers did not always agree

with him, but their affection and respect were obvious in more than 100 tours, when vast crowds around the world were drawn to his outdoor Masses.

He was the first pope to regularly pack up, hit the road and carry the banner of the church into his members' own back yards. His talent for languages allowed him to address each national constituency in its native language.

Catholics around the world loved him for this, and some of his critics in places like Cuba, Greece and Eastern Europe feared him for it.

"He brought the human face of the Vatican to people of every culture in every part of the world," said Detroit Cardinal Adam Maida. "He showed that the

Please see **Pope, A12**

Special 8-page section honors the life of Pope John Paul II
SECTION D
Related stories, Pages A8-10

60

THE BLADE

One of America's Great Newspapers

$1.50 ● 344 PAGES ●   TOLEDO, OHIO SUNDAY, APRIL 5, 2005   FINAL

SPECIAL REPORT

THE BLADE/LORI KING

Tom Noe says politics had nothing to do with the state's decision to invest with him. The state trumpets its relationship with Mr. Noe's firm, praising the returns on its investment.

Ohio agency sinks millions into rare coins

State gives investment business to prominent local Republican

By MIKE WILKINSON and JAMES DREW
BLADE STAFF WRITERS

Since 1998, Ohio has invested millions of dollars in the unregulated world of rare coins, buying nickels, dimes, and pennies.

Controlling the money for the state: Prominent local Republican and coin dealer Tom Noe, whose firm made more than $1 million off the deal last year alone.

The agreement to invest the money in rare coins is rare itself: The Blade could find no other instance of a state government investing in a rare coin fund. Neither the state nor Mr. Noe could provide one.

"I don't think I'd be excited to invest in rare coins," Vermont Treasurer Mike Ablowich said. "It's a little unusual."

The Ohio Bureau of Workers' Compensation has continued to be the sole investor in Mr. Noe's Capital Coin funds despite strong concerns raised by an auditor with the bureau about possible conflicts of interest and whether the state's millions were adequately protected.

And the state has maintained its stake in Capital Coin despite documented problems:

● Two coins worth roughly $300,000 were lost in the mail in 2003.

● The firm has written off $850,000 in debt over the last three years to cover a failed business relationship.

● Mr. Noe has loaned some of the state's money to a local real estate business that buys and sells central-city homes. A state auditor could not find documents to prove if the loans were sufficiently covered by the value of real estate that a Capital Coin subsidiary held as collateral.

Since the state first ventured into rare coins, Capital Coin has split $12.9 million in profits with the state, with Capital Coin keeping 20 percent, or nearly $2.6 million.

"It's probably one of the better investments in our portfolio," said Jim McLean, chief investment officer for the workers' compensation bureau — the state agency charged with paying medical bills and providing monthly checks to Ohio workers injured on the job.

Typically putting its billions to work in the stock and bond markets, the bureau decided in 1998 to take a portion of its reserves and invest in rare coins. Among the bureau's holdings: a 1792 silver piece estimated to be worth $2 million as well as 18th century nickels and pennies. One of the lost coins was an 1855 $3 gold coin; there are only two in the world.

The state trumpets its relationship with Mr. Noe, praising the returns on its investment. A few years ago, as the stock market tanked, most of its equity funds lost money. Capital

See **COINS**, Page 15

THE POPE, 1920-2005

John Paul II dead at 84

BLOCK NEWS ALLIANCE/MATT FREED

In the hours before the Pope's death, candles held by thousands of the faithful flicker in St. Peter's Square at the Vatican.

World mourns loss of beloved leader

By ANN RODGERS
BLOCK NEWS ALLIANCE

VATICAN CITY — Pope John Paul II died yesterday in his Vatican apartment as thousands of pilgrims gathered outside his lit windows and prayed by candlelight for his beloved Mary to guide him into the everlasting presence of her Son.

Born Karol Wojtyla on May 18, 1920, in Wadowice, Poland he succumbed finally to years of illness endured pain fully and publicly, ending an extraordinary, if sometimes polarizing, 26-year reign that remade the papacy.

"We are all orphans this evening," Undersecretary of State Archbishop Leonardo Sandri told the crowd of 70,000. There were tears for the 84-year-old Pope who had suffered greatly in his final years. They were not tears of anguish but of separation and loss.

"The angels welcome you,"

Vatican TV said after papal spokesman Joaquin Navarro-Valls announced the death of the Pope, who had for years suffered from Parkinson's disease and recently had been debilitated by the flu, breathing difficulties, and infections.

In contrast to the church's ancient traditions, Mr. Navarro-Valls announced the death to journalists in the most modern of communication forms, an e-mail that said: "The Holy Father died this evening at 9:37 p.m. [Rome time, 2:37 p.m. Toledo time] in his private apartment."

Cardinal Joseph Ratzinger, the German prelate who is the chief guardian of church doctrine, said John Paul had been aware that he was "passing to the Lord."

John Paul

The Vatican said the body of John Paul II will lie in state at St. Peter's Basilica no sooner than tomorrow. The Italian news agency ANSA reported that his funeral is expected no sooner than Thursday.

The Vatican has declined to say whether John Paul left instructions for his burial. Most popes in recent centuries have asked to be buried in the crypts below St. Peter's Basilica, but some have suggested the first Polish-born pope might have chosen to be laid to rest in his native country.

Members of the College of Cardinals were already headed toward the Vatican to prepare for the secret duty of locking themselves in the Sistine Chapel to elect the next pope. Tradition calls for the process to

begin within 20 days of death.

Hospitalized twice since Feb. 1, John Paul II's health hit its last crisis on Thursday, when the Vatican announced that a urinary tract infection had caused a high fever and unstable blood pressure. In the next day, his kidneys and cardio-respiratory system began to fail. Yesterday morning, Mr. Navarro-Valls announced grimly that the Pope had begun to fade from consciousness.

His last hours were spent, Mr. Navarro-Valls said in a statement early today, by "the uninterrupted prayer of all those who surrounded him."

He died almost immediately after the Mass of Divine Mercy Sunday — a feast John Paul himself had instituted — was celebrated in his room by his longtime aide and close friend, Archbishop Stanislaw Dziwisz.

See **POPE**, Page 9

MORE COVERAGE, PAGES 5-12.

■ Young Catholics mourn only leader they have known. Page 6.

■ Pontiff left mark on area leaders, residents. Page 7.

■ Man of peace inspired revolt against communism. Page 9.

■ Canon law spells out papal selection. Page 12.

■ The Pope was a man of letters, loved by media. Behind the News, Page B1.

AFTER A POPE DIES
Approximate timetable of the main events after the death of a pope:

Funeral, mourning, and election of a successor

Day 1	Days 2-4	Day 4, 5 or 6	
Pope dies.	Body lies in state at the Vatican's St. Peter's Basilica.	Single day for funeral and burial.	**Installation of new pope** Immediately after election.

Days 1-9	Days 15-20	Days 27-33
"Novemdiales," or nine days of mourning.	College of Cardinals begins meeting in secret conclave to elect a new pope. Voting continues until a pope is elected.	After 12 or 13 days of meeting, cardinals may choose to use simple majority, rather than two-thirds majority, to reach decision.

KNIGHT RIDDER

INSIDE

Weather

Partial sunshine and milder temperatures with a bit of a breeze.

HI 56°   LO 34°

Weather | Page E26

Watchdog's bone

Ohio's consumer watchdog on utility issues has taken on electric rates that have saddled northwest Ohioans for years.

Business | Page F1

Many tongues

With no hands to help them eat, birds rely on their tongues to sip nectar, drag worms from the lawn, or pick insects from a tree.

Toledo Magazine | Page B6

Daylight Saving Time

It's time to save some daylight as most of the nation's clocks spring ahead one hour, effective as of 2 a.m. today.

SPRING FORWARD

Then there were 2

It's now the Final Two: Illinois and North Carolina will meet tomorrow to determine the NCAA basketball champs.

Sports | Page E1

A day in the U.S.

For the latest in our series, "First Time," our staff writer Ryan E. Smith spent some time with Tarkan Mekik on his first day as a U.S. citizen.

Living | Page C1

www.toledoblade.com

Recycled and recyclable

Copyright © 2005 The Blade

Clean Care, Incorporated chose quality, commitment, service, and a lower price. Clean Care Incorporated chose Buckeye TeleSystem. We go beyond a phone company. 419-724-9881 –Adv.

Iraqi insurgents hit Abu Ghraib prison

44 GIs, 12 detainees reported hurt

WASHINGTON POST

BAGHDAD — Attacking in waves of car bombs, rockets, and gunfire, dozens of insurgents assailed Iraq's notorious Abu Ghraib prison yesterday in an hours-long onslaught that wounded 44 U.S. troops and 12 detainees, the American military said.

Attackers apparently did not penetrate the prison grounds, although some inmates were reported to have been seriously wounded. The second of two car bombs exploded as troops were trying to evacuate the in-

jured from the first, the Reuters news agency said.

In Baghdad, the latest prospects of defusing Iraq's Sunni-led insurgency by drawing the Sunni minority into the country's government and military looked shaky.

The Association of Muslim Scholars, the most prominent of dozens of groups speaking for disaffected Sunnis, distanced itself yesterday from an edict by 64 Sunni clerics and

scholars the previous day that had encouraged Sunnis to join Iraq's new security forces.

Politically, efforts by Iraq's ethnic Kurds and majority Shiite Arabs to form a national unity government threatened to stall again over finding a widely acceptable Sunni willing to accept a key post in the new government.

The U.S. military said between 40 and 60 insurgents attacked Abu Ghraib prison,

which became the focus of a U.S. military abuse-scandal last year when photos emerged of American troops taunting naked, contorted Iraqi detainees.

U.S. forces still maintain a base and a detainee center at the sprawling prison complex.

Insurgents kept up sporadic attacks for about four hours, firing rocket-propelled grenades into the prison grounds, said Lt. Col. Guy Rudisill, the military spokesman for detention operations. Americans fired

See **IRAQ**, Page 2

FINAL EDITION

THE ENQUIRER

SUNDAY, APRIL 3, 2005

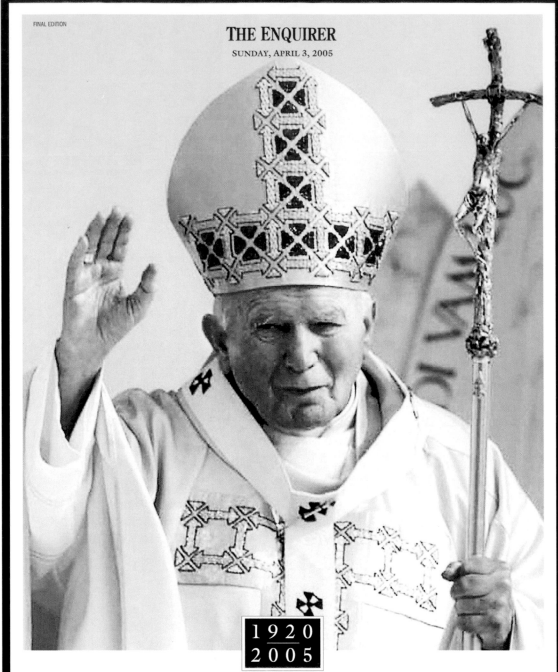

1920
2005

POPE JOHN PAUL II
Millions mourn His Holiness

Pope John Paul II, who changed the course of the world through faith and sheer dint of will, died Saturday after a grave illness. He will be remembered as a bold pontiff who towered over his century, then led his church into a new millennium.
Shaped by his childhood in rural Poland and fired in the kiln of World War II, young priest Karol Wojtyla rose to lead the world's largest church, striding the globe for more than a quarter of a century with an authority that transcended Catholicism.
Some in his own church complained that he was a throwback to an earlier kind of pope, imperial and autocratic, bent on quashing dissent. Others said he was ahead of his time, traversing the world many times over to spread his message, the first jet-set pope.
But few in any realm have wrestled with the leaders and movements of their eras the way Pope John Paul II did.

INSIDE / PAGES A5A-A10

■ Pope John Paul II obituary.
■ Editorial, Borgman tribute.
■ The pope's life and legacy.

■ The world mourns passing of the popular pope.
■ Looking ahead.

■ Cincinnati, N.Ky. mourn as basilica bells toll.
■ Local voices.

INDEX

Copyright, 2005, The Cincinnati Enquirer

WEATHER

High 58°
Low 40°
Mostly sunny.

COMPLETE FORECAST: B6

COMING
MONDAY
Faces – beyond the players – that you'll see around the ballpark on Opening Day and the rest of the season. **TEMPO**

Spring ahead
Did you remember to set your clocks ahead one hour last night?

In Indiana, does anybody really know what time it is? **LIFE F7**

Local News
Opening Day tickets worth the long wait
Nothing is harder to get or more in demand right now: tickets to the Reds' Opening Day.
For many in Cincinnati, standing in line for the hot tickets is tradition – and worth the 97 hours to get a seat.
"It's a holiday tied with Easter and Christmas," says one UC student.
LOCAL NEWS B1

Business
Experts: Cool your jets on investing in stocks
The stock market was down in the first quarter, but many financial experts say people aren't scared. And they think we should be.
In their mind, there's too much optimism for a stock market facing rising interest rates, rising oil prices and slower growth in profits.
BUSINESS J1

Sports
Baseball 2005 section digs in to new season
Is there life after Larkin? Can Junior have a big season? Who are all these new people? Find the answers to your burning Reds questions in today's special baseball section. We also offer a preview of the 2005 season, including forecasts and team schedules – plus a walk through Opening Day history.
SPECIAL SECTION

0 40901 20101 4

62

COLUMBUS, OHIO

The Columbus Dispatch

SUNDAY, APRIL 3, 2005

JOHN PAUL II 1920-2005

A servant above all

Pope dies at 84; world celebrates his life while mourning loss

By Victor L. Simpson
ASSOCIATED PRESS

VATICAN CITY — Pope John Paul II, who helped topple communism in Europe and left a deeply conservative stamp on the church that he led for 26 years, died last night in his Vatican apartment, ending a long public struggle against debilitating illness. He was 84.

"We all feel like orphans this evening," Undersecretary of State Archbishop Leonardo Sandri told the crowd of 70,000 that gathered in St. Peter's Square below the pope's still-lighted apartment windows.

In the massive piazza that stretches from St. Peter's Basilica, the assembled flock fell into a stunned silence before some people broke into applause — an Italian tradition in which mourners often clap for important figures. Others wept. Still others recited the rosary. A seminarian slowly waved a large Polish flag draped with black bunting for the Polish-born pontiff, the most-traveled pope in history.

At one point, prelates asked those in the square to stay silent so they might "accompany the pope in his first steps into heaven." But as the Vatican bells tolled in mourning, a group of young people sang, "Alleluia, he will rise again."

"The angels welcome you," Vatican TV said upon the announcement of the pope's death.

In contrast to the church's ancient traditions, papal spokesman Joaquin Navarro-Valls announced the death to journalists in the most modern of communication forms, an e-mail that said: "The Holy Father died this evening at 9:37 p.m. in his private apartment." The spokesman said church officials now would be following instructions that John Paul had written on Feb. 22, 1996. A precise cause of death was not given.

In the last two days of the pope's life, after it had become clear he would not recover, the tide of humanity near the Vatican had ebbed and flowed, swelling again last night.

"He was a marvelous man. Now he's no longer suffering," said a tearful Concetta Sposato, a pilgrim.

"My father died last year. For me, it feels the same," said Elisabetta Pomacalca, a 25-year-old Peruvian who lives in Rome.

"I'm Polish. For us, he was a father," said pilgrim Beata Sowa.

A Mass was scheduled for St. Peter's Square for 10:30 a.m. (4:30 a.m. EDT) today. The pope's body was expected to be taken to the basilica no earlier than Monday afternoon, the Vatican said.

It said the College of Cardinals — the red-robed "princes" of the Roman Catholic Church — would meet at 10 a.m. (4 a.m. EDT) Monday in a pre-conclave session. They were expected to set a funeral date, which the Vatican said probably would be between Wednesday and Friday.

Karol Joseph Wojtyla was a robust 58 when the last papal conclave stunned the

See **POPE** Page A2

INSIDE

▶ **A timeline of the pope's life** | A3

▶ **John Paul set a new standard for popes** | B1

▶ **The candidates to replace him** | B2

▶ **An essay on the pope's unique perspective, talents** | B3

Pope John Paul II prayed in the Blessed Sacrament Chapel in Cathedral Basilica during a visit to St. Louis in January 1999.

AMY SANCETTA | ASSOCIATED PRESS

JOSE MORE | UNITED PRESS INTERNATIONAL
On a visit to Mexico in 1979, a few months after his election, the pope was welcomed to the village of Cuilapam.

REFLECTIONS OF CENTRAL OHIOANS

Faithful recall service, spirit, humor of pontiff

By Kelly Lecker and Spencer Hunt
THE COLUMBUS DISPATCH

Twenty-five minutes after the world learned of Pope John Paul II's death yesterday, a Latino couple was married at Holy Name Church on E. Patterson Avenue.

A large photo of the pope and black bunting to signify his death joined the Easter candle and flowers that decorated the church.

"That's part of what life is all about. The church goes on," Monsignor James Ruef said. "I'm sure there are babies being baptized, weddings going on all over. That's the way the Holy Father would have wanted it."

Roman Catholics across central Ohio mourned the pope's death yesterday and celebrated his life. They honored him in Masses and looked back on cherished memories of their encounters with the church's charismatic leader.

Kathy Shannon isn't a regular churchgoer, but her grief over the death of John Paul drew her to St. Joseph Cathedral Downtown.

"With this kind of loss, I wanted to be surrounded," said Shannon, of Colum-

bus, who went to the cathedral with her sister-in-law, Kris Seitzer. "He was an inspiration."

About 250 people attended the 5:15 p.m. Mass.

That was a little bigger than the usual crowd, according to David Simmons, who handed out bulletins to people walking through the door.

"There are a lot of different faces," he added.

At Holy Name Church, about 100 Latinos gathered for a Spanish-language Mass last night. Their parish, Santa Cruz, worships at the church.

The Rev. Jose Perez dedicated the service to the pope, whose photo was displayed at the front of the altar. His sermon focused on the Easter message of faith and redemption, then turned to John Paul and how he was teaching Catholics to the end.

"He didn't go the hospital. . . . He died in his house. And he died with dignity," he said.

The congregation prayed for the cardinals who, the pastor said, will elect the next pope without prejudice and accord-

See **FAITHFUL** Page A2

THE PLAIN DEALER

LK GA LN SP ME LG ✩✩✩✩✩

SUNDAY, APRIL 3, 2005

JOHN PAUL II | 1920-2005

'Humble, human, holy'

GABRIEL BOUYS | AFP/GETTY IMAGES

Pope John Paul II's own suffering helped forge a strong bond of compassion for others. Here he celebrates a Mass of beatification of Anton Martin Slomsek in Maribor, Slovenia, in 1999.

After a quarter-century as pope, a frail John Paul II dies

Don't weep for me, he writes in final note

DAVID BRIGGS
Plain Dealer Religion Reporter

He touched the lives of lepers and heads of state, and hundreds of millions of people in between who saw in this stoop-shouldered mystic the vision of a better humankind. He also helped bring down the Berlin Wall and open up the world's largest church to dialogues with Jews and Muslims.

Pope John Paul II died at 9:37 p.m. Saturday, Rome time (2:37 p.m. EST), succumbing to heart and kidney failure after a bacterial infection weakened his body. He was 84.

In his last hours, he reportedly sent a note to his aides asking them not to weep for him

"I am happy, and you should be as well," the note said, according to an Italian newspaper. "Let us pray together with joy."

History's most traveled pontiff visited millions in more than 100 trips abroad, bringing the papacy to Eastern Europe, the Middle East and Cuba, where he was a strong voice for political freedom, and to the United States, where he defended the authority of his office against growing demands for a more democratic church.

Yet he will be remembered less for humbling the mighty, from Bill Clinton to Mikhail Gorbachev, than for lifting up the poor, people with AIDS and the disabled. John Paul was at his happiest surrounded by hundreds of thousands of young people at World Youth Days from Denver to Toronto, or in moments such as the one during a visit to Los Angeles in 1987 when he startled security guards by climbing over barricades to embrace and bless with a kiss a young man with no hands who was playing the guitar with his feet.

Tony Melendez, who was turned down for the seminary because he did not have a thumb or a forefinger with

which to hold the Eucharist, later would say that from the moment the pope embraced him, "it was for this that I was born. It was for this that I came into the world."

John Paul was a son of the Second Vatican Council that opened the windows of the church to the modern world.

He addressed Muslims as brothers, made the first visit by a pontiff to the Rome Synagogue and invited Buddhists, Hindus and representatives from all the world's faiths to a World Day of Prayer in Assisi.

SEE POPE | **A18**

FRANCO ORIGLIA | GETTY IMAGES

Worshippers in St. Peter's Square hear the news of the pope's death.

Stunned silence, then pilgrims' tears

VICTOR L. SIMPSON
Associated Press

VATICAN CITY — In the huge piazza that stretches from St. Peter's Basilica, the assembled flock fell into a stunned silence before some people broke into applause — an Italian tradition in which mourners often clap for important figures — when the pope died.

Others wept. Still others recited the rosary. A seminarian slowly waved a red and white Polish flag draped with black bunting for the Polish-born pontiff, the most-traveled pope in history.

"We all feel like orphans this evening," Undersecretary of State Archbishop Leonardo Sandri told the crowd of 70,000 that gathered in St. Peter's Square below the pope's still-lighted apartment windows.

At one point, prelates asked those in the square to stay silent so they might "accompany the pope in his first steps into heaven."

But as the Vatican bells tolled in mourning, a group of young people sang, "Alleluia, he will rise again." One strummed a guitar, and other pilgrims joined in singing "Ave Maria."

"The angels welcome you," Vatican TV said after papal spokesman Joaquin Navarro-Valls announced the death of the pope, who had for years suffered from Parkinson's disease and came down with a fever and infections in recent weeks.

In contrast to the church's ancient traditions, Navarro-Valls announced the death to journalists in the most modern of communication forms, an e-mail that said: "The Holy Father died this evening at 9:37 p.m. in his private apartment."

The spokesman said church officials now would be following instructions that John Paul had written for them on Feb. 22, 1996. A precise cause of death was not given.

SEE TEARS | **A21**

REFLECTION, REMEMBRANCE

A look back at the pope's life. **A19**

The front-runners to be the next pope. **A20**

Clevelanders pray after hearing the news. **A21**

Shaker Heights group in St. Peter's Square. **A23**

Clevelander worked with the pope. **A23**

COMMEMORATIVE EDITION

The Sunday Oregonian

APRIL 3, 2005   2001 PULITZER PRIZE WINNER FOR PUBLIC SERVICE ★★★ SUNRISE EDITION   PORTLAND, OREGON **$1.50**

John Paul II
1920 - 2005

GABRIEL BOUYS/AGENCE FRANCE-PRESSE

SLOVENIA, 1999: Pope John Paul II, who died Saturday at the Vatican, demanded discipline from the faithful while championing the cause of human freedom.

Oregonians heed call to pray for pope who suffered, showed them way to live

By SHELBY OPPEL WOOD and NANCY HAUGHT | THE OREGONIAN

MOUNT ANGEL —

The monks had just stopped singing about their Lord rising from the dead when the Catholic teens visiting Mt. Angel Abbey stepped out of the church and into the noonday sun.

Peter O'Brien told them to gather round.

"The Holy Father died about 10 minutes ago. I know that's hard to hear," said O'Brien, a deacon from Our Lady of Perpetual Help in Albany, who was leading two dozen high schoolers on an abbey tour as part of their confirmation class.

The teens took the news quietly, staring at O'Brien or at their feet. Later, Nicole Leeper said Pope John Paul II's death Saturday rattled her even though she expected it.

"He's been around for so long, you kind of take it for granted he's always going to be," said Leeper, 14. "And when he's not, it shocks you a little bit."

Many of Oregon's 426,000 Catholics heard about the pope's death at home, at

Please see **REACTION,** Page A14

Services

The Portland Archdiocese will hold two Masses for Pope John Paul II, both at St. Mary's Cathedral, 1716 N.W. Davis St

Today: Vigil at 7:30 p.m.

Monday: Memorial Mass at 7:30 p.m.

Inside

Leader in a troubled time: John Paul II, captivating his flock by sheer force of personality, would reshape the church with a vision of disciplined Catholicism/**A10**

The succession: With prayer and secrecy, the College of Cardinals will elect the next pope/**A13**

The long-serving pontiff, shepherd of the world's 1 billion Catholics, dies at age 84

By IAN FISHER and ELAINE SCIOLINO | NEW YORK TIMES NEWS SERVICE

VATICAN CITY —

Pope John Paul II died Saturday, succumbing to years of illness endured painfully and publicly, ending an extraordinary, if sometimes polarizing, 26-year reign that remade the papacy.

He died at 9:37 p.m. in his apartment three stories above St. Peter's Square, as tens of thousands of the faithful gathered within sight of his lit window for a second night of vigils, amid millions of prayers for his rapidly declining health from Roman Catholics around the world.

People wept and knelt on cobblestones as the news of his death spread across the square, bowing their heads to a man whose long and down-to-earth papacy was the only that many Catholics around the world remembered. For more than 10 minutes, not long after his death was announced, the largely Roman crowd simply applauded him.

"I have looked up to this man as a guide, and now it is like a star that has suddenly

Please see **POPE,** Page A12

ASSOCIATED PRESS

1978: Newly elected Pope John Paul II steps onto the balcony at St. Peter's Basilica on Oct. 16 to greet the crowd, which soon starts chanting "Viva il Papa!"

ARTURO MARI/ASSOCIATED PRESS

1983: Around Christmas, the pope meets with Mehmet Ali Agca in the prison where Agca was held after his 1981 attempt on the pope's life.

ASSOCIATED PRESS

1986: John Paul rides with Mother Teresa in February near her hospice in India. Years later, he began the process to have her named a saint.

PIER PAOLO CITO/ASSOCIATED PRESS

2005: In his final public appearance, Pope John Paul II offers a blessing for those gathered below his apartment window Wednesday in St. Peter's Square.

65

Pope John Paul II in a 1979 visit to Washington, D.C.

KRT PHOTO

THE GREATEST POPE

A 28-PAGE TRIBUTE

PHILADELPHIA

DAILY NEWS

THE PEOPLE PAPER

67

Pittsburgh Post-Gazette

SUNDAY

ONE OF AMERICA'S GREAT NEWSPAPERS

Vol. 78, No.246

***
FINAL
APRIL 3, 2005
$1.50

JOHN PAUL II DIES

Paul Hanna/Reuters

Pope John Paul II prays at a Mass that was dedicated to peace in the Balkans on June 3, 1999.

68

For thousands of mourners gathered in St. Peter's Square, there were tears of loss and separation, but not of anguish

By Ann Rodgers
Pittsburgh Post-Gazette

VATICAN CITY — Pope John Paul II died yesterday in his Vatican apartment, ending a sad vigil by the tens of thousands of pilgrims gathered outside and millions more across the world he had profoundly shaped in the 26 years of his papacy.

"We are all orphans this evening," Undersecretary of State Archbishop Leonardo Sandri told

■ Five pages of coverage on the pope's death begin on **Page A-15.**

the crowd of 70,000 in St. Peter's Square. There were tears for the 84-year-old pope who had suffered greatly in his final years. But they were not tears of anguish, but of separation and loss.

"It's not a tragic death, it was a holy death," said the Rev. James Farnan, 41, a Pittsburgh priest doing doctoral studies in Rome,

who was in the square when the pope died. The light in the papal apartment remained on, so no one knew until the announcement was made.

"The angels welcome you," Vatican TV said after papal spokesman Joaquin Navarro-Valls announced the death of the pope, who had for years suffered from Parkinson's disease and recently had been debilitated by fever and infections.

SEE **POPE**, PAGE A-15

Pontiff touched lives of millions around globe

By James O'Toole
Pittsburgh Post-Gazette

Pope John Paul II was remembered across the world yesterday as a leader who reached across religious and national boundaries to change history, an unbending champion of the teachings of Jesus Christ , and a very human pastor devoted particularly to children.

"Our sadness at his death is tempered ... with the realization of his extraordinary life and ministry," said the Most Rev. Donald W. Wuerl, bishop of the Ro-

SEE **REACTION**, PAGE A-18

Sunday Patriot-News

SUNDAY
April 3, 2005

$1.75
$1.60 home delivered

Volume 56, No. 31 Copyright © 2005, The Patriot-News Co. HARRISBURG, PA. **PENNLIVE.COM** FINAL EDITION

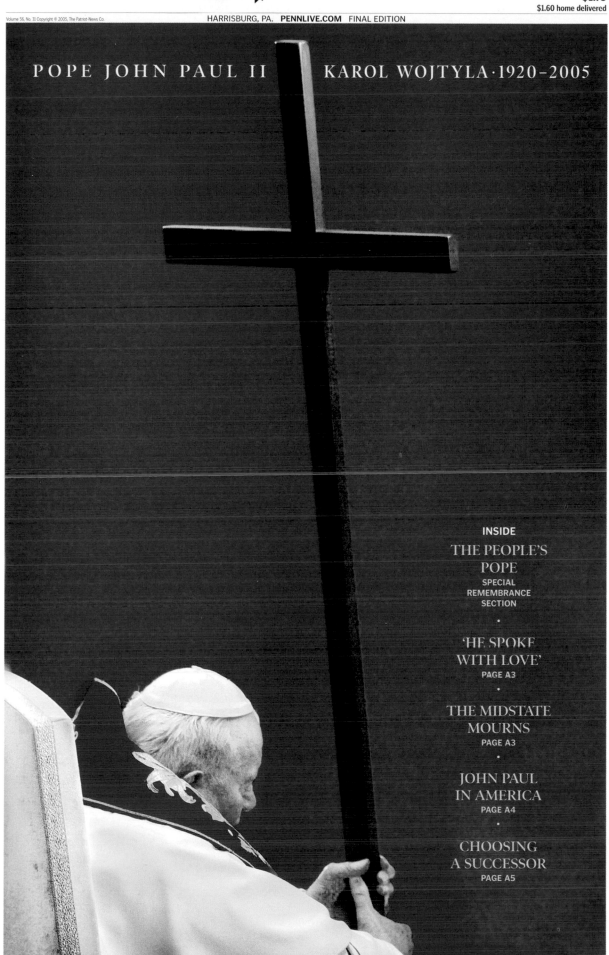

POPE JOHN PAUL II · KAROL WOJTYLA·1920–2005

INSIDE

THE PEOPLE'S
POPE
SPECIAL
REMEMBRANCE
SECTION

·

'HE SPOKE
WITH LOVE'
PAGE A3

·

THE MIDSTATE
MOURNS
PAGE A3

·

JOHN PAUL
IN AMERICA
PAGE A4

·

CHOOSING
A SUCCESSOR
PAGE A5

PATRICK HERTZOG, The Associated Press, 2004

69

SUNDAY
APRIL 3, 2005

The Philadelphia Inquirer

$1.50
$1.75 in some
locations outside the
metropolitan area

c   W W W . P H I L L Y . C O M   176th Year, No. 307

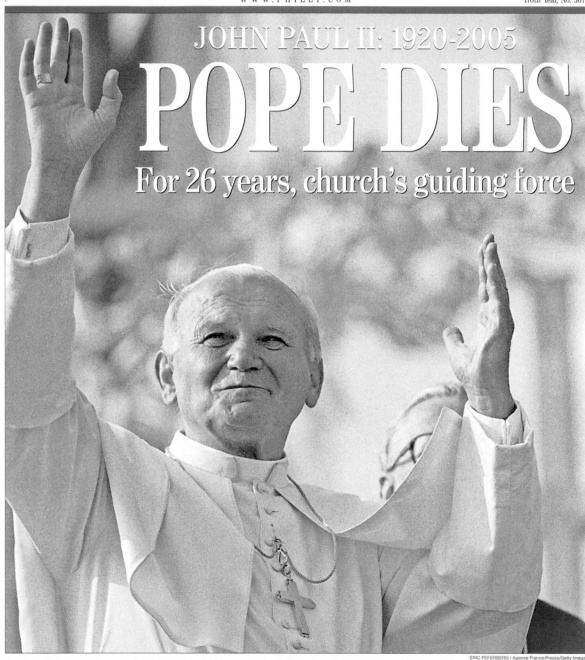

JOHN PAUL II: 1920-2005

POPE DIES

For 26 years, church's guiding force

ERIC FEFERBERG / Agence France-Presse/Getty Images

Pope John Paul II, who died yesterday, waves to Poles in 1987 in Krakow, in his home country. In 1978, he was chosen the first non-Italian pope in 455 years. He became history's third-longest-serving pontiff.

A remarkable journey from Poland to Rome

By David O'Reilly
INQUIRER STAFF WRITER

Pope John Paul II, spiritual leader of the world's one billion Roman Catholics for a quarter-century, was a giant of modern history, an uncompromising moral force who traveled the globe to champion human rights and conservative doctrine.

John Paul, who died yesterday at 84, was traditional in matters of morality and theology, passionately progressive on behalf of the poor, immigrants and world peace. Charismatic and media-savvy, he was widely admired even by those who disputed his orthodox teachings.

Even as ill health visibly overtook him, he proclaimed his message — slowed, but never stopped, by bullets, a tumor, a broken hip, arthritis, Parkinson's disease and advancing age.

His was the third-longest pontificate in church history, and he became so enduring an institutional presence that his views gradually supplanted much of the blueprint for change laid out by the historic Second Vatican Council.

He appointed virtually all the world's active bishops, and all but three of the 117 cardinals eligible to elect his successor, making it likely that his brand of orthodoxy will continue into the next pontificate.

As he took on such sensitive topics as abortion, euthanasia, immigration, capital punishment, worker rights, communist oppression and capitalist greed, he found himself allied with differ-

See **JOHN PAUL II** on A18

Full Coverage, A17-25

HINDA SCHUMAN / Inquirer Suburban Staff
The Lehman family of Buckingham prays at Our Lady of Czestochowa, a Doylestown shrine that felt a special connection with John Paul. Story on **A21.**

What's Next

Today: Requiem Mass in St. Peter's Square.
Tomorrow: Three days of lying in state probably will begin. Cardinals start assembling.
Later this week: John Paul's funeral will take place in the Basilica or St. Peter's Square.

VOICES: Readers react to the Pope's death. **B8.**

A shudder of sorrow as mourning begins

Below his window, thousands are stilled.

**By Ken Dilanian,
Matthew Scofield
and Patricia Montemurri**
INQUIRER STAFF WRITERS

VATICAN CITY — Pope John Paul II died yesterday, after an eventful 26-year papacy and a two-day end-of-life drama that focused the world's attention on his life, his legacy, and what lies ahead for the Roman Catholic Church.

News of his death, which occurred at 9:37 p.m. (2:37 p.m. Philadelphia time), was announced minutes later to the estimated 70,000 people gathered in St. Peter's Square. Some wept uncontrollably; others stood stunned or bowed their heads in prayer.

"We all feel like orphans this evening," Undersecretary of State Archbishop Leonardo Sandri told the crowd.

The bells of St. Peter's Basilica tolled in a solemn signal of mourning as people streamed into the square and the crowd overflowed into nearby streets.

Many said they knew what had happened when they saw the lights flicker in the windows of the papal apartment, three stories above Bernini's famous colonnade.

"He was so strong, and he always spoke about our problems," said Cotbrina Tosti, 26, who was born the year John Paul ascended to the papacy, and who stood in tears, in the packed, hushed

See **DEATH** on A17

The Providence Sunday Journal

APRIL 3, 2005

AP PHOTO / MASSIMO SAMBUCETTI

JOHN PAUL II

1920 - 2005

Karol Wojtyla of Poland, the first non-Italian pope since 1523, died yesterday in Rome.
He played a major role in the collapse of European Communism.

IN GOD'S HANDS

The pope died yesterday at 9:37 p.m. in his private apartment. "We all feel like orphans this evening," Archbishop Leonardo Sandri told a crowd of 70,000 gathered in St. Peter's Square.

PAGE A3

PICKING A NEW POPE

The end of a papacy sets in motion a highly ritualized and a deeply human process. Vatican officials step into carefully designated roles to carry out the choreography of funeral rites and the selection of a successor.

PAGE A6

WORLD, NATION, RHODE ISLAND REACT

"We will always remember the humble, wise and fearless priest who became one of history's great moral leaders."
— President Bush

PAGES A11-14, 17

THE IMAGES AND EVENTS OF HIS LIFE

Journal religion writer Richard C. Dujardin recalls his worldwide travels with the pope. Also, four pages on John Paul II's life in words and pictures.

SUNDAY EXTRA

The State

Sunday, April 3, 2005

114TH YEAR, NO. 93 | SOUTH CAROLINA'S LARGEST NEWSPAPER

COPYRIGHT © 2005 | COLUMBIA, S.C. | CAPITAL FINAL ++

I thestate.com I

POPE JOHN PAUL II | 1920-2005

POPE DEAD AT 84

'We all feel like orphans this evening'

By KEN DILANIAN,
MATTHEW SCHOFIELD
and PATRICIA MONTEMURRI
Knight Ridder Newspapers

VATICAN CITY — The light in the papal apartment, the bells of St. Peter's Basilica tolling in a solemn signal of mourning told the faithful what they didn't want to hear.

John Paul II, the Polish-born pope, was dead at age 84.

The pontiff died Saturday after a two-day end-of-life drama that sparked an unprecedented global outpouring of attention to his life, his legacy and what lies ahead for the Roman Catholic Church.

The first news of his death at 9:37 p.m. local time (2:37 p.m. EST) came via the papal spokesman's e-mail to journalists.

Then it was announced to an estimated 70,000 people gathered in St. Peter's Square.

"We all feel like orphans this evening," Undersecretary of State Archbishop Leonardo Sandri told the crowd.

The assembled flock fell silent before some people broke out in applause — an Italian tradition in which mourners often clap for important figures. Some wept uncontrollably, some stared in disbelief. Still others bowed their heads in prayer. People streamed into the square, and the crowd overflowed into nearby streets.

Many said they knew what happened when they saw the light go on in the window of John Paul's apartment, three stories above Bernini's colonnade.

"He was so strong, and he always spoke about our problems," said Cotbrina Tosti, 26, who was born the year John Paul ascended to the papacy, and who stood, in tears, in the packed, hushed crowd.

"He had his opinions and sometimes they were not ours, but he spoke without judgment and he always spoke with love."

SEE **POPE** PAGE **A7**

The obituary, A8

ONLINE

To post your condolences and to view a slide show of the pope's life, including his 1987 visit to Columbia, visit www.thestate.com.

A traditionalist pope shaped the church and its youth

The church wrapped itself in tradition under John Paul II, the only pope many young Catholics have known.

PAGE A9

South Carolina Catholics offer prayers for their pope

The pews of local Catholic churches filled late Saturday as their members came in prayer to remember Pope John Paul II.

PAGE A10

Pope charmed Columbia in only visit to Bible Belt

South Carolinians welcomed the first pope ever to visit when John Paul II came to Columbia in 1987.

PAGE A11

THE STATE ILLUSTRATION; PHOTOGRAPH BY PLINIO LEPRI/THE ASSOCIATED PRESS

Today: Breezy with a good deal of sun.
High: 60
Low: 42
Details: B2

$2
★★★★★
April 3, 2005

Sunday News Sentinel

Knoxville   KnoxN

COMIC CHANGES
Our funnies are taking on a different look — we've dropped some, added others.
Find your two 4-page sections inside.

Editor Jack McElroy explains the changes. **G4**

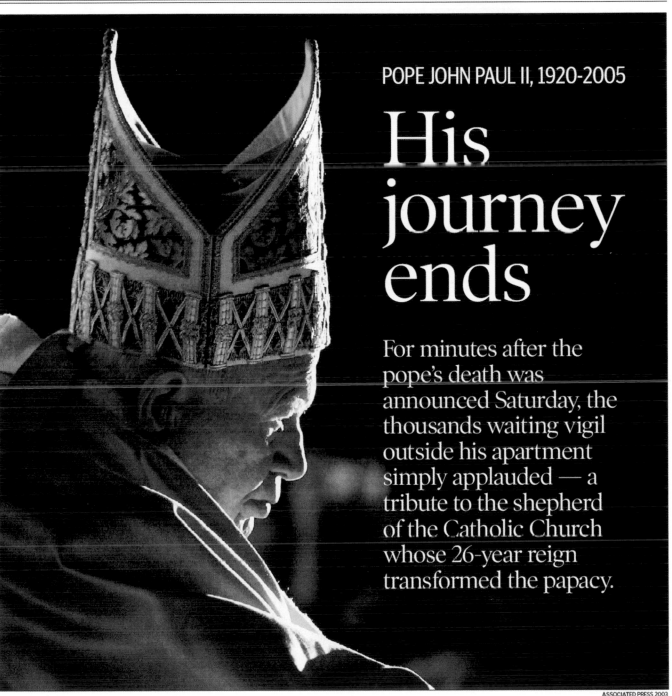

POPE JOHN PAUL II, 1920-2005

His journey ends

For minutes after the pope's death was announced Saturday, the thousands waiting vigil outside his apartment simply applauded — a tribute to the shepherd of the Catholic Church whose 26-year reign transformed the papacy.

ASSOCIATED PRESS 2003

HIS BELIEFS
Pope John Paul II held his ground on conservative issues. But did it cause the Catholic Church to lose support? **A2**

HIS LIFE
In his youth, he wanted to become an actor. But an accident detoured his plans toward priesthood and, ultimately, the papacy. **A16**

HIS HOMELAND
Poles said their goodbyes to their beloved native son Saturday, relieved that his suffering had ended. **A18**

HIS SUCCESSOR
There is only one certainty over who will be the next pope: The cardinals will decide if the papacy will be handed back to its traditional caretakers. **A22**

KNOXNEWS.COM
■ Mourning and election: what happens now.
■ View more photos, video and stories about the pope and learn how to share your thoughts.

73

EXPANDED COVERAGE ON PAGES A2, A16-A22

www.tennessean.com

NASHVILLE, TENNESSEE

THE TENNESSEAN

VOLUME 101, NO. 93   9 SECTIONS   C   © COPYRIGHT 2005   PERIODICALS POSTAGE PAID IN NASHVILLE, TN

POPE JOHN PAUL II • 1920-2005

A pilgrim goes home

3 PAGES INSIDE

World mourns
Mourners turn out in large numbers from Warsaw to cities of Latin America.
On Page 18A

The pope kisses Kamila Nosarzewski of Crossville, Tenn., last year.

Pontiff's travels
John Paul was a missionary on the move, traveling to more than 120 countries. **On Page 18A**

His legacy
Pope's motto, "Be not afraid," buoyed him through the fall of communism and inspired millions. **On Page 19A**

Remembrances
Nashville-area parishioners recall pope's message. **On Page 19A**

Next pope
No clear favorite for next pontiff when cardinals convene later this month. **On Page 20A**

John Paul II leaves world transformed by his papacy

By LARRY STAMMER
Los Angeles Times
and ROBERT D. McFADDEN
The New York Times

Pope John Paul II, whose indomitable will and uncompromising belief in human dignity — helped bring down communism in Eastern Europe and reshaped Christianity's relationship to Judaism, was indisputably the most influential pope of the 20th century. He died yesterday in his Vatican apartment at age 84.

The first non-Italian elected pope in 455 years, John Paul energized the papacy through much of his reign, traveling as evangelist and champion of religious freedom even as he imposed a rigorous moral discipline and more centralized authority on his sometimes rebellious 1 billion-member church.

In his final months, as his health declined markedly, he valiantly pressed ahead with his mission, choosing to project his gradual incapacitation as a final Christian message of redemption through suffering.

For the impoverished masses in the nations of Asia, Africa and Latin America that he so assiduously visited, John Paul was often a revolutionary icon demanding social justice: jobs, respect for human dignity, a decent standard of living, education and health care.

John Paul's pronouncements could have unmistakable political

Pope John Paul II, shown celebrating his first Mass in Cuba in January 1998, led the Roman Catholic Church for more than a quarter-century and became history's most-traveled pope. He died yesterday.
AP / FILE

and social consequences. He saw anything that impeded human dignity — including oppressive political and economic systems, as well as undisciplined personal freedom — as opposed to God's purposes and an obstacle to individual fulfillment.

"Nowadays it is sometimes held, though wrongly, that freedom is an end in itself, that each human being is free when he makes use of freedom as he wishes, and that this must be our aim in the lives of individuals and societies," he wrote in 1979. "In reality, freedom is a great gift only when we know how to use it con-

▶ Please see **POPE, 18A**

IN NASHVILLE

MICHAEL CLANCY
The Rev. Joseph P. Breen, center, leads the congregation of St. Edward Church in song during Mass after Pope John Paul II's death.

Pope remembered as leader who touched all faiths

By NATALIA MIELCZAREK
Staff Writer

Pope John Paul II was known around the world as the pilgrim pope, a shepherd of his flock, the people's pope.

And that's how local Catholics and spiritual leaders of various faiths eulogized the Polish-born pontiff yesterday after his death at age 84.

"There's a sense of sadness, of course, but also a sense of gratitude for having lived in a time that saw him as a leader of Catholics and the leader of the world," said the Rev. David Choby, administrator of the Diocese of Nashville.

"He certainly was accomplished as a person who had a strong respect for human dignity. He loved the people, and the people loved him."

The health of the pontiff, born Karol Wojtyla in Wadowice, Poland, had declined steadily in the past few

▶ Please see **CATHOLICS, 19A**

Local services

Father David Choby, the administrator of the Catholic Diocese of Nashville, will celebrate a special Mass at 7 p.m. Thursday at the Cathedral of the Incarnation, 2015 West End Ave. An evening prayer service for the general public will be held at 7 p.m. Monday, April 11, at the Cathedral of the Incarnation.

Pope John Paul II High School, 117 Caldwell Drive in Hendersonville, has planned 24-hour adoration of the Blessed Sacrament in the school's chapel during the nine-day period of mourning. The school invites the public to join in honoring the pope.

Source:
www.dioceseofnashville.com

Spring ahead
Did you remember to set your clocks an hour ahead?
AP

CONTENTS

Sections:

School piano brings 11¢ at auction

With no minimum bid, Rutherford sale a boon for buyers, if not district

By CLAY CAREY
Staff Writer

MURFREESBORO — The cash-strapped Rutherford County School System didn't get quite as much money as it had hoped for from this year's auction of unneeded items.

One reason was the bargains bidders got, including a piano bought for 11 cents, a 1997 Ford van that sold for $250 and a 32-inch Samsung television that went for $1.27.

Those rock-bottom prices have some school administrators wondering if the current surplus system is as good a deal for the county as it is for the bidders.

Rutherford County's school system has faced a growing need for money since the last property tax hike in 2003. Three new schools are expected to cost $36.3 million to build and about $3.5 million a year to run when they open in 2006. The building plan also calls for three more schools to open in 2007, as well as a major addition at Murfreesboro's Blackman High School. The county has even asked lawmakers to levy taxes on new homes and on home sales, in part to pay for the increasing demands explosive growth has put on schools.

And every year, the school system puts hundreds of items, ranging from damaged

▶ Please see **SURPLUS, 2A**

New today: 'Life' shifts focus, adds TV channels

To our readers:
It's a new Life section, starting today. Here are some of the improvements you can expect in the section each week:

• A focus on entertainment personalities and issues. Nashville has a significant and sophisticated entertainment landscape that transcends music, and we'll use Life to reflect what's happening here and issues that affect entertainment consumers.

• A pullout TV book featuring 27 additional channels, including most of the ones you've been asking us to add. The new, 65-channel lineup, by the way, includes virtually every cable channel viewed by at least 5% of the Nashville TV audience each month. Accommodating additional channels did require some reconfigurations, as you'll see in the weekday daytime listings. While it may take a little getting used to, know that you'll still find listings for 18 hours a day, seven days a week. We also cut the accompanying material, which more fully describes some of the movies on that night. However, the grids do provide enough information on those movies. The TV book begins with Ken Beck's column, on Page 23 this week.

• A new feature called Coming Attractions, which will give you a head start on the week's new movies, CDs, DVDs and video games. Check out Page 10.

• An expanded section of things-to-do listings, including tourist attractions and museums. See Page 35.

• The standalone Travel section is now folded into Life, with an emphasis on day trips and regional getaways, starting on Page 49.

• These changes mean a regular feature has moved elsewhere: Hints from Heloise will now appear in the Home section. (See Page 3H.)

We'd like to hear what you think about all these changes. Please contact reader editor John Gibson at 259-8228, or via e-mail at jgibson@tennessean.com.

— **Everett J. Mitchell II**,
Vice President News and Editor

Meet this year's Top 40 Under 40

The Midstate is a better place for having these 40 people in it.

They tirelessly work to make good things happen. They constantly look for ways to give back. Some have overcome great obstacles to make a difference, while others are driven to share their good fortune with the world.

The young men and women who were chosen as finalists in *The Tennessean*'s fourth annual Top 40 Under 40 contest come from diverse backgrounds, but their accomplishments in the community give them something in common. Chosen from hundreds of nominees in two rounds of judging by community leaders, they truly are an inspiration.

Take some time to get to know these movers and shakers who are making waves in Middle Tennessee.
On Pages 16-17A

To subscribe call:
242-NEWS
or (800) 342-8237

0 40901 05601 0

Austin American-Statesman

$1.60   Final   statesman.com   Sunday, April 3, 2005

1920-2005

Pope John Paul II

The world mourns death of beloved pontiff

Spiritual shepherd led Catholics for 26 years

Cardinals will gather for election of successor

Luca Bruno ASSOCIATED PRESS
Many of the 70,000 people gathered at the Vatican reacted with tears after the death of Pope John Paul II was announced in St. Peter's Square on Saturday. This woman received comfort from a nun.

Andrew Medichini 2002 ASSOCIATED PRESS

70,000 pay respects at St. Peter's Square

By Don Melvin
INTERNATIONAL STAFF

VATICAN CITY — All day the crowd in St. Peter's Square had been building, swelling with people who wanted to say good-bye to Pope John Paul II, the only pope some of them had ever known. When his death was an-nounced Saturday, the crowd of 70,000 fell silent and then burst

into long applause, an Italian tradition in which mourners show respect.

"He was a marvelous man. Now he's no longer suffering," Concetta Sposato, a pilgrim in the crowd, said tearfully.

After 26 years as head of the Roman Catholic Church, the pope died at 9:37 p.m. local time

See POPE, A8

Local Masses

A memorial Mass for the oc-casion of a pope's death will be celebrated at noon Monday at St. Mary Cathedral, the mother church of the Austin diocese, at 203 E. 10th St.

Two special Masses in memory of the pope will be held today at 4 p.m. and 5:30 p.m.

Read more about Central Texas responses to the pope's death, **A8.**

On statesman.com: Find more Central Texas photos and additional coverage.

More coverage

A chronology of the pope's life, **A6-7.**

For many Latin Americans, pope had special significance, **A8.**

Sorrow in John Paul's native Poland, **A8.**

Next pontiff is unlikely to be a carbon copy of John Paul II, church experts say, **A9.**

Editorial reflects on pope's contributions, **H2.**

An unwavering moral force who transformed the world

By Shelley Emling and Gayle White
INTERNATIONAL STAFF

Pope John Paul II left an in-delible mark on the Roman Catholic Church and the world with a papacy that spanned more than a quarter-century. A leader for his momentous times, he helped hasten the collapse of communism in Europe and presided over the church's

boom in popularity throughout much of the developing world, especially Africa and Latin America.

He symbolized a Catholicism that was shifting away from its Italian roots, but he was rock solid in his adherence to the church's traditional teachings. His unwavering stand against artificial birth control and for the all-male celibate priesthood

See FLOCK, A6

Among blacks, club was the place to be

Fire at Midtown Live left a major void in Austin's social scene

By Tony Plohetski
AMERICAN-STATESMAN STAFF

Austin businesswoman Jo Baylor took a vacation to France in the late 1980s and returned with an idea to bring to her hometown a European-style nightclub, a place where people could get a good five-course meal, dance and socialize under one roof.

Baylor studied the market and decided Austin's African American community needed a new club.

Phases, the popular all-purpose nightclub on Rosewood Avenue, had closed a couple of

On statesman.com: See related letters and reports on the Midtown Live proposal with this story online.

years before. Smaller bars had sprouted along 11th and 12th streets in East Austin, but many came and went with each pass-ing month.

Baylor also had the perfect building. She had been leasing a strip center on Cameron Road from a couple of Houston busi-nessmen, and a restaurant an-choring it had recently closed.

On Midtown Live's opening night nearly 18 years ago, cus-tomers stood in a line several dozen deep to get in.

"People were just so hungry

See FIRE, A10

IN THIS SECTION

Remembering Selena

Tributes on 10th anniversary of her death serve as remind-ers of the qualities that made her great.   **A17**

WEATHER

Mostly sunny, breezy.

High: 77   Low: 57
Details, B8 and online at statesman.com/weather

© 2005, Austin American-Statesman

FALLING SHORT

PROBLEMS IN TEXAS HIGHER EDUCATION

For Latinos, path to college is steep

Cultural and financial hurdles slow state's efforts to close the gap

Second in an occasional series

By Laura Heinauer and Ralph K.M. Haurwitz
AMERICAN-STATESMAN STAFF

LOS FRESNOS — Every sen-ior at Los Fresnos High School has applied to college, and more than three-fourths already have been accepted. That would be an impressive achievement at vir-tually any public high school, but it is an astonishing one here

in the Lower Rio Grande Valley, one of the poorest areas in the nation.

It required years of selling the idea of college not only to the students, nearly all of whom are Hispanic, but also to their par-ents, many of whom didn't complete high school. It re-quired dragging students out of class to work on applications. And it required working side by side with parents to help them fill out financial aid forms.

True, most of the colleges to which the students applied ac-cept virtually all comers. And it remains to be seen how many

See COLLEGE, A14

75

Good morning! **SUNNY, HIGH 76, LOW 56** / **PAGE C18**   **SCOTT, BURKE, TAVERAS MAKE ASTROS' FINAL CUT** / **PAGE C1**

HOUSTON ★ CHRONICLE

WWW.CHRON.COM   SUNDAY, APRIL 3, 2005   ★ ★ ★ ★   VOL. 104 • NO. 172 • $1.75

THE BP EXPLOSION

Workers could only watch in horror

■ Unknown to many victims, witnesses say, a gas eruption signaled trouble

By ANNE BELLI and TERRI LANGFORD
HOUSTON CHRONICLE

It was shortly after 1 p.m. on a sunny spring day, and contractors working on the gasoline-producing "ultracracker" unit had just finished eating fajitas brought in from Gringo's Mexican Cafe.

BP had catered lunch for the workers as a reward for completing another week's work without injuries. Now everybody was getting back to business — climbing scaffolding, getting in vehicles, moving equipment and operating generators.

More than a dozen contractors from JE Merit gathered in a nearby construction trailer for an afternoon staff meeting.

Unknown to many of the workers, part of a nearby isomerization unit — used to boost the octane level of gasoline — was about to be restarted after a long period of maintenance.

Please see **BP,** *Page A13*

INSIDE
Profiles of the 15 people who died in the blast.
PAGE A14

DeLay is losing support, poll finds

■ Schiavo case and ethics battles take a toll in his district

By SAMANTHA LEVINE and JOE STINEBAKER
HOUSTON CHRONICLE

House Majority Leader Tom DeLay's footing among his constituents has slipped drastically during the past year and a majority of his district disapproves of how he handled the Terri Schiavo case, according to a Houston Chronicle poll.

Nearly 40 percent of the 501 voters questioned Wednesday through Friday said their opinion of the powerful Sugar Land Republican is less favorable than last year, compared with 11 percent who said their view of him has improved.

Half of the respondents gave DeLay a somewhat or very favorable rating.

Yet 49 percent said they would vote for someone other than DeLay if a congressional election in the 22nd District were at hand; 39 percent said they would stick with him.

"There seems to be no question that there has been an ero-
Please see **POLL,** *Page A16*

JOHN PAUL II DIES AFTER REMARKABLE JOURNEY

MILLIONS MOURN INDOMITABLE SPIRIT

HIS YOUTH: John Paul as a young man in Poland.
TORONTO STAR

ELECTION: John Paul after being elected pope in 1978.
ASSOCIATED PRESS FILE

IN 1998: John Paul at his first Mass in Cuba.
ASSOCIATED PRESS FILE

ASSOCIATED PRESS FILE
THE PEACEMAKER: John Paul watches a white dove released by Roman youths in honor of his repeated calls for peace in St. Peter's Square at the Vatican in April 2003.

■ The priest from Poland who went to Rome helped bring communism's fall

By RICHARD VARA AND GREGORY KATZ
HOUSTON CHRONICLE

VATICAN CITY — With bells tolling and tens of thousands of mourners standing solemnly beneath his window in St. Peter's Square, Pope John Paul II's 26-year reign as spiritual leader of the world's 1.1 billion Roman Catholics came to an end Saturday.

John Paul, the first non-Italian pope in more than 450 years, died at 84. He used his papacy to preach faith, social justice and morality to an audience that extended far beyond his own flock.

"Our beloved Holy Father, John Paul, has returned to the house of the Father," said Archbishop Leonardo Sandri, the Vatican's undersecretary of state, when he announced the pope's death to the huge crowd. "We all feel like orphans this evening."

The mourners, who had flocked into the square all day as the pope's aides and doctors tended to him in his third-floor apartments, fell into tearful silence, broken only by the slow toll of one of the bells of St. Peter's Basilica. Within hours of the announcement, the crowd had swelled to about 130,000 people.

After a while the crowd slowly began ap-
Please see **POPE,** *Page A23*

8-PAGE SPECIAL SECTION
An in-depth look at the life and papacy of John Paul II.
SECTION N

Houston's diverse Catholic community unites in its grief

■ Some recall the honor, joy of seeing him in person

By CLAUDIA FELDMAN
HOUSTON CHRONICLE

The day Pope John Paul II died, thousands of Houston Catholics felt Polish.

Juanita Torres and her daughter, Elena, made a beeline for Our Lady of Czestochowa Catholic Church mid-afternoon Saturday, knelt near a painting of the youthful pope and said their prayers.

"I felt so grateful to the pope. He made many trips to Mexico," said Juanita Torres, 64.

The church on Blalock, glowing as the afternoon sun filtered through the stained glass windows, was mostly empty. During the calm before the packed 6 p.m. Mass, church members came and went in ones and twos. Some wanted to make sure the sanctuary was ready for the expected crowd; others came to pay their respects.

Barbara Ostrowski, 47, helped shroud the church doors in black bunting.
Please see **HOUSTON,** *Page A24*

■ **ONLINE:** Interactive history, photo galleries and video   ■ **EN ESPAÑOL:** La muerte del Papa y las reacciones de varios gobernantes latinoamericanos: PÁG. A23

SAN ANTONIO, TEXAS

SPECIAL REPORT: A SHEPHERD'S PASSING

8 PAGES OF COVERAGE INSIDE, 8A-15A

San Antonio Express-News

Sunday, April 3, 2005

Metro Edition

THE VOICE OF SOUTH TEXAS SINCE 1865

$1.50

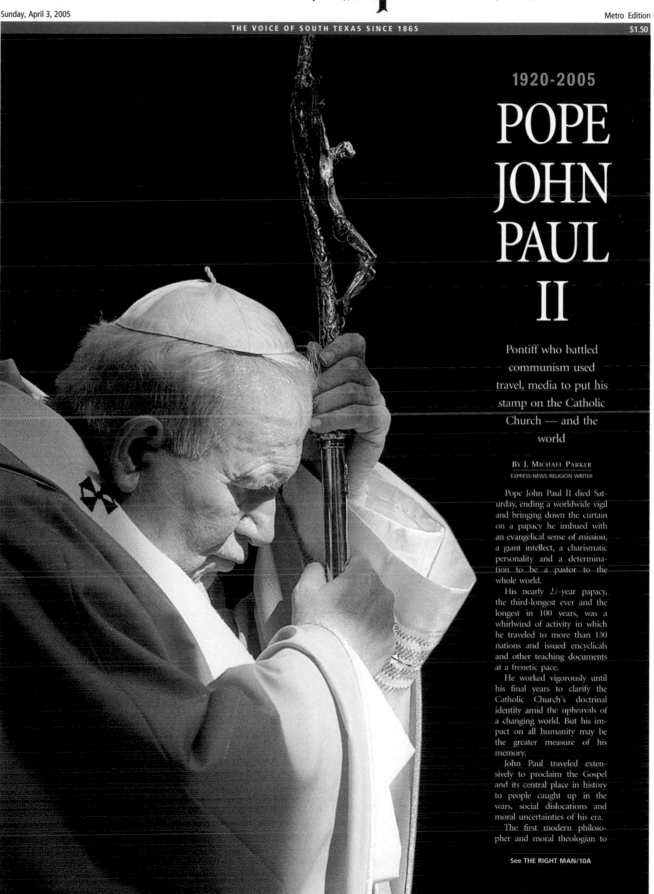

1920-2005

POPE JOHN PAUL II

Pontiff who battled communism used travel, media to put his stamp on the Catholic Church — and the world

BY J. MICHAEL PARKER
EXPRESS-NEWS RELIGION WRITER

Pope John Paul II died Saturday, ending a worldwide vigil and bringing down the curtain on a papacy he imbued with an evangelical sense of mission, a giant intellect, a charismatic personality and a determination to be a pastor to the whole world.

His nearly 27-year papacy, the third-longest ever and the longest in 100 years, was a whirlwind of activity in which he traveled to more than 130 nations and issued encyclicals and other teaching documents at a frenetic pace.

He worked vigorously until his final years to clarify the Catholic Church's doctrinal identity amid the upheavals of a changing world. But his impact on all humanity may be the greater measure of his memory.

John Paul traveled extensively to proclaim the Gospel and its central place in history to people caught up in the wars, social dislocations and moral uncertainties of his era.

The first modern philosopher and moral theologian to

See THE RIGHT MAN/10A

PIER PAOLO CITO/ASSOCIATED PRESS FILE PHOTO

GLOBAL GRIEVING
Mourning cloaks the world after pope's death

See A8

LOCAL DIOCESE
Brownsville bishop recalls time with pontiff

See A9

LASTING LEGACY
Recalling the remarkable life of Pope John Paul II

See A10

BROWNSVILLE
The Herald

SUNDAY, APRIL 3, 2005   BORN ON THE FOURTH OF JULY 1892 $1.50

P O N T I F F   P A S S E S

POPE JOHN PAUL II

World mourns loss of Holy Father

BY DON MELVIN
COX NEWS SERVICE

VATICAN CITY — All day long the crowd in St. Peter's Square had been building, swelled with people who wanted to say goodbye to Pope John Paul II, the only pope some of them had ever known. When his death was announced Saturday evening, the crowd, by now 70,000 strong, fell silent — and then burst into long applause, an Italian tradition in which mourners show respect.

"He was a marvelous man. Now he's no longer suffering," Concetta Sposato, a pilgrim who heard the pope had died as she was on her way to St. Peter's to pray, said tearfully.

John Paul II died at 9:37 p.m. local time (1:37 p.m. U.S. central) The news was relayed in an e-mail to journalists and then immediately announced to the crowd, even as the lights in

PLEASE SEE WORLD, A11

City holds vigils in remembrance

BY EMMA PEREZ-TREVIÑO AND LAURA B. MARTINEZ
THE BROWNSVILLE HERALD

In the church named after Mexico's patron saint that Pope John Paul II loved so dearly, the Rev. Francisco Acosta urged parishioners on Saturday not to feel they have lost a pontiff but gained a saint in heaven.

"Let's pray for (the pope) and for the church," Acosta said during Mass at Our Lady of Guadalupe Church on Lincoln Street.

Hours after the pope's death, mourners filled the church's pews and saw two photographs in front of the alter showing Acosta with the pope in 1984.

Next to the photos was a statue of San Juan Diego, an indigenous saint canonized by the pope during his fifth trip to Mexico in September 2002.

These were among several examples of the

PLEASE SEE FAITHFUL, A12

M A Y   1 8 ,   1 9 2 0   ~   A P R I L   2 ,   2 0 0 5

INSIDE: A special commemorative section — the pope in his own words

The Dallas Morning News

Texas' Leading Newspaper · Dallas, Texas, Sunday, April 3, 2005 · DallasNews.com · $1.50

POPE JOHN PAUL II: 1920-2005

He touched the world

Tireless traveler served poor, helped vanquish communism

© DAVID BURNETT/Contact Press Images

Pope John Paul II, visiting Paris in 1980, served as pope for 26 years — longer than all but two pontiffs. He also had a broader reach, traveling more than all the other popes combined. "He will go down in history as one of the most important world leaders in the second half of the 20th century," said the editor of a Catholic magazine.

Stunned silence, tearful prayers, a celebration of life by thousands

By TOD ROBBERSON
Europe Bureau

VATICAN CITY — Within minutes of the announcement that Pope John Paul II had died, the multitudes at St. Peter's Square grew from tens of thousands to possibly more than a million. And still more followed.

The deep-toned peal of a giant bell echoed across the vast plaza Saturday as thousands burst into tears and knelt in prayer, bidding farewell to the 84-year-old John Paul, whose popularity and impact were appreciated perhaps more in his final days than in the 26 years he spent as pontiff.

Giant flat-screen television screens and floodlights were interspersed with towering Roman columns and magnificent, ancient architecture around St. Peter's Square, reflecting one of the primary tasks of a 21st-century pope: to unite a rapidly changing, modern world with a Roman Catholic Church steeped in 2,000 years of tradition.

The impact of his papacy was evident among the Catholic faithful as well as non-Catholics such as Linda Williams and Keith Kusterer of Indianapolis, who caught a flight to Rome last week immediately after it became apparent the pope was in his final days.

"We decided to come over because of what he did for the world and the fact that he was the people's pope," Ms. Williams said. "He was so young and athletic when he started. He skied, hiked, climbed mountains. He communicated. He touched all religions — at least all Christian religions."

Mr. Kusterer said the pope's energy was best exemplified by the enormous number of trips he took around the world — more than any

See 'HE' Page 11A

INSIDE

How will the next pope be chosen? And will he be non-European? **11A**

Editorial: "monumental figure" **2A**

In Mexico, John Paul II enjoyed immense popularity. But Catholics continue to defect to evangelical Christian churches. **20A**

In the pope's Polish hometown, he was known as Karol Wojtyla. **19A**

Texans remember the pope. **13A**

ON THE WEB

Visit DallasNews.com/religion for photos, reader comments and reaction and news updates on the death of Pope John Paul II.

Advocate for peace held fast to conservative ideals

By SUSAN HOGAN/ALBACH
Staff Writer

Pope John Paul II, who played a central role in the collapse of communism and broke from papal tradition by preaching in 129 countries during his quarter-century reign, died Saturday. He was 84.

The Vatican released a statement on the death by e-mail Saturday night: "The Holy Father died this evening at 9:37 p.m. in his private apartment."

Vatican protocol dictates nine days of public mourning before a conclave convenes in Rome to elect a new pope by secret ballot. The conclave — made up of the princes of the worldwide church, known as cardinals — will almost surely select John Paul's successor from its own ranks.

The son of a Polish military officer, Karol Józef Wojtyla became one of the most influential pontiffs in the church's history, one whose conservative doctrinal legacy will live on for decades. In his 26 years as the "Vicar of Christ," he appointed nearly every prelate worldwide who sits as a cardinal or bishop today.

As leader of the world's 1 billion Catholics, John Paul was one of the world's most powerful men. His influence stretched beyond the spiritual to political circles, with leaders from Mikhail Gorbachev to President Bush seeking his ear.

"He will go down in history as

See PONTIFF Page 16A

METRO EDITION

DESERET
Morning News

VOL. 155/NO. 293

SUNDAY, APRIL 3, 2006

SALT LAKE CITY, UTAH

POPE JOHN PAUL II ✦ 1920 - 2005

In downtown Los Angeles

DAMIAN DOVARGANES ASSOCIATED PRESS

In St. Peter's Square, Vatican City

LUCA BRUNO ASSOCIATED PRESS

In Krakow, Poland

CZAREK SOKOLOWSKI ASSOCIATED PRESS

The world mourns

Julio Funes, left, Jose Franco and Baltazar Silva kneel and offer prayers at the Cathedral of the Madeleine in Salt Lake City on Saturday.

MICHAEL BRANDY, DESERET MORNING NEWS

Utahns join in prayer, tears for John Paul II

By Nicole Warburton
Deseret Morning News

As he sat weeping, huddled next to a friend from home, a sliver of light fell upon Jose Franco's face.

It was a moment of pain for the immigrant from Mexico. An hour earlier, the man he had known his whole life as pope — or holy father — had died.

"He always had that young spirit and always tried to instill that in us to be young and full of the spirit," said Franco, his eyes red-rimmed as he fingered a silver

Please see MASS on A14

PIER PAOLO CITO ASSOCIATED PRESS

Pope leans on staff at San Mattia church in 1999.

His dedication, love won hearts of millions

By Carrie A. Moore
Deseret Morning News

Utahns joined the world in mourning and reflection Saturday on the life of Pope John Paul II, whose dedication to moral principle and unprecedented outreach to people of all faiths and stations endeared him to millions around the globe.

With tens of thousands keeping a silent vigil in St. Peter's Square, Vatican officials announced that the pontiff, 84, died in his private apartment at 9:37 p.m.

GLOBAL TRIBUTES
Death prompts an outpouring of grief
A2, A9-14

Please see MOURN on A10

President Hinckley praises pontiff

President Gordon B. Hinckley of The Church of Jesus Christ of Latter-day Saints remembered Pope John Paul II during both general sessions of the faith's 175th Annual General Conference on Saturday.

In a brief preface to his opening address, during the pontiff's final hours, President Hinckley said, "I extend to our Catholic neighbors and friends our heartfelt sympathy at this time of great sorrow."

Pope John Paul II has worked tirelessly to lift the burdens of the poor, to speak fearlessly on behalf of moral values and human dignity. He will be greatly missed."

Word came that the pope had died shortly after noon Utah time, prompting President Hinckley to make the following statement when the afternoon session began:

"We join those throughout the world who mourn the passing of Pope John

Paul II, an extraordinary man of faith, vision and intellect, whose courageous actions have touched the world in ways that will be felt for generations to come.

"The pope's voice remained firm in defense of freedom, family and Christianity. On matters of principle and morality he was uncompromising. On his compassion for the world's poor, he has been unwavering. He will be greatly missed."

GENERAL CONFERENCE

LDS Church statistics
AS OF DEC. 31, 2004

CHURCH UNITS
Stakes	2,665
Missions	338
Districts	646
Wards & branches	26,670

CHURCH MEMBERSHIP
Total membership	12,275,822
Increase in children of record	98,870
Converts baptized	241,239

MISSIONARIES
Full time	51,067

TEMPLES
Temples dedicated during 2004	3
Temples rededicated during 2004	2
Temples in operation	119

SOURCE: LDS Church public affairs dept.

DESERET MORNING NEWS GRAPHIC

LDS hail a decade of great 'flowering'

By Twila Van Leer
Deseret Morning News

A decade of "remarkable flowering" in the history of The Church of Jesus Christ of Latter-day Saints was celebrated as the church opened its 175th Annual General Conference Saturday. The 10 years since Gordon B. Hinckley, Thomas S. Monson and James E. Faust were sustained as the First Presidency have been an era of "meaningful accomplishments," President Hinckley said in opening remarks Saturday morning.

Members sustained a new Primary general presidency, along with a number of other additions to the presiding quorums of the church during the second general session. Sister Cheryl C. Lant is the new Primary president.

Inside today's News
➤ Conference session summaries / A16
➤ New general authorities named / A17
➤ Draper temple lures homebuyers / B1

Please see CONFERENCE on A17

AUGUST MILLER DESERET MORNING NEWS

General Primary Presidency: Margaret S. Lifferth, left; Cheryl C. Lant, president; Vicki F. Matsumori.

INSIDE

Romney's faith could hurt an '08 run

Mormons not viewed as Christians by some faiths

By Michael McAuliffe
Newhouse News Service

Millions of Americans think John F. Kennedy put to rest the issue of religion in presidential politics when, in 1960, he became the first Roman Catholic to win the White House.

Another Massachusetts politician, Republican Gov. W. Mitt Romney, may find out that is not the case should he run for president in 2008,

Mitt Romney

as many people believe he is angling to do.

Romney is a devout member of The Church of Jesus Christ of Latter-day Saints, more commonly known as the Mormons. Its members, however, are not considered Christians by a number of other

denominations, including the Southern Baptist Convention and the United Methodist Church, the largest Protestant denominations in America and two faiths whose membership is heavily concentrated in the South.

Given that the South has become a GOP stronghold in recent presidential races, some believe Romney's religion would emerge as an issue should he seek to become the 44th president.

"I think it likely will matter," said Charles Reagan Wilson, director of the Center for the Study of Southern Culture at the University of

Mississippi. "I think he will have to be very savvy and skillful in talking with evangelicals, and I don't know what experience he has doing that."

Wilson, who has heard Baptist ministers denounce Mormonism from the pulpit, said the Latter-day Saints are viewed as "an odd religious phenomenon" by Southern evangelicals, most of whom are Republicans. Aggressive Mormon proselytizing has not helped the religion's image in the region, Wilson said.

"In the South we talk about reli-

Please see ROMNEY on A7

UTAH'S INDEPENDENT VOICE SINCE 1871

The Salt Lake Tribune

© 2005 THE SALT LAKE TRIBUNE   SUNDAY ❖ APRIL 3, 2005   s   WWW.SLTRIB.COM

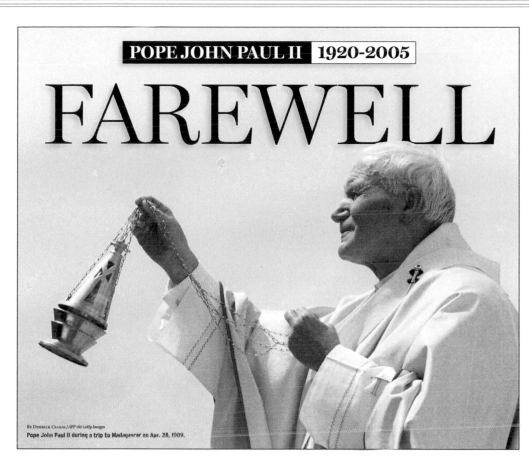

POPE JOHN PAUL II   1920-2005

FAREWELL

BY DERRICK CEYRAC/AFP via Getty Images
Pope John Paul II during a trip to Madagascar on Apr. 28, 1909.

Pope John Paul II revitalized Catholicism even as he confronted a world grown profoundly secular. He helped vanquish European communism and made human rights his lodestar. He drew tens of millions of young Catholics to his spiritual side, even if his orthodoxy was not universally popular. His humanity will never be forgotten.

Karol Wojtyla (the future pope) as a boy

A young Wojtyla on a hiking trip

Cardinal Wojtyla in 1969

Pope John Paul II in 2003

Beloved beyond the church
Theologian with allure and historic political sway

BY ROBERT D. MCFADDEN
The New York Times

When Cardinal Karol Wojtyla of Poland was elected pope in 1978, it was quickly evident that this was to be an extraordinary pontificate, one that would captivate much of humanity by sheer force of personality and reshape the church with a heroic vision of a combative, disciplined Catholicism.

It was to be the longest and most luminous pontificate of the 20th century, and (depending on how St. Peter is counted) the second- or third-longest in history — a 26-year era that would witness sweeping political changes around the world, the growth of the Roman church to 1 billion baptized members from 750 million, and the beginning of Christianity's Third Millennium.

The man who would call himself John Paul II was not the traditional papal figure, compassionate and loving but ascetic and remote behind the high walls and
See **JOHN PAUL II**, A12

Strength of spirit
Love, conviction, courage resonated with Utahns

BY PEGGY FLETCHER STACK
AND BROOKE ADAMS
The Salt Lake Tribune

The Rev. Colin Bircumshaw was in St. Peter's Square in Rome the day Pope John Paul II was shot by a would-be assassin. As word swept through the crowd, Bircumshaw was engulfed by sorrow and loss.

Those same emotions returned this week when the priest at St. Ann's Catholic Church in South Salt Lake learned that the pontiff was dying.

Bircumshaw was studying in Rome in 1978 when he saw the white smoke signifying a new pope's election spiraling above the square. And he even had a private conversation with John Paul II.

"Utah?" the pope asked the young priest in Italian. "Mormonis?"

The multilingual leader continued the conversation in German, then French and Spanish. Bircumshaw kept pace until the pontiff went to Polish.
See **UTAHNS**, A7

Inside

Utah Bishop George H. Niederauer reflects on his time with the pope. **A7**

The Roman Catholic Church sets in motion the choosing of a successor. **A8**

John Paul II is surrounded by his closest aides in his last moments. **A9**

His early life was a story of struggle and despair. **A10**

Karol Jozef Wojtyla adhered strictly to Catholic teachings and traditions. **A11**

Thousands of faithful mark the pope's passing in St. Peter's Square. **A14**

Mayhem at Abu Ghraib wounds GIs, detainees

Concerted assault: Attacks with car bombs, rockets and guns last for four hours

BY ELLEN KNICKMEYER
The Washington Post

BAGHDAD, Iraq — Attacking in waves of car bombs, rockets and gun fire, dozens of insurgents assailed Iraq's notorious Abu Ghraib prison on Saturday in an hours-long onslaught that wounded 44 U.S. troops and 12 detainees, the American military said.

Attackers apparently did not penetrate the prison grounds, although some inmates were reported to have been seriously wounded. The second of two car bombs exploded as troops were trying to evacuate the injured from the first, the Reuters news agency said.

In Baghdad, the latest prospects of defusing Iraq's Sunni-led insurgency by drawing the Sunni minority into the country's government and military looked shaky.

The Association of Muslim Scholars, the most prominent of dozens of groups speaking for disaffected Sunnis, distanced itself Saturday from an edict by 64 Sunni clerics and scholars the previous day that had encouraged Sunnis to join Iraq's new security forces.

Politically, efforts by Iraq's ethnic Kurds and majority Shiite Arabs to form a national unity government threatened to stall again over finding a
See **ABU GHRAIB**, A4

Spring forward: Did you set your clocks one hour ahead?

INSIDE

Business E1	Landers ... D15
Books D5	Lottery B3
Classifieds . W2	Movies D12
Crossword . D14	Obituaries ... B8
Editorials .. AA1	Puzzles ... D14
Horoscope . D14	Sports C1

WEATHER Page A9

Breezy, highs in mid-60s north, 70s south.

6 34945 02345 1
VOLUME 269
NUMBER 171

LDS General Conference
Hinckley lauds pope, pans gambling

LDS Church President Gordon B. Hinckley remembered Pope John Paul II as "an extraordinary man of faith, vision and intellect" Saturday on the first day of the church's 175th Annual General Conference in downtown Salt Lake City.

Mormon leaders at the two-day conference returned to familiar sermon topics: the importance of kindness, the contributions of missionary work, the value of tithing and the enticements of evil.

The 94-year-old Hinckley, who also reflected on his 10-year leadership of the church, warned about the dangers of gambling, mentioning the lure of Internet poker.

LDS Conference coverage B1

LDS Church President Gordon B. Hinckley speaks at the LDS General Conference on Saturday morning. Hinckley invoked Pope John Paul II's struggle hours before the pope died.

AL HARTMANN
The Salt Lake Tribune

Richmond Times-Dispatch

VIRGINIA'S NEWS LEADER
A MEDIA GENERAL NEWSPAPER

RICHMOND, VIRGINIA

SUNDAY, APRIL 3, 2005

$1.75

Pope John Paul II
1920-2005

ARNEL REYNON/TIMES-DISPATCH

The people's pope

SPECIAL TRIBUTE

The pope drew praise for fighting communism but stirred controversy with conservative doctrine. **A17**

In Richmond, the pope is honored as a champion of peace and justice. **A21**

As bells toll from the Vatican, thousands weep in St. Peter's Square. **A23**

You'll find more articles and photos online at **TimesDispatch.com**

Pope John Paul II, the one-time stone cutter who rose to become the first non-Italian pope in more than 400 years and one of the world's most beloved leaders, died yesterday in the Vatican.

After months of declining health, John Paul, 84, died in his Vatican City apartment overlooking St. Peter's Square at 2:37 p.m. EST.

Few people had as much impact on the world as John Paul. His influence transcended the Roman Catholic Church as he urged reconciliation with other faiths and helped reshape the world's political landscape.

Karol Wojtyla, the man destined to become the 264th pope of the Roman Catholic Church, was born on May 18, 1920, and grew up in Wadowice, Poland.

When he was elected pope on Oct. 16, 1978, at age 58, he was the first Polish pope and the youngest pontiff in more than 100 years.

Before he assumed the papacy, he attended an underground seminary after the Nazis invaded Poland. He became a stone cutter in a quarry and was active in the Christian underground and helped Jews secure refuge.

Wojtyla lived more than half his life under tyranny, as Poland fell to communist rule after World War II. As pope, he challenged authoritarian power with spiritual appeals for humanity, inspiring millions who soon witnessed the collapse of the Soviet Union.

The most widely traveled pontiff in history, John Paul II journeyed more than 750,000 miles to visit more than 120 countries — some of which no longer exist in the wake of the turbulent political reform he helped unleash.

"The claim to build a world without God has been shown to be an illusion," he said in Prague in 1990 as the last vestiges of communism crumbled in Europe.

Visitors the pope received at the Vatican include a 100-member delegation from the Catholic Diocese of Richmond in 1995, the year the diocese celebrated its 175th anniversary and the 25th anniversary of the ordination of its then bishop, the Most Rev. Walter F. Sullivan.

Richmond lawyer Tommy Baer, then president of B'nai B'rth International, met with the pope in 1996 to urge him to support Middle East peace and to open the Vatican's World War II archives to historians.

In his final years, John Paul said he regarded his growing infirmity, brought about by Parkinson's disease and a progression of ailments, as a test of his faith and a chance to teach the world about the dignity of the aged.

— Staff and wire reports

The News & Advance

$1.50

Sunday, April 3, 2005 — A Media General Newspaper — Vol. 140, No. 93

➤ **SPRING AHEAD:** In case you forgot, daylight-saving time began today at 2 a.m.

Lynchburg, Virginia

Faithful servant

Pope
John
Paul II
1920-2005

INSIDE:

Pope John Paul II passes away quietly Saturday

The Associated Press

VATICAN CITY — Pope John Paul II assailed moral perils as he traveled the world, a crowd-pleasing super-pastor whose 26-year papacy carried the Roman Catholic Church into Christianity's third millennium and emboldened eastern Europeans to bring down the communist system.

As the first non-Italian pontiff in 455 years and the first from Poland, John Paul brought a back-to-basics conservatism infused with a common touch and a longing to heal ancient religious wounds. And he survived an assassination attempt to become the third-longest-serving pope.

In his final days, the 84-year-old pontiff sought to set an example of a dignified death.

A letter released on Good Friday reflected on his hospitalization as "a patient alongside other patients, uniting in the Eucharist my own sufferings with those of Christ."

John Paul's Polish roots nourished a doctrinal conservatism — opposition to contraception, abortion, women priests — that rankled liberal Catholics in the United States and Western Europe.

A sex abuse scandal among clergy plunged his church into moral crisis, with allegations that he didn't react to it swiftly enough.

And while championing the world's poor, he rebuked Latin American priests who sought to involve the church politically through the doctrine of "liberation theology."

No pope ever traveled so much or so far: He visited more than 120 nations during the third-longest papacy in history.

No pope delivered so many speeches: He warned in vain against wars in Iraq and the Balkans, deplored the fate of Palestinians and called for reconciliation with Jews.

Please see **SERVANT**, Page A4

➤ **THE PAPAL INNOVATOR:** Almost from the start, John Paul reshaped the papacy, dusting off the managerial cobwebs that had accumulated over the centuries./**Page A4**

➤ **POPE SUCCESSION:** Soon after the pope's funeral, the College of Cardinals will assemble to begin the election process for the next pontiff./**Page A5**

➤ **WASHINGTON REACTION:** President Bush said during a national address the pontiff is 'an inspiration to us all' and reacted to his death by immediately ordering the flags over the White House to fly at half-staff./**Page A6**

➤ **THE AILING POPE:** The pontiff's very public battle with Parkinson's disease and its ramifications puts the travails of the elderly and infirm front and center./**Page A6**

➤ **THE WORLD REACTS:** Mourners around the world react to the news of the pope's death. Thousands flock to churches and other events in respect of the late religious leader, who also was an advocate for peace./**Page A6**

➤ **RELIGIOUS LEADERS LAMENT:** Pat Robertson expressed his remorse at the death of Pope John Paul II while the Rev. Jerry Falwell, from the hospital, said 'the world has lost a great moral leader.'/**Page A7**

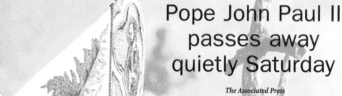

THE ROANOKE TIMES

SUNDAY APRIL 3, 2005 ===== roanoke.com ===== ROANOKE, VIRGINIA $1.50

HAYSOM MURDERS
20 YEARS AGO TODAY

FILE PHOTO I The Roanoke Times

In 1985, authorities from Bedford County and Lynchburg discuss the double slaying on the porch adjoining the kitchen where Nancy Haysom's body was found.

Blood, sweat and convictions

Starting in 1985, the Haysom double murder case ranged from Virginia to England and ignited a three-year legal battle.

By Jay Conley
jay.conley@roanoke.com
981-3114

Carl Wells remembers it clearly.

Retired now to his 200-plus-acre farm just outside Bedford, Wells, 69, was Bedford County's sheriff 20 years ago today when friends found the brutally stabbed bodies of Derek and Nancy Haysom in their Boonsboro home.

"It was about as bad a crime scene as you'd want to look at," he said.

The discovery of the bodies touched off a criminal investigation that led from Virginia to England and ignited a three-year legal battle.

Watch video of Jens Soering discussing views on his case, prison life and religion.

@roanoke.com

Beyond the sheer violence of the act came the shocking discovery that the affluent couple's college-age daughter, Elizabeth, and her German boyfriend, Jens Soering, both honor students at the University of Virginia, were responsible for the crime.

The slain couple's ties to South Africa and Canada, along with Soering's father being a West German diplomat, caused a flurry of national and international media attention.

In Bedford, the case was the talk of the town.

"Wherever you went, people were talking about it," said Carol Black, who has been the county's Circuit Court clerk for 21 years. "When you put it all together, it was all so different than anything else that had ever

See **HAYSOM, 8**

STEPHANIE KLEIN-DAVIS I The Roanoke Times

Carl Wells was sheriff of Bedford County at the time of the Haysom murders 20 years ago. The crime scene is still fresh in his mind. Today he is retired and lives on a farm outside Bedford.

Pope John Paul II 1920 ~ 2005

'The angels welcome you'

Associated Press I File 1983

Pope John Paul II in 1996 left instructions that the press be notified via e-mail upon his death. "The Holy Father died this evening at 9:37 p.m. in his private apartment," it read. He was 84 and served as pontiff for 26 years — the third-longest papacy in the history of the church.

Salem priest knew pope's Polish impact firsthand

By David Harrison
david.harrison@roanoke.com
981-3340

In 1978, the year Karol Wojtyla became Pope John Paul II, the Rev. Remi Sojka was in elementary school in Gliwice, Poland, an industrial city similar to Pittsburgh, he said.

The election of a Polish man to the papacy electrified people in Poland, Sojka, 39, recalled Saturday, and gave a glimmer of hope to a country still exhausted by World War II and living under a Communist regime that stifled opposition and jailed and tortured dissidents.

"When the pope was elected, it felt like God did not forget about Polish

"When the pope was elected, it felt like God did not forget about Polish people."

Rev. Remi Sojka
Our Lady of Perpetual Help

See **PRIEST, 6**

Shaped by his childhood in rural Poland and fired in the kiln of World War II, Pope John Paul II embodied the power and tradition of Catholicism.

By Steve Kloehn
Chicago Tribune

Pope John Paul II, who changed the course of the world through faith and sheer dint of will, died Saturday. He will be remembered as a bold pontiff who towered over his century, then led his church into a new millennium.

"The angels welcome you," Vatican TV said after papal spokesman Joaquin Navarro-Valls announced the death of the pope, who had for years suffered from Parkinson's disease and came down with fever and infections in recent weeks.

In contrast to the church's ancient traditions, Navarro-Valls announced the death to journalists in the most modern of communication forms, an e-mail that said: "The Holy Father died this evening at 9:37 p.m. in his private apartment."

Within minutes of the announcement that Pope John Paul II had died, the multitudes at St. Peter's Square grew from tens of thousands to possibly more than a million. And still more followed.

The deep-toned peal of a giant bell echoed across the vast plaza as thousands burst into tears and knelt in prayer, bidding farewell to the 84-year-old John Paul.

See **POPE, 6**

MORE INSIDE

Pope & mystic
Pope John Paul II spent much of each day in prayer, adoration and contemplation. **Page 3.**

Sistine conclave
When white smoke puffs out of the chapel, crowds in St. Peter's Square will scream "Viva Il Papa." **Page 5.**

@roanoke.com

See photos and a multimedia presentation of his life, hear local reaction, talk about his legacy and more.

KEEPSAKE
A special tribute
to Pope John Paul II
PAGES 2,7

IN REMEMBRANCE
Pope was influential
around the world
PAGE 3

LOCAL IMPACT
Opinions varied about
outspoken pope
PAGE 4

TIMELINE
Triumphs and trials
of a lifetime
PAGE 6

GLOBE-TROTTER
Pope visited more
than 115 countries
PAGE 8

85

Seattle Post-Intelligencer

A HEARST NEWSPAPER
SEATTLEPI.COM

50¢

KING, PIERCE, SNOHOMISH, ISLAND, KITSAP & THURSTON COUNTIES | ELSEWHERE 75¢

COMMENTARY
To survive at work, detach emotionally
BUSINESS C1

OPENING DAY
ICHIRO'S ENCORE
• Can he keep breaking records?
• M's host Twins today at 2:05
COMPLETE COVERAGE IN SPORTS D1, 7-9

CULTURE
Pierced and parenting: Staying punk, being a mom
LIFE AND ARTS E1

MONDAY, APRIL 4, 2005

A TIME TO MOURN

POPE'S FINAL MESSAGE ONE OF LOVE AND PEACE

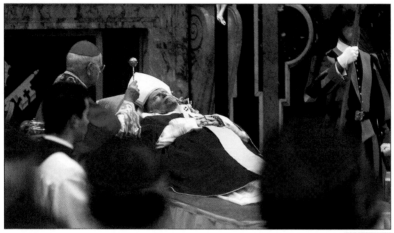

ASSOCIATED PRESS PHOTOS
The body of Pope John Paul II lies in state in the Clementine hall at the Vatican yesterday as thousands of people crowd St. Peter's Square, below.

P-I NEWS SERVICES

VATICAN CITY – His pale, folded hands intertwined with a rosary, Pope John Paul II was laid out inside the papal palace yesterday as the power in the Roman Catholic Church began its shift to his eventual successor. Millions prayed and wept at services across the globe.

Just 12 hours after he died Saturday night – after a urinary tract infection set off a fatal spiral of ailments – the majestic pageantry around the death of a pope began, with a huge public Mass in St. Peter's Square and then the first rites of John Paul's funeral.

The pope was laid out, dressed in white and red vestments, his head covered with a white bishop's miter and propped up on three gold pillows. Tucked under his left arm was the silver staff, the crosier he carried in public.

In death, after 26 years as pope, "his expression was serene," Francesco Rutelli, the former mayor of Rome, said after seeing the body.

About 80,000 people crowded into the square; 20,000 more spilled onto side streets for the Mass – the Sunday Mass that had been celebrated for more than 26 years by John Paul himself.

The most emotional moment of the day was when Archbishop Leonardo Sandri, the Vatican undersecretary of state, read the traditional Sunday noontime prayer, which John Paul had delivered throughout his pontificate.

Some in the crowd sucked in their breath, bowed their heads or

SEE SERVICES, A8

INSIDE

In his last minutes, the pope reportedly whispered "amen"
SEE A8

St. James Cathedral Masses draw throngs
SEE A9

Seattle police restrict Taser use

Policy urges caution in turning stun guns on vulnerable people

BY HECTOR CASTRO
P-I reporter

The Seattle Police Department is tightening its use of Tasers, urging officers to take particular care before using the electric-shock devices on pregnant women, the very young, the very old and the infirm.

The need to stop criminal or risky behavior "should clearly justify" the additional risks posed when a Taser is used against a pregnant, sick or otherwise vulnerable person, the new directives say.

The directives, presented over the weekend to the 220 officers who carry Tasers, also require a supervisor to be called to the scene whenever a Taser is used three or more times on a person.

"I think it's healthy that they're looking at the policy," said Pete Holmes, a member of a citizens police review panel, when told of the changes.

While Tasers have not officially been blamed for any deaths, some 74 deaths have occurred after Taser use in the United States and Canada, including deaths in Silverdale, Auburn and Olympia. Although an Amnesty International report said the Taser effects cannot be ruled out as contributing to death in at least seven of the cases, Taser International insists the stun guns it manufactures have been proven safe.

There also has been controversy about the use of Tasers on handcuffed people and about multiple shock-

SEE TASERS, A7

P-I REPORT ONLINE

A two-day P-I special report last fall looked at criticisms of how Tasers are being used by law enforcement agencies around the state. Among the complaints: that officers are too quick to use them. But police agencies say they are a lifesaving alternative to firearms.

seattlepi.com/specials/tasers/

Safeco Field's lineup also eager for opening day

Behind the scenes (mostly), they make M's games possible

BY CLARE FARNSWORTH
P-I reporter

For 300 of the Mariners' biggest supporters, there will be no need to take them out to the ballgame this afternoon.

They will already be there. Some for hours. Others for days.

Before Jamie Moyer makes his first pitch in the Mariners' 2:05 p.m. season opener against the Minnesota Twins at Safeco Field, the mound and field will have been meticulously manicured by head groundskeeper Bob Christofferson and his crew.

Before the first fan passes through the turnstile, Scot Mabry will have positioned himself, and his wheelchair, at the Terrace Club gate to pass out promotional giveaways

SEE LINEUP, A7

INSIDE

Collect 'em! Trade 'em! Here's your opening day lineup for Safeco Field
SEE A7

Foie gras leaves activists with a bad taste

Lawmakers asked to ban force-feeding of birds for delicacy

BY KATHY GEORGE
P-I reporter

Foie gras is a delicacy on the finest of menus, baked in rock salt at Rover's, dressed up with apples, currants and candied ginger at Cafe Juanita, or sprinkled with truffle oil at Maximilien in the Market.

A month ago, when Union chef and co-owner Ethan Stowell was featured as a "rising star of American cuisine" at the prestigious Beard House in New York, the Seattle restaurateur made foie gras part of the $115-per-dinner affair.

But is this gourmet chef's staple (pronounced "fwah grah") also an atrocity?

Around the country, animal rights activists have been pressuring restaurants to stop serving foie gras – and pushing lawmakers to ban it altogether – saying it involves force-feeding ducks to make their livers swell painfully.

Activists and restaurateurs agree it is only a matter of time before the movement spreads to the Seattle area, where one protest group already has about 1,000 members on its mailing list.

"Foie gras means fatty liver. It's a diseased state," said Matt Rossell, Northwest coordinator of In Defense of Animals, whose members have demonstrated outside pricey Portland restaurants with gruesome photos of dead ducks. "I believe it's at the extreme end of cruelty."

Already, California activists have sent a video and brochures to Maximilien in the Market. "They were

SEE FOIE GRAS, A6

INDEX

TODAY'S WEATHER
Morning showers, then partly sunny. High 53. **B6**

★★★

To subscribe to the P-I, call 206-464-2121
© 2005 SEATTLE POST-INTELLIGENCER

MIDEAST
One step forward in Iraq's politics
A Sunni Muslim has been selected speaker of Iraq's recently elected Parliament, a breakthrough in the ethnic and sectarian debate over a new government, but lawmakers again failed to name a new president.
WORLD A4

MOVIES
Aussie export's mind games
Radha Mitchell has played the distraught wife and the disapproving wife. Now she's playing alternating versions of the same woman – not a wife – in Woody Allen's latest film, "Melinda and Melinda."
LIFE AND ARTS E1

RELIGION
How big is too big?
A megachurch's plan for a "satellite" near Bellevue's Spiritridge Park has run into some opposition from neighbors who worry about the building's "visibility."
SEATTLE AND THE NW B1

THE NEWS TRIBUNE

THE NEWSPAPER FOR THE SOUTH SOUND • SUNDAY, APRIL 3, 2005 • TACOMA, WASH. • THENEWSTRIBUNE.COM • $1.50

Sunday
MORE THAN $143 WORTH OF COUPONS INSIDE

NCAA'S FINAL TWO: ILLINOIS AND NORTH CAROLINA SPORTS, C1

PLAY BALL!
A 99-loss season left the Mariners in need of a makeover. This year's blueprint calls for lots of changes.

SPECIAL 20-PAGE SECTION INSIDE

POPE JOHN PAUL II
1920-2005

THE LIFE AND LEGACY OF POPE JOHN PAUL II

SPECIAL EIGHT-PAGE SECTION INSIDE

---

10 PAGES OF SPECIAL COVERAGE INSIDE

AT REST AT LAST

John Paul II's death ends years of pain and sickness, third-longest papacy

The Associated Press file

Pope John Paul II, shown in 1983, led the Roman Catholic Church for 26 years. The first non-Italian pope in 455 years, he won an outpouring of global affection with his world travels.

SOUTH SOUND PARISHES

Local Catholics mourn his death but honor his life

With pain and sadness, the area's faithful turn to their churches to grieve over the death of their spiritual leader, Pope John Paul II.

News Tribune staff

Henry Wroblewski knelt Saturday night in the back pew at Tacoma's Polish Catholic parish, clutched a rosary and grieved over the death of Pope John Paul II.

He's glad the pope's pain is over. But for Wroblewski and others at Sts. Peter & Paul Catholic Church who revere the Polish pope as their spiritual father and a national hero, the pain of mourning is just beginning.

Wroblewski recalled how the pope – then archbishop of Krakow – confirmed him as a teenager in Poland in 1972, putting his hand on Wroblewski's head. On Saturday, Wroblewski called the pope "my bishop" and credited him with destroying communism in Poland.

"We lost somebody who is very important for us," said the 46-year-old Wroblewski, a

Please see LOCAL, back page

RUSS CARMACK/The News Tribune

Henry Wroblewski remembers how Pope John Paul II – then the archbishop of Krakow, Poland – put his hand on Wroblewski's head during his confirmation in 1972. "We lost somebody who is very important to us," Wroblewski said.

POPE JOHN
PAUL II
1920-2005

INSIDE

'VIVA IL PAPA!': Italians, the world mourn popular pope. **A10**

DECISION TIME: Who could be the next pope, and how he will be chosen. **A11**

POPE OF THE PEOPLE: Warm personality earned John Paul enormous appeal. **A16**

AMONG HIS PUBLIC: The pope's tenure in photos. **A19**

BELOVED FATHER: Northwest youth charmed by charismatic leader. **A20**

WORLD TRAVELER: Pope made 104 trips to 120 countries around the globe. **A21**

UNDERSTANDING THE PAPACY: Poster of papal history and traditions. **A22**

■ Share your thoughts about the pope's life and legacy on our Web site, www.thenewstribune.com.

84-year-old pope finally succumbs

BY RICHARD BOUDREAUX
Los Angeles Times

VATICAN CITY – Pope John Paul II died Saturday night, ending a long, painfully public struggle against debilitating ailments and a globetrotting reign that made him one of the towering figures of his time. He was 84.

The Polish prelate who led the Roman Catholic Church for 26 years succumbed in his apartment in the Vatican's Apostolic Palace at 9:37 p.m., papal spokesman Joaquin Navarro-Valls announced.

Weakened for more than a decade by Parkinson's disease, the pope was overcome by fever, infections and heart and kidney failure last week after two hospitalizations in as many months. He slipped in and out of consciousness Saturday, surrounded by the only family he had – five Polish priests and bishops and four Polish nuns who had looked after him for years.

The Vatican gave no precise cause of death.

"Our holy father John Paul has returned to the house of the father," Archbishop Leonardo Sandri, the Vatican undersecretary of state, told 60,000 people standing vigil in St. Peter's Square below the pope's still-lighted third-floor apartment windows.

The crowd fell into stunned and tearful silence, then into applause – an Italian sign of respect.

"We all feel like orphans this evening," Sandri said.

Bells tolled in mourning across Rome, and condo-

Please see POPE, back page

THE SUNDAY
JOURNAL SENTINEL

FINAL EDITION ★ SUNDAY, APRIL 3, 2005 ★ WWW.JSONLINE.COM

POPE JOHN PAUL II 1920-2005

At peace

For quarter-century, pontiff traveled the world with message of human dignity and freedom

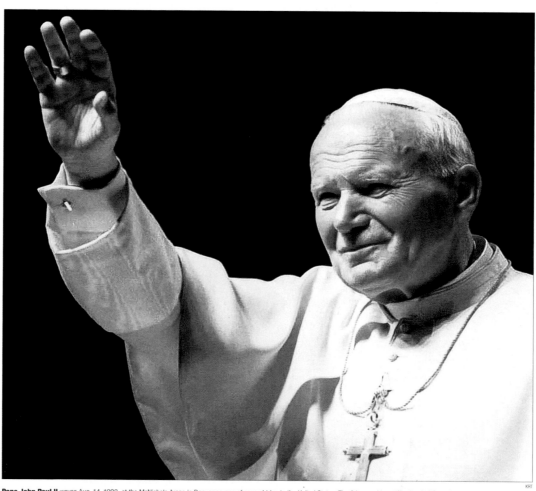

Pope John Paul II waves Aug. 14, 1993, at the McNichols Arena in Denver on one of several trips to the United States. The 84-year-old pontiff, who died Saturday, made 104 trips abroad, stopping in more than 120 countries in 26 years.

By TOM HEINEN
theinen@journalsentinel.com

Ranging far beyond the paths trod by St. Peter the Apostle in spreading the early church, Pope John Paul II flew the equivalent of 30 times around the world in a papacy that was unprecedented in outreach, prolific in teaching and exceptional in endurance.

His story is one of epic proportions, a saga intertwined with the Second Vatican Council's new stance toward the modern world, the Roman Catholic Church's subsequent upheavals, and the collapse of European communism.

That he has left remarkable footprints in history is unquestionable. Just how deep the imprints are, what they mean, and where they will lead his successors in the 21st century are the questions of the hour,

and of years to come.

John Paul, who led the church since his election in 1978, died at 9:37 p.m. Saturday (1:37 p.m. CST) in his Vatican apartment after a long, public struggle against debilitating illness.

"We all feel like orphans this evening," Undersecretary of State Archbishop Leonardo Sandri told a crowd of 70,000 that had gathered Saturday in St. Peter's Square below the pope's still-lighted apartment windows.

A number of historians, political scientists and biographers say the pope played a pivotal role in the breakup of the former Soviet Union. Born Karol Wojtyła on May 18, 1920, at Wadowice, Poland, he stood up to communist leaders during his years as archbishop of Krakow. His deep love of his homeland and his faith-inspired emphasis on human dignity fueled a spirit of resistance in Poland that set an example for the rest of Eastern Europe.

John Paul and President Ronald Reagan — who admired and respected each other — reportedly coordinated efforts to topple communism in Poland in correspondence that is still classified.

His impact on the worldwide church also has been profound.

A host of statistics underlie the legacy he leaves behind: First non-Italian pope since 1523; first pope from Poland, or any Slavic country; third-longest serving pope; Second Vatican Council participant and shepherd of its aftereffects; unprecedented advocate of ecumenical and interfaith dialogue and reconciliation; first pope to enter a Jewish synagogue; first pope to enter a mosque; most widely traveled pope; giver of more than 3,000 speeches; seen by more than 17 million pilgrims at weekly general audiences; pope who far surpassed previous records by beatifying more than 1,300

Please see POPE, 8A

COVERAGE ON PAGES 8A-27A, AND 8B

■ **Wisconsin ties:** Lee S. Dreyfus credits future pope's visit to Stevens Point in 1976 with helping him win governorship. **11A**

■ **Local reaction:** At area churches, loss mourned. **12A**

■ **Elsewhere:** Thousands gather in prayer at St. Peter's Square; President Bush, other leaders offer praise for pontiff. **13A**

■ **Images:** The pope's life in photographs. **18A**

■ **What comes next:** Cardinals will meet in secrecy to choose a new leader. **19A**

SUNDAY

Wisconsin State Journal

APRIL 3, 2005   MADISON, WISCONSIN   WWW.MADISON.COM

POPE JOHN PAUL II 1920-2005

LONG REIGN ENDS

John Paul II dies after his 26 history-making years as pope

Candles illuminate a picture of Pope John Paul II in St. Peter Square in the Vatican after the death of the pope was announced.

Alessandra Tarantino – Associated Press

The young reflect on the only pope they've ever known

By Ed Treleven
Wisconsin State Journal

Barely a half-hour after news that Pope John Paul II had died, the sanctuary of St Paul's University Catholic Center was quiet as the faithful prayed.

Candles glowed on the altar and throughout the sanctuary, mostly young people sat alone or huddled in small groups, heads bowed, hands folded. The silence was broken only by the faint sound of bongo drums from the State Street Mall outside.

The church, near the UW-Madison campus, was host Saturday to workshops for young Evangelical Catholics — the age group that many say Pope John Paul II reached very effectively during his 26-year reign. But it also served as a place where young Catholics could be together to reflect on the only pope that many of them had ever known.

"He was just a world leader, not just for Catholics but for all people," said Sarah Keyes, 20, a UW-Madison sophomore who attended the Evangelic Catholic Institute on Saturday. "He reached lots of nations, lots of religions. In his death we can celebrate his life, too."

"I was sad because he is the only pope I've

Please see YOUNG, Page A6

John Maniaci – State Journal

UW-Madison students, from left, Victoria Stiegel, Steph Place, Sarah Keyes and Maria Walker huddle together and sit with Matt Faltynski in front of a shrine to Pope John Paul II at St. Paul's University Catholic Center, 723 State St. The students were at St. Paul's to attend workshops for young Evangelical Catholics on Saturday when they received word of the pope's death.

By Victor L. Simpson
Associated Press

VATICAN CITY — Pope John Paul II, who helped topple communism in Europe and left a deeply conservative stamp on the church that he led for 26 years, died Saturday night in his Vatican apartment, ending a long public struggle against debilitating illness. He was 84.

"We all feel like orphans this evening," Undersecretary of State Archbishop Leonardo Sandri told the crowd of 70,000 that gathered in St. Peter's Square below the pope's still-lighted apartment windows.

In the massive piazza that stretches from St. Peter's Basilica, the assembled flock fell into a stunned silence before some people broke into applause — an Italian tradition in which mourners often clap for important figures. Others wept. Still others recited the rosary. A seminarian slowly waved a large red and white Polish flag draped with black bunting for the Polish-born pontiff, the most-traveled pope in history.

At one point, prelates asked those in the square to stay silent so they might "accom-

Please see POPE, Page A6

STRONG LEADER	CONCLAVE	'GREAT COUNTRYMAN'	AT ST. PETER'S SQUARE
Rembrance of pope a boost to church's image	Cardinals will gather to choose next pope	Karol Wojtyla's native Poland mourns.	Thousands gather to show appreciation for pope.
Page A4	Page A5	Page A7	Page A10

Suffering Pope ... page 11

NATIONAL · CATHOLIC
REGISTER

From Sorrow, Love ... back page

VOLUME 81 NO. 15   SPECIAL EDITION, APRIL. 10-16, 2005 $1.95 USA / $2.95 CANADA

The Pope's Final 'Amen'

by **EDWARD PENTIN**
Register Correspondent

ROME — Pope John Paul II wanted to teach us how to die.

That's what Vatican Archbishop J. Michael Miller said, shortly before John Paul's death.

The Pope wanted to make his death a powerful teaching moment — and it was. Pope John Paul was said to have been "extraordinarily serene" in death.

The Holy Father is reported to have died looking toward the window as he prayed, raising his right hand shortly before his last breath, a gesture of blessing, as if he became aware of the crowd of faithful present in St. Peter's Square who in those moments were reciting the rosary.

Then, at 9:37 p.m., just after the prayer ended, the Pope made a huge effort and pronounced the word "Amen" and died.

It was the vigil of Divine Mercy Sunday, a feast the Pope himself had instituted. It was also a first Saturday — making it a day at once related to St. Faustina Kowalska of *continues on page 14*

A 'Prophet, Priest and King' for Our Time

by **FR. RAYMOND J. DE SOUZA**
Register Correspondent

When Pope John Paul II died on April 2 at age 84, he had spent more than half of his life as a bishop. Consecrated at 38, Karol Wojtyla was 20 years a bishop before his election as Pope on Oct. 16, 1978.

The year of his election, 1978, was known as the year of three popes (Paul VI, John Paul I and John Paul II). John Paul can be perhaps better understood as the man of three pontificates.

When Karol Wojtyla was solemnly installed as Pope on Oct. 22, 1978, he declined (like his immediate predecessor) to be crowned with the traditional triple tiara.

In his homily, the new Pope said the ancient crown was the wrong symbol, too easily mistaken for the political claims of a secular potentate. But he said that the triple tiara could perhaps be understood in a better way, as reflecting the *triplex munus* — the threefold mission or service — of Jesus Christ.

Christ was king, prophet and priest. So too, John Paul said, should every Christian be, according to his or her state in life. For the Pope, the *triplex munus* can also serve as a powerful interpretative key — the king who governs, the prophet who teaches, and the priest who sanctifies.

In the pages that follow, we'll look at the three "decades" of the Pope's long pontificate with these three emphases in mind.

Father Raymond J. de Souza is the Register's former Rome correspondent.

JOHN PAUL, PRAY FOR US

CNS PHOTO

POPE JOHN PAUL II
1920-2005
A Life That Changed the World

A REGISTER EDITORIAL

What God Did With This Man

It's easy, with a man like Pope John Paul II, to make a crucial mistake: to make him superhuman. The achievements in his life seem great and effortless, both at once.

Coming into the Church in the middle of a crisis of faith, he said "Open the doors to Christ," and many of us — eventually — did, as his prodding reached down to us, through the Church.

He wasn't the great condemner many wanted him to be. Instead, he searched for the distorted truth at that core of modern errors, and recovered it. He answered Marxism and Madison Avenue with the same message: "Work was made for man, not man for work." He answered the sexual revolution with a revolution in Catholic thought about the beauty and necessity of authentic sexual expression.

Just as the Church was being mocked as something that only the elderly bothered with anymore, he gathered the largest crowds in the history of the planet at his World Youth Day events — even as a frail old man.

It all seemed so perfect. He helped topple communist tyranny in the '80s. He presided over a flowering of Catholic doctrine in the 1990s with the publication of the Catechism and encyclicals whose very names sum up the key elements missing from the intellectual life of our times and our Church: *The Gospel of Life, The Splendor of Truth, Faith and Reason.*

Those who rejected his magisterium wanted to say the Church was adrift: With his Jubilee Year and plan for the new millennium, he stole their chance.

The truth is, his pontificate *was* perfect in a way — and it was more than Karol Wojtyla was capable of.

Yes, Karol Wojtyla was a talented man, but not *that* talented. As a playwright, he learned about the importance of drama and the power of arresting insights — but he wasn't a great playwright. As a poet, he learned to reflect the beauty of God's creation in words — but he wasn't a great poet. As a writer, he was philosophically rich and theologically deep in a way that will change the course of the Church — but he was a dense writer who is difficult to read.

The sum total of the talents of this Pole from Wadowice couldn't possibly be credited with all that Pope John Paul II did, any more than the fisherman Peter's management expertise can be credited with the Church's success during its rocky beginnings.

Above all, God deserves our praise and our gratitude for Pope *continues on page 10*

Inperson   Moments — Private and Public — With the Pope

REGISTER
WWW.NCREGISTER.COM

George Weigel was given unprecedented access to Pope John Paul II while he prepared his biography.

But after 1999's *Witness to Hope* was on the bookshelves, he found that the Pope had moved him in a far deeper way than merely as the subject of research for a book. He spoke with Father Raymond J. de Souza for the Register.

You have spent many years of your professional life reporting on and writing about Pope John Paul II. What has his impact been on you?

The impact has been enormous, and on many levels.

Intellectually, the Pope offered me a way of thinking about being Catholic in the modern world that was both faithful to the great tradition and fully alert to the possibilities to be teased out of contemporary thought. Spiritually, the Pope was a shining example of a life lived according to the Gospel without compromise. Professionally, of course, the Pope changed my life by agreeing to cooperate with my rather brash proposal that I write his biography.

I'll certainly be thinking about John Paul II for the rest of my life, and not only because I intend to finish *Witness to Hope*, bringing the story to a close. I'll be thinking about John Paul because he has been one of the decisive influences in my life.

During the course of your work, you had many private encounters with John Paul II. Is there a memory that stands out as particularly revealing of the man?

Everybody asks this and, of course, there isn't a simple or single answer.

But one encounter I'll never forget took place in early January 2000. Some 150 graduates of the seminary in which I've taught in Poland since 1994 came to Rome for a reunion and to see the Jubilee Year in together. I had asked Bishop Stanislaw Dziwisz, the Pope's secretary, if the Holy Father would receive the group briefly.

I swore that it would only take 10 minutes.

"They'll sing the Holy Father a Christmas carol, he can greet the group and give them his blessing, and that'll be that." To which Bishop Dziwisz agreed. So we had everybody gathered in the Sala Clementina, the Pope came in, we sang a Polish Christmas carol — and then the Pope insisted on greeting every single person in the group, one by one, giving each person his blessing and a rosary. It lasted almost 45 minutes, perhaps more.

I couldn't look at Bishop Dziwisz, but when Dziwisz saw how much the Pope was enjoying himself with the students, he invited the seminary faculty to lunch the next day, so I assumed that all was forgiven.

Still, what does this tell us about the Pope? It reminds us that, for John Paul II, everybody was somebody for whom the Son of God had entered the world, suffered and died. This meant that everybody was a somebody, with infinite, indeed eternal, value.

Many great admirers have spoken of John Paul II as their hero. But often heroes seem less *continues on page 8*

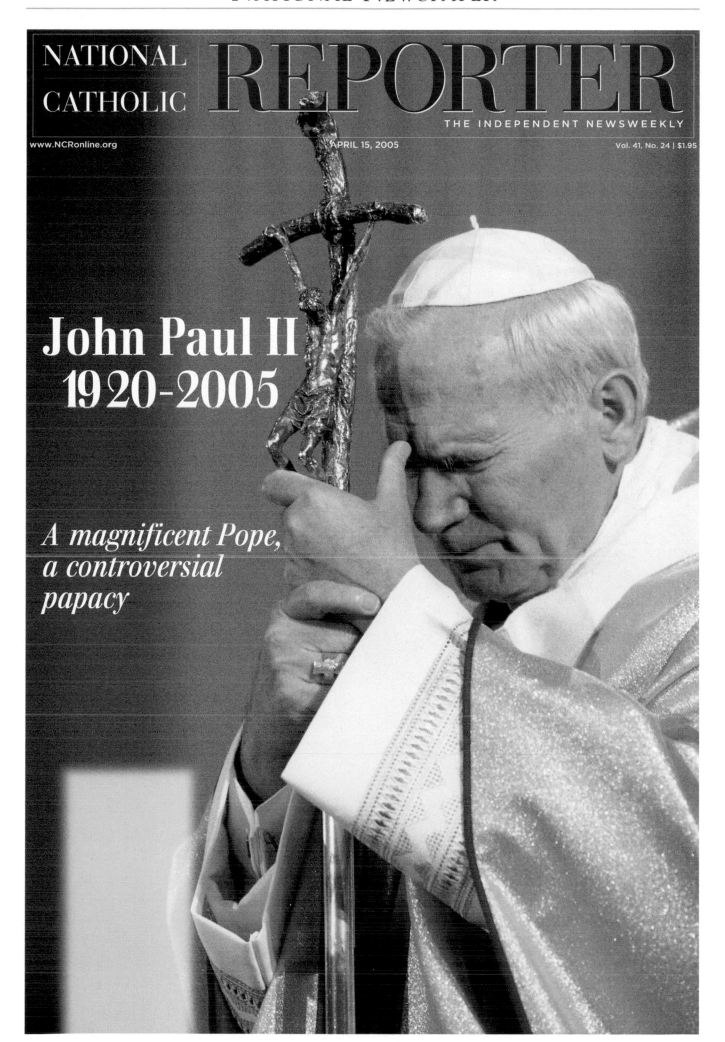

NATIONAL CATHOLIC **REPORTER**

THE INDEPENDENT NEWSWEEKLY

www.NCRonline.org

APRIL 15, 2005

Vol. 41, No. 24 | $1.95

John Paul II 1920-2005

A magnificent Pope, a controversial papacy

DELIVERED TO POST OFFICE ON SUNDAY, APRIL 3, 2005

nowydziennik

60c

ROK XXXV NEW YORK www.dziennik.com **POLISH DAILY NEWS**

Nr 9340 PONIEDZIAŁEK 4 KWIETNIA – MONDAY, APRIL 4, 2005

- **Jak Karol Wojtyła został biskupem**
  "Wezwanie" – fragment książki Jana Pawła II "Wstańcie, chodźmy!" – s. 14

- **26 lat Jana Pawła II**
  Fotoreportaż – s. 15

- **Jan Paweł Wielki**
  Wywiad z Andrzejem Nowakiem o dorobku intelektualnym Papieża – s. 16

Ojciec Święty spocznie w Watykanie

Jan Paweł II
1920-2005

Jan Paweł II spocznie w Watykanie, a jego pogrzeb odbędzie się w środę lub czwartek – poinformowała w niedzielę włoska telewizja publiczna RAI. Ojciec Święty zmarł w sobotę wieczorem czasu lokalnego w swoim apartamencie w Watykanie – otoczony polskimi przyjaciółmi.

"Nasz Ojciec Święty Jan Paweł II powrócił do domu Ojca" – tak o śmierci Papieża poinformował w sobotę wieczorem 60 tys. wiernych na placu św. Piotra arcybiskup Leonardo Sandri. W niedzielę, podczas mszy św. na placu przed watykańską bazyliką, 200 tys. wiernych oddało hołd Zmarłemu. Trumna z ciałem Jana Pawła II została wystawiona w sali Klementyńskiej, skąd będzie przeniesiona na widok publiczny do Bazyliki św. Piotra. Trumna pozostanie tam 3-4 dni. W pożegnaniu Papieża może wziąć udział 2-4 mln ludzi. Będzie to najbardziej masowe wydarzenie w historii Włoch. Wśród głów państw z całego świata swój przyjazd zapowiedział prezydent George Bush.

Jan Paweł II zmarł w sobotę, po dwóch dniach agonii, o godzinie 21:37 czasu lokalnego w swoim prywatnym apartamencie. Zgon nastąpił w wigilię bliskiego sercu Papieża święta Miłosierdzia Bożego. Przyczyną śmierci Ojca Świętego był szok septyczny i nieodwracalna zapaść sercowo-naczyniowa. W dokumencie podkreślono, że schorzeniem, które doprowadziło Papieża do śmierci, była też choroba Parkinsona. Jeden z lekarzy z zespołu opiekującego się Janem Pawłem II ujawnił, że zrobili oni wszystko, by Go uratować, ale nie stosowali tak zwanej uporczywej terapii.

Cały świat opłakuje "Papieża zwykłych ludzi". We Włoszech zarządzono od niedzieli trzydniową żałobę narodową. Polski rząd, na nadzwyczajnym posiedzeniu zwołanym w nocy z soboty na niedzielę, zdecydował o wprowadzeniu żałoby narodowej do dnia pogrzebu. "Ufamy, że Jan Paweł II powiększy grono świętych i już dziś modli się za nas u tronu Bożego" – napisał Episkopat Polski. Media w Polsce podały, powołując się na ks. infułata Janusza Bielańskiego, proboszcza parafii wawelskiej, że kardynał Franciszek Macharski zwróci się do Watykanu, by papieskie serce trafiło do wawelskiej katedry. "To byłaby najwspanialsza relikwia i najbardziej drogocenny skarb" – powiedział Bielański. Tymczasem na mszę celebrowaną w niedzielę po południu przez księdza prowincjała Krzysztofa Wieliczkę w katedrze św. Patryka na Manhattanie przyszło około 3 tys. Polaków.

zb, (r)

Więcej na str. 2–8

Foto: PAP/AP/Massimo Sambucetti

Ciało Papieża Jana Pawła II ułożono w niedzielę na katafalku w sali Klementyńskiej Pałacu Apostolskiego w Watykanie

THE CHRISTIAN SCIENCE MONITOR

'To injure no man, but to bless all mankind'

BOSTON · MONDAY
APRIL 4, 2005

VOL. 97, NO. 90   COPYRIGHT © 2005 THE CHRISTIAN SCIENCE PUBLISHING SOCIETY — All rights reserved

Currents *Fish aficionados get some extra help at the market today, as a new seafood labeling law kicks into effect.* **Page 11**

Work&Money *Why efforts to reform US bankruptcy laws are likely to hurt women more than men.* **Page 13**

www.csmonitor.com   **$1.00**

A statement from The Christian Science Board of Directors

PEACE AND THE POPE

As one of earth's tireless pilgrims, Pope John Paul II rightly will be remembered for going where the world's people live and worship – circling the globe in his travels; embracing a spiritually burgeoning Southern Hemisphere; and in heartfelt openness, reaching out to fellow Christians, Jews, Muslims, and many other faith families.

The Christian Science Monitor's founder, Mary Baker Eddy, could have been writing about John Paul II when she paid tribute to Pope Leo XIII in 1903: "The intellectual, moral, and religious energy of this illustrious pontiff have animated the Church of Rome for one quarter of a century.... I sympathize with those who mourn, but rejoice in knowing our dear God comforts such with the blessed assurance that life is not lost; its influence remains in the minds of men, and divine Love holds its substance safe in the certainty of immortality" (The First Church of Christ, Scientist, and Miscellany, pp. 294-295).

John Paul once described heaven as "the fullness of communion with God," adding that it is "neither an abstraction nor a physical place in the clouds." In his, and each child of God's, inseparable connection with divine Love, heaven's peace can be tasted today.

A strong pope, a broad impact

■ In his 26-year reign, John Paul II proved a charismatic, sometimes divisive, church leader.

By JANE LAMPMAN
STAFF WRITER

A charismatic, yet controversial, leader who captured the attention and admiration of the world for more than a quarter century, Pope John Paul II died on Saturday, ending one of the longest papal reigns in history.

During his 26 years, he redefined the papacy as that of pastor and evangelist, extending the reach of the church with his savvy use of the media and indefatigable travels to more than 130 nations.

"No human being in history ... had ever spoken to so many people, in so many different cultural contexts," according to papal biographer George Weigel, who was close to the pope.

While deeply disappointed by the decline of Catholicism in Europe, John Paul II presided over rapid growth of the church in Africa and Asia, which fueled a 40 percent increase worldwide, according to church statistics.

Yet while widely respected for his courage and personal holiness, John Paul II was often a controversial figure globally for his conservative stance on issues such as contraception. He stirred dissent within the church as well, presiding over a growing polarization

See **LEGACY** *page 10*

GUILLERMO ARIAS/AP

THIERRY GOUIGNON/REUTERS

INTERNATIONAL RESPONSE: Above, Mexicans in Guadalajara City lit candles to mark the passing of Pope John Paul II on Saturday. The pope visited more than 130 nations. Left, an Ivorian man prays at a church in Abidjan.

World pays tribute
From Manila to Mexico City, people reflect on a pope who traveled more than any other in history. **See page 7.**

Private volunteers patrol a porous border

ROBERT HARBISON

IN ARIZONA: Phillip Orth says the Border Patrol needs more support.

■ In April, a slice of Arizona will be monitored by 1,500 'minutemen.'

By DANIEL B. WOOD
STAFF WRITER

TOMBSTONE, ARIZ. – With lawn chairs, two-way radios, and binoculars, they've come to save the Union. All volunteers, age four to 86, they've descended here from all 50 states via RV, motorcycle, sidecar, and sport coupe.

Across a remote corner of the American Southwest – a honeycombed terrain that helped Apache leader Geronimo elude the US government for years – they are providing eyes, ears, and vacation time to another cause they feel has

long eluded the same government: effective immigration law enforcement.

Some 1,500 self-selected volunteers will begin fanning out to designated outposts along the Arizona border today in a highly visible – and controversial – bid to help reclaim part of the US-Mexican border. If successful, similar projects are planned in neighboring states in coming months.

"We are lighting the fuse to a grass-roots grass fire using the Constitution, the First Amendment, and Martin Luther King's philosophy to pursue our objective in a peaceful, rational way," says James Gilchrist, a former marine and cofounder of the so-called Minuteman Project. "This is just the beginning."

See **BORDER** *page 4*

95

CLAVES DE SU VIDA

1920
►Hijo de un militar, nace en una pequeña ciudad de Cracovia.

1978
►Lo eligen Papa después del breve pontificado de 33 días de Juan Pablo I.

1979
►Su primer viaje a Polonia conmueve al mundo comunista.

1981
►Lo balea un terrorista turco en el Vaticano. Se recuperó y fue a la prisión a perdonarlo.

2004
►Su último viaje fue a Lourdes en agosto. Llegó a sumar 104 visitas por todo el mundo.

ClarínX

UN TOQUE DE ATENCION PARA LA SOLUCION ARGENTINA DE LOS PROBLEMAS ARGENTINOS

Buenos Aires
República Argentina
Año LX Nº 21.278

Domingo 3
Abril de 2005

Precio en Capital Federal y GBA: $ 3,20
• Recargo envío al interior: $ 0,30.
• Uruguay: $ 45 • Brasil: R$ 10,00.
• Paraguay: G$ 11.000.
Precios de opcionales, en el índice de la página 2

MASSIMO SAMBUCETTI / AP

LA MUERTE DE JUAN PABLO II

Adiós al peregrino

SUPLEMENTO ESPECIAL
El viajero de la fe
16 PAGINAS

►**Karol Wojtyla fue el primer Papa no italiano que tuvo la Iglesia en 455 años.** Su pontificado de 26 años reconoce varias claves: la lucha contra el comunismo, que terminó en la caída del Muro; el atentado que casi le cuesta la vida; su crítica al capitalismo salvaje y su férreo apego a la ortodoxia tradicional. Pero también fue un peregrino: viajó más que todos sus antecesores juntos, el equivalente a dar la vuelta al mundo 30 veces. **P.18**

FRASE DEL DIA: JUAN PABLO II, EN ARGENTINA, SOBRE EL CONFLICTO DE MALVINAS: "HAGAN CON SUS MANOS UNA CADENA MAS FUERTE QUE LAS CADENAS DE LA GUERRA". SUP. ESP.

LA NUEVA PROVINCIA

BAHÍA BLANCA, DOMINGO 3 DE ABRIL DE 2005 · WWW.LANUEVA.COM · AÑO CVII - NÚMERO 36.869

JUAN PABLO II
EMPRENDIÓ EL ÚLTIMO VIAJE

El Papa Juan Pablo II, quien gobernó la Iglesia Católica durante 26 años, murió ayer a los 84 años de edad y en sus aposentos, tal como lo había decidido él mismo al pedir no ser internado en una clínica. El "Papa viajero" sucumbió tras un brusco deterioro de su salud, que duró 54 horas.

"El Santo Padre murió esta noche a las 21.37 en su apartamento privado. Se pusieron en práctica los procedimientos previstos en la Constitución apostólica, promulgada por Juan Pablo II el 22 de febrero de 1996", fue la escueta comunicación brindada por el portavoz vaticano Joaquín Navarro-Valls para la noticia más temida en los últimos días por toda la humanidad.

Mientras los líderes mundiales hicieron llegar sus condolencias al Vaticano, destacando por sobre todo la personalidad y la amplitud del líder católico fallecido, los fieles lo lloran en cada rincón del planeta.

EL MUNDO LLORA AL PAPA

En la Casa del Padre

El deceso físico del Santísimo Padre Juan Pablo II nos deja naturalmente sensibilizados desde el punto de vista humano, pero la muerte de un bienaventurado siempre, para los fieles de la Iglesia Católica Apostólica Romana, no es una partida definitiva sino la llegada a la Casa del Padre en el Paraíso.

Bien lo escribió San Pablo Apóstol en su Epístola a los Romanos, capítulo 6-5, cuando postula durante su ministerio por el mundo latino y pagano: "Si nos unimos a Cristo, también estaremos en su resurrección". La llamada a la fidelidad y a la conversión resulta más que obvia: es el camino de los llamados al Cielo.

Juan Pablo II fue un héroe del amor de caridad y un visionario acerca del futuro que correspondería a quienes lo sobrevivimos merced a la gracia de Dios, a las familias piadosas, a los gobernantes decentes, a los trabajadores leales en sus labores. No es un programa meramente práctico, es una responsabilidad.

Ahora nos incumbe rezar para que el Espíritu Santo fortalezca a la Iglesia, para qué se sostenga y genere más bienaventurados, como en vida lo fue Karol Wojtyla, sucesor de San Pedro Apóstol.

MÁS INFORMACIÓN EN LAS PÁGINAS 2, 3, 4, 5 Y 6

Pronóstico
Máxima **21/23°** · MAÑANA Frío y soleado
Mínima **5/7°** · TARDE Templado y soleado

Juan Pablo II entre nosotros. Suplemento especial para recordar un momento único para la ciudad y la región.
RECLAME GRATIS

Edición
Ejemplar de 64 páginas
Suplemento Juan Pablo II
Revista "Nueva"
Insert Hipertehuelche
PRECIO: $ 2.80. Recargo aéreo y/o terrestre: $ 0,10

FACES OF NAVY CHOPPER DISASTER REPORTS Pages 1, 4 and 5, News Section 2

The Sydney Morning Herald

Monday April 4, 2005 — TRIBUTE EDITION — First published 1831 No. 57, 256 $1.20 (inc GST)

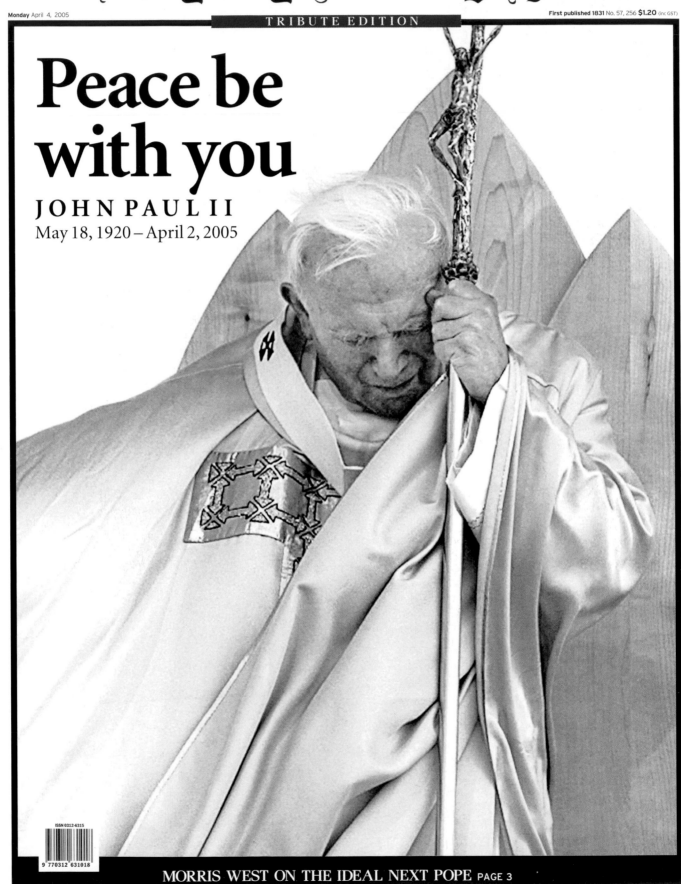

Peace be with you

JOHN PAUL II
May 18, 1920 – April 2, 2005

ISSN 0312-6315
9 770312 631018

MORRIS WEST ON THE IDEAL NEXT POPE PAGE 3

UNABHÄNGIGE TAGESZEITUNG FÜR ÖSTERREICH | GEGRÜNDET 1848

Montag, 4. 4. 2005 | www.diepresse.com | Mo 14 / Nr. 17.142 / 1,20 Euro***

Die Presse

15 Seiten Sonderberichte, Kommentare, Analysen

| Die besten Aktien der vergangenen Woche | ATX ▲ betandwin + 13,88 % | Dow Jones ▼ Hewlett Packard + 9,70 % | Eurostoxx 50 ▲ Sanpaolo .+ 7,17 % | DAX ▲ Continental + 9,35 % | FT-SE 100 ▼ Prudential + 6,81 % | Der neue CLUB SUXESS macht Preise attraktiver. http://clubsuxess.ba-ca.com. |

 Die Karriere
Vom Krakauer Theologen zum Papst.

 Polen ohne Vater
Der „Presse"-Korrespondent berichtet aus Warschau.

TV-Liebling, Popstar
Sein Geheimnis: Zuneigung für die Jugend der Welt.

Johannes Paul II. 1978 – 2005
Karol Józef Wojtyla 1920 – 2005

„Ich bin heiter – seid ihr es auch!"

▶ **WELTWEITE TRAUER.** *Johannes Paul II. im Petersdom aufgebahrt. Kardinäle aus allen fünf Kontinenten nach Rom gerufen. Wahl des neuen Papstes frühestens in zwei Wochen.*

Giovanni Paolo, Giovanni Paolo!" Der Ruf nach dem verstorbenen Heiligen Vater wollte am Sonntag nicht verstummen. 130.000 Menschen versammelten sich auf dem Petersplatz, um sich von ihrem Papst zu verabschieden. Sie weinten. Sie beteten. Und sie riefen immer wieder seinen Namen.

„Ich bin heiter, seid ihr es auch", soll eine der letzten Botschaften des Papstes gewesen sein. Sich an diese Aufforderung zu halten, fiel den Gläubigen am Sonntag schwer.

Papst Johannes Paul II. war am Vorabend um 21.37 Uhr von seinen Leiden erlöst worden. „Septischer Schock" (Blutvergiftung) steht auf seinem Totenschein zu lesen.

Wie eine Schockwelle breitete sich auch die Nachricht vom Tod des 84-Jährigen rund um den Erdball aus. Auf allen fünf Kontinenten strömten Millionen Gläubige in die Kirchen, um dem Pontifex die Ehre zu erweisen. Spitzenpolitiker aller Konfessionen und Ideologien zollten ihm Respekt. Ob Katholiken, Protestanten oder Orthodoxe, ob Moslems, Juden oder Atheisten – alle würdigten den Heiligen Vater. Als Friedensapostel die einen, als Bezwinger des Kommunismus die anderen.

Im Vatikan begann das minuziöse Procedere abzulaufen, das für den Fall des Ablebens des Papstes exakt vorgegeben ist. Joseph Ratzinger, der Leiter der Glaubenskongregation, berief die Kardinäle aus allen Teilen der Welt nach Rom. 117 von ihnen sollen einen neuen Papst wählen. Doch frühestens erst in 14 Tagen. Die Zeit davor ist der Trauer gewidmet. Bis Donnerstag vermutlich ist Johannes Paul II. im Vatikan aufgebahrt. Dann soll er in der Krypta des Petersdoms beigesetzt werden. Sein Herz aber, so berichtet die „Gazeta Wyborcza", wird möglicherweise in seiner polnischen Heimat bestattet.

[Fotos: ap (3), epa]

PREISE: Deutschland, Italien € 2.-, Belgien € 2,80; SIT 460, HRK 14, KČ 60, SK 80, Ft 390. „DIE PRESSE", 1015 Wien, Parkring 12a; PF 6. ℗ 514 14. Fax: DW 400 (Redaktion); DW 250 (Anzeigen). ABO: ℗ 514 14 DW 70, Fax: DW 71. Verlagspostamt: 1010 Wien, P.b.b. Zulassungsnummer: 022032748T

O GLOBO

80 anos

IRINEU MARINHO (1876-1925)   RIO DE JANEIRO, DOMINGO, 3 DE ABRIL DE 2005 • ANO LXXX • Nº 26.172 • www.oglobo.com.br   ROBERTO MARINHO (1904-2003)

Efe/7-6-1997

NESTA EDIÇÃO, CADERNO ESPECIAL

Adeus, João de Deus

A lenta e comovente agonia do Papa João Paulo II, de 84 anos, chegou ao fim às 21h37m de ontem (16h37m em Brasília), encerrando 26 anos de pontificado, o terceiro mais longo da História. As últimas palavras do Papa peregrino, que visitou três vezes o Brasil, foram dirigidas aos jovens: "Eu busquei vocês. Agora vocês vêm a mim. Eu agradeço", relatam DEBORAH BERLINCK e GINA DE AZEVEDO MARQUES, do Vaticano. Na Praça de São Pedro, 60 mil fiéis reagiram com um longo aplauso, um sinal de respeito na Itália, seguido de silêncio e choro. O sepultamento deve ocorrer quarta-feira.

COMO SERÁ ESCOLHIDO O NOVO PAPA

Editoria de Arte

1 Após a morte

O Camerlengo (cardeal que governa interinamente a Igreja até que o Papa seja escolhido) anuncia a morte, sela os apartamentos papais e prepara o enterro.

2 Preparativos

Cardeais de todo o mundo viajam ao Vaticano para eleger o novo pontífice num processo que se inicia de 15 a 20 dias após a morte do Papa. Durante o conclave eles ficarão totalmente isolados.

3 O processo

Cada cardeal dá seu voto secreto por escrito na Capela Sistina. Depois da contagem, os votos são queimados com substâncias químicas para produzir as fumaças preta (quando não há vencedor) ou branca (quando o papa é escolhido).

4 O resultado

A votação continua até que um candidato receba mais de dois terços dos votos. Se não houver vencedor depois de 30 votações, o novo Papa é eleito por maioria simples.

5 O novo Papa

Depois que o vencedor aceita sua escolha, um cardeal declara "Habemus Papam!" (Temos papa!) da sacada do Vaticano.

CHICO

— Podem deixar que daqui pra frente eu dirijo...

Dois policiais militares suspeitos da chacina na Baixada são detidos

● Dois policiais militares do 24º BPM (Queimados) foram detidos sob suspeita de terem participado da chacina na Baixada. Os dois foram apontados como autores da matança de 30 pessoas na noite de quinta-feira em informações passadas ao Disque-Denúncia, que já recebeu 172 ligações sobre o caso. Segundo promotores, há outros sete policiais sendo investigados. ● Em Niterói, Marcelo de Oliveira Carvalho, de 22 anos, foi morto a tiros na madrugada de ontem durante uma festa na Faculdade de Direito da UFF. **Páginas 19 a 23**

zh.clicrbs.com.br

ZERO HORA

ANO 41 - Nº 14.466 · PORTO ALEGRE, **DOMINGO**, *3 DE ABRIL DE 2005* · R$ 1,00

EDIÇÃO EXTRA

VINCENZO PINTO, REUTERS/ZH – 18/08/2002

Morre João Paulo II

O homem que comandou a Igreja Católica por 26 anos, cinco meses e 17 dias morreu às 16h37min deste sábado (horário de Brasília), encerrando uma dramática luta pela vida e deixando lições que mudaram o mundo

■ **As últimas horas de João Paulo II e a comoção no mundo**

■ **Como Karol Wojtyla mudou a história da Igreja e do planeta**

■ **A histórica visita a Porto Alegre que fez o Papa virar gaúcho**

32 PAGES OF COVERAGE, INCLUDING A SPECIAL TRIBUTE SECTION

OTTAWA CITIZEN

SUNDAY, APRIL 3, 2005 · ESTABLISHED IN 1845 · 93 CENTS + GST

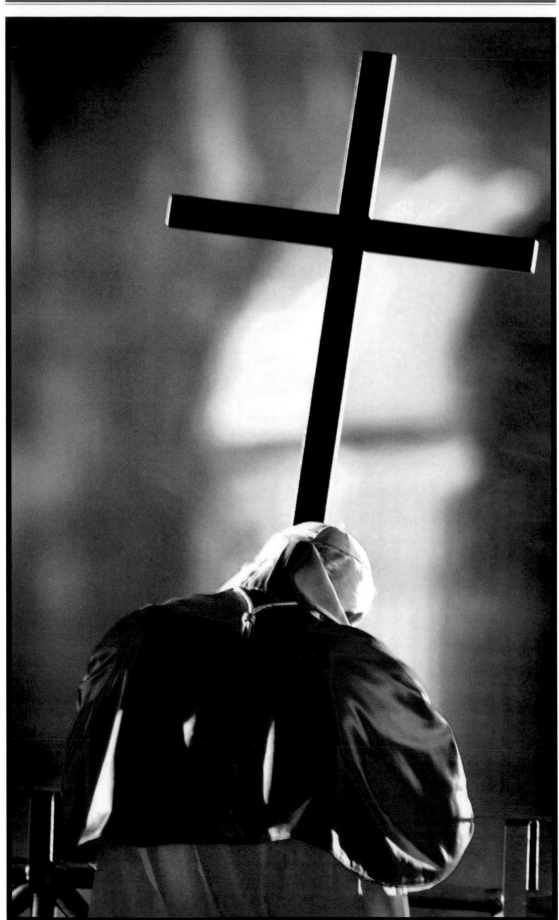

ONTARIO EDITION · TORONTO WEATHER: SUNNY WITH CLOUDY PERIODS, HIGH 10. MAP AND DETAILS, S10

BIG OIL'S BIG DIG: Patrick Brethour reports on Alberta's $87-billion project.   **B1**

THE GLOBE AND MAIL

CANADA'S NATIONAL NEWSPAPER ■ FOUNDED 1844 ■ GLOBEANDMAIL.COM ■ MONDAY, APRIL 4, 2005

A long farewell for John Paul

The remains of Pope John Paul II lie in the Clementine Hall of the Vatican yesterday. Cardinals will meet today in the Vatican to discuss funeral arrangements for the 84-year-old pontiff.

ENRICO OLIVERIO/ASSOCIATED PRESS

IIII **CHOOSING A SUCCESSOR**

117 cardinals gather in Rome for a conclave unlike any other

BY MICHAEL VALPY

It will be a pope vote like no other in history, and the politicking isn't going to wait until the Roman Catholic Church's 117 cardinal electors get frisked for cellphones and Palm Pilots and locked up in the Vatican's Sistine Chapel in a fortnight's time.

As Pope John Paul lay in state at the Vatican's Apostolic Palace last night, the princes of the church from 53 countries began to gather in Rome. They may not all know each other well through face-to-face encounters, but they are the most me-

IIII **ST. PETER'S SQUARE**

Doug Saunders reports from Vatican City on preparations for what will likely be the biggest funeral in history. **A6**

dia-savvy group of cardinals ever assembled to elect a pope.

They will have been bombarded by the same books, magazine articles and television reports as the

public about the church's global problems and the sort of man it needs sitting on St. Peter's Throne next. They will be familiar with the biographies and track records of the leading *papabile* — those considered pope material (by the news media, at least).

They'll have the better part of two weeks to sound each other out, immerse themselves in what the pundits are saying and even chat up the *papabile* before they enter the chapel conclave to begin voting: two ballots in the morning, two ballots in the afternoon until a candidate wins

two-thirds-majority support.

Only three of 117 cardinals — those who are under the age of 80 — have participated in a conclave.

There is no obvious front-runner.

For the first time in more than 800 years, the cardinals will have comfortable living quarters with en suite bathrooms in the newly built Domus Sanctae Marthae, rather than iron cots, chamber pots and the thin dividers that would separate a snoring eminence from a flatulent one in the Apostolic Palace.

See CONCLAVE on page A4

IIII **IN JOHN PAUL'S HOMELAND**

Poland mourns its greatest son

ALAN FREEMAN

KRAKOW, POLAND

As they had done so many times before, they came in their thousands to the square facing Krakow's Bishop's Palace to wait for him to appear at the second-floor window and talk to

them. Only this time, they knew that Pope John Paul II would never come.

Poland was a country bereft this weekend, and in Krakow, as elsewhere, regular life came to a virtual standstill. Shops, cinemas and theatres closed to honour John Paul's passing. LOT Polish Airlines suspended films on its flights as a sign of respect.

Poles gathered by the thousand to chant hymns and ponder their collective loss in this picturesque city along the Vistula River, where Karol Wojtyla attended seminary, was ordained and became a cardinal.

See POLAND on page A7

Ontario discriminates against parents, students with autism, judge rules

BY KIRK MAKIN, JUSTICE REPORTER

Ontario has violated the constitutional rights and "human dignity" of autistic schoolchildren by denying them treatment they desperately need in order to cope and thrive, an Ontario Superior Court judge has ruled.

Madam Justice Frances Kiteley found discrimination based on age and disability, bringing a dramatic end to a lawsuit launched by 29 groups of parents whose autistic children were denied autism treatment in the education system at the age of 6.

"I find that the age cutoff reflects

and reinforces the stereotype that children with autism over age 6 are virtually unredeemable," Judge Kiteley said. "To deny the plaintiff children the opportunity to have [treatment] after the age of 5 is to stereotype them, to prejudice them and to create a disadvantage for them."

She awarded the litigants damages that will run into the millions of dollars for past and future treatment. She also refused the province's request for a grace period in which to repair its delivery of autism programs, saying it has had ample time to fix the problem.

See RULING on page A9

Countdown to V-E Day

The Globe and Mail
YANKS 140 MILES FROM BERLIN

On April 4, 1945, The Globe reported another sign the war was drawing to a close: the BBC had broadcast its first weather forecast since 1939. Casualties listed by the Canadian armed services:
Dead 29, Wounded 118

Story on page A3

For the full front pages, please visit
globeandmail.com/national

SOURCE: THE NATIONAL ARCHIVE

Testimony at Gomery published on blogs

Brault's evidence leads to speculation of more criminal charges, snap election

BY JANE TABER
SENIOR POLITICAL WRITER

The explosive testimony given out of the public eye last week at the Gomery commission began appearing on websites yesterday, capping a weekend of frenzied rumours about snap elections and covert political meetings in Ottawa.

Conservative deputy leader Peter MacKay even suggested yesterday that the testimony, which is under a publication ban, could lead to criminal charges against senior Liberals.

"I have no doubt in my mind that more charges could be laid," Mr. MacKay said yesterday.

"If this thing breaks loose, the ripples on the water could be felt right up to the highest levels of this government, and then it begs the question, are they going to pull the pin themselves or orchestrate their own demise to avoid all of this coming out? This goes to the No. 1 issue, which I think is going to be the defining issue in the next election, that's ethics."

See GOMERY on page A8

K-os reigns at Junos

K-os, a soul-rap musician whose real name is Kheaven Brereton, took three Juno Awards last night, including single of the year, and tied with Avril Lavigne for the highest number received for 2004. **A9**

Full index, page A2

Births & Deaths, **S9**

$1
including tax
in metro
areas.
Price may
be higher
outside.

7 73552 00101 5

www.elmercurio.com

EL MERCURIO

EDICIÓN DE 184 PÁGINAS
REVISTAS 32 PÁGINAS

$600
I, II, XI Y XII REGIÓN $820

FUNDADO EN VALPARAÍSO EL 12 DE SEPTIEMBRE DE 1827 / AÑO CLXXVIII N° 61.092 / MCR · SANTIAGO DE CHILE, DOMINGO 3 DE ABRIL DE 2005 · FUNDADO EN SANTIAGO EL 1 DE JUNIO DE 1900 / AÑO CV N° 37.895 (ES PROPIEDAD)

Murió Juan Pablo II

VATICANO:
Un e-mail avisó su muerte a las 21:37 horas en Roma (15:37 de Chile).

A 4

NACIONAL:
Cardenal Errázuriz oficiará una misa hoy al mediodía en la Plaza de Armas.

C 5

IGLESIA:
J. Medina, Cardenal protodiácono: "Todo Papa debe ser conservador".

D 6

ESCRIBEN:
J. M. Ibáñez, F. Montes, C. Peña, A. Fermandois y H. Beyer.

C 6, D 14 y D 15

EN INTERNET
Su vida, su legado y los detalles del tercer pontificado más largo de la Iglesia Católica en http://especialpapa.emol.com

7 806616 000020

La Cuarta

EL DIARIO POPULAR

Santiago, domingo 3 de abril de 2005. Año XXI, Nº 6.811

www.lacuarta.cl

Calvario de Juan Pablo II estremeció al mundo

EL PAPA VIAJÓ AHORA AL CIELO

Iglesias de todos los credos rinden homenaje al campeón de la paz. Recorrió más de un millón de kilómetros en 26 años, llevando el bíblico mensaje de "Amaos los unos a los otros". Multitud lo despidió con ovación en la Plaza San Pedro.

PÁGINAS 2 A 12

Duelo nacional de tres días.

$250
Reg. I-II-XI y XII: $350

107

LA TERCERA

"El diario que quieres"

DOMINGO

Conéctese hoy a
www.latercera.cl

SUSCRIBASE A LA TERCERA Y OBTENGA IMPORTANTES BENEFICIOS: 550 7110

3 DE ABRIL DE 2005   FUNDADO EL 7 DE JULIO DE 1950, AÑO 55 N° 20.031

Juan Pablo II (1920-2005)

Muere el Papa que marcó la historia del fin de siglo

▶ A las 15.37 de ayer, y tras casi tres días de agonía, falleció Juan Pablo II. Más de 100 mil personas lo lloraron en la Plaza de San Pedro y millones en todo el mundo.

▶ En Chile, el Presidente Lagos expresó las condolencias y decretó tres días de duelo oficial.

▶ En 26 años de pontificado manejó con mano de hierro la Iglesia Católica, fue factor clave en el fin del comunismo e impuso una doctrina conservadora.

MUNDO ■ PAGINAS 2 A 23

REPORTAJES ■ PAGINAS 4 A 15

SUPLEMENTO ESPECIAL

40 PAGINAS

La vida, el pontificado y el legado de Karol Wojtyla

Santiago
HOY: Mínima **9** · Máxima **25**
MAÑANA: Mínima **11** · Máxima **26**
RESTRICCION VEHICULAR: **No rige**

Precio: **$ 500**
Regiones I-II-XI y XII: **$ 650**

7 806611 000063

108

EL COLOMBIANO

MEDELLÍN, **LUNES** 4 DE ABRIL DE 2005

$1.200

Año 94. Nº 31.446. 36 páginas en cuatro cuadernillos. Internet: www.elcolombiano.com Correo electrónico: elcolombiano@elcolombiano.com.co ISSN 0122-0802. Tarifa postal reducida Adpostal Nº 77. Vence Dic. 31 de 2006

Vitrina

Lo dicen los arcanos
Lea hoy las predicciones del Tarot del Caminante

El Tarot que cada semana les ofrece EL COLOMBIANO a sus lectores se publica hoy en la sección D. Una visión de la semana que comienza.

Tarot del Caminante 4D

Crédito de fomento
El BID prestaría un millón de dólares al Banco de la Mujer

Su directora, Margarita Correa, gestiona un crédito con el BID, por US$1 millón, para seguir apoyando la gestión de las microempresas.

Economía y Negocios 2B

Sufragio seguro
El voto electrónico se alista para llegar a Colombia

En el país ya existe el marco normativo para automatizar una elección popular. La tecnología podrá garantizar confianza para el ciudadano.

Informática 4B

Llegó para quedarse
Treinta policías se instalaron en San José de Apartadó

Treinta policías se instalaron ayer, a pesar de la posición en contra, en la comunidad de paz. Los niños fueron los menos prevenidos.

Paz y D.H. 6B

Fuentes de luz y vida
Alegran los parques de la ciudad con sus juegos

Área Metro 1D

El Editorial
Las batallas de Juan Pablo II

Este líder mundial se ganó un lugar en la historia. Durante su pontificado se armó de coraje y convicción para destronar los ideales del nazismo y el comunismo, contrarios a la dignidad y la libertad del hombre.

5A

Hoy / Mañana
Hoy: Lluvias aisladas. T. mín. 19 °C. T. máx. 26 °C.
Mañana: Lluvias aisladas. T. mín. 18 °C. T. máx. 27 °C.

7 704354 000039 $ 1200

Juan Pablo, el Grande

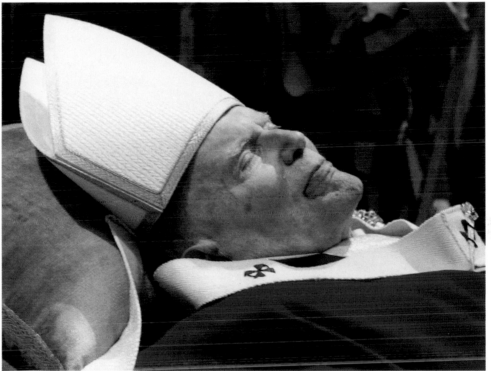

Reuters, Ciudad del Vaticano, El Vaticano

El cardenal Angelo Sodano calificó al Papa como "Juan Pablo el Grande", un título reservado a los pontífices dignos de la santidad y que le rinde homenaje al legado de Juan Pablo II.

● DESDE HOY, los fieles visitarán el cuerpo del Papa en la Basílica San Pedro.

● EL GOBIERNO de Colombia decretó dos días de duelo. Misas en su honor.

● UN REPASO a los Papas del siglo XX. Fueron nueve líderes en momentos clave.

● EL ATLETA de Dios fue deportista en su juventud y un viajero incansable.

● EL COLOMBIANO tendrá fascículo sobre su vida desde el miércoles 6.

Muere el hombre, nace un Santo 2A a 12A

Nuevos alcaldes para tres municipios

En calma transcurrió ayer la jornada electoral en los municipios de Cañasgordas, Hispania y San Vicente, en los que sus habitantes eligieron en las urnas a sus nuevos gobernantes, que irán hasta el año 2007.

Miriam Higuita en la primera, Nelsy Luz Bonilla en la segunda y Roberto Jaramillo en la tercera tomarán posesión de sus cargos en mayo al resultar vencedores.

Hechos Políticos 5B

Eln sigue con plagio: Antonio García

En respuesta al presidente Álvaro Uribe, que pide cesar los secuestros para reunirse en un país con ese grupo guerrillero, Antonio García, uno de los jefes del Coce, del Eln, anunció que ese grupo armado continuará con la práctica de secuestros, porque es su forma de financiación.

Paz y D.H. 6B

Verdes y naranjas dominan el torneo

Henry Agudelo

Con el triunfo 1-0 sobre Junior en el Atanasio Girardot, el DIM ascendió al sexto puesto en la Copa Mustang. Nacional es líder y Envigado, segundo.

Sólo Goles 1C, 2C y 3C

Marcadores

Medellín	1	Junior	0
Envigado	2	Santa Fe	1
Cali	3	Nacional	3
Bucaramanga	2	Caldas	1
Millonarios	1	Cartagena	1
Magdalena	0	Tolima	0
Huila	2	Quindío	0
Pereira	1	América	2
Chicó	3	Pasto	4

● Medellín venció al Junior; Envigado, a Santa Fe. Y Nacional sacó empate en Cali.
P. 1C, 2C y 3C

● Suramericano Sub-17: Colombia, que cayó con Chile, busca revancha con Uruguay.
P. 4C

● Renault continúa la fiesta con Alonso líder, en el campeonato mundial de F-1.
P. 5C

Fernando Alonso ganó en Bahrein y se mantuvo líder en la F-1.

Mejora el centro de menores infractores la Pola

Según autoridades, jueces, internos, familiares y educadores, las condiciones de los menores de edad recluidos en el Centro de Atención al Menor Infractor Carlos Lleras Restrepo, conocido como la Pola, mejoran de manera considerable.

Beatriz White, secretaria de Solidaridad de Medellín expresó que el nuevo contrato con Partenón, entidad que realiza el trabajo de reeducación, fijó unas exigencias concretas que se están cumpliendo.

Área Metro 2D

El TLC sí tiene ambiente en E.U.: embajador Moreno

El Tratado de Libre Comercio que se negocia con Estados Unidos deberá firmarse antes de julio próximo, estimó el embajador de Colombia en Washington, Luis Alberto Moreno Mejía. Destacó el ambiente político que reina en el Congreso americano para la firma del acuerdo, pero recordó que no todo está asegurado.

Economía y Negocios 1B

LA NACIÓN

San José,
Costa Rica
DOMINGO
3 de abril del 2005
¢400

www.nacion.com

HOY EN EL EDITORIAL
El gladiador de la fe
Juan Pablo II, de joven resistió el nazismo; como obispo se enfrentó con el comunismo, y como papa se entregó a la defensa de los derechos humanos. P.31

← **Deportes:** Yanquis y Medias Rojas abren la temporada 2005

DOMINGO
La mejor oferta para toda la familia
172 páginas

Proa
REVISTA
Stephen Hawking, algo más que una mente brillante

Áncora
SUPLEMENTO
El escritor danés Hans Christian Andersen: vocero de las hadas

Viva
SUPLEMENTO
La agrupación Cantares llega ya a 25 años de vida artística

Tema del domingo P. 4

Juan Pablo II emprendió su último peregrinaje

Consternación
El mundo llora su muerte; Gobierno tico decreta 4 días de duelo nacional

Arranca ritual
Sus restos estarán en capilla ardiente en la basílica de San Pedro mañana

Palabras finales
Papa evocó a los jóvenes y les agradeció su apoyo durante la agonía

Listín Diario

RD$15.00 | N° 31,540 | LUNES, 4 DE ABRIL DEL 2005 | AÑO CXVI | SANTO DOMINGO REPÚBLICA DOMINICANA | FUNDADO EL 1° DE AGOSTO DE 1889 | LISTINDIARIO.COM.DO

1920 - 2005

DESCANSE EN PAZ

AP

El cuerpo del Papa Juan Pablo II yace en capilla ardiente en el Palacio Apostólico del Vaticano.

Juan Pablo II recibe gran tributo mundial

CIUDAD DEL VATICANO (AP).- En descanso eterno después de años de enfermedades debilitantes, el cuerpo del Papa Juan Pablo II yacía ayer en la capilla ardiente en el Palacio Apostólico, mientras el mundo le tributaba un emotivo adiós.

Unas 100,000 personas se congregaron para asistir a una misa matutina y otros miles, entre feligreses, turistas y curiosos, siguieron llegando durante el día, en una oleada que colmó la avenida que conduce a la Basílica de San Pedro.

En tanto, el Vaticano se preparaba para escoger a su sucesor. La posibilidad de que el nuevo pontífice provenga de Latinoamérica, África o Asia crea una vibrante expectativa desde México hasta Manila y de Tegucigalpa a Kinshasa. **8D**

Agencias citan López en lista de "papables"

NÉSTOR MEDRANO

SANTO DOMINGO.- El cardenal Nicolás de Jesús López Rodríguez, quien es mencionado por agencias internacionales como uno de los posibles sucesores de Juan Pablo II, viaja hoy al Vaticano, donde asistirá a la reunión del Colegio de Cardenales, que hará la elección.

El Cardenal ofició una misa por el alma del Pontífice fallecido, con la asistencia del vicepresidente Rafael Alburquerque y funcionarios. En tanto la nación sigue en duelo por el Papa. **5A**

CORRUPCIÓN

PC pide investigar Mejía por caso 50 invernaderos

VIVIANO DE LEÓN

SANTO DOMINGO.- El coordinador de Participación Ciudadana, Luis Shécker, planteó que el ex presidente Hipólito Mejía debe ser investigado por la distribución irregular de 50 invernaderos, con lo que se estafó al Estado por RD$500 millones, según el Depreco.

El dirigente del movimiento cívico planteó también que no hay voluntad política para sancionar la corrupción, posición con la que coincide el director ejecutivo de Finjus, Servio Tulio Castaños Guzmán. **6A**

Hipólito Mejía

GINECOLOGÍA

Padre Billini consultará por cáncer

DORIS PANTALEÓN

SANTO DOMINGO.- El hospital Padre Billini ofrece un nuevo servicio de oncología-ginecológica, con el equipo de médicos que hacían esa labor en el Instituto Heriberto Pieter, informó su director, el doctor Rafael Rojas. **8A**

DIFICULTADES

Otro fuego devasta 25 mil tareas de bosque en Cotuí

PILAR MORENO
ANDRÉS VÁSQUEZ
SANTO CASTRO

SANTO DOMINGO.- Unas 25 mil tareas de bosque fueron arropadas por un incendio, al parecer intencional, que se originó desde el sábado en el Cruce de Maguaca, en Cotuí, informó el jefe de bomberos, Lucas Otáñez.

Mientras, el subsecretario de Medio Ambiente y Recursos Naturales, Héctor Miguel Abreu, explicó que las dificultades para el acceso a las zonas de incendios, la altura y la cercanía de las montañas obstaculizan el trabajo de los helicópteros venezolanos para lanzar agua sobre las áreas encendidas. **14A**

A **La República**

Medicinas siguen caras

Aunque han bajado alrededor de 25%, los medicamentos para el corazón continúan con precios elevados, inalcanzables para la mayoría de esos pacientes. **8A**

EDITORIAL
Juan Pablo II y la Iglesia dominicana. **12A**

B **El Deporte**

Alonso gana otra vez F-1

El español Fernando Alonso se adjudicó inapelablemente ayer el Gran Premio de Bahrein, su segunda victoria sucesiva en lo que va del mundial de Fórmula Uno. **2B**

C **La Vida**

El comilón emocional

¿Come cuando está solo, aburrido o insatisfecho? Este trastorno, que pone en peligro la salud y la silueta, ha originado un nuevo patrón psicológico: el glotón emocional. **1C**

D **El Dinero**

Los combustibles, con precios de agosto 2004

Los precios de los combustibles retrocedieron hasta la posición que tenían en la semana del 21 al 27 de agosto del año pasado, cuando un galón de gasolina premium costaba 107.80 pesos y de regular, 97.40. **1D**

D **Las Mundiales**

Otro cura haitiano será candidato a Presidencia

El padre Gerard Jean-Juste, un cura católico populista leal al derrocado presidente Jean-Bertrand Aristide, está considerando postularse a la presidencia de Haití. **7D**

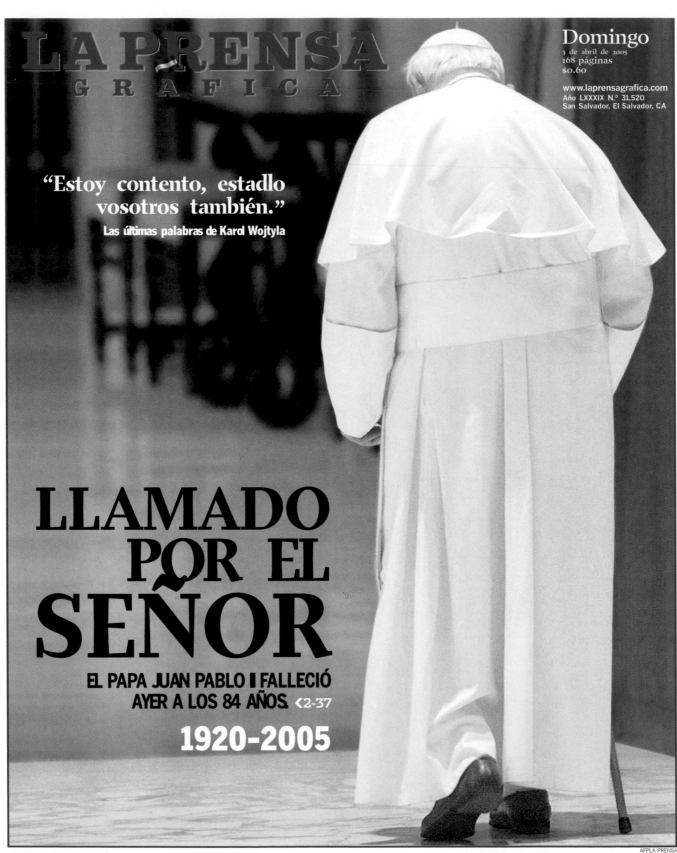

LA PRENSA GRAFICA

Domingo
3 de abril de 2005
168 páginas
$0.60

www.laprensagrafica.com
Año LXXXIX N.º 31,520
San Salvador, El Salvador, CA

"Estoy contento, estadlo vosotros también."

Las últimas palabras de Karol Wojtyla

LLAMADO POR EL SEÑOR

EL PAPA JUAN PABLO II FALLECIÓ AYER A LOS 84 AÑOS. ‹2-37

1920-2005

AFPLA PRENSA

Sunday 3 April 2005   www.observer.co.uk   £1.50

The Observer

FREE SPORT MAGAZINE

HEYSEL'S LEGACY - 20 YEARS ON,
THE TRAGEDY THAT CHANGED FOOTBALL
ERNIE ELS ON THE INTENSE RIVALRIES
AT THE TOP OF WORLD GOLF

I'M WITH THE BRIDE

LYNN BARBER CELEBRATES
CAMILLA – A WOMAN IN LOVE
REVIEW, PAGE 5

The final farewell

Pope John Paul II, 18 May 1920–2 April 2005

INSIDE

News, pictures and global
reaction, 2-4

**PLUS FOUR-PAGE
SPECIAL REPORT**
Cristina Odone on the man
who changed the world,
13-15
Peter Stanford on the
succession, 16

Observer Comment: Man
who loved humanity, 24
The Pope they loved, 25

The Pope pictured during a
mass of beatification in
Maribor, Slovenia, on
19 September 1999.
Photograph by
Gabriel Bouys/AFP

9 770029 771724   No 11,138

TELEVISION Inside The Observer Magazine; **WEATHER** This section, back page; **CROSSWORDS** Azed Escape, 23; **Everyman** Review, 20; **Speedy** This section, 12; **COMMENT** This section, 22-28

THE DEATH OF JOHN PAUL II

INTERNATIONAL
Herald Tribune
THE WORLD'S DAILY NEWSPAPER PUBLISHED BY THE NEW YORK TIMES EDITED AND PRINTED IN PARIS
MONDAY, April 4, 2005

Huge crowds share in somber pageantry

A public end for an extraordinary papacy

Pool photo by Massimo Sambucetti

The body of Pope John Paul II was laid out in the Vatican on Sunday for a private viewing by church officials. A public viewing outside St. Peter's Basilica will take place Monday.

Private viewing in Vatican; Pilgrims converge for rites

By Ian Fisher

VATICAN CITY: His folded hands intertwined with a rosary, the body of Pope John Paul II was laid out inside the papal palace on Sunday as the balance of power in the Roman Catholic Church began its shift to the unnamed man who will soon replace him.

Just 15 hours after he died on Saturday night, the great pageantry around the death of a pope began Sunday morning, with a huge public Mass in St. Peter's Square and then the first rites of his funeral: The 84-year-old John Paul was laid out in Clementine Hall, dressed in white and red vestments, his head covered with a white bishop's miter and propped up on three dark gold pillows.

Tucked under his left arm was the silver staff, called the crow's ear, that he had carried in public.

"He suffered a lot, and he suffered for many years," Francesco Rutelli, the former mayor of Rome and a key opposition leader in Italy, said after seeing the body of the pope, whom he had met with often over the years.

In death, after 26 years as pope, "his expression was serene," Rutelli said.

The viewing ceremony — broadcast live over Italian television — was a private one for cardinals, bishops and other church officials, as well as prominent officials in this nation where the Catholic church is a central and ancient pillar. The guests included Prime Minister Silvio Berlusconi and President Carlo Azeglio Ciampi. Archbishop Stanislaw Dziwisz, the pope's personal secretary for decades and by proximity one of the most powerful men in the church, sat in a rear pew receiving condolences and wiping away tears.

The public part of the mourning for Pope John Paul II, who died after a urinary tract infection on Thursday set off a fatal chain of ailments, begins on Monday. Then, the pope's body will be displayed at the top of the steps outside the huge bronze doors of St. Peter's Basilica, designed in part by Michelangelo. Already on Sunday, several hundred chairs were set up in two sections — broken up by an open surface of stone where his body will lay for three for four days starting on Monday — in front of the basilica.

On Sunday, huge crowds continued to flock to St. Peter's Square, after two nights of vigils for the pope, who died during a crowded prayer service for his health at 9:37 p.m. on Saturday. At a memorial Mass on Sunday morning, Archbishop Leonardo Sandri, who served as the public voice for the pope in the last stages of his illness, announced to the crowd of tens of thousands that he would be reading a message prepared by the pope himself for the day, a week after Easter.

"It is love which converts hearts and gives peace," the pope said in the blessing read by Sandri. "Lord, who with your death and resurrection reveal the love of the Father, we believe in you and with faith we repeat to you today: 'Jesus, I trust in you, have pity on us and on the entire world.' "

But the mood had begun to change slightly from what had been an anxious death watch: On a beautiful sunny day, there were banners and music and a self-conscious awareness of being close to history, with some Romans and tourists posing in front of St. Peter's with copies of newspapers with headlines announcing John Paul II's death.

Still, there remained a strong sense of loss and mourning for a pope who had ruled for so long and inspired many Catholics — whether or not they agreed with his conservative stances on social issues — with the idea that his papacy had been different from others.

POPE, Continued on Page 4

Rome's immigrants embraced pope

By Elisabeth Rosenthal

ROME: On Sunday, as Italy remembered Pope John Paul II formally and officially for his role as head of the Catholic Church, this city's teeming Catholic immigrant community bid a far more emotional and intensely personal goodbye to a charismatic man who many said had transformed their lives.

"You can't forget a person like this," said Charles Boliko at Rome's Congolese church, which opened its doors 10 years ago. "He came to Africa. He said, 'I know you suffer. I know you exist.' We are very emotional and this is so important to us."

Boliko recalled that when he was young, Mass was in Latin. "It was so strange, I couldn't relate at all," he said. But this pope, he continued, "encouraged us to celebrate in an African way — we sing, we dance, we clap, we use our drums. We will always, always be grateful to him."

There is an old saying here in Rome: "When the pope dies, make another one." In that spirit, the Italian media has been filled with somewhat mechanical memorials, delivered by black-clad politicians and celebrities. Indeed, for most Italians, the church is an institution of far greater importance than the pope. But for the millions of immigrants who fill this country's low-wage jobs, it seemed the other way around on Sunday.

John Paul II was a man — a foreigner himself — who left behind the formal vestiges of the Vatican and related to ordinary people wherever he went. He came to their countries. He hugged their children. He brought to life a church that had previously seemed dead and distant to them.

"Our country has always been Catholic, but this is the first pope to visit our country with all its troubles — the church seems so much closer and more human now," said Germania Betancourt, an Ecuadorian who has worked as a baby sitter in Rome for the past eight years.

At Santo Stanislao dei Polacchi, Rome's largest Polish church, hundreds of believers joined in religious folk songs beneath a picture of the young Pope John Paul II at 8 a.m. on Sunday. Andrea and Lucia Cliycko — he is a construction worker and she is a housekeeper — drove 90 minutes into Rome after a sleepless night in order to join in the mourning.

"Last night on television, I heard the Italian President and George Bush, too — but this is different for us," said Andrea Cliycko.

"With the death of the pope, the world as we know it ends, and another will have to start," he said. "We'll see what it's like."

In some ways, all popes belong to Rome. "This pope was Polish, but became Italian," said Rita Ausanio, who had driven hours to be in St. Peter's Square on Sunday.

But immigrants see things differently.

Italy is home to millions of foreigners — legal and illegal — the vast majority of them Catholics. One fifth of applications for residency in Italy cite religious commitment as a motivation.

ROME, Continued on Page 4

Karol Wojtyla, 1920-2005

- **The man who would call himself John Paul II was not the traditional papal figure, compassionate and loving but ascetic and remote behind the high walls and elaborate ceremony of the Vatican. Here was a different kind of pope: complex, schooled in confrontation, theologically intransigent but deftly politic, full of wit and daring. An obituary.** *Pages 6 and 7*
- **World leaders reflect on the passing of an enormously influential pontiff. President Bush was said to be making plans to attend the funeral.** *Page 5*
- **In his final hours, the pope was described as serene in the knowledge that soon he would be in heaven.** *Page 4*

Start of a life's journey

A town remembers its most famous son

By Richard Bernstein

WADOWICE, Poland: From inside the Basilica of the Mother of God of Constant Help, the sound of the special Mass being said for the pope on Sunday morning spilled out onto what some time ago was already named John Paul II Square, filled with hundreds of townspeople and visitors, their faces glowing in the pale morning sun.

Special Masses were said all over Poland on Sunday, the morning after the pope died, but the Mass in Wadowice, where Karol Wojtyla began his extraordinary life's journey 84 years ago, was naturally special — not least because of the large numbers of television satellite trucks parked around the square, beaming the ceremony live to viewers all over this country.

It seemed as if the entire population of the town, which lines the wooded hills south of Krakow, came out to say goodbye to the historic figure whose connection with their town clearly fills them with pride.

They prayed, they remembered; they told stories of the pope's three visits to Wadowice to their children and friends and to inquiring reporters looking for anecdotes. They signed the thick remembrance book placed on a flower-strewn terrace outside the basilica, where the fire department's brass band, which went to Rome no fewer than six times during John Paul II's papacy, played Polish Catholic melodies.

Behind the church a smaller crowd was spilling out of a shop labeled "Opominki," or souvenirs, waiting for those inside to finish buying pictures of the pope, bas-relief brass plaques showing him in a prayerful pose and desk ornaments saying "John Paul II and Wadowice" on them.

It is a big thing for a small town like Wadowice to have produced one of the most famous people in the world, and so, not surprisingly perhaps, the atmosphere on the morning after his death had a curious mix of elements. There were deep reverence and solemnity. There were also the activities associated with what one townsman, who gave his name only as Jan, called "The cult of John Paul II," which has been emerging for several years in Wadowice.

"For several years now," Jan said, "the tourists and pilgrims have made business boom here."

Some people prayed and lit candles and knelt on the cobblestones outside the church. Others wandered around the square, looking at the yellow house where Wojtyla was born, the large building, now the Town Hall, where he went to school.

POLAND, Continued on Page 4

Spanish cardinal fills empty seat

78-year-old becomes interim Vatican chief

By Elaine Sciolino

ROME: The Regime of the Vacant See has begun.

At the moment of Pope John Paul II's death on Saturday night, the power structure that governed the Roman Catholic hierarchy for the past 26 years fell away, and an ultraconservative, 78-year-old Spanish cardinal temporarily became the leading decision-maker in Catholicism.

Cardinal Eduardo Martínez Somalo, the "camerlengo" or "chamberlain" of the Vatican, will be the administrative — although not the spiritual — father of the world's more than one billion Catholics until a new pope is elected sometime within the next few weeks.

As the pope's body lay at the Vatican's Apostolic Palace on Sunday morning, it was Martínez Somalo who recited prayers in Latin and sprinkled holy water over the pope's body.

In his red robe and lace-trimmed white cassock, the little-known cardinal suddenly was propelled into the world's spotlight, as Italian as well as foreign television channels carried the event live.

There is no "deputy" or "acting" pope in Catholicism, so the transition period before a new pope is elected comes with a traumatic bureaucratic shakeup.

The heads of the agencies of the Vatican, essentially the cabinet of the Vatican, and John Paul's inner circle of aides automatically lose their power.

Until the pope's death Saturday night, for example, Archbishop Stanislaw Dziwisz, the pope's personal secretary and a trusted aide from their days together in Poland, was one of the most powerful men in Vatican City.

Archbishop Dziwisz slept near the pope's bedroom, controlled his schedule, told him what papers to sign and was with him during most of every day and at the moment of his death.

Cardinal Angelo Sodano, an Italian, lost his job as the Vatican's Secretary of State, but will play an important role in preparing for the conclave, the gathering of cardinals that will elect the next pope.

Cardinal Joseph Ratzinger, a German, no longer is head of the powerful Congregation for the Doctrine of the Faith, the "ministry" in the Vatican that helps shape and enforce Catholic doctrine. However, as Dean of the Cardinals, he will wield extraordinary influence in guiding the cardinals in the stewardship of the church until a new pope is in place.

"The seat of Peter is now empty, the throne is vacant," said Giovanni Maria Vian, a Vatican historian at La Sapienza University in Rome. "The government of the church now is regulated by norms that go back to the medieval times."

"The church of Rome is perhaps the last absolute monarchy in the world," he said, "and when the pope dies, all the curial offices are decapitated. All the heads fall, and only a few special ones remain."

The cleric of the moment, however, is Martínez Somalo. It was he who had the responsibility to make sure that the pope was dead. He also took charge of organizing the lying in state of the pope's body in the Vatican basilica and the pope's funeral and, if tradition prevails, of putting seals on the pope's bedroom and study.

Martínez Somalo's primary responsibility is to organize the still unscheduled papal conclave of all the cardinals.

TRANSITION, Continued on Page 4

Newsstand prices

France € 2.00

Algeria	Din 70	Ivory Coast	CFA 1.700
Andorra	€ 2.00	Reunion	€ 3.50
Cameroon	CFA 1.800	Antilles	€ 2.30
		Senegal	CFA 1.700
Gabon	CFA 1.700	Tunisia	Din 2.700

For information on delivery, or to subscribe in France, call toll-free:
00 800 44 48 78 27
or email us at subs@iht.com

UPDATE

In other news

- **In former Soviet states, leaders watch uneasily as the call for democracy widens.** *Page 3*
- **Rebellion at La Scala ends as Riccardo Muti resigns as musical director after 19 years.** *Page 8*
- **A UN envoy says Syria has vowed to pull out all military and intelligence units from Lebanon by the end of April.** *Page 9*
- **Iraqi lawmakers elect a Sunni Arab as speaker of Parliament.** *Page 9*

Daring to create

Mayor Bertrand Delanoë has worked hard to make his city a contemporary masterpiece. "Paris is a museum, and that is a privilege," he says. "But if it wants to be loyal to its history, it needs to innovate, to dare — it needs to move into the 21st century." *Page 2*

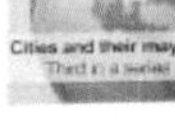

On the Web: *www.iht.com*

Le Monde

DIMANCHE 3 - LUNDI 4 AVRIL 2005

Le pape des multitudes

JEAN PAUL II

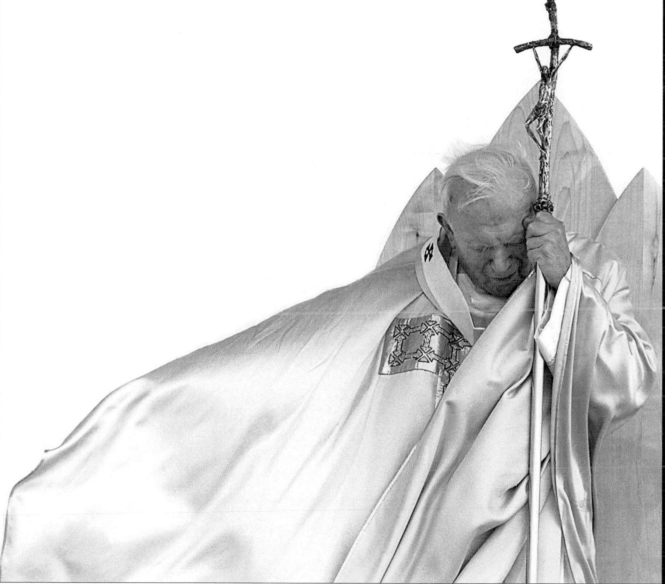

GABRIEL BOUYS/AFP

Jean Paul II a livré son ultime combat au terme de vingt-six ans et presque six mois de pontificat. Avant lui, un seul pape, Pie IX (1846-1878), avait gouverné aussi longtemps l'Eglise. Malgré les rigueurs de l'âge et de la maladie, le Polonais Karol Wojtyla, élu le 16 octobre 1978, à la surprise du monde entier, premier pape non italien depuis plus de quatre siècles, premier pape slave de l'Histoire, aura mené sa mission, dans la souffrance, jusqu'à son terme.

C'est la fin d'un destin hors du commun et tragique. Dans la Pologne où Karol Wojtyla est né en 1920, a passé son enfance, fait ses premières armes de prêtre et d'évêque, son tempérament a été forgé à l'épreuve du feu : celui des deux totalitarismes – le nazisme et le communisme – du XXe siècle. Il a connu les nuits de l'occupation, travaillé de ses mains, étudié en cachette, joué sur des scènes clandestines, mais aussi fait du sport, écrit des poèmes, enchanté des amis.

Cette humanité expliquera la popularité de cet « athlète de Dieu », arpenteur infatigable du monde, agitateur des consciences, mort dans le dépouillement de la maladie comme le « serviteur souffrant » de la Bible.

Son règne sur le trône de Pierre fut non seulement le plus long, mais le plus dense du XXe siècle. Il restera une voix parmi les plus fortes à la charnière de deux millénaires, et le pape des multitudes. Car aucun pape avant lui n'avait donné une dimension aussi universelle à son rôle. Aucun n'avait fait autant de kilomètres hors de Rome, croisé autant de foules, écrit et prononcé autant de discours, rencontré de responsables chrétiens et non chrétiens, ambassadeurs, savants, intellectuels, chefs d'Etat et de gouvernement.

Ses voyages dans la Pologne communiste ont été une contribution, qu'aucun historien ne discute, à l'éclatement du système derrière le rideau de fer. Les dialogues qu'il a ouverts avec les autres confessions, notamment avec les juifs, ses « frères aînés » dans la foi, pour lesquels il a exprimé le repentir de l'Eglise, resteront aussi au crédit de ce pape hors du commun qui, à Assise ou à la tribune de l'ONU,

n'aura cessé de répéter que la paix du monde passe par la paix des religions. Cette paix, de sa voix depuis longtemps lasse et angoissée, il en aura été l'apôtre à Beyrouth, à Sarajevo, à Jérusalem et lors des deux guerres du Golfe.

Jean Paul II a réaffirmé l'autorité et la visibilité d'un catholicisme bousculé par les incertitudes et les tensions qui avaient suivi le concile Vatican II (1962-1965). Ses cent quatre voyages dans les cinq continents ont permis à ce pape missionnaire de proclamer sa foi en l'homme, ses droits, sa liberté, sa dignité, de défendre sa conception du respect absolu de la vie contre la « culture de mort ».

À l'heure du bilan, faut-il opposer un pape progressiste sur les questions sociales et politiques et conservateur sur la morale sexuelle et familiale, bravant l'impopularité par sa dénonciation de l'IVG, du divorce, de l'union libre, du préservatif ? Pour ses fidèles, il n'y a pas de contradiction entre deux attitudes également fondées sur la dignité de l'homme et la condamnation de tout ce qui porte atteinte à

la vie : la guerre ou le terrorisme, l'avortement ou les manipulations génétiques. Pour les autres, il laissera le souvenir d'un pape incapable de s'adapter à la modernité, préférant l'autorité du magistère romain aux risques de la nouveauté.

Jean Paul II laisse une Eglise en état de crise. Il aura été un pape de gestes et de paroles, pas de réformes. C'est à son successeur qu'il appartiendra de prendre la mesure des urgences ; la menace de l'islam extrémiste ; les pannes du dialogue avec les orthodoxes et les anglicans ; les contestations liées à la centralisation et au déficit de démocratie dans l'Eglise, au statut des femmes, à l'obligation du célibat des prêtres, à une morale sexuelle jugée archaïque. Aucun des défis lancés à l'homme n'est aujourd'hui étranger à l'Eglise catholique. C'est à ce pape qui vient de mourir qu'elle le doit, et les cardinaux-électeurs de son successeur, qui se réuniront dans trois semaines en conclave, l'auront présent à l'esprit.

Henri Tincq

CAHIER DU « MONDE » DATÉ DIMANCHE 3 - LUNDI 4 AVRIL 2005, N° 18721. NE PEUT ÊTRE VENDU SÉPARÉMENT

PRENSA LIBRE

UN PERIODISMO INDEPENDIENTE, HONRADO Y DIGNO

AÑO LIV, NO. 17,671 • Q3.00 LOS DOMINGOS   www.prensalibre.com   GUATEMALA, DOMINGO 3 DE ABRIL DE 2005

Termina agonía del Santo Padre

ADIÓS

Luto en el mundo por el fallecimiento de Juan Pablo II

A las 13.37

El Papa expiró a las 21.37 horas de Roma. Reloj marcaba las 13.37 en Guatemala ▶ Pág. 2

Gran vacío

Generalizado pesar por deceso. Líderes ponderan personalidad y logros del Papa Peregrino ▶ Pág. 4

Funeral

Restos serán llevados mañana a Basílica de San Pedro. Cardenales fijarán fecha de sepelio ▶ Pág. 12

Foto Prensa Libre: MYNOR DE LEÓN

En la Plaza Juan Pablo II, en esta capital, católicos rezan por el eterno descanso del alma del fiel amigo de los guatemaltecos.

GRATIS Busque en esta edición el Suplemento Especial sobre la vida y obra del Papa

Lágrimas y ovaciones en Plaza de San Pedro

Decenas de miles de fieles portando velas y flores se congregan en señal de respeto, recuerdo y fidelidad hacia el Papa ▶ Pág. 2

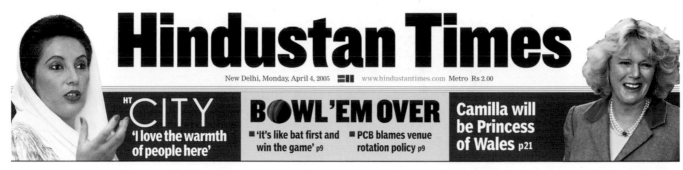

Hindustan Times

New Delhi, Monday, April 4, 2005 ▮▮▮ www.hindustantimes.com Metro Rs 2.00

HT CITY
'I love the warmth of people here'

BOWL 'EM OVER
- 'It's like bat first and win the game' p9
- PCB blames venue rotation policy p9

Camilla will be Princess of Wales p21

A man who changed the world

On Pope John Paul II's watch, USSR collapsed, Berlin Wall came down, Catholic church spread to Asia, Africa

Ian Fisher
Vatican City, April 3

ON SUNDAY morning, on a bright spring day, tens of thousands gathered at St. Peter's Square for a commemorative mass for Pope John Paul II.

As they waited on stones still spattered with colourful wax from Saturday night's candlelight vigil, video screens flashed pictures of the pope bearing the inscription "In Your Hands."

"Our soul is shaken by a painful fact," said Cardinal Angelo Sodano in his homily. "Our father, shepherd, John Paul II, has left us."

He was 84 years old. He was born Karol Wojtyla on May 18, 1920 in Wadowice, Poland.

In his last public appearance, from his apartment window on Wednesday, he looked weak and gaunt, unable to pronounce a blessing to the crowd. Still recovering from a tracheotomy on February 24, a pope known for his great ability as a communicator could hardly speak.

In 1978, he came to office as a fit and handsome 58-year-old, blessed with a charisma, intellectual vigour and energy that took him to 129 foreign countries as the pulse of the Catholic Church moved away from an increasingly secular Europe to Africa, Asia and Latin America.

A Pole chosen as the first non Italian pope in 455 years, he transformed the papacy into a television ready voice for peace and life, from the womb to the wheelchair. He also reached beyond religion into human rights and politics, encouraging his fellow Poles and other Europeans to reject Communism. Many historians say he deserves part of the credit for the subsequent collapse of the Soviet Union.

Even as his own voice faded away, his views on the sanctity of all human life echoed unambiguously among Catholics and Christian evangelicals on issues from abortion to the end of life.

"This pope will have a place in history," Giancarlo Zizola, an Italian Vatican expert, said on Saturday after his death. "Not just for what he is glorified for now, for attracting the great masses, as a sporty pope — this won't last. Not even the fall of Berlin Wall, the defeat of communism, because he himself said it would destroy itself.

"But he will be remembered for the seeds he laid," he added. "He will be remembered for his great favouring of dialogue between different religions, for the culture of peace, and the courage to speak against wars. For having saved the values of the West from the West itself. And the human form he gave to the papacy. It is not negative or positive: it is a complete pontificate."

John Paul's detractors were often as passionate as his supporters, criticising him for what they said was tradition-bound papacy in need of a bolder connection with modern life if the church wanted to bring back to the faith people in more secular Western nations.

Among liberal Catholics, he was criticised for his strong opposition to abortion, homosexuality and contraception, as well as the ordination of women and married men.

Though he was never known as a strong administrator of the dense Vatican bureaucracy, he kept a centralising hand on the selection of bishops around the world and enforced a rigid adherence to many basic church teachings among the clergy and Catholic theologians.

But he defied easy definition: For all his conservatism on social and theological issues, he was decidedly forward looking — too much so even for some cardinals — on the delicate question of other religions.

While never veering from his belief that Jesus Christ alone was capable of saving the souls of human beings, he reached out tirelessly to other faiths, becoming the first pope to set foot in a synagogue as well as in a mosque.

"He came across in some ways as a regular guy," said Michael Walsh, a British biographer of the pope and a former Jesuit priest. "Famous for looking at his watch. What pope looks at his watch? In Britain we're proud that he used to wear Doc Martin boots. He would watch football, drink a glass of wine."

There is, at the moment, no favourite in the running, no obvious inheritor to John Paul II's formidable legacy. But in making their choice, the cardinals will have to weigh the range of issues facing the church — many of which, critics as well as some supporters argue, have been left languishing in the pope's illness, especially these last few months of virtual incapacitation.

(The New York Times)
More on P21

SO BE IT: The body of Pope John Paul II lies in state at the Clementine Hall of the Apostolic Palace at the Vatican on Sunday. His last word was "Amen". AP

> " In Britain, we're proud that he used to wear Doc Martin boots, would watch football and drink a glass of wine — *The pope's biographer* "

What will **happen** now

Process outlined in a 1996 document, Universi Dominici Gregis, to be followed

Funeral
Pope to be buried 4-6 days after death (probably in St Peter's Basilica). College of Cardinals to meet on Monday to set date

Vatican freeze
Cardinals holding Vatican posts lose jobs. Most important official, papal chamberlain, arranges funeral, conclave

Conclave
Conclave must begin 15-20 days after pontiff dies. Cardinals vote in utmost secrecy in Sistine Chapel. Can go on for days

Smoke signal
Ballots burned after every round of voting. The smoke can be seen from St Peter's square. Black smoke signals deadlock, white shows new pontiff has been elected

---

>> INBOX

Bihar moves

LJP CHIEF Ram Vilas Paswan on Sunday rejected JD(U) leader Nitish Kumar's support offer. He said he would favour continuation of central rule. **P13**

Choose a career that you want.
Call 3050 5555

NIIT *CareerScope*
Fri-Sun, 10am - 6pm

HindustanTimes.com poll

Was Sourav Ganguly's captaincy a factor in India's one-day international victory in Kochi?

Yes 30.72%
No 66.56%
Can't Say 2.72%

Today's Question
Should homosexuality be legalised in India?
www.hindustantimes.com

>> WEATHER

MONDAY
Pleasant morn, sunny day. A cool night. High 35°C, low 18°C. Max rel humidity 44%

TUESDAY
Pleasant morn, warm day. Night remains cool & windy. High 36°C, low 19°C.
Detailed report on p4

28 pages, including six pages of *HT City*.
Vol. LXXXI No. 80

JAIPUR GOLDEN
TRANSPORT COMPANY PVT. LTD.
XII/4735, Roshanara Road, Delhi-110007
Tel: 23827906-12, Fax: 011-23821816
E-mail : enquiries@jglcl.com www.jglcl.com
We carry your trust

Bus travellers in safehouse

HT Correspondent
Jammu, April 3

FOUR DAYS before the April 7 Srinagar-Muzaffarabad bus leaves on its historic journey, carrying members of divided families from either side of the LoC, 13 passengers from Poonch and Rajouri districts find themselves under the protection of a tight security cover in Jammu.

Said Mohammad, 90, and his eight family members from Rajouri's Muradpur have been allowed to venture out to buy gifts for the relatives they will see after years of separation — but only in the vicinity of the hotel to which they have been relocated.

Mohammad's wife, Sher Bibi, 85, had been worried that they may have to travel empty-handed after all — they hadn't expected the security cover to be in place so soon.

But the DIG for Rajouri and Poonch area, S.P. Sahai, and Director-General of Police (Jammu) Gopal Sharma didn't want to leave anything to chance in light of the March 30 threats by four militant organisations — the Save Kashmir Movement, Al-Nasreen, Al-Afreen and Farzandan-e-Millat — to the travellers, warning them not to board the "coffin" to Muzaffarabad.

The militant organisations — who see the opening of the road after 57 years as a cause for worry for the people of Kashmir since it is an "effort of India to take over the state" — have urged people to boycott the bus or face the consequences.

But the passengers remain intent on travelling — the threats (to their property while they are away or to the bus) are dwarfed by the longing to see their loved ones.

More on P13

Safety first
- 13 passengers from Poonch and Rajouri districts are being kept under tight security in Jammu
- They will be taken to Srinagar on April 5 for their onward journey to Muzaffarabad
- On March 30, militant outfits warned people against travelling by the Srinagar-Muzaffarabad bus

---

Makeover for Prasar Bharati

Kumkum Chadha
New Delhi, April 3

THE GOVERNMENT has decided to take a "relook" at the functioning of Prasar Bharati and examine the possibility of redefining its role as a public broadcaster.

Information and Broadcasting Minister Jaipal Reddy has constituted a committee under the chairmanship of I&B Secretary Navin Chawla to propose a financial structure for Prasar Bharati, assess its role and make suggestions to strengthen its functioning.

On the anvil is a "focus shift", with greater emphasis on content. Sources say Prasar Bharati is getting more and more "technology-driven" and ignoring programme content altogether.

Amid growing concern over the erosion of DD's "maximum-reach edge" over private channels, sources feel Prasar Bharati needs to address the content issue on a war footing. The committee — given a three-month deadline to submit its report — will have a panel of external experts to examine this and fine tune recommendations.

While proposing a viable capital

On the agenda

Content: Has been suffering. Experts to examine issue and fine-tune recommendations

Finances: Panel to work on maximising Prasar Bharati's revenue-earning potential through commercial operations

and financial structure for Prasar Bharati, the committee will address the broadcaster's need to maximise its revenue-earning potential. It is in this context that Prasar Bharati's role as a public broadcaster will come into focus.

This aspect had also come under scrutiny at a recent meeting between the Planning Commission and the I&B Ministry. It was felt that a redefinition would help end the ambiguity about Prasar Bharati's role — between being a public broadcaster and a commercial player in a competitive market.

It was suggested that the corporation could be geographically divided between revenue and non-revenue generating states. While in the latter bracket, Prasar Bharati could perform the role of a public-service broadcaster, in the former it could be a commercial player.

THE IRISH TIMES

€1.50 (INCL. VAT) 75p STERLING AREA.   MONDAY, APRIL 4, 2005   WWW.IRELAND.COM

Pope John Paul II 1920-2005

Special supplement on his extraordinary life and times

THE IRISH TIMES

A great leader of this world

The death of Pope John Paul II leaves the whole world in mourning for one of the great leaders of our time. He was an inspirational figure who practised what he preached, even if his pleas for social justice, strict standards of sexual morality and the rejection of unbridled capitalism were more often than not ignored. He was an outstanding pastor who visibly wore himself out in his mission to make this a better world and convince men and women of all faiths and none that their ultimate destiny transcends the joys and sorrows of everyday life.

Even for those who did not share his strongly held Christian beliefs, there was inspiration in itself to watch him defy debilitating illnesses to preach a unifying message of solidarity to a world divided between differing creeds. It was an impossible task humanly speaking but he never shirked it.

He was consistent in his pro-life stance which not only condemned abortion but also the death penalty and war as an instrument of foreign policy. He believed the medieval concept of the "just war" was outmoded and he spoke out against the two Gulf wars in spite of US displeasure. He campaigned with some success for the cancellation of official debts incurred by the poorest countries.

He saw himself as Christ's representative on earth and reached out to people of all religions and cultures in a way none of his predecessors would have dreamed of. He seemed to be indeed a Man of Destiny as he inspired, first his native Poland during the Solidarity rebellion, and then the rest of central and eastern Europe under communist domination, to struggle nonviolently to replace the harsh regimes controlled from Moscow. He was arguably the single most important figure in reuniting Europe and bringing the Cold War to an end.

His vision of a Christian Europe to replace the division of the Cold War period, in which east and west would unite under a vaguely defined slogan of "solidarity", has not come to pass. He saw the enlarged European Union which has become a reality as a poor substitute imbued with materialistic and godless values. But he believed it still has the potential to rise to its true vocation.

He narrowly survived an assassination attempt in St Peter's Square and later visited his would-be murderer in prison to offer forgiveness in the true Christian spirit. He did more than any other pope to try to undo centuries of anti-semitism which tainted official Catholicism for far too long. He apologised humbly in the name of the Catholic Church for its historical wrongs. He was the first to visit a Muslim country and open a dialogue with that religion. In this he was an inspiring figure in an age which had seen the depths to which so-called civilised man could descend and which wondered was there any place for a loving God.

Behind this charismatic figure who had once been a poet, an actor and an athlete before he dedicated his life to God, there was a strict moralist whose conservatism disappointed many Catholics hoping for a greater understanding of what it is to live in the real world of broken marriages, dwindling clergy, sexual freedom and Aids-stricken African countries. In this area of Catholic morality, Pope John Paul would brook no dissent. Theologians who tried to re-interpret traditional Catholic teaching on sexual matters to accommodate these developments in the world of the 20th and 21st centuries and in the spirit of the Second Vatican Council were silenced.

Where Pope Paul VI had shown compassion to priests seeking release from their vows and permission to marry, Pope John Paul for years set his face against what he saw as betrayal. Even to discuss priestly celibacy or the ordaining of women priests would not be tolerated under a pope who had once written plays about the tenderness of human love.

He was capable of change, however, in other matters. At first in his long pontificate, he showed little sympathy for the dilemma of the clergy in Latin American countries ministering to a peasantry and urban proletariat shamefully exploited by nominally Catholic dictators or plutocrats who often had the favour of the official Church. Liberation theology which drew on Marxist philosophy to illustrate the class divisions in Latin America gradually became more acceptable to him. As he put it, "if there is no hope for the poor, there will be no hope for anyone, not even for the so-called rich".

Pope John Paul's dream of a reconciliation, or "common house", between Rome and the Orthodox churches of eastern Europe – a split in Christianity which long pre-dated the Reformation – was one of his most painful failures. Centuries of mutual distrust and even antagonism would take more than the sudden collapse of the communist regimes of central and eastern Europe to heal.

As with any human endeavour, Pope John Paul's life and work was a mixture of success and failure, but with him it was on a heroic scale across the world. He saw his latter years as a final phase where, in his own words, "the Pope has to suffer so that every family and the world may see that there is a higher gospel, the gospel of suffering by which the future is prepared".

World unites in tribute

The body of Pope John Paul II in the Clementine Hall at the Vatican's Apostolic Palace yesterday.
Photograph: Gianni Giansanti/Vatican Pool/Getty Images

At least two million to attend funeral

**PADDY AGNEW
IN ROME**

The mortal remains of Pope John Paul II went on display in the Vatican yesterday. This morning in Rome, cardinals will turn their minds to his last will and testament and plans for his funeral.

It is assumed – but not confirmed – that the Pope will, like his predecessors, be buried in the crypt beneath St Peter's Basilica. At least two million people are expected to descend on Rome in the coming days in the expectation of attending what may be the largest such gathering in modern times.

The numbers travelling to the Italian capital will be boosted by the advent of cheap air travel and inspired by the most travelled Pope in history. Tens of thousands are expected from Poland, where the Pope's death has aroused great emotions, and very many young people are also expected to make the journey.

Vatican and Roman authorities have begun to grapple with the logistical problems of transport and accommodation. Yesterday the city laid on extra trains and fresh water supplies and began to erect hundreds of tents in expectation of a massive influx of mourners.

They plan to erect giant screens across the city for pilgrims to follow celebrations, and the Ancient Roman Circus Maximus – once used for chariot races – was designated a gathering point for the mourners. Two stadiums will be opened for pilgrims, with food and water points.

Officials said more than 150,000 people streamed into St Peter's Square throughout yesterday. The crowds blocked roads to the Vatican but the authorities are bracing themselves for the arrival of, on their own estimate, about two million

What happens next?

Today
10am: Cardinals hold first pre-conclave meeting to read papal will and agree funeral arrangements.
5pm: Pope's body transferred to St Peter's Basilica, where it will lie in state.

Thursday or Friday
Funeral expected on either day.

April 17th/22nd
Expected start of conclave in which 117 cardinals under 80 years of age will elect new Pope.

people by the end of the week.

Mayor Walter Veltroni warned that Rome faced one of the biggest organisational tasks in its history.

"For us it is an extraordinary test, of the most tremendous importance. It's going to be like organising the Jubilee in just 48 hours," he told reporters. During the Jubilee Year of 2000 some 30 million people visited the Vatican.

Yesterday the world got its first glimpse of the late Pope. Clad in crimson and white vestments, his body lay on a bier under a simple crucifix with his bishop's staff under his arm.

Those allowed to view the Pope included church dignitaries and Italian politicians. Today, members of the public will get their turn at 5pm Rome time.

The Vatican yesterday gave formal confirmation of the cause of death at 8.37pm Irish time on Saturday. It said the Pope, who was 84, died of heart failure and septic shock – an overwhelming infection leading to low blood pressure and low blood flow which can stop vital organs.

Tributes to the Pope came from all over the world. His funeral is expected to be attended by at least 100 of the world's heads of state and government, including President Bush of the US, President Chirac of France, British prime minister Tony Blair and the UN secretary general Kofi Annan among others. President McAleese will represent Ireland.

Taoiseach Bertie Ahern said the selection of the other members of the Irish delegation would depend on the final protocol decisions made by the Vatican.

Mr Ahern said the national flag would fly at half mast until the funeral was over but there would be no day of mourning.

Officials were last night trying to assess the public appetite for such a gesture after former MEP Dana Rosemary Scallan criticised the decision not to declare an official day of mourning, and some members of the public telephoned Government Buildings suggesting one.

Throughout the world yesterday Sunday religious services were dominated by thoughts for the late Pope.

In Rome around 130,000 worshippers gathered at St Peter's Square to hear the Pope's own words read out at Mass.

"It is love which converts hearts and gives peace," said the text, which was prepared for the Sunday after Easter and was read out by an archbishop.

Under a lamplight in the centre of the great square, a makeshift shrine to him was adorned with flowers, candles, photographs of the him, rosary beads and messages of gratitude.

"Papa, ti voglio bene, Francesco" – I love you, from Francesco" – the succinct message was written in pencil on a post-it note and in a very young hand.

Inside: pages 8 to 15

ידיעות אחרונות

העורך לשעבר: ד"ר ח. רוזנבלום ז"ל | יו"ר ההנהלה הראשי: יהודה מוזס ז"ל | העורך האחראי הראשון: נח מוזס ז"ל | העורך האחראי: ארנון מוזס | עורך המשנה: יואל אסתרון

Yedioth Ahronoth | ידיעות אחרונות | דפוס גלעד רח' מוזס 2, תל-אביב | יום א', כ"ג באדר ב', תשס"ה | 3.4.2005 | גליון מס' 23875 | 4.80 ש"ח (כולל מע"מ) | 4.10 ש"ח (ללא מע"מ)

ישראל: יוחנן פאולוס השני היה ידיד גדול לעם היהודי

הלך לעולמו

3 ימים נאבקו הרופאים על חייו של האפיפיור, ומאות מיליוני קתולים ברחבי העולם התפללו לנס ● אבל אמש נדם ליבו ● בוותיקן נשלמות ההכנות להלוויה ולבחירת יורש ●
יוסי בר, רומא / עמ' 2‑5

שלום לך חברי, קרול

למדנו יחד מכיתה א' בעיירה ואדוביצה בפולין: אני, יוסף בינגשטוק, ילד יהודי ואתה, קרול ויטולה, שהסבת לימים לאפיפיור יוחנן פאולוס השני.

היית תלמיד מבריק וחבר טוב שלי. העתקתי ממך שעורים. גם כשהתבגרת, רבים מחבריך היו יהודים. במכתבים ששלחת לי בחגים, חזרת תמיד על הערכה שלך לעם היהודי וסיפרת כמה גדול כאבך על השמדת היהודים בשואה.
יוסף בינגשטוק, חבר ילדות
(ראו עמ' 5)

ראש להביט מכאבים

לאחר נתק של חודשים:

מתנחלי גוש קטיף באים לפגוש את שרון

יגיעו מחרתיים ללשכת רה"מ, לראשונה מאז אישור תוכנית ההתנתקות ● איציק סבן, עמ' 6

הפורצים נתפסו על הסנופלינג

מארב באזור הבורסה ברמת-גן הבתין בפורצים משתלשלים על סנופלינג בדרך למפעל תכשיטים והזיק שוטרים. בתמונה: אחד הפורצים. בוקי נאה, עמ' 15

רעידת האדמה במשטרה:

המפכ"ל: אם נצ"מ לוי סיע לעבריינים – שילך לכלא

משה קראדי מדבר לראשונה על החקירה נגד מפקד היחידה המרכזית במחוז הדרומי ● רונן טל, עמ' 8

איך להיפטר מכאבים

בחיים, כמו במחזה

רגע לפני בכורת המחזה הטראגי שלה, גילתה השדרנית: יש לה סרטן ● עמ' 14

il manifesto

quotidiano comunista - anno XXXV n. 84   DOMENICA 3 APRILE 2005

euro 1,10
con Le Monde Diplomatique un euro in più
con il dvd "I tamburi dell'Amazzonia" 4,50 euro in più

Un po' di silenzio

ROSSANA ROSSANDA

Che la terra gli sia leggera, più di quanto lo sono stati i media. Giovanni Paolo II si è spento, dopo giorni di patimento mentre l'Italia era sommersa da un mare di parole, immagini rubate, indiscrezioni. Un indecente voyeurismo. L'ultima fotografia del suo volto sfigurato nell'inutile tentativo di parlare alla folla ha campeggiato sulle prime pagine. Chi lo diceva morto, chi lo sentiva parlare in italiano e in tedesco, chi lo assicurava vigile e chi in coma. Se avessero potuto tenere le telecamere a mezzo metro dal letto e captare in audio l'ultimo respiro, lo avrebbero fatto. I soliti vescovi della tv non erano inginocchiati a pregare, stavano negli studi della Rai o di Mediaset a invitare alla preghiera gli altri. In un crescendo alimentato dai soliti conduttori siamo stati informati che piangevano e pregavano tutti i cattolici, anzi tutte le chiese cristiane, tutto l'ebraismo, tutti i musulmani; ci mancavano solo i sentimenti dei buddisti. Il presidente della Repubblica della quale sono anch'io cittadina, ha partecipato alle messe di veglia e fatto dichiarazioni un tempo impensabili per uno stato laico e che non mi rappresentano.

Non so se questa spettacolarizzazione sia stata da lui desiderata o se sia frutto della curia e dei personaggi che lo circondavano. Certo Karol Wojtyla ha accettato e cercato tutti i media - per introdurre la Chiesa nel terzo millennio, ci dicono i vaticanisti - e alla fine è stato vittima delle loro smoderatezze, che nessuno ormai ignora. Così sono scomparse dalle prime pagine e dai telegiornali tutte le altre notizie, a meno che riguardassero la Formula 1. E forse questa massificazione di una religione facile ha guidato buona parte di quelli che da sabato hanno riempito piazza san Pietro per poter dire, come il nonno al tempo delle battaglie, «anche io c'ero», allo spegnersi delle luci delle due famose finestre.

Come rimproverarli? Non è questo che mette a disagio chi, non credente, considera il cristianesimo un grande evento dell'umanità. E' l'uso che se ne sta facendo. Perché parlare di via crucis per un vecchio che stava morendo di pesanti malattie, come capita a milioni di altri al mondo, e senza essere arrivati alla sua età, e senza le cure che a lui sono state prodigate? Di martirio? L'ebreo di Nazareth, convinto di essere figlio di Dio, accettò di essere flagellato e morire di un orrendo supplizio, e solitario, come l'ultimo degli schiavi, per salvare il mondo. Karol Wojtyla, da quando è stato eletto papa, non si è sentito più un uomo, ma la voce di Cristo, fino a parlare di sé in terza persona.

Ma era un uomo e ci ha fatto un'immensa pena questo suo proporsi come simbolo di una via d'uscita per un'umanità non solo secolarizzata ma che dichiara ogni giorno di essere priva di ideali e di idee. Lo si è consumato come una rockstar quando lo si sarebbe dovuto proteggere. Morire è un duro lavoro, e più in una fibra come la sua che sfidava la montagna e le nevi, e ha a lungo resistito. Andava accompagnato con discrezione e pietà.

Non pensiamo che ce ne saranno molte al suo funerale e alla sua sepoltura. Verranno i grandi del mondo che non si sono sognati di dargli ascolto quando parlava per la pace e contro la ricchezza. E' stato la sola autorità morale per chi non ha più avuto cura di un'etica terrena. Adesso viene il tempo per una riflessione sul papato di Giovanni Paolo II, anch'esso enfatizzato da elogi e dichiarazioni di primati e insostituibilità, che neanche Gregorio Magno. Ora si potrà misurare il suo apporto teologico, forse non così rilevante, il suo insegnamento etico, forse non così innovativo, il suo peso politico moltiplicato dal crollo dei comunismi, il suo ruolo non privo di ombre sulla comunità ecclesiale. C'è un giorno per vivere e un giorno per morire, dice il *Qoelet*. Che almeno questo sia lasciato al silenzio.

Foto Stefano Montesi

Karol Wojtyla è morto. Ieri sera, alle 21,37, è finita la lunga agonia del papa, e con essa un'era. La notizia piomba su una piazza san Pietro gremita di persone in preghiera. Da tutto il mondo arrivano a Roma i cardinali per un difficile Conclave: sarà una successione quasi "impossibile"

Non se ne fa un altro

Oggi e domani al voto: trema il regno del centrodestra

Oggi e domani si vota in 13 regioni. Nella quattordicesima, la Basilicata, l'apertura delle urne è stata rinviata al 17 e 18 aprile. Rinnovo anche per 366 comuni, tra cui Venezia, Taranto, Lodi, Mantova e Pavia. Il rinnovo dei consigli provinciali riguarderà invece Viterbo e Caserta. Nel complesso dovrebbero andare alle urne quasi 42 milioni di elettori.

La campagna elettorale è stata chiusa con 24 ore di anticipo per l'agonia del papa, ma l'importanza del test rimane inalterata, per quanto riguarda sia le amministrazioni regionali che la ricaduta sul governo centrale. Per la Cdl è essenziale mantenere almeno le cinque regioni principali tra quelle che attualmente governa. Ma se la riconferma appare probabile in Lombardia e in Veneto la partita è apertissima in Piemonte, Lazio e Puglia.

L'esito del voto influirà inevitabilmente anche sugli equilibri all'interno delle singole coalizioni. La vittoria di Vendola in Puglia rafforzerebbe non solo la sinistra radicale ma anche la linea di Romano Prodi e probabilmente lo spingerebbe a insistere per procedere ovunque col metodo delle primarie. Mentre una sconfitta complessiva del polo, soprattutto se Roberto Formigoni dovesse invece essere confermato per la terza volta governatore della Lombardia, indebolirebbe la linea del premier.

Determinate, anche per le polemiche che hanno flagellato la campagna elettorale, il risultato nel Lazio.

ALLE PAGINE 4 E 5

IMMIGRATI

In tutta Europa contro i cpt

In piazza in migliaia   **A PAG. 6**

ZIMBABWE

Vince Mugabe, ma è polemica

L'opposizione: «Brogli»   **A PAG. 7**

SCALA

Riccardo Muti si è dimesso

«Una scelta obbligata»   **A PAGINA 9**

la Repubblica

Fondatore Eugenio Scalfari

Direttore Ezio Mauro

Anno 30 - Numero 79 € 0,90 in Italia

domenica 3 aprile 2005

SEDE: 00147 ROMA, Via Cristoforo Colombo, 90
tel. 06/49821, fax 06/49822923.
Sped. abb. post., art. 1, legge 46/04 del 27 febbraio 2004 - Roma.
Concessionaria di pubblicità:
A. MANZONI & C. Milano - Via Nervesa, 21 - tel. 02/574941.

PREZZI DI VENDITA ALL'ESTERO: Portogallo, Spagna € 1,20
(Azzorre, Madeira, Canarie € 1,40); Grecia € 1,60; Austria, Belgio,
Francia (se con D o Il Venerdì € 2,00), Germania, Lussemburgo,
Monaco P., Olanda € 1,85; Finlandia, Irlanda € 2,00; Albania
Lek 280; Canada $1; Costa Rica Col 1.000; Croazia Kn 13;

Danimarca Kr.15; Egitto EP 15,50; Malta Cents 53; Marocco
MDH 24; Norvegia Kr. 16; Polonia Pln 8,40; Regno Unito Lst. 1,30;
Repubblica Ceca Kc 56; Slovacchia Skk 71; Slovenia Sit. 280;
Svezia Kr. 15; Svizzera Fr. 2,80; Svizzera Tic. Fr. 2,5 (con il Venerdì
Fr. 2,80); Tunisia TD 2; Ungheria Ft. 350; U.S.A $ 1.

www.repubblica.it 1 2

["Il Santo Padre è deceduto questa sera alle 21.37 nel suo appartamento privato" **]**

Il portavoce vaticano Joaquin Navarro Valls, 2 aprile 2005

Da domani il corpo di Giovanni Paolo II esposto in Vaticano, i funerali giovedì. Tre giorni di lutto nazionale. Bush: ha lottato per la libertà

Addio Wojtyla

Il mondo piange il Papa. Si è spento dicendo "Amen"

LA DOPPIA ANIMA DEL REGNO

EUGENIO SCALFARI

QUANDO si dice la Chiesa, si dicono tante cose e tante diverse realtà con una sola parola: la comunità dei fedeli, le congregazioni religiose, i sacerdoti che amministrano i sacramenti, i vescovi successori degli apostoli, la Curia dei ministeri vaticani, il Papa che guida, decide, rappresenta in terra il legame tra le anime credenti e il Cristo che venne per indicare la via della salvezza e della nuova alleanza.

Ieri, mentre il Papa moriva, la Chiesa è stata tutte queste cose insieme. Il mondo dei fedeli, le famiglie, i giovani, i vecchi, i bambini, hanno pregato, hanno pianto, sperando irragionevolmente ma fervidamente di poter riascoltare quella voce nelle basiliche, nelle parrocchie, nelle piazze di tutto il mondo. Non solo i fedeli cattolici, ma i cristiani delle osservanze evangeliche, ortodosse, anglicane, gli ebrei delle sinagoghe, "fratelli maggiori" come li definì Giovanni Paolo.

SEGUE A PAGINA 26

E A SAN PIETRO SCENDE IL SILENZIO

GIUSEPPE D'AVANZO

«IL PAPA è tornato nella casa del Padre». Gli altoparlanti diffondono nella piazza gremita queste otto secche parole che lasciano increduli, nonostante tutto, nonostante fosse ormai vana ogni speranza, nonostante ognuno già fosse preparato all'addio. Centomila volti cercano con un solo movimento la "sua" finestra. Per la prima volta si illumina in questo sabato di attesa, e ora di morte, mentre la campana di Sant'Andrea comincia a battere lenta e solenne il suo annuncio. C'è un applauso. Senza un perché. Come un'onda attraversa la piazza. Irragionevole come ogni maledizione figlia della televisione. I prelati, che conducono la veglia, invitano ad accompagnare con il silenzio «i suoi primi passi nel cielo». Finalmente un silenzio denso invade San Pietro. I volti si impietriscono. C'è chi piange. Chi cade in ginocchio. Chi si segna, mormorando tra sé il suo addio. I più giovani, tanti tra i più giovani, salmodiano: «Alleluja, risorgerà». Una ragazza piange a dirotto stretta ad un'amica.

SEGUE A PAGINA 4

MARCO POLITI

CITTÀ DEL VATICANO — Karol Wojtyla si è spento sereno come un patriarca, straziato come un martire. Alle 21 e 37 di ieri la sua vita si è spezzata. Sui fedeli in piazza San Pietro, sui romani, sul mondo è caduto il colpo di un flash dell'Ansa. «Il Papa è morto».

SEGUE A PAGINA 2
SERVIZI DA PAGINA 2 A PAGINA 27

---

all'interno

Ciampi in tv "Perso un padre"

JERKOV e MAROZZI

Oltre le mura nella sua città

VITTORIO ZUCCONI

Sede vacante riti e liturgia

FILIPPO CECCARELLI

domani

Un volume di 172 pagine

L'Atlante sul Pontefice

Domani in edicola con "Repubblica", l'Atlante su Giovanni Paolo II: un volume di 172 pagine a 2,90 euro in più

Urne aperte anche domani fino alle 15. L'incognita dell'affluenza

Regionali, oggi si vota è un test su Berlusconi

ALLE PAGINE 28 e 29 con un commento di ILVO DIAMANTI

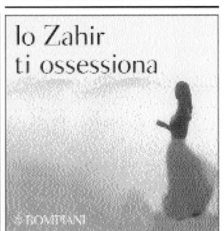

lo Zahir ti ossessiona

BOMPIANI

121

LA STAMPA

DOMENICA 3 APRILE 2005. ANNO 139. N. 91. € 0,90 IN ITALIA [PREZZI TANDEM ED ESTERO IN ULTIMA] ● SPED. ABB. POST. - D. L. 353/03 (CONV. IN L. 27/02/04 N. 46) ART. 1 COMMA 1, DCB - TO
www.lastampa.it

PER I GIOVANI LE ULTIME PAROLE DEL PONTEFICE: «GRAZIE, VI HO CERCATO E ORA SIETE VENUTI DA ME». LO SPORT SI FERMA, ANNULLATE PARTITE E DIRETTE TV

IL MONDO PIANGE IL PAPA

Giovanni Paolo II è morto alle 21,37. Domani la data dei funerali. Una folla commossa riunita nella notte davanti a San Pietro
Il messaggio di Ciampi: «Ha segnato la storia». Bush: «È stato un campione di libertà». Proclamati tre giorni di lutto nazionale

LA GIUSTIZIA IL MALE E IL PERDONO

Barbara Spinelli

LUI che parlò così spesso di luce, perché nessun racconto edificante ma solo la visione nitida può sconfiggere il male quando si nasconde, si dissimula. Lui che di chiarità aveva quasi sete, al punto che un giorno disse nella preghiera ecumenica di Assisi: «Le tenebre non si dissipano con le armi; le tenebre si allontanano accendendo i fari di luce». Lui che era sempre in cerca, mai come chi è già pervenuto alla verità ma come chi non cessa di essere in cammino, Papa itinerante anche quando si chiudeva nel silenzio e se ne stava inginocchiato ore, raccolto nella piccola cella in Vaticano. Lui che non si stancava di parlare della via, di come fosse importante mettersi in movimento, non sedersi, non abdicare: e la via era per lui la sostanza più vera dell'essere, era la parola che ricorreva nelle omelie e negli angelus, nelle encicliche e nelle lettere apostoliche. Perché tutto stava a esser pronti, a offrire ogni giorno il proprio corpo al destino di morte, a rispondere alla chiamata, a non indugiare come le vergini folli o come chi deve ancora prendere i sandali o la cintura o gli averi affastellati in terra. Lui che ripeteva: «In un viale senza uscita, l'unica uscita è nel viale stesso».

Di tutto questo si sente già oggi la mancanza. Di quello sguardo particolarissimo, che coglieva alla sprovvista e sembrava come sboccato da arco inatteso. Di quel volto che esprimeva fedeltà contadiana ininterrotta, senso del servizio, e quella maestà speciale che non scaturisce dalla certezza delle cose ultime ma dall'attitudine a obbedire e tremare nel medesimo istante, a credere e a disperare della ragioni del credere. Di quel segnale di partenza si sente la mancanza, che Giovanni Paolo II impersonò fin dai primi giorni del pontificato e in questi ultimi anni, che sono stati di svuotamento e di pienezza, di morte quotidiana accettata e di morte vinta. «Muoio ogni giorno - cotidie morior»: le parole di San Paolo rivivevano in lui e si congiungevano ai versi sublimi di Orazio, che citò un giorno di settembre, nel 2003, quasi sussurrandole a se stesso: «Non omnis moriar...» - «Non morirò del tutto: gran parte di me sfuggirà alla funebre dea...» (Odi III-30,v.6). Gerusalemme e Roma accostate, intrecciate: lì era la via, la sua via.

Il primo segnale di partenza fu lanciato a chi ancora viveva il totalitarismo comunista, e ne era prigioniero anche con la mente. Il Papa andò nella sua terra polacca per dire solo tre parole: «Non abbiate paura!», e le ripeté più volte, e fu la prima grande crepa nel muro che per decenni aveva cinto il male più durevole del secolo.

CONTINUA A PAGINA 5 PRIMA COLONNA

Il pianto e il dolore in tutto il mondo

Ansaldo, Beccantini, Buccheri, Condio, Corbi, Cotto, Galeazzi, Gawronski, Giovannini, Martinetti, Mastrolilli, Ruotolo, Vergnano, Zaccaria DA PAGINA 2 A PAGINA 17

E NELLA PIAZZA E' SCESO IL SILENZIO

Igor Man

IL Papa venuto dal freddo ci ha lasciati. Il suo grande cuore s'è fermato alle 21 e 37 minuti del 2 di aprile, nella notte di Roma, col primo alito di primavera. Quella primavera romana ch'egli definiva «capricciosa ma allegra». Quando la notizia è piombata sulla folla che allagava la piazza dei suoi tanti trionfi, la poltiglia di consonanti che aveva raggiunto la stanza del Papa s'è taciuta. Di colpo. Con la terribilità della mannaia che tronca tutti i fili della speranza. Già da molte ore, Wojtyla alternava momenti di rifugio nel sopore a momenti di cauta vigilanza.

Sabato mattina aveva ricevuto i cardinali Silvestrini e Touran, utili suoi compagni di viaggio («ministri degli esteri») innumerevoli volte. Il Papa respirava senza l'ausilio dell'ossigeno, non c'era la flebo nella mano destra che il cardinale Silvestrini ha baciato dicendogli: «Santo Padre, siamo qui per ringraziarla. Di quello che vostra santità ha fatto per l'uomo, con la Parola evangelica, con l'esempio. Per aver fatto conoscere Gesù agli altri. Grazie di tutto, santità». I due cardinali s'erano inginocchiati: quando si sono levati in piedi per congedarsi («non senza particolare emozione») il Papa ha accennato un gesto tra il saluto e la benedizione.

Come diceva Paolo VI, il tratto ultimo della vita spesso procede a strappi siccome un vecchio treno. E c'è sempre qualcuno che aspetta al terzo binario, il «binario morto» dove il viaggio finisce. Ora è chiaro che mentre quel cardinale ci dice che Giovanni Paolo s'approssima all'ultima boa, e quell'altro porporato ci dà per praticamente avvenuta la morte «clinica» (encefalogramma piatto eccetera) è chiaro, miracolosamente chiaro, che Papa

CONTINUA A PAGINA 7 PRIMA COLONNA

SERVIZI

IL PARROCO DELL'UMANITA'

Difensore della fede tradizionale, ma aperto a ogni modernità

Marco Tosatti A PAGINA 14

IL DIALOGO APERTO CON LE ALTRE FEDI

Una svolta per la Chiesa il riconoscimento degli errori del passato

Enzo Bianchi e Fiamma Nirenstein A PAG. 10

GLI UOMINI E I TEMI DEL CONCLAVE

Italiani in minoranza ma favoriti nella corsa alla successione

Luigi La Spina A PAGINA 11

ALMENO UN MILIONE DI PELLEGRINI

Roma pronta all'invasione La Protezione civile prepara stadi e tendopoli

Francesco Grignetti A PAG. 9

UN PONTE DI PACE TRA EST E OVEST

Fassino: protagonista del mondo che cambia Urbani: sfida per i liberali

INTERVISTE DI R.Barenghi e F.Geremicca A PAG.15

VOTANO 41 MILIONI, SEGGI APERTI OGGI E DOMANI FINO ALLE 15

Alle urne per scegliere i presidenti di 13 Regioni

LA CAMPAGNA

INSULTI E RICORSI POI COMMOSSO SILENZIO

Le sfide condizionate dalle scelte dei Tar E il lutto oscurerà l'impatto mediatico

Fabrizio Rondolino A PAGINA 19

ROMA. Oggi e domani 41 milioni di italiani sono chiamati alle urne per scegliere 13 governatori, due presidenti di Provincia e 366 sindaci. La campagna elettorale è stata condizionata dai Tribunali Amministrativi, che hanno bloccato la consultazione in Basilicata, rinviandola al 17 aprile, e hanno dovuto decidere, a vario titolo, in Lombardia, Lazio, Piemonte e Liguria. Comunque vada il voto, l'impatto mediatico del risultato sarà oscurato dal lutto per il Papa.

Bruzzone E ALTRI SERVIZI A PAGG. 18 E 19

LA SCALA

RICCARDO MUTI SI E' DIMESSO

L'addio del direttore: una scelta obbligata

Beria di Argentine, Cappelletto, Minervino e Poletti ALLE PAG. 30 E 31

Amman, Jordan

THE JORDAN TIMES

SUBSCRIPTION COPY 200 Fils
Published by the Jordan Press Foundation
Volume 30 | Number 8939

TODAY

Sunday, April 3, 2005
Safar 23, 1426 Hijri

TAFILEH

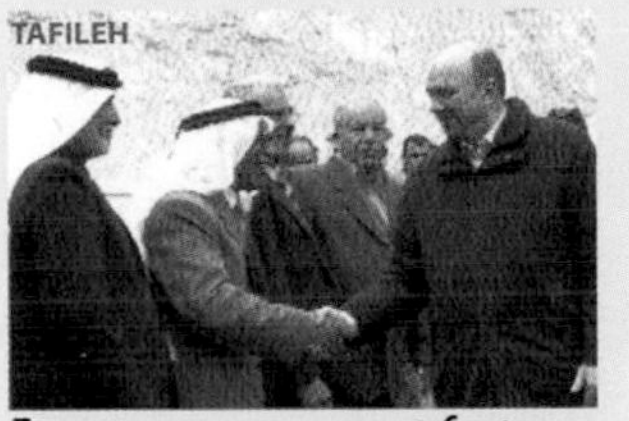

Fayez opens garment factory

Facility expected to offer immediate employment to 180 women and 100 men | 2

EGYPT

Gov't defends 'unnecessary' emergency laws

Activists argue that September's presidential elections will be unfair if the restrictive laws are in place | 4

ECONOMY

Gulf states most competitive in Arab world'

Population growth will push Jordan's 13% jobless rate to 24% in a decade if something isn't done —Muasher | 11

WEATHER

A slight drop in temperature is forecast for today with cloudy to partly cloudy skies, accompanied with a chance for scattered showers, particularly in the northern and central parts of the Kingdom. In Aqaba, it will be fair with winds northerly moderate to brisk and seas calm.

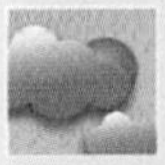

Min./Max. temp.

Amman	06/13	Jordan Valley	10/20
Aqaba	14/23	Hilly Areas	04/09
Deserts	05/16		

VATICAN

Pope dies; world mourns

VATICAN CITY (Reuters) — Pope John Paul II, the man known as "God's Athlete," who transformed the papacy by taking his message to every corner of the world, died on Saturday aged 84, felled by ailments that left him lame and voiceless.

"Our beloved Holy Father John Paul has returned to the house of the Father," Archbishop Leonardo Sandri, said announcing the death to a huge crowd that had gathered under the pontiff's windows to pray for a miraculous recovery that never came.

The Vatican said the Pope died in his apartments at 9:37pm (1937 GMT), just as the crowd was serenading the charismatic Polish churchman who led the world's 1.1 billion Catholics.

As the news spread through Rome, thousands upon thousands of faithful streamed up to the Vatican to join those already there, paying respects to a man who helped undermine Communism in Europe while upholding traditional church orthodoxy.

The exact cause of death was not immediately given but the Pope's health had deteriorated steadily over the past decade with the onset of Parkinson's disease and arthritis. Earlier this year, it took a sharp turn for the worse.

He had an operation in February to ease serious breathing problems, but never regained his strength and last Thursday developed an infection and high fever that soon precipitated heart failure, kidney problems and ultimately death.

"The Catholic Church has lost its shepherd. The world has lost a champion of human freedom and a good and faithful servant of God has been called home," US President George W. Bush said in a televised address from the White House.

The slow mourning toll of one of the great bells of St Peter's Basilica made the only sound to cut the stunning, tearful silence in the Vatican.

Necks craned up towards the lighted windows of the Pope's apartments where his once vigorous body now lay lifeless.

Funeral

According to pre-written church rules, the Pontiff's mourning rites will last 9 days and his body laid to rest in the crypt underneath St Peter's Basilica.

Italian media said the funeral would be held on Wednesday.

The conclave to elect a new Pope will start in 15 to 20 days, with 117 cardinals from around the world gathering in the Vatican's Sistine Chapel to choose a successor.

There is no favourite candidate to take over. The former Archbishop Karol Wojtyla of Krakow was himself regarded as an outsider when he was elevated to the papacy on October 16, 1978.

In his native Poland bells tolled across the country and sirens wailed in the capital Warsaw as news of the Pope's death dashed any lingering hopes of a miraculous recovery.

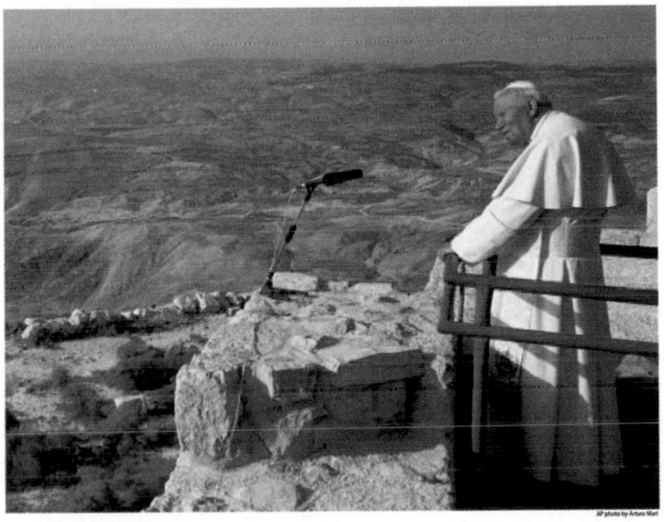

AP photo by Arturo Mari

Pope John Paul II stands on top of Mount Nebo during a March 2000 visit to Jordan

"I am overwhelmed by pain. I have prayed for two days and thought that a miracle will happen, but it didn't happen and now we can only weep," said Teresa Swidnicka in Krakow, where Wojtyla was once a bishop.

Apart from his battle against communism, John Paul will be also be remembered for his unyielding defence of traditional Vatican doctrines, drawing criticism from liberal Catholics who opposed his proclamations against contraception, abortion, married priests and women clergy.

In death, tributes poured in from around the world.

"John Paul II was one of the greatest men of the last century. Perhaps the greatest," said Henry Kissinger, former US secretary of state.

Former British Prime Minister Margaret Thatcher said: "By combating the falsehoods of communism and proclaiming the true dignity of the individual, his was the moral force behind victory in the Cold War."

Vigorous papacy

The first non-Italian Pope in 455 years, John Paul threw off the stiff trappings of the papacy, meeting ordinary people everywhere he travelled. In over a quarter century on the world stage, he was both a champion of the downtrodden and an often contested defender of orthodoxy within his own church.

But as the years passed, so his energy faded.

Continued on page 3

PALESTINE

Abbas sacks national security chief

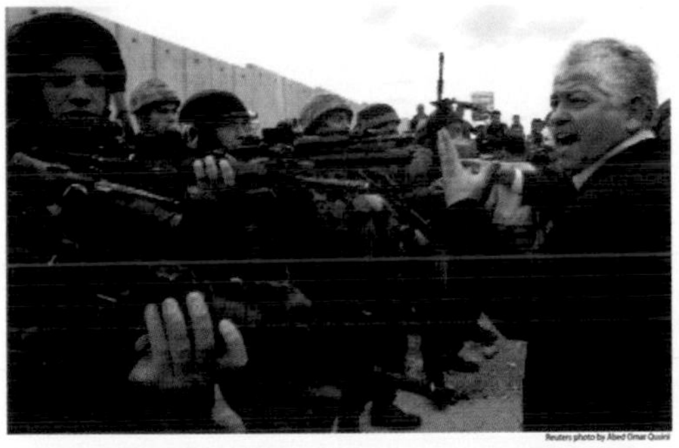

Reuters photo by Abed Omar Qusini

A Palestinian demonstrator on Saturday shouts at Israeli forces during a protest against the seperation barrier near the West Bank village of Nazlat Eisa

RAMALLAH (AFP) — Palestinian leader Mahmoud Abbas on Saturday placed West Bank security services on a "state of alert" in a bid to curb rampant security chaos, a Palestinian security official told AFP.

Troops began deploying across main West Bank cities late Saturday, just hours after the Palestinian leader ordered similar measures in Ramallah following an incident earlier this week in which gunmen opened fire inside his Muqata compound. The order was given at top-level meeting between Abbas and his security chiefs late Saturday, the official said on condition of anonymity.

At the meeting, Abbas also gave the order for all branches of the sprawling Palestinian security services to be immediately relocated outside his Muqata compound. The order, effective immediately, will see the offices of the national security, military intelligence and police, among others, being rehoused on a large tract of land located about a kilometre away from the Muqata, an official who attended the meeting told AFP.

Continued on page 3

Mulki says Israel to release prisoners

By Alia Shukri Hamzeh

AMMAN — Foreign Minister Hani Mulki on Saturday said Israel was expected to release Jordanian prisoners held on political and security charges by the end of this week.

Mulki and other Foreign Ministry officials said the release of the prisoners was "in its final stages," noting that Israeli authorities, namely the justice ministry, "approved it."

He said the government did not spare any effort to secure the release of around 25 prisoners, some of whom were held before the 1994 peace treaty with Israel.

"We are still working on the release of the prisoners. It's one of our top priorities and we will not stop until we release all of them," Mulki told The Jordan Times.

An Israeli justice ministry recommendation on the prisoners was expected to be presented to the Israeli Cabinet.

Foreign Ministry Spokesperson Rajab Sukayri said around 14 prisoners were expected to be released.

Some observers and officials saw the expected release as an Israeli "goodwill gesture" after Jordan reinstated its envoy to Tel Aviv.

They said the move would pave the way for the repeatedly postponed visit of Israeli Foreign Minister Silvan Shalom to the Kingdom.

Mulki to visit Lebanon, Syria

Meanwhile, Mulki confirmed that he plans to visit Beirut and Damascus after the Lebanese elections, expected in May, to follow up on decisions made during the Arab summit in Algeria.

Continued on page 3

IRAQ

20 US troops hurt in mass Abu Ghraib attack

BAGHDAD (Reuters) — Dozens of insurgents mounted a sustained attack on Abu Ghraib prison outside Baghdad on Saturday, detonating two suicide car bombs and firing rocket-propelled grenades before US troops repelled the assault.

At least 20 US soldiers and 12 detainees were wounded in the carefully planned attack, which began at around 1500 GMT and lasted for around an hour, the US military said. "A group of between 40 and 60 insurgents attacked the US forward operating base at Abu Ghraib," Lieutenant Colonel Guy Rudisill, spokesman for detainee affairs, told Reuters.

"They detonated two VBIEDs [suicide car bombs] and also fired rocket-propelled grenades into the prison camp... it was a sustained attack," he said. Mortars and small arms fire were also directed towards the prison, on Baghdad's western edge. "The attacks were intermittent. They would fire RPGs and then stop, then they would attack again," Rudisill said. US forces responded with heavy weapons, eventually bringing the situation under control. It was not known how many insurgents were wounded or killed in the battle.

Witnesses said the second car bomb was detonated against US forces as they were trying to evacuate casualties from the first. US troops sealed the prison grounds. It was not believed any insurgents penetrated the perimeter.

Abu Ghraib, notorious for the US prisoner abuse scandal that emerged last year, is one of three US-run detention facilities in Iraq and holds around 2,000 prisoners.

The jail has been attacked in the past, but the latest assault was believed to be the largest and most determined. It is also the first against the prison for some time, and comes amid recent signs that Iraq's insurgency was calming down.

Assembly to meet

The attack and a suicide car bomb blast north of Baghdad that killed five, were reminders of the profound security challenges Iraqi leaders face as they attempt to form a government more than two months after elections were held.

Senior Iraqi officials have raised concerns that the longer it takes to form a government the more it will fuel the insurgency by making elected authorities appear indecisive.

There is also growing frustration among ordinary Iraqis, more than eight million of whom braved the threat of violence to vote on January 30 and have yet to see any results emerge.

Continued on page 3

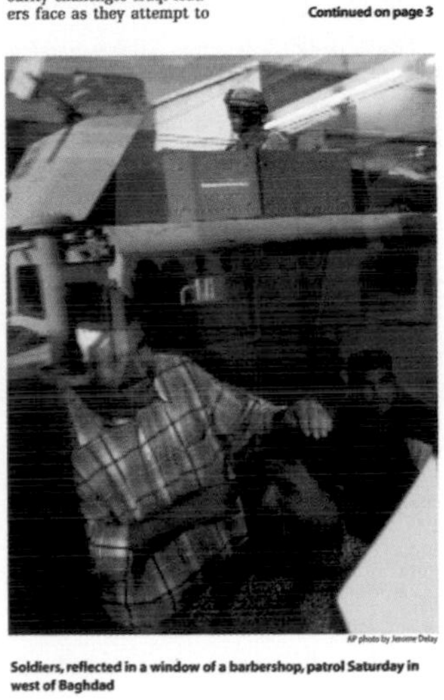

AP photo by Jerome Delay

Soldiers, reflected in a window of a barbershop, patrol Saturday in west of Baghdad

LEBANON

Elections in danger as blast injures 9

BEIRUT (AFP) — Lebanon's pro-Syrian forces on Saturday went on the counter-attack with a demand that could delay elections due in May, as the country was shaken by another bombing amid a quickening Syrian troop withdrawal.

In Damascus, an official said that Foreign Minister Farouk Sharaa would unveil a timetable for a full pullout after talks with UN special envoy Terje Roed-Larsen on Sunday.

Prime minister-designate Omar Karameh, at a meeting late Friday with his pro-Syrian allies, decided to stay on, despite having failed over the past three weeks to form a new government to ease Lebanon's political crisis.

Karameh, who said Tuesday he would resign, was tasked with forming a Cabinet "to save the country," following the opposition's refusal to join a national unity government, said Parliament Speaker Nabih Berri.

Continued on page 3

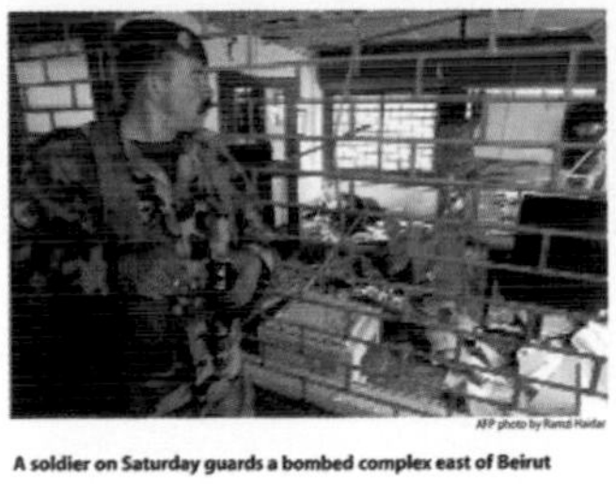

AFP photo by Ramzi Haidar

A soldier on Saturday guards a bombed complex east of Beirut

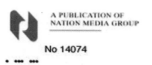

THE NEWSPAPER THAT SERVES THE NATION

A PUBLICATION OF
NATION MEDIA GROUP

No 14074

www.nationmedia.com

SUNDAY NATION

Nairobi, April 3, 2005

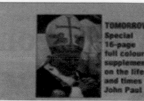

TOMORROW
Special
16-page
full colour
supplement
on the life
and times of
John Paul II

Ksh40/00 (Tsh600/00; Ush900/00)

Rest in Peace

Pope John Paul II: 1920–2005

124

DOMINGO 3 *de abril de 2005*

EL MAÑANA

LA VERDAD SIN FRONTERAS

VERBO LIBRE

El trabajo más importante no es la transformación del mundo, sino la transformación de nosotros mismos. –JUAN PABLO II

DEPORTES
SAN ANGELO venció anoche a Bucks de Laredo para emparejar la serie de playoffs por bando **(1D**

LOCAL
DOS HOMBRES armados balean al abogado Anselmo Guarneros y un acompañante **(1B**

Amén

Fotos: AP

Sembrador de esperanza

➤ Fue actor, deportista, huyó de los nazis y finalmente, se convirtió en uno de los Papas más influyentes del siglo XX. En sus 104 viajes, Juan Pablo II pisó todo el planeta y se relacionó especialmente con los jóvenes **(Suplemento**

Tristeza internacional

➤ Líderes del mundo y millones de católicos despiden con tristeza a Juan Pablo II tras su muerte, han elogiado su carisma y su lucha por la libertad durante 26 años al frente de la Iglesia Católica. **(11B**

Va Norberto al cónclave

➤ El próximo Papa será elegido por 118 cardenales. Norberto Rivera, de México, participará en el proceso para la designación del Pontífice y es uno de los candidatos. **(16B**

➤ **Juan Pablo II acaba su peregrinar** ➤ **Impacta su muerte a mil 100 millones de creyentes alrededor del mundo**

CIUDAD DEL VATICANO.- El camino llegó a su fin tras 26 años de peregrinar.

Juan Pablo II, el Papa que recorrió el mundo extendiendo su fe, murió ayer a los 84 años, tras 48 horas de agonía.

El doblar de las campanas, que confirmó su muerte, transformó los rezos en un nutrido aplauso de los más de 70 mil fieles que desde el pasado jueves lo acompañaban en la Plaza de San Pedro, pendientes de su ventana.

"El Santo Padre ha muerto esta noche a las 21:37 horas de Italia (13:37 horas de México) en su apartamento", informó su portavoz, el español Joaquín Navarro-Valls, a través de un comunicado.

Poco antes de morir, el Papa recibió la extrema unción y falleció tomado de la mano del Arzobispo polaco Stanislaw Dziwisz, su secretario personal.

"Todos nos sentimos huérfanos esta anoche", expresó el Arzobispo argentino Leonardo Sandri, sustituto de la Secretaría de Estado, encargado de comunicar la muerte del Pontífice a las miles de personas que esperaban en la explanada del Vaticano.

Desde el 24 de febrero, Juan Pablo II respiraba gracias a una traqueotomía, el 30 de marzo le fue colocada una sonda para alimentarlo y su condición se agravó un día después.

Para los teólogos, el polaco Karol Wojtyla fue un hombre que revolucionó la fe; para los historiadores, alguien que ayudó a derrotar al comunismo, y para los mil 100 millones de católicos un pastor carismático.

De acuerdo con el protocolo, su muerte debió ser certificada por el Cardenal español Eduardo Martínez Somalo, el Camarlengo, que según la tradición repitió 3 veces su nombre de pila –Karol, Karol, Karol- y golpeó su frente con un martillo de plata.

Posteriormente se destruyó el anillo del pescador, acto con el que se puso fin oficialmente a su Pontificado.

MÉXICO TRISTE

"Esta noche he perdido un amigo y sobre todo un padre. Imagino que para México debe ser una tristeza infinita", comentó

a Reforma el cardenal eslovaco Josef Tomko, uno de los pocos que tuvo acceso anoche a la habitación del Pontífice, apenas murió.

El cardenal mexicano Javier Lozano Barragán, Ministro de Salud del Vaticano, dijo en entrevista que el Papa estuvo inconsciente desde las 18.30 horas, tiempo de Italia.

"Luego fue apagándose. Murió en serenidad, con absoluta tranquilidad", expresó.

Fue en México, País que visitó cinco veces entre 1979 y 2002, que Juan Pablo II inició su "Pontificado itinerante" durante el cual realizó 104 viajes por 129 naciones.

"Durante su última visita se despidió de México diciendo: 'Me voy y no me voy'. Hoy efectivamente el Papa se va pero no se va, porque en México su mensaje, su presencia y ejemplo restará para siempre", recordó el Embajador ante la Santa Sede, Javier Moctezuma Barragán.

(Esteban Israel / Agencia Reforma)

➤ **¿Qué idioma se habla en el cielo?** ➤ **Milagro en Zacatecas** ➤ **Sus últimos minutos (10 - 16A**

EL PAPA Y SU LEGADO SECCIÓN ESPECIAL

El inicio — Octubre '78
Karol Wojtyla es elegido como el primer Papa no italiano en 455 años.

En tierra regia — Enero '79
En su primera visita a Monterrey, el Papa saluda a la multitud en el Río.

El atentado — Mayo '81
El turco Mehmet Ali Agca dispara tres tiros al Pontífice en la Plaza de San Pedro.

Cumbre histórica — Dic. '89
El encuentro con Gorbachov fue el primero entre un Papa y un líder soviético.

La despedida — Marzo '05
El Papa apareció por última vez en la Plaza San Pedro, pero no pudo hablar.

Domingo
3 de Abril
del 2005

194 páginas,
12 secciones, $12

EL NORTE

Hoy inició el Horario de Verano:
¿Ya adelantó 1 hora su reloj?

Año LXVII
Número 24,227
Monterrey, N.L., México

www.elnorte.com

Muere Juan Pablo II
Acaba su peregrinar

Termina la agonía del Pontífice

Por **ESTEBAN ISRAEL**
EL NORTE / ITALIA

1920-2005

CIUDAD DEL VATICANO.- El camino llegó a su fin tras 26 años de peregrinar.

Juan Pablo II, el Papa que recorrió el mundo extendiendo la fe católica, murió ayer a los 84 años tras 48 horas de agonía.

El doblar de las campanas, que confirmó su muerte, transformó los rezos en un nutrido aplauso de los más de 70 mil fieles que desde el pasado jueves lo acompañaban en la Plaza de San Pedro, pendientes de su ventana.

"El Santo Padre ha muerto esta noche a las 21:37 horas de Italia (13:37 horas de México) en su apartamento", informó su portavoz, el español Joaquín Navarro-Valls, a través de un comunicado.

Poco antes de morir, el Papa recibió la extremaunción y falleció tomado de la mano del Arzobispo polaco Stanislaw Dziwisz, su secretario personal.

"Todos nos sentimos huérfanos esta noche", expresó el Arzobispo argentino Leonardo Sandri, sustituto de la Secretaría de Estado, encargado de comunicar la muerte del Pontífice a las miles de personas que esperaban en la explanada del Vaticano.

Desde el 24 de febrero, Juan Pablo II respiraba gracias a una traqueotomía, y el 30 de marzo se le colocada una sonda para alimentarlo, pero su condición se agravó un día después.

Para los teólogos, el polaco Karol Wojtyla fue un hombre que revolucionó la fe; para los historiadores, alguien que ayudó a derrotar al comunismo, y para los mil 100 millones de católicos, un pastor carismático.

De acuerdo con el protocolo, su muerte debió ser certificada por el Cardenal español Eduardo Martínez Somalo, el Camarlengo, quien según la tradición, preguntó tres veces al Papa su nombre de pila tocando suavemente su frente con un martillo de plata.

Posteriormente se destruyó el anillo del pescador, acto con el que se puso fin oficialmente al Pontificado de Juan Pablo II.

"Esta noche he perdido un amigo y, sobre todo, un padre", comentó a Grupo REFORMA el Cardenal eslovaco Josef Tomko, uno de los pocos que tuvieron acceso anoche a la habitación del Pontífice apenas murió. "Imagino que para México debe ser una tristeza infinita".

El Cardenal mexicano Javier Lozano Barragán, Ministro de Salud del Vaticano, dijo en entrevista que el Papa estuvo inconsciente desde las 18:30 horas.

"Luego fue apagándose", expresó Lozano Barragán. "Murió en serenidad, con absoluta tranquilidad".

Fue en México, País que visitó cinco veces entre 1979 y el 2002, donde Juan Pablo II inició su "Pontificado itinerante", durante el que realizó 104 viajes por 129 naciones.

"Durante su última visita se despidió de México diciendo: 'Me voy, pero no me voy'", recordó el Embajador ante la Santa Sede, Javier Moctezuma Barragán. "Hoy efectivamente el Papa se va, pero no se va, porque en México su mensaje, su presencia y ejemplo estarán para siempre".

Los católicos deberán observar nueve días de estricto luto. Se tiene previsto que el entierro del Pontífice se lleve a cabo en la Basílica de San Pedro entre el próximo miércoles y viernes.

Ayer el Presidente Vicente Fox pronunció un mensaje en el que invitó a los mexicanos a honrar la memoria del Papa y a recordar el legado humanista y espiritual que dejó al mundo.

EN ROMA *La Plaza de San Pedro recibió ayer a miles de personas que se congregaron para despedir a Juan Pablo II.*

EN MONTERREY *Ante la imagen del Papa en el altar de la Basílica de Guadalupe, regios iniciaron una noche de vigilia.*

Cuatro mexicanos tendrán voto

■ México tendrá cuatro Cardenales entre los 117 que elegirán al nuevo Pontífice. Ernesto Corripio no votará por ser mayor de 80 años.

Norberto Rivera Carrera
Arzobispo Primado de México

Adolfo Suárez Rivera
Arzobispo Emérito de Monterrey

Juan Sandoval Íñiguez
Arzobispo de Guadalajara

Javier Lozano Barragán
Ministro de Salud del Vaticano

▶ **NACIONAL** ▶ **EDITORIALES** ▶ **GENTE!** ▶ **VIDA!** ▶ **DEPORTES** ▶ **LOCAL** ▶

¿Qué sigue?

▶ Tras la muerte del Papa, los Cardenales de todo el mundo viajarán a Roma para la ceremonia del velorio y la sepultura.

▶ El cuerpo de Juan Pablo II, embalsamado y vestido con los hábitos pontificios, será colocado en una capilla privada para que los Cardenales y los miembros de la Casa Pontificia puedan verlo.

▶ La fecha del entierro deberá ser entre el cuarto y el sexto día después de su muerte, es decir, entre este miércoles 6 y el viernes 8 de abril.

▶ El cónclave para elegir al sucesor no podrá realizarse antes de 15 días ni después de 20 días de la muerte del Papa.

▶ Serán 117 Cardenales – en el interior de la Capilla Sixtina– quienes designarán al nuevo Papa.

▶ Si después de 21 votaciones no hay un elegido, el sistema se cambia de mayoría calificada (dos tercios) a mayoría absoluta (la mitad más uno).

▶ Cuando alguien alcance la mayoría, se le preguntará al elegido si acepta su designación y se le pedirá que diga cómo quiere ser llamado.

▶ Las papeletas de votación serán quemadas con paja seca para producir humo blanco y anunciar al mundo que hay un nuevo Papa.

elnorte.com
Cobertura en línea, gráficos animados, fotogalerías, videos y más sobre la muerte del Papa.

Llega Navidad a Texas en Semana Santa

Quitan triunfo a los Rayados

2-0 Deportes

Rompen regios récord de compras en McAllen, Laredo y San Antonio

Por **ROBERTO GUERRERO**

Codos, codos, pero no tanto. Los regiomontanos que aprovecharon el periodo vacacional de Semana Santa para viajar a Texas salieron de compras a lo grande.

El fortalecimiento del Peso, las ofertas de temporada y el aumento temporal en la franquicia para traer mercancías por hasta 300 dólares libres de impuestos provocaron que en la Semana Santa llovieran dólares, sobre todo de regiomontanos, en los comercios de Texas.

Las tiendas de esa zona aumentaron sus ventas a niveles no vistos en los mismos periodos vacacionales de los últimos años, según las Cámaras de Comercio de Laredo, McAllen y San Antonio, que estiman aumentos promedio de entre 30 y 40 por ciento en comparación a la Semana Santa del 2004.

René González, secretario de relaciones externas de Laredo, atribuyó a los regiomontanos el éxito de la temporada.

"Nos fue muy bien este año, sobre todo con los regiomontanos, que siempre frecuentan la ciudad (Laredo) en esta temporada", sostuvo González.

"Tuvimos muy buenas ventas en este periodo. El tráfico que se veía en la frontera era inmenso. El incremento en las ventas, que se espera sea del 40 por ciento, llegó a ser hasta del 70 por ciento en algunas tiendas".

En el caso de McAllen, la afluencia de vacacionistas mexicanos llevó a la tienda Target de esa ciudad al primer lugar nacional de ventas, desplazando inclusive al Target Super Center de Chicago, estableciéndose que ofrece alimentos y tiene un restaurante, dijo Manuel Montemayor, gerente de la sucursal fronteriza.

"Desde enero le ha ido muy bien a McAllen", dijo Silvia Garza, vicepresidenta de la Cámara de Comercio de esa ciudad, "pero más aún en esta temporada, cuando se ven todas las tiendas llenas, y mucho mejor que en Navidad, el Día de Acción de Gracias o el Día del Presidente".

Garza estimó que el incremento en las ventas en McAllen fue de un 30 por ciento y lo atribuye a un Peso fuerte y a las numerosas promociones que ofrece la mayoría de las tiendas

departamentales de la localidad.

Además a que, del 11 al 28 de marzo, los mexicanos que regresaron de Estados Unidos por carretera disfrutaron de una franquicia de 300 dólares por persona, en lugar de los 50 dólares que permiten regularmente las autoridades.

Para Raúl González, director general de Casa San Antonio en Monterrey, aún es prematuro reportar los niveles de ventas derivados de la Semana Mayor, aunque tiene un pronóstico optimista.

"Esperamos que (al tener los números reales) haya un incremento tanto en la cantidad de visitantes como en las ventas de entre el 30 y 40 por ciento en relación con el año anterior, principalmente de habitantes de las ciudades de Monterrey, Torreón y Saltillo".

EL PAPA Y SU LEGADO SECCIÓN ESPECIAL

El inicio Octubre '78
Karol Wojtyla es elegido Papa, el primero no italiano en 455 años.

En México Enero '79
Besa por primera vez suelo mexicano, al que regresó cuatro veces más.

El atentado Mayo '81
El turco Mehmet Alí Agca dispara al Pontífice en la Plaza de San Pedro.

Cumbre histórica Dic. '89
El encuentro con Gorbachov es el primer encuentro entre un Papa y un líder soviético.

La despedida Marzo '05
El Papa aparece por última vez en San Pedro y ya no puede hablar.

Domingo 3 de Abril del 2005
México, D.F.
222 Páginas
12 Secciones, $ 12.00
SECCIÓN A

REFORMA
CORAZÓN DE MÉXICO

¿YA ADELANTÓ **1 HORA** SU RELOJ?

Año 12, Número 4125
www.reforma.com

MUERE JUAN PABLO II

Acaba su peregrinar

Termina la agonía del Pontífice entre plegarias de todo el mundo

POR ESTEBAN ISRAEL
REFORMA / ITALIA

CIUDAD DEL VATICANO.- El camino llegó a su fin tras 26 años de peregrinar.

Juan Pablo II, el Papa que recorrió el mundo extendiendo su fe, murió ayer a los 84 años, tras 48 horas de agonía.

El doblar de las campanas, que confirmó su muerte, transformó los rezos en un nutrido aplauso de los más de 70 mil fieles que desde el pasado jueves lo acompañaban en la Plaza de San Pedro, pendientes de su ventana.

"El Santo Padre ha muerto esta noche a las 21:37 horas de Italia (13:37 horas de México) en su apartamento", informó su portavoz, el español Joaquín Navarro Valls, a través de un comunicado.

Poco antes de morir, el Papa recibió la extremaunción y expiró tomado de la mano del Arzobispo polaco Stanislaw Dziwisz, su secretario personal.

"Todos nos sentimos huérfanos esta noche", expresó el Arzobispo argentino Leonardo Sandri, sustituto de la Secretaría de Estado, encargado de comunicar la muerte del Pontífice a las miles de personas que esperaban en la explanada del Vaticano.

Desde el 24 de febrero, Juan Pablo II respiraba gracias a una traqueotomía; el 30 de marzo le fue colocada una sonda para alimentarlo, y su condición se agravó un día después.

Para los teólogos, el polaco Karol Wojtyla fue un hombre que revolucionó la fe; para los historiadores, alguien que ayudó a derrotar al comunismo, y para los mil 100 millones de católicos, un pastor carismático.

Según el protocolo, su muerte debió ser certificada por el Cardenal español Eduardo Martínez Somalo, el Camarlengo, que según la tradición repitió 3 veces su nombre de pila: "Karol, Karol, Karol", y golpeó su frente con un martillo de plata.

Posteriormente destruyó el Anillo del Pescador, acto con el que se puso fin oficialmente a su Pontificado.

"Esta noche he perdido un amigo y sobre todo un padre. Imagino que para México debe ser una tristeza infinita", comentó a REFORMA el Cardenal eslovaco Josef Tomko, uno de los pocos que tuvo acceso anoche a la habitación del Pontífice apenas murió.

El Cardenal mexicano Javier Lozano Barragán, Ministro de Salud del Vaticano, dijo en entrevista que el Papa estuvo inconsciente desde las 18:30 horas.

"Luego fue apagándose. Murió con serenidad y tranquilidad", expresó.

Fue en México, país que visitó cinco veces entre 1979 y el 2002, que Juan Pablo II inició su "Pontificado itinerante", durante el cual realizó 104 viajes por 129 naciones.

"Durante su última visita se despidió de México diciendo: Me voy, pero no me voy. Hoy, efectivamente, el Papa se va, pero no se va, porque en México su mensaje y ejemplo estará para siempre", recordó el Embajador ante la Santa Sede, Javier Moctezuma Barragán.

El mundo católico observa desde hoy nueve días de estricto luto. Se tiene previsto que su entierro se lleve a cabo en la Basílica de San Pedro entre el miércoles y el viernes próximos.

A las 18:00 horas, tiempo de México, el Presidente Vicente Fox pronunció un mensaje a la nación en el que invitó a los mexicanos a honrar la memoria del Papa y a recordar el legado humanista y espiritual que dejó al mundo.

EN EL VATICANO *Católicos de todo el mundo se congregaron en la Plaza de San Pedro para acompañar a Juan Pablo II, con la oración, en sus últimos momentos.*
Foto: Reuters

EN LA VILLA *Al saber de la muerte del Papa, cientos de personas se volcaron a La Villa.*

Cuatro mexicanos tendrán voto

■ México tendrá 4 Cardenales entre los 117 que elegirán al nuevo Papa. Ernesto Corripio no votará por ser mayor de 80 años.

Norberto Rivera Carrera
Arzobispo Primado de México

Adolfo Suárez Rivera
Arzobispo Emérito de Monterrey

Juan Sandoval Íñiguez
Arzobispo de Guadalajara

Javier Lozano Barragán
Ministro de Salud del Vaticano

¿QUÉ SIGUE?

▶ Los Cardenales de todo el mundo deben viajar a Roma para la ceremonia del velorio y la sepultura.

▶ El cuerpo de Juan Pablo II, embalsamado y vestido con los hábitos pontificios, será colocado en una capilla privada para que los Cardenales y los miembros de la Casa Pontificia puedan verlo.

▶ La fecha del entierro deberá ser entre el 6 y el 8 de abril.

▶ El cónclave para elegir al sucesor no podrá realizarse antes de 15 días ni después de 20 tras la muerte del Papa.

▶ Serán 117 Cardenales –en el interior de la Capilla Sixtina– quienes designarán al nuevo Papa.

▶ Si después de 21 rondas de votación no hay un elegido, el sistema se cambia de mayoría calificada (dos tercios) a mayoría absoluta (la mitad más uno).

▶ Cuando alguien alcance la mayoría, se le preguntará al elegido si acepta su designación y se le pedirá que diga cómo quiere ser llamado.

▶ Las papeletas de voto serán quemadas con paja seca para producir humo blanco y anunciar al mundo que ya hay un nuevo Papa.

Bendecidos por el Papa (Gente! 2E) **Un filósofo en el Vaticano (El Ángel)** siga los acontecimientos en el Vaticano *reforma.com*

Ordenan aprehensión de Nahum

Un juez federal giró ayer orden de aprehensión contra el ex director de Giras de la Presidencia Nahum Acosta Lugo por el delito de delincuencia organizada.

Fuentes cercanas al caso dijeron que no se dio la aprehensión por delitos contra la salud porque la PGR no ofreció evidencias suficientes.

Nacional (2A)

Cierra PRD filas con AMLO

REFORMA / REDACCIÓN

LAS DIFERENTES CORRIENTES AL INTERIOR del PRD cerraron filas para defender a Andrés Manuel López Obrador, de cara al juicio de desafuero que enfrenta.

Las principales corrientes perredistas pactaron votar a favor de una reforma estatutaria que permitiría a López Obrador ser candidato presidencial del partido, aun si estuviera sometido a proceso penal.

Con ese propósito, y a propuesta del presidente electo del partido, Leonel Cota, en el Congreso Nacional que se efectuará dentro de tres semanas se reformarían los artículos 3 y 14 del estatuto del PRD.

La corriente Izquierda Democrática Nacional –que encabeza René Bejarano– propuso que en el Congreso Nacional del partido se aclame a López Obrador como candidato a la Presidencia.

Los dirigentes del PRD en el DF acordaron tener un solo esquema para la resistencia civil, y afirmaron que López Obrador llegará a las boletas electorales del 2006 aun si su nombre tiene que ser escrito de puño y letra de sus simpatizantes.

Organizaciones campesinas anunciaron bloqueos de carreteras y de edificios públicos, en el marco de las acciones pacíficas de resistencia civil contra el desafuero.

▶ **Caen sospechosos en casa de Camacho ...(7A)**

...Y su remoción depende de un juez

LA DECISIÓN DE SEPARAR DE SU CARGO al Jefe de Gobierno del DF, Andrés Manuel López Obrador, quedó en manos de un juez.

El dictamen de la Sección Instructora establece que, de acuerdo con la Constitución, sólo cuando López Obrador esté en proceso penal, es decir con orden de aprehensión, dejará de ser gobernante de la ciudad.

La priísta Rebeca Godínez y el perredista Horacio Duarte, miembros de la Instructora, estimaron que aunque se le retire el fuero, mientras no haya orden de aprehensión, seguirá siendo Jefe de Gobierno.

Ayer, los dos diputados del PRI y uno del PAN que determinaron el desafuero concluyeron la redacción del dictamen en el cual establecieron que el tabasqueño es culpable de desobediencia a un juez, violó una suspensión judicial y, por lo tanto, cometió un delito equiparable al abuso de poder.

Además, establecieron, fue omiso, actuó con dolo, tuvo participación directa en la violación a la Ley de Amparo, presentó una argumentación ineficaz y no dio elementos para refutar las acusaciones de la PGR.

Por Claudia Guerrero y Andrea Merlos

LIMA, SÁBADO 2 DE ABRIL DEL 2005   DIRECTOR GENERAL: ALEJANDRO MIRÓ QUESADA G.   DIRECTOR: ALEJANDRO MIRÓ QUESADA C.   AÑO 165 N° 85,264 • PRECIO EN LIMA S/. 2,00

El Comercio

INDEPENDENCIA Y VERACIDAD

AL SERVICIO DEL PAÍS DESDE 1839

▶ www.elcomercioperu.com ◀

---

temadeldía MÉDICOS DEL VATICANO CONFIRMAN QUE SITUACIÓN ES IRREVERSIBLE

Todo está consumado

TODOS PENDIENTES. Una larga procesión de fieles desfiló por la Plaza de San Pedro todo el día, así como por las numerosas iglesias de Roma.

▌▌ Salud de Juan Pablo II empeoró e incluso perdió el conocimiento

▌▌ Más de 70 mil personas llegaron hasta la Plaza de San Pedro para orar

▌▌ Una agencia de noticias dijo que el Papa había muerto, pero fue desmentida

▌▌ En la Catedral de Lima y en el interior del país se oficiaron misas por su salud

CIUDAD DEL VATICANO [EL COMERCIO/AGENCIAS]. El papa Juan Pablo II continuaba al cierre de esta edición en su lenta agonía, mientras millones de personas en el mundo rezaban en las iglesias ante la inminencia del desenlace fatal.

En el último comunicado oficial, divulgado ayer a las 17:00 GMT (12 m. en Perú), el portavoz del Vaticano, Joaquín Navarro-Valls, había afirmado que el cuadro clínico del pontífice había empeorado en las últimas horas. "Las condiciones generales y cardiorrespiratorias del Santo Padre se han agravado. Los parámetros biológicos están notablemente comprometidos", precisó el español, quien aseguró que el Papa presenta un cuadro clínico de insuficiencia respiratoria y renal e hipotensión arterial.

Por su parte, el anestesista italiano Vincenzo Carpino dijo: "En estas condiciones no hay esperanzas y hay una pérdida de conocimiento".

En la Plaza de San Pedro, sentados sobre las piedras, algunos fieles inclinaban la cabeza para rezar. Envueltos en mantas, otros alzaban la vista a las ventanas, donde las luces permanecían encendidas. Era tal el silencio entre la multitud de 70.000 personas que se escuchaba el ruido del agua en las fuentes. **Miles de peruanos rezaron por la salud del Papa.** [A2,4,6,7]

Así lo dijo

❝ Esta noche, Cristo abrirá las puertas al Papa. Con seguridad, allá le estará esperando María ❞

Monseñor Angelo Comastri, vicario del Papa

▶ **EL DATO**
El jefe de la Iglesia Católica visitó el Perú en 1985 y 1988, en plena época del terrorismo

Así lo dijo

❝ Estamos en la premuerte porque el Papa agoniza. Los médicos del Vaticano me dicen que situación es irreversible ❞

Cardenal Javier Lozano, ministro de Sanidad del Vaticano

▶ **EXPECTATIVA EN LA WEB**
La página oficial del Vaticano colapsó ayer por el exceso de consultas.

VIGILIA EN SU TIERRA NATAL. En Polonia sus compatriotas también elevaron plegarias acompañando al santo padre en su etapa final.

---

buenosdías

Expectante angustia

Y ENTONCES LAS CAMPANAS TAÑERON, ALGUNOS se santiguaron y muchos otros rompieron a llorar. El Papa había muerto anunciaban en las radios, repetían los flashes televisivos, insistían en las páginas de Internet. Ya descansa en paz, decían, y los locutores buscaban sus frases más rebuscadas para tratar de explicar el dramático momento.

Pero a los pocos minutos la historia empezó a cambiar: El Vaticano no hace comentarios, se preocupaban en los canales de cable; hay versiones contradictorias, afirmaban los noticieros; sería muerte cerebral, sería... hasta que la Santa Sede dio por fin su versión: El Papa no había muerto.

Y tras las disculpas y recriminaciones, nuevamente los comentarios de los analistas, la Plaza de San Pedro repleta, las misas alrededor del mundo, el testimonio de los doloridos fieles y el dramático relato de cómo se marchitaba la vida del hombre más querido del mundo.

Imposible encontrar un viernes más largo que el vivido ayer. Fue una agonía para todos.

ÁNGELES DE LA PLAYA

Salvavidas rescataron a 1.639 bañistas este verano

El verano estuvo movido para los efectivos de la Unidad de Salvamento Acuático de la Policía, quienes salvaron a 1.639 personas de morir ahogadas. Los 500 guardianes del mar seguirán vigilando las playas limeñas hasta el 17 de abril. **Unos 250 efectivos** vigilarán los fines de semana las playas peligrosas. [A13]

ARDUA TAREA

JNE verificará padrones de partidos en dos semanas

Vencido el plazo para la presentación de los padrones de afiliados de los partidos políticos ante el Jurado Nacional de Elecciones, el ente electoral deberá verificar la autenticidad de las firmas y comprobar que no haya doble o triple afiliación. **Cuestionan si** el JNE tiene medios para verificación. [A10]

ECONOMÍA

La Bolsa de Valores de Lima fue la más rentable de la región

Primer trimestre del 2005 [B1]

PERÚ

Deslizamiento de desechos minerales sepulta cementerio

Pesar en Cerro de Pasco [A18]

SOMOS

Salve su matrimonio con sesiones de baile besos y abrazos

El 'boom' de la caricioterapia

DEPORTE TOTAL

Alianza Lima con suplentes goleó 6-2 al Cienciano

Gonzales Vigil hizo 4 goles [A28]

SUN●STAR

CEBU

NO. 1 IN READERSHIP

Scenes from the papacy

A4

Monday, April 4, 2005   Cebu City, Philippines   www.sunstar.com.ph/cebu/   44 Pages   P8

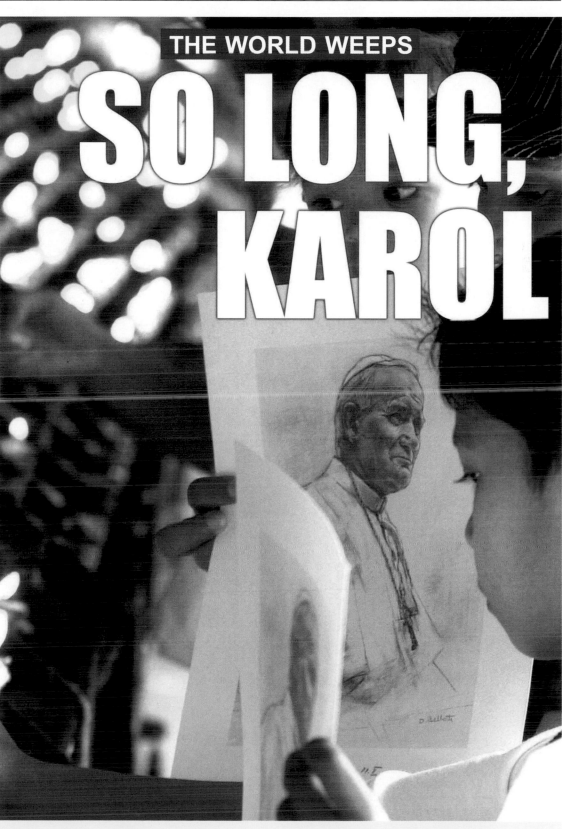

THE WORLD WEEPS

SO LONG, KAROL

- • Cardinals begin meeting today to prepare for pope's funeral, anytime from Wednesday to Friday; public viewing begins today, as Vatican City braces for millions of pilgrims
- • Official text of homily for requiem mass addresses pontiff as "John Paul the Great," a title reserved for popes worthy of sainthood
- • Vatican lists 84-year-old pope's cause of death as septic shock, irreversible cardio-respiratory collapse
- • In Cebu, Cardinal Vidal comforts his flock, pays tribute to the pope's gift of bridging differences, but holding fast to doctrine (A2)
- • Other fotos, stories: Worldwide, an outpouring of grief (A24)

VATICAN CITY—Finally at rest after years of debilitating disease, Pope John Paul II's body lay in state yesterday in the Apostolic Palace.

The world mourned his passing and the Vatican prepared for the ritual-filled funeral and conclave that will elect his successor.

An estimated 100,000 people turned out for a morning mass. Thousands more—tourists, Romans, young and old—kept coming throughout the day, a sea of humanity filling the broad boulevard leading to St. Peter's Basilica. They clutched rosaries and newspaper photos of John Paul as they stood shoulder-to-shoulder to pray for the

: LESSON, A29

LEADING LIGHT. Candles are lit around the world, including this young boy's suburban parish in Manila, in memory of Pope John Paul II, born Karol Wojtyla, the most dominant moral figure of his time. (AP FOTO)

129

Cebuanos recall encounters with the pope A6

Project delays cost govt $7.5M; DPWH leads pack BusinessB1

The Manila Times

MONDAY
APRIL 4, 2005 VOL. 106 ■ NO.170

Founded 1898

Php 15.00
3 SECTIONS 22 PAGES

5 MORE BOYS TO TESTIFY AT JACKSON TRIAL
NewsA2

DAN MARIANO NEW TIMES COLUMNIST
OpEdA6

IPU SIDELINES MYANMAR ISSUE
NewsA8

BATA REIGNS AGAIN AS SMB 9-BALL CHAMP
SportsB8

THE POPE IS DEAD

Pope of life and love

THE death of John Paul II robs mankind—not just the Roman Catholic Church and its 1.25 billion members—of the foremost advocate of the Culture of Life and the Culture of Love.

John Paul II defined the Culture of Death to include abortion, euthanasia, human cloning, terrorism, war and genocide. He also saw oppression, poverty, unjust distribution of wealth and the tendency of power holders to trample on the dignity of other human beings as maladies brought about by the Culture of Death.

In his 26 and a half years as Bishop of Rome and Supreme Pontiff of the Catholic Church, the Polish Pope came to be loved not just by members of his flock. Christians of other denominations, even people of other religions, went to his rallies and joined him in pilgrimages to shrines of the Blessed Virgin Mary, to whom he was most particularly devoted.

He made apostolic trips to 179 countries. He was a globally attractive and lovable figure.

He had the ability to make everyone in the audience feel being personally addressed when he called on his listeners not to be afraid to imitate Christ's willingness to carry the cross for the common good and the salvation of souls. That ability came from his holiness and his spiritual energy.

See LOVE A2

TODAY

PESO-DOLLAR RATE
US$1 = PHP54.760
Closing price last Friday

EDITORIAL
Can the BIR deliver this time?
IT'S difficult to get excited over the much-publicized crusade of the Bureau of Internal Revenue to file tax-evasion cases every week.

April 3, 2005
Lotto Results 6/49
P11,073,757.80

04 06 13 16 19 37

WEATHER
Partly Cloudy
Temp: 24˚- 33˚C

■ Pope John Paul II, 1920-2005

Pall of deep loss envelops the world

POPE John Paul II, spiritual leader of the world's 1.25 billion Roman Catholics, died on Saturday, two days after suffering heart failure brought by two months of acute breathing problems and other infections.

News of the Pope's death touched not only Catholics from his native Poland to the Americas, from Africa to Asia, but untold numbers of other admirers of one of the most popular and recognizable popes in history.

Tribute from world leaders, related stories
Page A8

The death of the 84-year-old Polish-born Pontiff was announced to a huge crowd of pilgrims who had gathered for a vigil under John Paul II's apartment windows in Saint Peter's Square.

The dead Pope's secretary of state, Cardinal Angelo Sodano, intoned the "De Profundis [Out of the Depths]," a Latin prayer for the dead, to an eerily hushed Saint Peter's Square.

See POPE A2

RP enters period of mourning

PRESIDENT Arroyo declared a period of national mourning beginning Monday until Pope John Paul II is laid to rest.

All government offices have instructions to fly the flag at half-staff.

The President, a devout Catholic, expressed a "deep sense of grief" over the death of the 84-year-old Pontiff.

"We mourn with the world the passing of Pope John Paul II. His death brings to all a deep sense of grief and loss," she said.

"He was a holy champion of the Filipino family and of the profound Christian values that make everyone of us contemplate, everyday, what is just, moral and sacred in life," Mrs. Arroyo added.

See MOURNING A2

Nationality of successor heightens guessing game

BY BRIAN MURPHY
AP Religion Writer

VATICAN CITY: The intense guessing game over who will be the next Pope has only one certainty: the cardinals must decide whether to follow John Paul II with another non-Italian or hand the papacy back to its traditional caretakers.

The Polish-born John Paul was the first Pope from outside Italy in 455 years. He brought a new vitality to the Vatican and challenged parochial attitudes across the church. One view holds that the papal electors will want to maintain the spirit by recognizing the Roman Catholic centers of gravity outside Europe, led by Latin America and Africa.

See GAME A2

Sin remembers days with a cardinal named Wojtyla

BY WILLIAM B. DEPASUPIL
Reporter

FOR Jaime Cardinal Sin the death of Pope John Paul II meant the loss of a brother and a dear friend.

Sin on Sunday recalled the fond memories 27 years ago with a cardinal from Poland, Karol Josef Wojtyla, while attending the conclave of cardinals to choose the successor of Pope John Paul I, who died after only 33 days in pontificate.

"I will never forget the conclave of 1978 which elected him [Wojtyla] Supreme Pontiff. We were lodged together because we were among the youngest [cardinals]," Sin said. "From there blossomed a warm friendship and fraternal bonding."

See CARDINAL A2

■ Milestones in the life of an extraordinary man

1920-1946
A wartime childhood
Karol Jozef Wojtyla born in Wadowice May 18, 1920. Studied philosophy in Jagiellonian University in Krakow in 1938. Followed clandestine classes for priesthood in Krakow's underground seminary.

1946-1958
A Polish priest
Ordained as a priest on November 1, 1946, trained abroad. Returned to Poland in 1948, did parish work, sponsored students and had a university career.

1958-1978
Rising through the ranks
In 1958 Pius XII appointed him Auxiliary Bishop to Archbishop of Krakow. In 1964 named Archbishop Archbishop of Krakow by Paul VI. In 1967, made a cardinal by Paul VI.

1978
The globe-trotting pope
On October 16, 1978, became first Polish pope in history. Named John Paul II. Succeeded John Paul I who died after 33 days as pope. Throughout his papacy he made 104 trips outside Italy and 146 visits inside Italy.

1981
Attempt on his life
On May 13 John Paul II was victim of an assassination attempt in Rome. He was shot in the abdomen, left hand and the right arm.

1986
Open to other religions
On April 13 made the first ever visit to a synagogue by a pope. Throughout his papacy he supported dialogue between the religions.

1987
Fight against communism
On June 11 met Lech Walesa in Gdansk. John Paul II contributed to the fall of communism by defending the Solidarity movement and its Polish leader.

1997
Canonizations and beatifications
On May 20 Mother Teresa visited the Vatican. Six years later, John Paul II beatified her. During his papacy he declared 1,338 beatifications and 487 canonizations.

1994-2005
The decline
In 1992 John Paul II was operated on for a benign intestinal tumor. In 1994, he breaks a thigh bone, and from then on appears increasingly frail and will never walk with ease again. Parkinson's disease worsens his physical state. Early 2005, he is hospitalized twice at the Gemelli hospital. On April 1, 2005, he has a urinary tract infection, septic shock and a heart attack, and is given his final rites.

DATA/PHOTOS FROM AFP

GAZETA**Krakowska**

niedziela, 3 kwietnia 2005   Rok CCX   WYDANIE NADZWYCZAJNE

TOTUS TUUS
† 2005

WYDANIE SPECJALNE
BEZPŁATNE

NIEDZIELA
3 kwietnia 2005

NAKŁAD 338 TYS.

WYDAWCA AGORA SA
NUMER INDEKSU 350141

gazeta
WYBORCZA

18 maja 1920 | 2 kwietnia 2005

JAN PAWEŁ II
odszedł

Zanim stąd odejdę, proszę was, abyście całe
to duchowe dziedzictwo, któremu na imię „Polska",
raz jeszcze przyjęli z wiarą, nadzieją i miłością
– taką, jaką zaszczepia w nas Chrystus na chrzcie świętym,
– abyście nigdy nie zwątpili i nie znużyli się, i nie zniechęcili,
– abyście nie podcinali sami tych korzeni, z których wyrastamy.
Proszę was:
– abyście mieli ufność nawet wbrew każdej swojej słabości,
abyście szukali zawsze duchowej mocy u Tego,
u którego tyle pokoleń ojców naszych i matek ją znajdowało,
– abyście od Niego nigdy nie odstąpili,
– abyście nigdy nie utracili tej wolności ducha,
do której On „wyzwala" człowieka,
– abyście nigdy nie wzgardzili tą Miłością, która jest „największa",
która się wyraziła przez Krzyż, a bez której życie ludzkie
nie ma ani korzenia, ani sensu.
Proszę was o to przez pamięć i przez potężne
wstawiennictwo Bogarodzicy z Jasnej Góry
i wszystkich Jej sanktuariów na ziemi polskiej,
przez pamięć św. Wojciecha, który zginął
dla Chrystusa nad Bałtykiem, przez pamięć
św. Stanisława, który legł pod mieczem
królewskim na Skałce.
Proszę was o to. Amen

Kraków, 1979

14 marca 1999 r., Jan Paweł II wsparty na pastorale
w parafialnym kościele św. Mateusza
na przedmieściach Rzymu

Spotkanie z młodzieżą w Paryżu. Niedziela, 1 czerwca
1980 r., stadion Parc des Princes

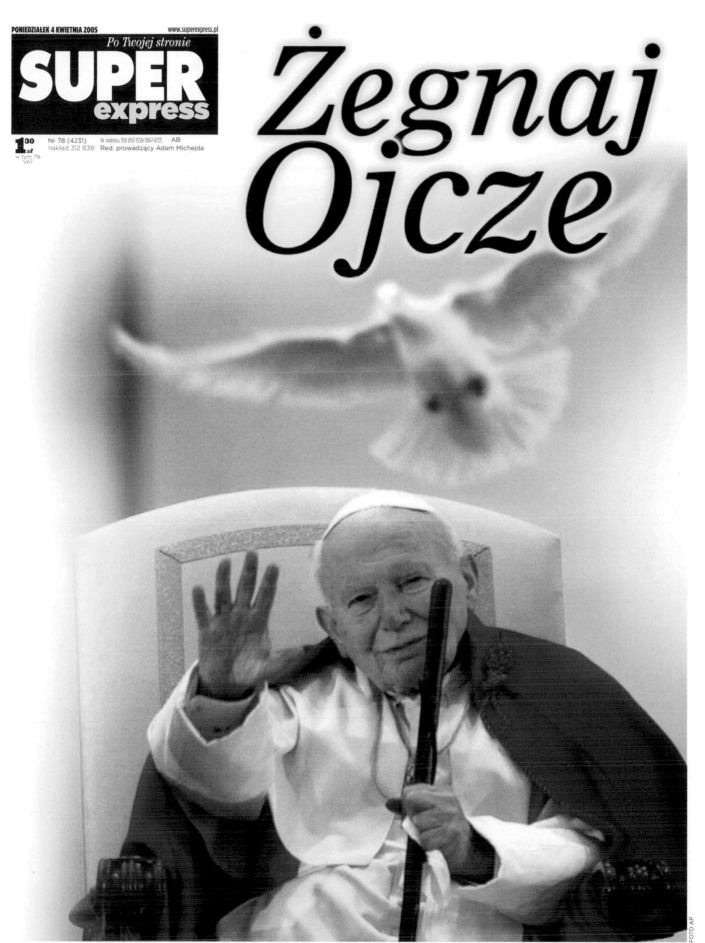

PONIEDZIAŁEK 4 KWIETNIA 2005   www.superexpress.pl

Po Twojej stronie

SUPER express

1³⁰ zł
w tym 7%
VAT

Nr 78 (4231)   Nr indeksu 350 850 ISSN 0867-8723   AB
nakład 312 838   Red. prowadzący Adam Michejda

Żegnaj Ojcze

Dziś w „Super Expressie" rozpoczynamy cykl dodatków o życiu Ojca Świętego

133

FOTO AP

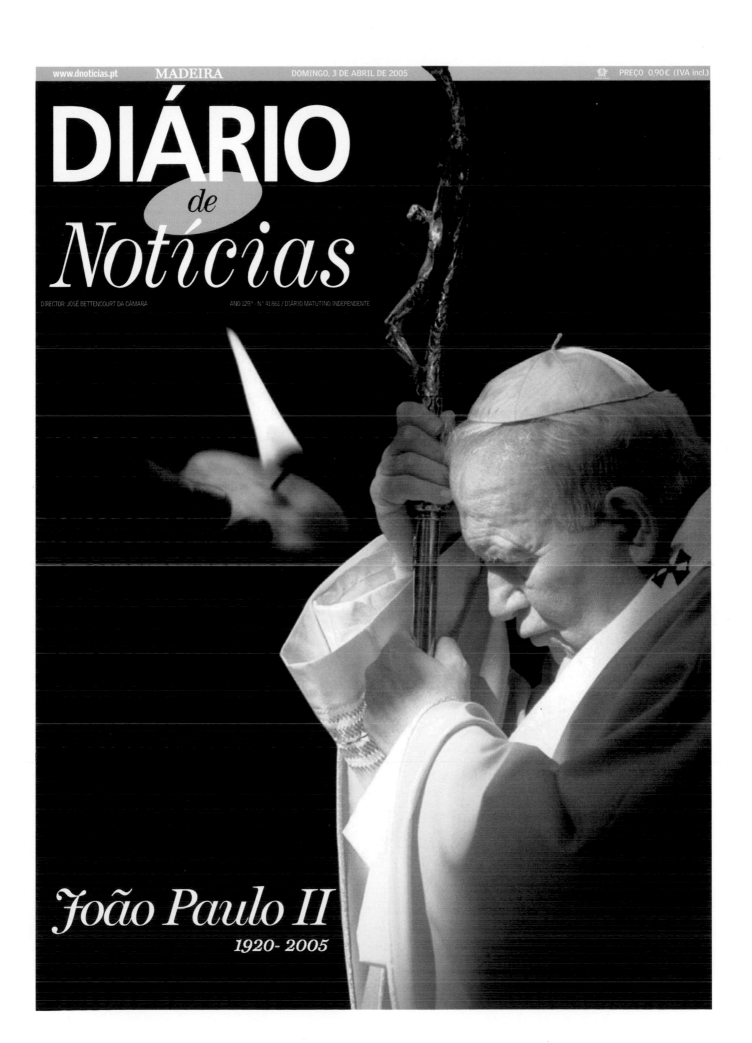

www.dnoticias.pt MADEIRA DOMINGO, 3 DE ABRIL DE 2005 PREÇO 0,90€ (IVA incl.)

DIÁRIO *de* Notícias

DIRECTOR: JOSÉ BETTENCOURT DA CÂMARA

ANO 129.º - N.º 41 861 / DIÁRIO MATUTINO INDEPENDENTE

João Paulo II
1920- 2005

PÚBLICO

www.publico.pt

DOMINGO

EDIÇÃO LISBOA

3 de Abril de 2005
Ano XVI • Nº 5487
€1,20 (IVA incluído)

Director **JOSÉ MANUEL FERNANDES**
Directores adjuntos: NUNO PACHECO
e MANUEL CARVALHO

e-mail: publico@publico.pt

PÚBLICA

O charme discreto de

Teresa Patrício Gouveia

ITÁLIA

Eleições regionais difíceis para Berlusconi

As eleições regionais que se realizam hoje e amanhã em Itália poderão ser bastante desfavoráveis ao primeiro-ministro Berlusconi. A sua coligação de centro-direita poderá perder, segundo as sondagens, pelo menos duas das oito regiões que controla actualmente. Em todo o caso, Berlusconi já garantiu que não se vai demitir. **P20/21**

ÍNDICE

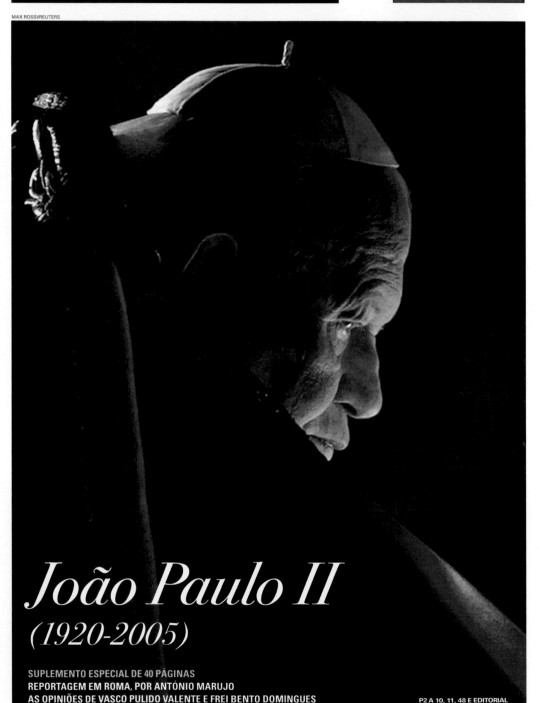

MAX ROSSI/REUTERS

João Paulo II
(1920-2005)

SUPLEMENTO ESPECIAL DE 40 PÁGINAS
REPORTAGEM EM ROMA, POR ANTÓNIO MARUJO
AS OPINIÕES DE VASCO PULIDO VALENTE E FREI BENTO DOMINGUES

P2 A 10, 11, 48 E EDITORIAL

الرياض
AL RIYADH - 13432 - 42nd Year - SUNDAY-3-4-2005

٥

شؤون دولية

الأحد ٢٤ صفر ١٤٢٦هـ - ٣ إبريل ٢٠٠٥م - العدد ١٣٤٣٢ - السنة الثانية والأربعون

البابا في المستشفى بعد تعرضه لمحاولة اغتيال عام ١٩٨١م — صورة تجمع البابا مع الرئيس الروسي غورباتشوف عام ٢٠٠٠م — يوحنا بولس الثاني في طفولته — صورة أرشيفية للبابا تعود للعام ١٩٨١م — البابا في صورة تعود لأكتوبر ٢٠٠٣م (رويترز)

★ بوش: فقدنا بطلاً ★ شيراك: فرنسا حزينة ★ عنان: رجل سلام ★ أبو مازن: مدافع عن القضية الفلسطينية

وفاة البابا يوحنا بولس الثاني بعد معاناة طويلة مع المرض

اجتماع ١١٧ كردنيالاً من أنحاء العالم لانتخاب رئيس للكنيسة خلال ٢٠ يوماً

مثل سابق وكاتب مسرحيات ومحارب ضد الإجهاض ومنع الحمل:

البابا ساهم في تقويض الشيوعية من أوروبا وواجه كوارث واتهامات أخلاقية في الكنيسة

الكنيسة الكاثوليكية في أرقام

137

The Star
WITH BUSINESSREPORT

MONDAY APRIL 4 2005   Established October 17 1887   R3,50 inc VAT (R4,50 outside Gauteng)   Annual subscribers: R2,91   www.star.co.za

At the side of Saint Peter
John Paul II likely to be buried in tomb next to first pope

SAPA-AFP, SAPA-AFP AND REUTERS
Vatican City

The man who changed the Catholic Church over the last 26 years will most probably be laid to rest next to its first pope.

The College of Cardinals convened this morning to finalise details of Pope John Paul II's funeral, which is expected to draw the greatest tide of pilgrims and heads of state to the Vatican in its history.

Although there was still no official confirmation on where the pope will be buried – whether in St Peter's Basilica, as tradition dictates, or in his native Poland – Italy's *Corriere della Sera* reported the pope had chosen to be buried in a crypt underneath the church.

John Paul is likely to take the tomb of Pope John XXIII – who was moved up from the crypt to the basilica itself after his beatification in 2000. It is a highly-privileged spot since it is one of the two closest to the tomb of Peter, Christ's apostle and the church's first pontiff, the daily reported.

It quoted Cardinal Franciszek Macharski, the archbishop of Krakow, denying rumours that the pope's heart was to be interred in the city where he was bishop before becoming pontiff.

Polish pilgrims holding vigil in St Peter's Square said they nonetheless hoped that he would be buried in a Polish flag.

John Paul himself set an imposing agenda for the cardinals in instructions he drafted in 1996, including the reading of any final documents he may have left for them, including directives on where he wanted to be interred.

In addition, the cardinals were expected to arrange the destruction of John Paul's Fisherman's Ring and the dies used to make lead seals for apostolic letters – formal gestures meant to symbolise the end of his reign and to prevent forgeries.

The body of John Paul emerges from an inner sanctum of the Vatican this afternoon for the public to bid farewell. It was displayed yesterday for prelates, ambassadors and other dignitaries.

After a solemn procession across St Peter's Square, the embalmed corpse was to be laid before the altar, guarded by Swiss guards, at

least until Wednesday.

The procession is expected to begin at 4pm and the public will be allowed into the basilica an hour later and for three days and nights.

Traditionally the funeral has to happen four to six days after a pope's death, in this case between Wednesday and Friday.

It is expected to draw up to 2-million people and some 200 state and religious leaders.

Some young pilgrims, eager to be the first to see the pope's body, staked out positions in cobblestoned St Peter's Square today.

"If it hadn't been for this pope, I would have completely lost my faith. I always trusted him, and needed to come here today to see him," said 22-year-old Silvia Mazzacani, who took an overnight train from northern Italy.

The body was laid out in the

palace yesterday for cardinals, officials – and television cameras – after a huge mass in the square celebrating the 26-year pontificate of the leader of the world's 1,1-billion Catholics.

He was pictured dressed in red and white robes and a white mitre, a serene expression on his face, while his pale hands clutched rosary beads. A crucifix lay alongside his body.

The body was laid out in the

US media said President George Bush, a devout Methodist who clashed with the pope over the Iraq war, was expected to attend the funeral. No US president has ever attended a pope's funeral.

Italian authorities said they would deploy more than 6 400 police to ensure public security and protection of the dignitaries. Nato warplanes and helicopters will enforce a no-fly zone over Rome.

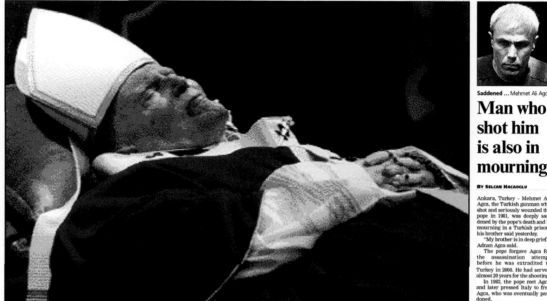

MASSIMO SAMBUCETTI/ REUTERS

Lying in state ... the body of Pope John Paul II rests in the Vatican yesterday and will be brought out this afternoon for a procession across St Peter's Square before being laid before the basilica's altar.

Saddened ... Mehmet Ali Agca

Man who shot him is also in mourning

BY SELCAN HACAOGLU

Ankara, Turkey – Mehmet Ali Agca, the Turkish gunman who shot and seriously wounded the pope in 1981, was deeply saddened by the pope's death and is mourning in a Turkish prison, his brother said yesterday.

"My brother is in deep grief," Adnan Agca said.

The pope forgave Agca for the assassination attempt before he was extradited to Turkey in 2000. He had served almost 20 years for the shooting.

In 1983, the pope met Agca and later pressed Italy to free Agca, who was eventually pardoned.

He is serving a 17-year prison sentence for earlier crimes in Turkey. – Sapa-AP

Last prayer and final words: Hallelujah, amen

Grieving ... a Lebanese woman cries during a mass in Saint George's Church in Beirut.   PHOTO: REUTERS

SAPA-AP, SAPA-AFP, REUTERS AND WASHINGTON POST

Vatican City – Pope John Paul's own words rang out across St Peter's Square the day after he died as an archbishop read out an address the pontiff had prepared for the regular Sunday mass at the Vatican.

The faithful gathered in the huge oval piazza wept as archbishop Leonardo Sandri read the pope's last message to the world, focused on the hope provided to Christians by Jesus' death and resurrection.

"To all humanity, which today seems so lost and dominated by the power of evil, selfishness and fear, our resurrected Lord gives us his love which forgives, reconciles and

reopens the soul to hope," the pope's words said.

"The glorious Hallelujah of Easter rings out. Today's Gospel reading from John shows how the resurrected Christ appeared to the Apostles and showed them his hands and his feet, the signs of the painful passion indelibly imprinted on his body even after his resurrection."

The pope urged the faithful to "contemplate with the eyes of Mary the immense mystery of merciful love that springs from the heart of Jesus Christ. Hallelujah!"

As his life ebbed away, he stared from his bed at his open window overlooking the crowds gathered in St Peter's Square and with great effort whispered the word "amen".

Pontiff's views on women caused ire among feminists

BY GINA DOGGETT

Vatican City – The late Pope John Paul II, who lost his mother at age nine and devoted himself to the Virgin Mary, had deep-seated views on the role of women that drew the ire of modern feminists.

While his affection and respect for women marked a shift from the traditional arms-length attitude of the all-male clergy, who are sworn to celibacy, the advancement of women was not on his agenda.

"A woman must give priority to her role as mother before any other

public or professional activity," he wrote in an exhortation entitled *Familiaris Consortio* (The Christian Family in the Modern World).

"Her original mission, for which she cannot be replaced, is to stay at home to raise children."

His 1999 letter *Mulieris Dignitatem* (The Dignity of Women) did little to appease those who objected to his rigid stance against abortion, divorce and women as priests.

Three years earlier he wrote: "To remain celibate with serenity, the priest must develop for himself an image of the woman as a sister."

His rejection of the ordination of women was a source of frustration among many in the American Catholic Church, where the idea gained wide currency in the 1970s.

Yesterday, the US-based Women's Ordination Conference said it mourned his death but grieved "for the actions (he) left undone for

women's equality in the church."

Joanna Manning, co-founder of Catholic Organisations for Renewal, criticised him for trying to re-establish humility and subordination as the traditional virtues of women.

The connection between John Paul II's views on women and his childhood loss is a matter of conjecture, but his single-minded devotion to Mary knew no bounds.

The motto of his papacy, "Totus Tuus", is a reference to the Madonna meaning "entirely yours".

The ailing pope invoked the motto following his February 24 throat

surgery, scribbling a note to aides saying: "I am forever Totus Tuus."

John Paul II was convinced that he owed his survival from the 1981 attempt on his life to Mary, whom he said guided the assassin's bullet away from any vital organs.

In only one instance was affection for a woman the source of wagging tongues. Polish actress Halina Kwiatkowska, in her book *Wielki Kolega* (The Great Friend), sought to lay to rest speculation of a romantic attachment with the future pope, who maintained a lifelong friendship with her. – Sapa-AFP

MORE REPORTS AND PICTURES – Pages 4, 5 and 9

FULL STORY IN **BUSINESS REPORT**   Clothing employers flout the law

9 771016 370005

Johannesburg
Beeld
Jou wêreld, Jou koerant

Maandag 4 April 2005 R3,50

'Amen' – toe sterf hy

Miljoene rou, wag om te hoor oor opvolger

Neels Jackson en Sapa-AFP-DPA

Die wêreld het gister verenig in rou ná die dood van een van die merkwaardigste godsdiensleiers nog: pous Johannes Paulus II, 26 jaar lank die geestelike leier van meer as 'n miljard lidmate van die Rooms-Katolieke Kerk.

Bespiegelings het ook toegeneem oor wie hom sal opvolg en die moontlikheid is selfs genoem dat 'n Afrikaan, kardinaal Francis Arinze van Nigerië, die volgende pous kan wees. (Berig op bl. 4.)

Die Vatikaan het eergisteraand bekend gemaak dat die 84-jarige pous om 21:37 dood is aan septiese skok en onomkeerbare hartversaking.

Die laaste sakramente is kort voor sy dood vir 'n tweede keer aan hom bedien.

Die pous was die afgelope tyd twee keer in die hospitaal en kon in die laaste weke nie meer sy openbare pligte nakom of selfs 'n seën uitspreek nie.

Gistermiddag het sy lyk in staatsie gelê in die Genadesaal van die Vatikaan. Die gestorwe pous was gekleе in rooi met 'n wit hoofbedekking met die pouslike staf in sy linkerarm. Sy kop het op goue kussings gerus.

Kardinale, ander kerklui en Italiaanse politici was onder die mense wat by sy oorskot verbybeweeg het. Verskeie van hulle het gekniel of saggies gebid.

Buite was daar 'n see van emosionele gesigte in die St. Pietersplein, waar 'n skare mense 'n mis vir die pous bygewoon het. Ook in Pole het groot skares mense hul beroemdste landgenoot se dood gedenk.

Wêreldwyd het Katolieke op die Sondag saamgetrek om te bid in die blommekranse is voor katedrale en kerke neergelê.

Huldeblyke het ingestroom. Selfs die Turk Mehmet Ali Agca, wat 'n mislukte sluipmoordpoging op die pous uitgevoer het, was in sy tronksel "diep bedroef" oor die pous se dood, het sy broer gesê.

Wêreldleiers het die pous geloof vir sy bydrae tot die val van die kommunisme, sy sterk standpunte teen onreg en oorlog en sy werk vir versoening en vrede.

Pres. Thabo Mbeki het gesê: "Ons is dankbaar vir die pous se rol om wêreldvrede, ontwikkeling en samewerking te bewerkstellig, waaronder sy steun vir Afrika se ontwikkeling en vernuwing."

Alle plaaslike politieke partye het ook aan hom hulde gebring.

Intussen het kardinale van oor die wêreld gister na die Vatikaan begin stroom. Dié "prinse van die kerk" moet besluit oor begrafnisreëlings en 'n opvolger kies.

Te midde van gerugte dat die pous self gevra het om in sy vaderland, Pole, begrawe te word, het die Poolse media gister bespiegel dat sy hart daarheen gebring sal word terwyl hy, soos gebruiklik, in die Vatikaan self begrawe sal word.

Volgens die Vatikaan se webwerf was daar gister wêreldwyd 117 kardinale jonger as 80. Dit sal hul taak wees om 'n nuwe pous te kies. Dit sal waarskynlik een van hulle self wees, al het tegnies mag hulle enige gedoopte Katolieke man kies.

Kardinaal Wilfrid Napier, Suid-Afrika se enigste kardinaal, vertrek dalk vandag na Rome om aan die proses deel te neem.

■ Nog berigte en foto's op bl. 4 en 14.

Pous Johannes Paulus II lê gister in staatsie in die Genadesaal van die Vatikaan.   Foto: AP

Die pous se heel laaste, moeisame woord

Oomblikke voordat pous Johannes Paulus II dood is, het hy sy hand opgelig terwyl 'n gebed op die St. Pietersplein in Rome gelei is.

Die oomblik toe die gebed verby was, het hy met groot moeite die woord "Amen" uitgekry.

Oomblikke later het hy gesterf, het vader Jarek Cielecki, redakteur van die Vatikaan se nuuediens, volgens die Britse Sondagkoerant The Observer gesê.
– Sarel van der Walt

Raad skuld baie oor ongeldige padboetes

Die Ekurhuleni-metroraad skuld glo meer as R100 000 aan mense wat verkeersboetes betaal het wat later teruggetrek is.

Die meeste van dié honderde mense weet nie dat die raad hulle geld skuld nie.

Luidens Boksburg se terugbetalingsregister, waarvan Beeld 'n gedeeltelike afskrif het, is daar terugbetalings wat al in 2003 gemagtig is, maar wat nou nog nie uitbetaal is nie.

Honderde van die inskrywings is blykbaar nooit betaal nie. En dit behels net boetes wat weens verkeersoortredings in Boksburg uitgereik is.

Dit is nie duidelik wat die stand van terugbetalings in die ander Oos-Randse dorpe is nie.

Die redes wat in die register vir die terugbetalings aangevoer word, is meestal dat die sake teruggetrek is of dat die landdros die terugbetaling gemagtig het.

Luidens 'n verklaring van mnr. Zweli Dlamini, woordvoerder van Ekurhuleni se metroraad, kan 'n landdros om verskeie redes gelas dat boetes aan mense terugbetaal word.

Geldige redes sluit in 'n dagvaarding wat nie behoorlik ingevul is nie of 'n boete wat meer as 30 dae ná die datum van die oortreding uitgereik is. Daar is ook gevalle waar mense dieselfde boete twee keer betaal het.

Volgens Dlamini word 'n tjek vir die terugbetaling aangevra sodra die landdros se bevel ontvang is. "Ons hanteer hierdie situasies soos en wanneer dit voorkom," lui sy verklaring.

Volgens Dlamini is dit moeilik om te sê wat die omvang van die agterstand met terugbetalings is. Hy kon ook nie uitwei oor die moontlike redes nie.

Hy het gesê die raad sal die saak behoorlik ondersoek.

Mnr. Bernard Spiers is een van die mense aan wie 'n terugbetaling in 2003 gemagtig is. Spiers was baie verbaas toe hy hoor die raad skuld hóm geld. "Gewoonlik is dit andersom."

Volgens Spiers kan hy onthou dat hy 'n boete aan die Oos-Rand betaal het, "maar ek kan nie eens onthou wat die bedrag was nie".

Spiers het gesê dit sal 'n "wonderwerk" wees as hy ooit die terugbetaling kry.

"Ek glo nie ek sal dié geld ooit sien nie," het hy gesê.
– Marida Fitzpatrick

Binne:

■ Binnegeveg in SA sending na Zim kring uit – bl. 2

■ Zoid, KKNK pak mekaar oor dronkes – bl. 5

Pavarotti se nat afskeid kortgeknip weens koors

Nat en kort.

In elk geval korter as wat Luciano Pavarotti se aanhangers verwag het.

Die Italiaanse tenoor se vaarwel-konsert Saterdagaand op SuperSport-park in Centurion is met 'n uur verkort omdat hy olik gevoel het. Die sowat 18 600 kaartjiekopers moes ook deurdringende reën trotseer.

En 'n erge verkeersprobleem. 'n Tou motors het vanaf drie uur vóór die Tot siens in Afrika-konsert 2,5 km ver op die N1-noord by die John Vorster afrit opgedam soos mense probeer het om die stadion te bereik. Twee uur later het dit steeds nie veel beter gelyk nie.

Sambreelloos, rigtingloos, uitsigloos en – vir dié wat nie gaste van die borg was nie – losielos, het sommige mense in die stadion maar later handdoek ingegooi en huis toe gegaan.

Duisende aanhangers het wel deurgedruk tot die bittereinde om tot siens te sê aan die maestro.

Aan entoesiasme was daar nie 'n gebrek nie, ondanks die weer. Al het die einde vroeër gekom as verwag.

"Ek is jammer, ek kan nie meer nie," het Pavarotti omstreeks 21:30 volgens Sapa gesê. "Ek het koors."

Hy het die konsert daarna afgesluit met 'n aria uit La Traviata wat hy saam met sy landgenoot Simona Todaro gesing het en saam met die plaaslike soprane Sibongile Khumalo en Sibongile Mngoma, asook die tenore Given Mabena, Agos Moahi en Lucky Sibande.

Die gehoor, wat op 'n toegif gewag het, moes tevrede wees met 'n vuurwerk-vertoning wat die einde aangekondig het.

Die tenoor Luciano Pavarotti eergisteraand in Centurion.   Foto: ALET PRETORIUS

No temáis, abrid las puertas a Cristo (Juan Pablo II)

EL ⊕ MUNDO

DEL SIGLO VEINTIUNO

DOMINGO 3 DE ABRIL DE 2005
Año XVII. Número: 5.591

EDICION: **MADRID**
Precio: 1 euro. Con Magazine: 1,70 €. Con videojuego: 4,95 € más

EL OBITO SE PRODUJO A LAS 21.37 DE AYER AL CABO DE 26 AÑOS Y 168 DIAS DE PONTIFICADO

Muere Juan Pablo II, el Papa que cambió la historia del siglo XX

Karol Wojtyla, cuyo papado es el tercero más largo de la Historia, tenía 84 años y su funeral no será antes del jueves

En la mañana de ayer nombró arzobispo de Zaragoza a Manuel Ureña Pastor en sustitución de monseñor Elías Yanes

El Rey y Zapatero enviaron telegramas de condolencia y miles de madrileños se congregaron en la plaza de Colón

RUBEN AMON
Corresponsal

ROMA.– Juan Pablo II ha muerto mientras 70.000 fieles murmuraban el rosario a los pies del palacio apostólico. Todavía no sabían la noticia. Se enteraron cuando irrumpió en la noche la luz que provenía de las habitaciones pontificias. Era la señal para que monseñor Leonardo Sandri, la voz del Papa cuando estaba mudo, anunciara la noticia al pueblo. «Nuestro Santo Padre Juan Pablo ha regresado a la casa del Padre», dijo.

El Papa había muerto a las 21.37, apenas 10 minutos antes de que el portavoz vaticano, Joaquín Navarro Valls, remitiera el correo electrónico de la defunción a las principales agencias. Tenía que ser un *mail*, símbolo de esa aldea global que Juan Pablo II custodiaba como un patriarca. Y tenía que ser un sábado, porque el tercer secreto de Fátima advierte que la Virgen se le aparecería para anunciar su muerte el primer sábado de cualquier mes.

Sigue en **página 26**
Editorial en **página 5**
Obituario en **páginas 6 y 7**
Más información en **Supl. Madrid**

ENTREVISTA

Monseñor Herranz: «Ninguno de los cardenales tenemos la ambición de ser el nuevo Papa»

«Seré el primero en pedir la beatificación de Juan Pablo II», asegura el prelado del Opus Dei   **Página 33**

DOCUMENTOS

EL PAPA MISIONERO

JUAN PABLO II 1978-2005
Documentos 16 páginas

AVISO A LOS LECTORES: debido al incremento de tirada por el fallecimiento del Papa, algunos ejemplares de EL MUNDO se distribuyen hoy excepcionalmente sin MAGAZINE y los otros suplementos

Juan Pablo II, con gesto cansado, celebrando en 2000 en la basílica de San Pedro del Vaticano una misa por los cardenales y los obispos fallecidos. / ALESSANDRO BIANCHI / EPA

Rajoy exige a Zapatero que frene la «nueva marca de ETA»

Para López Aguilar es «absurdo ilegalizar todo lo que Batasuna dice que hay que votar» / El partido 'abertzale' considera «una nueva oportunidad» la lista de PCTV

BILBAO/MADRID.– El presidente del PP, Mariano Rajoy, exigió ayer a José Luis Rodríguez Zapatero que frene la candidatura del Partido Comunista de las Tierras Vascas (PCTV), que identificó como «nueva marca de ETA». Sin embargo, el ministro de Justicia, Juan Fernando López Aguilar, confirmó ayer que el Gobierno no ve aún motivos para proceder contra esta lista. Explicó que sería «absurdo» pedir su ilegalización por el hecho de que Batasuna la apoye.   **Páginas 8 a 10**

140

EL PAIS

DIARIO INDEPENDIENTE DE LA MAÑANA

DOMINGO 3 DE ABRIL DE 2005
Año XXX. Número 10.164
www.elpais.es
EDICIÓN MADRID
Precio: 1,90 euros

Muere el Papa

Juan Pablo II, de 84 años, falleció a las 21.37 en su apartamento privado del Vaticano ● El Pontífice dirigió la Iglesia católica desde 1978

ENRIC GONZÁLEZ, Roma

El corazón de Karol Wojtyla latió por última vez anoche, mientras en la plaza de San Pedro, bajo la ventana de su habitación, 70.000 personas rezaban un rosario. La noticia fue anunciada en plena oración y la multitud reaccionó con un aplauso. Tras el aplauso se hizo un silencio de muerte, estremecedor, en la plaza y en muchos corazones de todo el mundo que respetaban al Papa desaparecido. En la explanada vaticana prosiguió un rezo bañado en lágrimas y se iluminó el mosaico con la efigie de la Virgen que el propio Wojtyla, que dedicó sus 26 años de pontificado a María con el lema *Totus tuus (Todo tuyo)*, había hecho instalar en la fachada del Palacio Apostólico. El pontificado y la vida de Juan Pablo II, que tenía 84 años, se apagaron tras dos días de dolorosa agonía.

El portavoz de la Santa Sede, Joaquín Navarro-Valls, dio a conocer el fallecimiento con un comunicado: "El Santo Padre ha fallecido esta noche a las 21.37 horas en su apartamento privado. Se han puesto en marcha todos los procedimientos previstos en la Constitución Apostólica *Universi Dominici Gregis*, promulgada por Juan Pablo II el 22 de febrero de 1996".

La Constitución de 1996 se limitó a actualizar los ritos tradicionales. El camarlengo del Colegio Apostólico, el cardenal español Eduardo Martínez Somalo, encargado de dirigir el interregno, había golpeado ya la frente del difunto, le había invocado tres veces por su nombre de pila, Karol, había certificado la falta de vida y había destruido el anillo y el sello papales. **Pasa a la página 2**

Más información en **páginas 3 a 9**

Juan Pablo II, durante la misa en la catedral de Estrasburgo (Francia) en octubre de 1988. / AFP

El guardián de la tradición

El largo e intenso pontificado de Juan Pablo II ha marcado la historia reciente, como queda reflejado en los textos que componen el suplemento especial que EL PAÍS ofrece hoy a sus lectores. **Juan Arias** recorre su biografía, marcada desde temprano por la cercanía de la muerte y el amor a la Virgen. Varios corresponsales del periódico analizan la influencia del Pontífice que, entre otras cosas, contribuyó de manera decisiva a la mayor transformación del mundo contemporáneo: la caída del comunismo.

Lech Walesa y **Mijaíl Gorbachov** evocan su relación con Juan Pablo II, cuyo peso político y su marcada personalidad lo convierten, según el periodista italiano **Eugenio Scalfari**, en un Papa sin sucesor.

Los teólogos **Enrique Miret Magdalena**, **Juan José Tamayo-Acosta** y **José Ignacio González Faus** destacan las facetas más controvertidas de Wojtyla: su afinidad con el Opus Dei, su combate a la *teología de la liberación* y la centralización de la Iglesia.

Suplemento especial de 24 páginas

Juan Pablo II, atlante del milenio
Artículo de José M. Martín Patino
Página 19

EDITORIAL
Carisma contradictorio
Página 18

ENTREVISTA CON PASQUAL MARAGALL

"Volveré a presentarme porque nuestra reforma necesita dos mandatos"

"Volveré a presentarme" a las elecciones, "porque creo que el programa de reformas que hemos iniciado las izquierdas catalanistas necesita dos mandatos". El presidente de la Generalitat de Cataluña, el socialista Pasqual Maragall, despeja así la incógnita abierta sobre su futuro inmediato, en la primera entrevista concedida a un periódico tras la *crisis del Carmel*, desatada tras unas declaraciones suyas en el Parlamento catalán. Maragall asegura también que agotará su mandato y que no remodelará su Gobierno. **Páginas 24 y 25**

Zapatero se reúne por sorpresa con el 'número dos' de Condoleezza Rice
Página 32

Cuentos Infantiles
'Pulgarcito'
Hoy, por 1 euro, con el EL PAÍS.

HISTORIA UNIVERSAL
Hoy, por sólo 9,95 euros, el volumen número 13 de la obra.

141

Der Zürcher Zeitung
226. Jahrgang

Montag, 4. April 2005
Nr. 77

Neue Zürcher Zeitung

Heute mit NZZ FOLIO
Thema: Beim Zahnarzt

SCHWEIZER AUSGABE

Fr. 2.50 inkl. MWSt · € 2.20 NZZ Online: www.nzz.ch

Redaktion und Verlag: Neue Zürcher Zeitung, Falkenstrasse 11, Postfach, 8021 Zürich, Tel. 01 258 11 11 · Redaktion: Telefax 01 252 13 29, E-Mail: redaktion@nzz.ch · Verlag: Telefax 01 258 13 23, E-Mail: verlag@nzz.ch
Abonnements: Tel. 01 258 15 30, Telefax 01 258 18 39, E-Mail: leserservice-schweiz@nzz.ch · Anzeigen: Tel. 01 258 16 98, E-Mail: anzeigen@nzzmedia.ch · Weitere Angaben im Impressum (Inlandteil)

Die Welt trauert um Papst Johannes Paul II.

Das Oberhaupt der katholischen Kirche nach 26-jährigem Pontifikat gestorben

Am Samstagabend ist Papst Johannes Paul II. gestorben. In aller Welt wurde der Pontifex als eine der einflussreichsten Persönlichkeiten der letzten Jahrzehnte gewürdigt. Die Begräbnisfeier, zu der zahlreiche Staats- und Regierungschefs und über eine Million Gläubige erwartet werden, wird diese Woche im Petersdom stattfinden.

Tz. Rom, 3. April

Am späten Samstagabend verkündete das Geläut von St. Peter und schliesslich aller Kirchenglocken von Rom den Tod von Papst Johannes Paul II. und das Ende seines 26-jährigen Pontifikats. Der 263. Nachfolger Petri starb, wie in einem Communiqué des Vatikans später festgehalten wurde, genau um 21 Uhr 37 in seinen Privatgemächern. Wie der polnische Priester Cielecki berichtete, soll der Papst seinen Blick zuletzt dem Fenster zugewandt und seine Hand nochmals wie zur Segnung der Gläubigen erhoben haben, die unten auf dem Petersplatz mit dem Rosenkranz und im Kerzenlicht traurig-still Nachtwache hielten. Dann habe sich der Papst auf seinem Sterbebett von seinen engsten, pausenlos betenden Vertrauten mit einem «Amen» verabschiedet.

Unterschiedliche Würdigungen

Wie ein Lauffeuer verbreitete sich darauf um den ganzen Globus die am Petersplatz verbreitete Nachricht, dass der geliebte Heilige Vater Johannes Paul II. in das Haus des Vaters zurückgekehrt sei. In aller Welt wurden die Fernseh- und Radiosendungen unterbrochen, und von überall trafen bald Kondolenzbotschaften zahlreicher Staats- und Regierungschefs und von Führern anderer Religionen und Konfessionen ein. Zu würdigen war ein Mann, der zweifellos als eine der einflussreichsten Führungspersönlichkeiten der zweiten Hälfte des 20. Jahrhunderts in die Geschichte eingehen wird und der vor allem auch, wie etwa der Kardinal Walter Kasper treffend erklärte, «ein Petrus war, ein Fels, an dem man sich festhalten und unter Umständen aber auch stossen konnte».

Der seit 455 Jahren erste Nichtitaliener auf dem Stuhl Petri hat jedenfalls einen fast übermenschliche Kräfte erfordernden Marathon zurückgelegt, den er im Oktober 1978, nach dem nur 33-tägigen Pontifikat von Johannes Paul I., als 58-jähriger, ungewöhnlich jugendlich-dynamischer «Athlet Gottes» angetreten hatte. Durch die Förderung der Dissidentenbewegung Solidarnosc in seiner Heimat Polen hat der neue Oberhirte zweifellos zum Zusammenbruch des gesamten Ostblocks beigetragen, so dass weiterhin anzunehmen, wenn auch nicht klar erwiesen ist, dass der Papst im Mai 1981 das Opfer eines vom Kreml in Auftrag gegebenen Mordanschlags wurde. Bei seinen Besuchen in nahezu jeder Ecke der Welt setzte sich der polnische Papst aber auch sonst stark für Menschenrechte, soziale Gerechtigkeit und Frieden ein.

Erwartungsgemäss unterschiedlich waren denn auch die Akzente, die in den Würdigungen aus aller Welt gesetzt wurden. Der amerikanische Präsident Bush hob die Rolle des «Verfechters der menschlichen Freiheit» hervor. Uno-Generalsekretär Annan lobte den Papst als «unermüdlichen Anwalt für den Frieden», während der frühere Staats- und Parteichef Gorbatschew daran erinnerte, dass der Verstorbene nicht nur den Kommunismus bekämpft, sondern auch dem Kapitalismus mit erheblichen Vorbehalten begegnet sei. Tatsächlich erinnert man sich an die Warnungen vor der «Vergötzung des Marktes».

«Ganz Italien weint»

In Italien, wo sogleich eine dreitägige Staatstrauer angekündigt wurde, erklärte Präsident Ciampi, dass der Papst ein wahrer Apostel für Gerechtigkeit und Frieden gewesen sei. Ministerpräsident Berlusconi sagte, dass ganz Italien zusammen mit der katholischen Kirche weine. Alle seien dankbar für das Wirken von Johannes Paul II. gegen jede Form von Totalitarismus, Gewalt, Unterdrückung und moralischem Zerfall. Tatsächlich schien in Italien nicht nur offiziell grosse Trauer bekundet zu werden. Weit über hunderttausend Personen, die sich schon bald nach der Todesnachricht auf dem Petersplatz eingefunden hatten, bezeugten das auf eindrücklichste Weise.

Besonders die Römer hatten den Papst aus Polen tief in ihre Herzen geschlossen. Sie anerkannten nicht nur, dass er sich wie kaum einer seiner italienischen Vorgänger auch intensiv um die pastoralen Aufgaben als Bischof von Rom gekümmert hatte. Abgesehen von der grossen Kontaktfreude und menschlichen Wärme bewies der Slawe auch mit seiner starken Marienverehrung und seiner Schwäche für die Volksfrömmigkeit viel Seelenverwandtschaft mit den Italienern. Ganz zu schweigen davon, dass zu den 482 Glaubensbrüdern und -schwestern, die er heilig gesprochen hatte, auch der in Rom und Umgebung besondern stark verehrte Padre Pio zählte. Der Kapuzinermönch soll schon dem Studenten Wojtyla 1947 prophezeit haben, dass er einmal Papst werde; dabei soll Pio aber auch Blut und Gewalt vorausgesehen haben.

Ein Idol in einer säkularisierten Welt

Beeindruckend war in Rom am Wochenende aber auch, wie viele Jugendliche um Johannes Paul II. trauerten. Dabei hatte der Generalvikar von Rom, Kardinal Ruini, vor rund zehn Jahren noch beklagt, dass die Ewige Stadt bereits «entchristianisiert» sei. Weit entfernt schien auch das Jahr 1996 zu liegen, als jugendliche Störefriede dem Heiligen Vater in Berlin «Kondome statt Dome» entgegengejohlt hatten. Denn auch in anderen Industrieländern schien dieser Papst Jugendlichen in letzter Zeit wieder verstärkt spirituellen Halt zu bieten, obwohl auch diese neue Generation beileibe nicht jener Moral nachlebt, die Johannes Paul II. in seinen 14 Enzykliken, 44 Apostolischen Schreiben und unzähligen Diskursen gepredigt hat.

Dem Pontifex kamen in der modernen Mediengesellschaft aber nicht nur ein ungewöhnliches Charisma und Kommunikationstalent zugute. Ergriffen hat dieser Statthalter Christi selbst seine Kritiker damit, wie er seine Botschaft gerade in den letzten qualvollen Jahren vorlebte. Und Kritiker hatte dieser konservative, recht autokratisch waltende Papst, der auch etwa den Geheimbund Opus Dei förderte, gewiss nicht wenige. Gerade auch innerhalb seiner eigenen Kirche und bei den anderen christlichen Glaubensgemeinschaften war dies der Fall, die er nicht als Schwestern, sondern bloss als Töchter akzeptieren wollte.

Die ökumenischen Beziehungen blieben jedenfalls unterkühlt, wogegen sich Johannes Paul II. zugunsten des Weltfriedens, aber nicht zuletzt auch im Kampf gegen die Säkularisierung stark um den Dialog mit anderen Religionen gekümmert hat. Besonders bemühte er sich mit zahlreichen Versöhnungsgesten auch um eine Verbesserung des Verhältnisses zum Judentum. So schien Johannes Paul II. von jüdischen Führern am Wochenende zuweilen herzlicher gewürdigt zu werden als etwa von Vertretern reformierter Kirchen.

Aufbahrung und Begräbnis im Petersdom

Am Sonntag durften Prominente Johannes Paul II. die letzte Ehre in der vatikanischen «Sala Clementina» erweisen, wo der in ein rotes samtenes Messgewand gekleidete Leichnam des Papstes aufgebahrt wurde. Zudem wurde am Vormittag auf dem Petersplatz vor einer Riesenschar von Gläubigen und Pilgern eine erste grosse heilige Messe für den Verstorbenen gefeiert, dessen sterbliche Überreste am Montag in den Petersdom übergeführt und dort aufgebahrt werden sollen, so dass auch noch Gläubige aus aller Welt dem toten Papst die letzte Ehre erweisen können. Die Trauerfeiern, zu denen zahlreiche Staats- und Regierungschefs und weit über eine Million Gläubige erwartet werden, dauern insgesamt neun Tage. Die eigentliche Beisetzung erfolgt nach den Regeln des Vatikans vier bis acht Tage nach dem Tod. Der genaue Zeitpunkt der Bestattung, die nach Angaben der italienischen Medien voraussichtlich in den vatikanischen Grotten des Petersdoms stattfinden wird, soll am Montag durch die Kardinalskongregation festgelegt werden.

Mit dem Tod des Papstes ist die Leitung der Kirche in die Hände des Kardinalskollegiums gefallen. Die Regeln für die Abläufe, Rituale, Kompetenzen und Pflichten während der Sedisvakanz, das heisst für die Zeit, in welcher der Stuhl Petri unbesetzt ist, sind von Johannes Paul II. selber in der Apostolischen Konstitution «Universi Dominici Gregis» von 1996 minuziös festgelegt worden. Dabei wurden im Besonderen für die Papstwahl, die frühestens am 15. und spätestens am 20. Tag nach dem Tod beginnen soll, einige Neuerungen eingeführt. So können sich die wahlberechtigten Kardinäle, das heisst jene, die das 80. Altersjahr noch nicht überschritten haben, bei ihrem hermetisch abgeschirmten Konklave in der Sixtinischen Kapelle für einfache Mehrheitsabstimmungen entscheiden, falls nach 31 Abstimmungen keine Zweidrittelmehrheit für einen neuen Papst zustande gekommen ist.

Gutachten über Todesursache

Mit dem Tod des Papstes verlieren Kardinäle, die eine Abteilung der römischen Kurie leiten, wie auch der Staatssekretär ihr Amt. Einzige Ausnahmen sind der Camerlengo (Kardinalkämmerer), der Grosspönitentiar und der Generalvikar von Rom. Der Camerlengo, zurzeit Kardinal Somalo, ist dabei der wichtigste Beamte während der Sedisvakanz. Er vernichtet nicht nur den Fischerring und das Bleisiegel des toten Papstes, er übernimmt auch die Verantwortung für die zeitlichen Güter und Rechte des Heiligen Stuhls und bereitet das Konklave vor, zu dem die derzeit 117 wahlberechtigten Purpurträger (ohne den Kardinal «in pectore») am Sonntagmorgen offiziell vom Dekan des Kardinalskollegiums, Kardinal Ratzinger, in den Vatikan berufen wurden.

Am Sonntagmorgen war es aber die erste traurige Pflicht des Camerlengo, den Ritus der offiziellen Feststellung des Todes des Pontifex vorzunehmen. Zudem stellte der päpstliche Leibarzt Buzzonetti ein medizinisches Gutachten aus, das vom Vatikan bemerkenswerterweise vollständig veröffentlicht wurde. Danach ist Papst Johannes Paul II. an septischem Schock und Kreislaufversagen gestorben, nachdem er bereits unter Morbus Parkinson, wiederholten akuten Atemkrisen, den Folgen eines Luftröhrenschnitts sowie gutartiger, doch durch Harnvergiftung verschlimmerter Prostatavergrösserung sowie Kardiopathie gelitten habe. Der Tod sei mittels einer elektrokardiographischen Aufzeichnung von über 20 Minuten Dauer festgestellt worden.

Nach dem Tod Karol Wojtylas

Reaktionen aus aller Welt	*2*
Wojtyla und die Würde der Person	*3*
Der Papst, der aus der Kälte kam	*3*
Zeuge mit historischer Wirkung	*11*
Papst und Pole	*27–29*

Der Leichnam des Papstes ist im Vatikan aufgebahrt worden. (Bild Reuters)

Warnung der USA im Streit um Waffenhandel mit China

Riga, 3. April. (Reuters) Die USA haben die Europäische Union vor einer Belastungsprobe gewarnt, sollte Europa wie geplant das Waffenembargo gegen China aufheben. «Dies hätte natürlich Auswirkungen auf unsere Rüstungsbeziehungen, weil die Art von Vereinbarungen, die wir mit Rüstungsfirmen in Europa haben, erschüttert würde», sagte der stellvertretende Aussenminister der USA, Robert Zoellick, am Sonntag bei einem Besuch in Lettland. Eine Aufhebung des Embargos wäre ein Fehler und nicht vorteilhaft für die gegenseitigen Beziehungen. In Europa wollen insbesondere Deutschland und Frankreich das Verbot des Waffenhandels mit China aufheben.

HEUTE

Umfang 52 Seiten

Gegen Explosion der Ärztekosten

Krankenversicherer und Ärzte wollen den Kostenschub beim neuen Arzttarif mit einer Vereinbarung verhindern, wonach die Tarife auch künftig gesenkt und regionale Unterschiede verringert werden können.

INLAND 11

Viel Geld für US-Manager

Die Bezahlung der amerikanischen Spitzenmanager ist 2004 im Durchschnitt auf 9,84 Millionen Dollar gestiegen. Dies entspricht einer Erhöhung um 12 Prozent.

WIRTSCHAFT 17

Exportschlager Jumbo-Pfandbriefe

Geweckt durch den Erfolg der (Jumbo-)Pfandbriefe, entdecken immer mehr europäische Länder diese Anleihen, die nun das grösste Segment in Europa bilden.

GELD UND ANLAGE 26

Der Lyriker Thomas Kling gestorben

Der deutsche Lyriker Thomas Kling ist 47-jährig gestorben. Der vielfach ausgezeichnete Dichter war unter anderem der erste Träger des Ernst-Jandl-Lyrik-Preises.

FEUILLETON 30

5800 Läufer am 3. Zürich-Marathon

Letzte Kraftreserven müssen manche Athleten anzapfen, wenn sie die 42,195 Kilometer lange Strecke bewältigen wollen. Ein Augenschein kurz vor dem Ziel.

ZÜRICH UND REGION 37

BEILAGEN

TAP Portugal auf Höhenflügen

Lange hat Portugals Staats-Airline TAP horrende Verluste erlitten. Jetzt hat das Unternehmen die Gewinnzone erreicht und sich der Star Alliance angeschlossen.

LUFTFAHRT 9

Smarter Mini mit Pfiff von Peugeot

Mit der vor drei Jahren am Pariser Autosalon präsentierten Studie Sésame hat Peugeot das Publikum begeistert. Bald wird der einstige Sésame als 1007 verkauft.

AUTO · MOBIL 42

Wetter 16 · Börsen 19 · Briefe an die NZZ 32 Fernseh-/Radioprogramme 33 · Sportresultate 51 Impressum 10

Anzeigen: Finanzmarkt 20 · Dienstleistungen 22 · Fahrzeuge 25 · Kino 35 · Veranstaltungen 36 · Immobilien 38, 42 · Bildung 48 Todesanzeigen 40

9 771420 531009 05077

Your gateway to Turkey on the way to Europe

www.turkishdailynews.com.tr

turkish **daily news**

Turkey's first and only English daily

"peace at home, peace in the world" Kemal Atatürk

Monday, April 4, 2005 YEAR: 44 No: 14793 YTL: 1.25 TL: 1,250,000

Mumcu enters the fray with guns blazing
Page 2

Erkan Mumcu

World mourns pope

Some 130,000 worshipers gather at St. Peter's Square to hear the pope's words read out at a Mass for the world's best known religious leader, who wielded political influence but failed in the eyes of critics to reform the Church

VATICAN CITY - Reuters

Pope John Paul's body was laid in view of the world on Sunday and his words echoed across St. Peter's Square as faithful mourned the Pole who helped topple Communism in Europe but left a riven Church.

Streams of pilgrims converged on Rome in a spontaneous outpouring of affection for the pontiff, who died on Saturday evening aged 84 in his Vatican bed after an extended struggle with ill health that slowly sapped his strength.

"He died with the serenity of the saints," Cardinal Angelo Sodano told a huge crowd assembled for a sombre Requiem Mass.

The pope's corpse, clad in crimson and white vestments, was put on view for the world by Vatican TV. He lay on a bier under a simple crucifix with his bishop's staff under his arm.

Some 130,000 worshipers gathered at St. Peter's Square to hear the pope's own words read out at the mass for the world's best known religious leader, who wielded political influence but failed in the eyes of critics to reform the Church.

John Paul's words resonated through the square when an archbishop read his text prepared for the Sunday after Easter.

"It is love which converts hearts and gives peace," the text said. Another message from the pope was read out to 60,000 worshipers in Krakow, Poland, where Karol Wojtyla was archbishop before being elected pope in 1978.

News of his death set off one of the greatest influxes of pilgrims in Rome's memory -- fitting tribute to a traveler who spent a lifetime meeting people around the globe.

"He has called us and we have come," said Giuseppe Incarnati, who rushed to the tiny Vatican City from Naples to be close to the deceased pope who transformed the papacy by taking his message of reconciliation to all corners of the globe. *More on page 5*

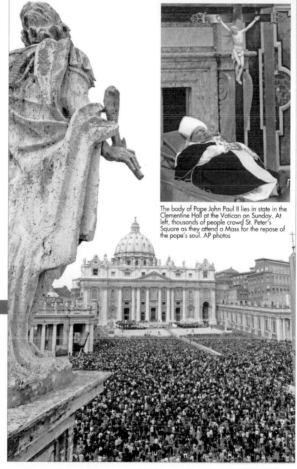

The body of Pope John Paul II lies in state in the Clementine Hall at the Vatican on Sunday. At left, thousands of people crowd St. Peter's Square as they attend a Mass for the repose of the pope's soul. AP photos

Turkey lauds late pontiff's efforts for world peace

Turkey extends condolences

ANKARA - Turkish Daily News

The Turkish leadership yesterday extended condolences to the Catholic world, which lost its spiritual leader, Pope John Paul II, over the weekend. President Ahmet Necdet Sezer, Prime Minister Recep Tayyip Erdoğan and Foreign Minister Abdullah Gül all sent separate messages to the Vatican expressing sadness over the pontiff's passing. "He will also be remembered for his arduous efforts for the maintenance of world peace," said Gül in his message.

Fener Greek Patriarch Bartolomeos expressed grief over the death of the pope and said his death was a loss to all Christianity. Bartolomeos praised the pontiff's efforts to reach reconciliation between the Roman Catholic and Greek Orthodox churches. Turkish gunman Mehmet Ali Ağca, who gravely wounded Pope John Paul in a failed assassination attempt in 1981, was reported to have been grief stricken over his death. *More on page 3*

One village guard killed by PKK

At least two PKK terrorists and one village guard were killed in clashes in southeastern Turkey on Saturday, a military official says.

2

Turkish businesses eye Chinese market

Several Turkish companies assert that China's market does indeed offers big opportunities both for investment and trade. Kibar Dış Ticaret Southeast Manager Mehmet Karataş said his firm exported $100 million worth of steel and iron products in 2004, roughly one-sixth of Turkey's exports to China.

7

Three warnings, then towed away

The police department has issued a directive asking all traffic policemen to tow cars that park in illegal spots after issuing three warnings to any motorist.

2

British PM Blair readies to call May 5 election

Britain's governing Labour Party told voters on Sunday it would build on the country's economic stability while its opponents would wreck it as Prime Minister Tony Blair prepared to call an election, expected on May 5.

6

MÜSİAD warns gov't of 'EU fatigue'

While the Turkish government has been insistently dismissing any slowing down in the process of Turkey's preparations for upcoming negotiations with the European Union, the pro-Islamic Independent Industrialists and Businessmen's Association urged the government on the creation of a team and the naming of a chief negotiator to coordinate the talks.

3

Ousted Kyrgyz president says he will resign today

Kyrgyz President Askar Akayev, who fled the country last month after demonstrators stormed his offices, said he will resign today.

6

■ Kurds and disappointment

Doğu Ergil

We are a nation that often confuses results with reasons. However, we are not unique in this flaw, otherwise there would be no social science or social theory. Yet when a nation collectively chooses to deal with results without pondering on reasons, problems mount up, change shape and, at times, turn into intractable conflicts. *Page 9*

TOMORROW

Cüneyt Ülsever

Prolific columnist Cüneyt Ülsever will continue writing his weekly column for Turkish Daily News readers on Tuesdays.

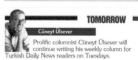

Newly elected Iraqi Parliament Speaker Hajim al-Hassani, a Sunni Arab, center, sits with new deputies Hussain al-Shahristani, a Shiite, left, and Kurdish leader Aref Taifour, right, at the National Assembly in Baghdad on Sunday. AP photo

Iraqi lawmakers elect speaker

BAGHDAD - The Associated Press

Iraqi lawmakers elected Industry Minister Hajim al-Hassani, a Sunni Arab, as parliament speaker on Sunday, ending days of deadlock and clearing the way for the formation of a new government two months after the country's historic elections.

The decision was a step toward repairing the tattered image of the newly elected National Assembly, which had bickered for days over who would take the speaker post. *Page 6*

Turkish mosque in Holland vandalized

AMSTERDAM - Associated Press

A group of youths smashed the windows of a mosque in the southern Netherlands, setting off a street brawl with Turkish immigrants, Dutch police said Sunday.

One person was hurt, and police arrested one man after the Saturday night disturbance in the city of Venray, police said. One man suffered unspecified injuries in Saturday's fight and was hospitalized overnight, police said.

Local media reported that the fight involved approximately 60 Turkish immigrants and 20 Dutchmen. *Page 2*

Compromise on İncirlik air base in the cards

WASHINGTON/ANKARA - Exclusive by TDN Defense Desk

The United States is expected to withdraw up to 70,000 troops from overseas bases within the next 10 years, but part of the remaining forces will be deployed in new locations. Turkey's critical southern base of İncirlik is naturally part of the plan, however the Turkish government seems a bit undecided on the matter.

"The Turks have told us that their decision will come soon on İncirlik. The base's use as a logistical hub will be good," said one State Department official in response to the expected Turkish move. "This is just better than nothing," said one U.S. source.

Meanwhile, Foreign Minister Abdullah Gül was quoted as saying yesterday that NATO ally the United States could be given permission to expand its use of Turkey's İncirlik air base for humanitarian purposes. *Page 4*

143

A healthy change

Villager Hasan Basri Aktan: We've lost our health to smoking, but the younger generation shouldn't lose theirs' *Page 16*

'Tulipomania' by Sevgi Çağal

Painter Sevgi Çağal opened her 25th exhibition at the Atatürk Culture Center in Istanbul on April 1. *Page 12*

Resurgent Clijsters takes second title in a row

Victory over Sharapova means that Clijsters, who was ranked 133 at the start of Indian Wells, will move back into top 20. *Page 15*

L'OSSERVATORE ROMANO

Via del Pellegrino 00120 CITTÀ DEL VATICANO – Segreteria di Redazione 0669883461 / 0669884442 - fax 0669883675
Servizio fotografico 0669884797 – Marketing e Diffusione 0669899470 - fax 0669882818 – ABBONAMENTI 0669899483
0669899480 – fax 0669882818 – Ufficio amministrativo 0669899489 – fax 0669885164 – e-mail: ornet@ossrom.va
WWW.VATICAN.VA/news_services/or/home_ita.html

SPEDIZIONE IN ABBONAMENTO POSTALE - ROMA
CONTO CORRENTE POSTALE N. 649004

GIORNALE QUOTIDIANO   POLITICO RELIGIOSO

UNICUIQUE SUUM   NON PRAEVALEBUNT

Copia : 0,90
Copia arretrata : 1,58

ABBONAMENTI
VATICANO E ITALIA
Quotidiano
L'Osservatore della Domenica
Cumulativo
ESTERO (VIA ORDINARIA)
Quotidiano
L'Osservatore della Domenica

Anno CXLV - N. 76 (43.913) – EDIZIONE STRAORDINARIA   CITTÀ DEL VATICANO   Domenica 3 Aprile 2005

Oggi, sabato 2 aprile, alle ore 21.37

il Signore ha chiamato a Sé

IL SANTO PADRE

GIOVANNI PAOLO II

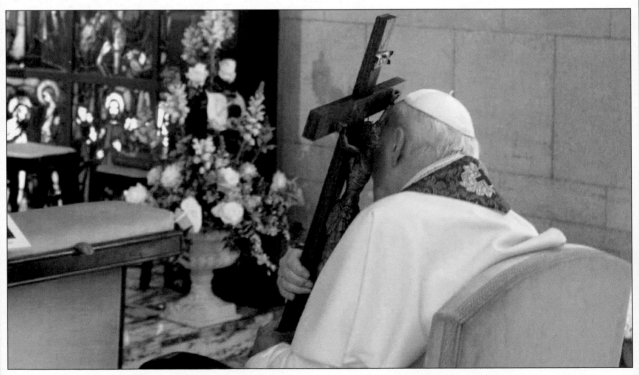

Ci hai lasciati, Padre Santo.
Ti sei consumato per noi.
In quest'ora — per Te gloriosa, per noi
dolente — ci sentiamo abbandonati.

Ma Tu prendici per mano e guidaci
con quella Tua Mano che in questi mesi
si è fatta in Te anche parola.
Grazie, Padre Santo!

m. a.

144

EL MUNDO

DIARIO DE LA TARDE

Banesco

LUNES / Caracas, 4 de Abril de 2005 / Año 48 / N° 13440 / www.cadenaglobal.com / www.elmundo.com.ve   Bs. 800

Vivas, Simonovis y Forero en audiencia

El tribunal 7° de control del estado Aragua podría enviar hoy a juicio a los comisarios Henry Vivas, Iván Simonovis y Lázaro Forero si el juez Francisco Ramón Mota acepta los elementos acusatorios presentados por la fiscal 6° con competencia nacional, Luisa Ortega Díaz, quien espera que se ratifique la medida de privación de libertad ya que los imputados intentaron huir del país.

La defensa de Simonovis, el abogado Carlos Bastidas, considera que el proceso judicial que se les sigue a los comisarios es eminentemente político y no hay elementos de convicción en la acusación. **P20**

Piden aumento en medicinas genéricas

Revisar el precio de unos 1.100 medicamentos genéricos regulados exigen los laboratorios, los cuales argumentan que los costos atentan contra la viabilidad de su producción. El presidente de la Cámara Nacional de Medicamentos Genéricos y Afines, Jorge Rivas, informó que a pesar de lo accesible al bolsillo, la elaboración de los medicamentos genéricos está siendo perjudicada porque tienen dos devaluaciones acumuladas y no se han hecho los ajustes necesarios. Además señala que la tardanza en el otorgamiento de divisas y registro sanitario retrasa la distribución. **P6**

Proponen 20% del ingreso anual para pago de vivienda

La banca plantea que la porción de salario del deudor hipotecario destinada al pago del crédito de vivienda principal, se actualice anualmente, para que sea el 20% del salario anual del trabajador el destinado para este fin. Andrés Azpúrua, de Banpro, señaló que de esta forma se evitaría el deterioro monetario y se garantizaría el acceso al beneficio a quienes aún no tienen una vivienda propia. Indicó que, tal como lo establece la ley, la cuota es muy baja. **P6**

Existen 61 mil cédulas "clonadas" P2

El Papa reposará en el Vaticano

El vocero de la Santa Sede anunció que el funeral será el viernes. El corazón de Juan Pablo II podría ir a Polonia

El papa Juan Pablo II será enterrado este viernes en el Vaticano. Así lo decidió hoy la Congregación General de Cardenales durante su primera sesión, la cual acordó que la ceremonia fúnebre tendrá lugar a las 10:00 am, hora local.

El Sumo Pontífice será sepultado en la cripta situada bajo la Basílica de San Pedro, informó este lunes el portavoz del Vaticano, Joaquín Navarro- Valls, quien puso fin a las especulaciones sobre la posibilidad de que Juan Pablo II fuera enterrado en su patria, Polonia.

Sin embargo, el corazón de Karol Wojtyla podría ser enterrado en Cracovia, la ciudad de la que fue arzobispo, afirma el diario **Gazeta Wyborcza**, el cual señala que representantes de la Iglesia de Cracovia y el secretario personal del Papa, Estanislao Dziwisz, han negociado un acuerdo para que Juan Pablo II repose en el Vaticano, según la tradición papal, pero que su corazón regrese a su país natal. **P8**

✓ **Decretados cinco días de duelo** P2
✓ **Templo de Don Bosco listo para exequial oficial** P19

Recta final para elegir candidatos

Los partidos políticos deberán definir esta semana los 5.800 candidatos que los representarán en las elecciones municipales del próximo 7 de agosto. El chavismo irá en un bloque donde el MVR lanzará el 70% de los candidatos. Los opositores irán en dos bloques, uno integrado por AD, Copei, MAS, Izquierda Democrática y Convergencia y otro compuesto por Primero Justicia, Proyecto Venezuela y La Causa R. **P2**

Terrazas del Este ofrece tranquilidad

Como la mayoría de las nuevas urbanizaciones construidas en el eje Guarenas-Guatire, Terrazas del Este es un parque residencial que sirve de "dormitorio" a familias jóvenes de clase media que trabajan en Caracas. Sus habitantes aseguran que es la mejor del sector, tiene grandes extensiones de áreas verdes y mucha tranquilidad. **P18**

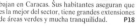
URBANO

En la tarjeta está la clave

Para enfrentar con éxito las venideras elecciones parroquiales y municipales, oposición y gobierno se debaten en el diseño de fórmulas que van desde el uso de las "morochas" a la "alianza perfecta". El resultado podría ser impredecible si los ciudadanos hacen su escogencia basándose en los programas de los candidatos y en su potencial. Analistas estiman que la esencia del proceso electoral está en la participación. **P5**

El juego no se acaba...

Los Yanquis de Nueva York no olvidan el revés de 2004 ante Boston y han hecho de todo por reverdecer su gloria. Amparados en el pitcheo de Randy Johnson ganaron el juego inaugural de Grandes Ligas . El mítico ex catcher Yogi Berra, el de la famosa frase "el juego no se acaba hasta que se termina", hizo el primer lanzamiento y fue el talismán de la victoria. **P11-12**

Carlos Capriles Ayala conquista a España

Pasó por Caracas e informó de sus triunfos en Madrid con sus textos, como **Sola a través de la selva amazónica**, considerado el libro mejor editado en la península ibérica. Además, reescribió especialmente su **Sexo y poder**, para incluir los deslices del rey Juan Carlos. Allista un ensayo sobre los golpes de Estado y magnicidios en Venezuela. Carlos Capriles Ayala, pues, está en la cresta de la ola. **P10**

Schumacher sigue desconocido

Las cosas han cambiado. La vida ya no es tan fácil para Michael Schumacher, quien ayer se retiró del Gran Premio de Bahrein y apenas acumula dos puntos en la clasificación de pilotos del mundial de Fórmula Uno. Por el contrario, el español Fernando Alonso comienza a mostrar madera de campeón y repitió triunfo para consolidar su liderato, con 26 unidades. **P11**

"Paras" tenían plan contra Chávez

Las autoridades de Colombia temen que en el municipio de San Onofre, donde fueron hallados 40 cadáveres, se encuentren al menos 500 cuerpos de personas asesinadas por las Autodefensas. La información fue suministrada por Feliciano Yepes, "para" detenido en Venezuela. Dijo que Castaño pretendía desestabilizar el gobierno del presidente Hugo Chávez. **P9**

DESTACADOS

Postergado concierto de Bisbal

El concierto que debía ofrecer este jueves el cantante español David Bisbal en la ciudad de Maracay fue postergado para el próximo domingo debido al duelo nacional que decretara el presidente Hugo Chávez tras la muerte del Santo Pontífice, Juan Pablo II.

Representa a cómicos, actúa y enseña

La actriz Flor Núñez vive en Miami, donde ha tenido éxito en la televisión y actualmente se presenta en un teatro de la calle 8. Fundó una escuela para el desarrollo actoral y además trabaja en la representación legal de los comediantes. **P17**

Música venezolana... no hay mucha

El director de Kys FM, Oswaldo Yépez, jura que le encanta la música venezolana. Sobre todo la de Héctor Cabrera, Mario Suárez, Ilan Chester y Franco de Vita. Pero pronostica que, con la puesta en práctica de la Ley Resorte, el repertorio se agotará en tres meses. **P15**

145

EL UNIVERSAL
SUPLEMENTO ESPECIAL

LUNES 4 DE ABRIL DE 2005   www.eluniversal.com

Adiós... Juan Pablo II
Karol Wojtyla 1920 | 2005

Llenó estadios y grandes descampados como si de una superestrella de rock se tratara, y en los casi 27 años que duró su pontificado llevó a todos los rincones del planeta su mensaje de amor, tolerancia y respeto por la vida, la familia y los valores cristianos. Viajó más y llevó a los altares a un mayor número de santos y beatos que todos sus antecesores. Logró derrumbar, desde bastidores, al gigante soviético. Su muerte deja un vacío no sólo entre los millones de católicos del mundo, sino también entre todos aquellos a quienes llevó su palabra en los cinco continentes. El Trono de Pedro no es lo único que tendrá que llenar su sucesor. Karol Wojtyla dejó una huella profunda.

ACKNOWLEDGMENTS

In addition to thanking the journalists whose work appears on these pages, we thank their employers, who provided the pages for use royalty-free. We are also grateful to The Associated Press, which approved the use of its material without reimbursement in support of Poynter's mission: training journalists. Poynter will use revenue from the book to subsidize that training in the United States and around the world.

We owe a special debt to friends and colleagues who helped make this book possible. Among other things, they helped us overcome computer problems in Kenya, provided Internet access in Italy, opened doors near and far, and provided translations of various sorts in various places. They include Alan Abbey, Magda Abu-Fadil, John Allen Jr., Bob Andelman, Bun Booyens, Hutch Craig, Carlo de Lucia, Jonathan Dube, Margo Hammond, Tom Heneghan, Stacy Meichtry, Debbie Hodges and the International Center for Journalists, Alessandro Morgantini, Churchill Otieno, Rev. Paul S. Quinter, Joanna Rix, Massimo Russo, David Sislen, Roberto Toma, Rabbi Michael Torop, Maria A. Velez, Ewa Wierzynska and Maciek Wierzynski.

At Andrews McMeel Publishing, we thank Chris Schillig, vice president and editorial director, for her strong support and enthusiasm from the start. We also thank John Carroll, who helped make the transition from newspaper page to book page a smooth and painless process.

Finally, we thank our colleagues at Poynter. They helped us conceive of this project and, once it was under way, they helped us by tracking down contact information, permissions and front pages, updating databases, troubleshooting our e-mail and computers, and being patient as we set aside other important projects to focus on this one. We appreciate all of the support we received from the faculty, staff and administration, including especially Bobbi Alsina, Andy Barnes, Fanua Borodzicz, Roy Peter Clark, Karen Dunlap, Rick Edmonds, Howard Finberg, Jill Geisler, Bob Haiman, Sandy Johnakin, Kelly McBride, Lanette Miller, Jim Naughton, Dave Pierson, Sara Quinn, Jeff Saffan, Monique Saunders, David Shedden, Al Tompkins and Keith Woods.

This book owes a special debt to the marketing, publications and online staff who worked tirelessly, with energy and care: Elizabeth Carr, Maria Jaimes, Vicki Krueger, Larry Larsen, Steve Outing, Nicole Sarsfield, Ola Seifert, Anne Van Wagener and Cary Pérez Waulk. And Bill Mitchell, who always keeps us inspired and laughing.

Julie Moos
Publications Manager
The Poynter Institute

ABOUT THE POYNTER INSTITUTE

The Poynter Institute is a school dedicated to teaching and inspiring journalists and media leaders. Through its seminars, publications and Web site (www.poynter.org), the Institute promotes excellence and integrity in the practice of craft and in the practical leadership of successful businesses. Poynter stands for a journalism that informs citizens, enlightens public discourse and strengthens the ties between journalism and democracy.

The school offers about 50 professional development seminars at its Florida campus each year. Poynter also teaches via its online training portal, News University (www.newsu.org). Poynter faculty and staff work with journalists—and journalism students—at various locations around the nation and the world.

The Institute was founded in 1975 by Nelson Poynter, chairman of the *St. Petersburg Times* and its Washington affiliate, *Congressional Quarterly*. Before his death in 1978, Mr. Poynter willed the controlling stock in his companies to the school. As a financially independent, nonprofit organization, The Poynter Institute is beholden to no interest except its own mission: to help journalists seek and achieve excellence.

Poynter.